# CANADA AND THE FIRST WORLD WAR:
## ESSAYS IN HONOUR OF ROBERT CRAIG BROWN

D1216184

The First World War is often credited with being the event that gave Canada its own identity, distinct from that of Britain, France, and the United States. Less often noted, however, is that it was also the cause of a great deal of friction within Canadian society. The fifteen essays contained in *Canada and the First World War* examine how Canadians experienced the war and how their experiences were shaped by region, politics, gender, race, class, and nationalism.

Editor David MacKenzie has brought together some of the leading voices in Canadian history to take in-depth looks at the tensions and fractures the war caused and to address the way some attitudes and perceptions about the country were changed while others remained the same. The essays vary in scope, but are strongly unified so as to create a collection that treats its subject in a complete and comprehensive manner.

*Canada and the First World War* is a tribute to esteemed University of Toronto historian Robert Craig Brown, one of Canada's greatest authorities on the war, and the authors include a cross-section of his friends, colleagues, contemporaries, and former students. Together, they provide a fitting tribute to a scholar who has contributed greatly to Canadians' understanding of their past. The collection is a significant addition to the ongoing re-examination of Canada's experiences in war.

DAVID MACKENZIE is an associate professor in the Department of History at Ryerson University.

Robert Craig Brown (Office of the Dean of Arts and Sciences, University of Toronto)

# Canada and the First World War

## Essays in Honour of Robert Craig Brown

*Edited by David MacKenzie*

UNIVERSITY OF TORONTO PRESS
Toronto Buffalo London

© University of Toronto Press Incorporated 2005
Toronto Buffalo London
Printed in Canada

ISBN 0-8020-3573-6 (cloth)
ISBN 0-8020-8445-1 (paper)

Printed on acid-free paper

**Library and Archives Canada Cataloguing in Publication**

Canada and the First World War : essays in honour of Robert
Craig Brown / edited by David MacKenzie.

Includes bibliographical references and index.
ISBN 0-8020-3573-6 (bound)     ISBN 0-8020-8445-1 (pbk.)

1. World War, 1939–1945 – Canada.   I. Brown, Robert Craig, 1935–
II. MacKenzie, David (David Clark), 1953–

D547.C2C3423  2005      940.53'71      C2004-903996-2

University of Toronto Press acknowledges the financial assistance to
its publishing program of the Canada Council for the Arts and the
Ontario Arts Council.

University of Toronto Press acknowledges the financial support for
its publishing activities of the Government of Canada through the
Book Publishing Industry Development Program (BPIDP).

This book has been published with the help of a grant from the Canadian
Federation for the Humanities and Social Sciences, through the Aid to
Scholarly Publications Programme, using funds provided by the Social
Sciences and Humanities Research Council of Canada.

# Contents

## IV The Aftermath

# Illustrations

# Preface

This book is a Festschrift for Robert Craig Brown. It sprang from two relatively simple ideas: first, that a book on Canada and the Great War would be a fitting tribute to a historian who has contributed so much to our present understanding of that experience and, second, that such a book could make a contribution to the on-going re-examination of Canada's experiences during the First World War. It has been a quarter of a century since Craig Brown and Ramsay Cook's *Canada: A Nation Transformed* first appeared, and since that time a new generation of historians and scholars has examined and challenged the way we think about the Great War. New territory has been explored and new questions have been asked about the past, and we believe that the time is right to bring together a collection of essays on Canada and the Great War that reflects the changing times. We all agreed that this is the best way to honour Craig and to acknowledge his contribution to the study of Canadian history.

We are taking a different approach to the Festschrift. Rather than the usual collection of disparate essays, in *Canada and the Great War* each author was assigned a specific topic on Canada and the war and given enough freedom to explore what he or she believes to be important for the subject. Together, the chapters constitute a broad history of Canada's experience in the First World War while honouring someone who has made a significant contribution to the study of history in Canada. The fifteen authors represent a cross-section of Craig's friends, colleagues, contemporaries, and former students. As individuals they have won virtually every major regional, national, academic, and non-academic book prize, and together they represent the leading scholars on Canada and the Great War, a subject that was, and still is, the focus for much of

Craig Brown's scholarship. These authors were selected because of their scholarship as historians and as specialists in the field and, by focusing on one subject of broad interest to Canadians, we hope to have produced a book with a longer shelf life than the usual Festschrift.

The different contributors to this book examine how Canadians experienced the Great War and how their experiences were shaped by region, politics, economics, gender, class, ethnicity, and nationalism. In different ways the writers look at the impact of the war on Canadians, at the tensions and fractures in Canadian society, at the upheaval and death, and at the way some attitudes and perceptions about the country changed while others remained the same.

Many people need to be thanked for their help in seeing this book through to publication. First, I must thank all of the contributors for devoting so much time and effort to their chapters over the past few years. In particular, I would like to thank Donald Avery for agreeing to contribute a chapter on western Canada to this project at the last minute. On very short notice, Don graciously agreed to take a chapter from his book *Dangerous Foreigners* and to update, revise, and shape it into a new chapter that fits so well into this volume.

Len Husband, of the University of Toronto Press, has guided this book through the various stages of publication, and this final product would not have been possible without his effort and his support. For that I am most grateful. Thanks also to Jill McConkey of the University of Toronto Press for her help at the beginning of this project. I would also like to thank Frances Mundy of the University of Toronto Press, Catherine Frost for copy-editing the manuscript, and Anita Levin for her work in preparing the index. This work has been supported in part by a manuscript preparation grant from Ryerson University.

My friends Patrice Dutil and Paul Litt, who evolved as advisers and contributors, provided feedback and humour over the duration of this project. They were always forthcoming with their views, and their support made the work that much easier – although our discussions of things historical can hardly be called work. Finally, I would like to thank my wife, Terry, and daughters, Claire and Beth, for their help, patience, and advice as this project evolved slowly from a nice idea into this book.

# Part I
# Introduction

# Introduction: Myth, Memory, and the Transformation of Canadian Society

DAVID MACKENZIE

The First World War touched the lives of every Canadian man, woman, and child, whether they remained at home or served overseas, and it continues to be one of the most fascinating periods in Canadian history. No one who seriously studies Canada in the modern era can ignore the First World War. But it is one of those peculiar historical truths that despite the impact of the Great War on all aspects of Canadian life, Canadians played practically no role in its outbreak. In 1914 war came to Canadians, as it did to Europeans, 'out of a cloudless sky, to populations which knew almost nothing of it and had been raised to doubt that it could ever again trouble their continent.'[1] Canadians had no choice about their involvement in the war, but they did have a voice when it came to deciding on the extent of their participation. The effect of the choices Canadians made at home and overseas is still reflected in Canadian society.

In the literature on Canada and the Great War, Craig Brown and Ramsay Cook's *Canada: A Nation Transformed* is a standard work. The focus of that book is much broader than the one found here; Brown and Cook begin their story in 1896 and examine Canadian society through the First World War and beyond to 1921. Canada in these years 'was a country being transformed' by a process of rapid modernization, industrialization, urbanization, and social and cultural upheaval. It was a transformation that 'must be measured by more than numbers and size,' the authors write, and it grew from 'seeds planted in previous decades, even centuries.'[2] This theme of transformation and the impact of war on Canadian society, as Ramsay Cook reminds us in his chapter, is central to the work of Craig Brown.

At the heart of their book is the Great War – a traumatic event, seen

by many to be a major catalyst of transformation. In a recent history of
the Great War, Michael Howard writes that 'events on the battlefield
ultimately determined what happened on the home front, and were
responsible for the vast transformation that resulted in the entire structure of European society.'[3] Is it possible to say that the entire structure of
Canadian society underwent a 'vast transformation' because of the First
World War? It is clear that the war has had a profound impact on
Canadian memory. Monuments, memorials, and cenotaphs can be found
in nearly every city and small town across the country, and our book-
stores are stocked each year with new titles examining different aspects
of the war.[4] In Canadian literature, the First World War has attracted
writers of early romance novels, such as Ralph Connor and Robert
Stead, through to the more literary works of Hugh MacLennan, Timothy Findley, and Robertson Davies, and its themes continue to be mined
by contemporary writers.[5] Every 11 November we are reminded that
something important happened in 1914–18, and that importance still
resonates with Canadians today.

But was the country transformed by the war and were Canadians
different after the war than before? How has the memory of the war
coloured the way we understand what happened? And how can the
war be credited or blamed for the changes that did occur? The economic developments, women's suffrage, linguistic strife, emerging autonomy and Americanization – would these changes have taken place
in any event, without the war? This theme of transformation – collective
and individual, national and regional, political, economic, and social –
forms the underlying structure of this book. This is not surprising; for
change, the factors that perpetuate it, and its effects have always been a
primary focus of historical enquiry. The First World War is a special case,
however; it was a cataclysm that affected all quarters of society, creating a
perception that change had been unusually rapid and profound.

This book is organized around several general sections, but inevitably some themes transcend these somewhat arbitrary divisions. All the
contributors examine the larger question of how Canadians experienced the First World War and challenge the way we think and write
about it. As Douglas McCalla notes in his chapter on the economy, the
First World War is a good illustration of how 'the power of established
stories and images' can 'dominate understanding long after research
has called them deeply into question.' These 'stories' include the standard interpretations that Canada's society was transformed by the war;
that Canadians responded to the call with enthusiasm; that the economy

industrialized and prospered; that Canadian nationalism was born in the trenches; that Canadian women found a degree of liberation through war work; and that conscription was essentially a political issue dividing French and English Canadians. Other questions are raised as well: What did Canadians know about the war? Did they make conscious decisions to fight or work or protest, or were they swept away by forces beyond their control?

Part One consists of this introduction and a chapter by Ramsay Cook on Craig Brown. Cook offers a snapshot of Brown's career and pays particular attention to his work on the First World War, especially his two-volume biography of Robert Borden.[6] It is this scholarship on the Great War that has made Craig Brown one of Canada's leading historians. As Cook explains, it was Brown's view that Prime Minister Borden put the 'national interest' above 'national unity' when it came to the war and conscription. Others in this volume put that idea to the test.

Part Two comprises five essays that examine in a broad way and from a variety of perspectives – military, political, and economic – how Canadians fought the war. Terry Copp situates his chapter on the Canadian military effort in the most recent literature and challenges interpretations that describe the war as an exercise in futility and portray Canadians as victims of impersonal and malevolent economic, military, and governmental forces. Copp argues that Canadians, by and large, were aware of what was happening in the war, including its devastation. Yet thousands of English-speaking Canadians still believed it to be a just war. As Copp writes, 'The Canadian Corps and the Canadian people had accomplished great things together in what they believed to be a necessary and noble cause.' Here conscription becomes a popular cause, at least in parts of English Canada, long before the politicians moved to introduce it.

The centrality of conscription in the Canadian war experience is underlined in several chapters. It was an issue that cut across all levels of Canadian society. J.L. Granatstein, who has written more on the subject than anyone else over the last forty years, takes a fresh look at conscription, especially at his own views on the matter, and argues, contrary to his earlier writings, that it was necessary to repair a military system that was breaking down. Conscription was a politically divisive issue that polarized Canadians for more than a generation, but, Granatstein reminds us, it became necessary, owing to difficulties in recruitment that arose from the unwillingness of both French- and English-speaking Canadian men to serve.

Streetcar: Step aboard, free trip to Europe, 1915 (City of Toronto Archives, Fonds 1244, Item 728)

In his chapter on political leadership, John English inevitably comes back to conscription, and he shows how the intellectual and cultural context of Canada's political leaders influenced their wartime decision-making. They were, by and large, British Protestant males, centred mainly in Ontario, and they represented the views of their community. The government was essentially 'democratically elected but unrepresentative in character,' English writes, and therefore was insensitive to the views of francophone or ethnic minorities. In this context, the decision on conscription, however difficult to make, becomes a logical one. British-Canadian nationalism won its last triumph in 1917, but it was 'profoundly dangerous in a nation where those of non-British background were over 40 per cent of the population and where many of British background themselves did not share the particular expression of British-Canadian nationalism so strongly expressed in English Canada's urban centres.'

Like Granatstein, English takes a fresh look at an area of scholarship that he and Craig Brown know well[7] and re-evaluates Canadian political leadership in the light of newer literature on memory and loss, painting a richly textured portrait of Canada's federal political leaders, in particular Robert Borden. Rather than looking through a modern prism, English sets these politicians in their Victorian and Edwardian contexts and, in the process, takes aim at present-minded critics of wartime leadership. Like Copp, English takes the perspective of the leaders themselves and examines what they believed and the context within which they lived. To examine these wartime leaders from a modern perspective, with modern sensibilities as a guide, English argues, makes them 'easy targets, uttering, as they so often did, phrases about duty, honour, and democracy, while the modern age with its ironic, discontinuous, and anti-traditional ways was successfully storming the heights of western life.' It is a valuable reminder of the importance of context in any effort to understand and explain the experience of the war. As Copp explains, 'the men and women who participated in events like the First World War were not concerned with the views of later generations. The meaning of their war was constantly changing, and since no one knew the outcome or the consequences of decisions that needed to be made, they relied upon the best information available at the time and tried to act in ways that did not violate their shared values.'

The chapters by Copp, Granatstein, and English help us to understand more clearly the context for, motives of, and pressures on Borden and the other wartime leaders and English-speaking Canadians generally. Conscription and the recruitment issue are considered from a different perspective by Patrice Dutil, who examines French Canada's role in the war through the prism of Napoléon Belcourt and his fight against Regulation 17, the provincial government regulation that severely curtailed use of the French language in Ontario schools. To understand attitudes about the war in Quebec and French Canada generally, Dutil argues, it is necessary to take into consideration Quebec's profound isolationism, which although not necessarily anti-British, affected the way French Canadians perceived the war and the outside world. For someone like Belcourt, isolationism was something to be feared and opposed, because in the context of the war it played two ways and could intensify both the isolationism of French Canadians with respect to the outside world and the isolation of French Canadians within Canada. Here, social transformation had negative effects; in the effort to create a national consensus, a new sense of citizenship, and a new national unity, French Canada was isolated and the result was national disunity. As Dutil puts it, 'A war that many thought could unite French and English Canadians, had proved everything to the contrary.'

Questions of myth and transformation are central to Douglas McCalla's chapter on the wartime economy. McCalla takes direct aim at the idea that the war helped to industrialize Canada's economy and produced permanent structural changes within it. McCalla turns this thinking on its head, arguing that Canada produced few new things during the war, shells and munitions being the exception, and that most of the changes to industry, urbanization, and governmental intervention in the economy were either temporary disruptions or part of longer term trends already occurring in the economy. There was no 'vast transformation' here. Historians generally have got the story backward, McCalla argues; these developments were not the product of the war, but rather, 'they actually reflect what the Canadian economy had become by 1914.' In the light of these arguments, he notes, it will be necessary to re-examine post-war protest, especially in western Canada, where the war has been singled out as the impetus for over-specialization in grain production and for the expansion of existing farms and the opening of marginal land.

McCalla argues that 'the war reinforced trends; it did not initiate them.' These views are echoed in Part Three, where the focus is the home front and how Canadians individually and collectively experienced the war. In her chapter on mobilizing women for the war, Joan Sangster challenges the image of the First World War as a 'political turning point' for Canadian women and questions the 'myth of unity, patriotism, and homogeneity.' The lives of working-class Canadian women were hardly transformed by the war, Sangster argues; if anything, these women experienced the 'acceleration of existing trends.' But pre-war attitudes about gender, family, and work persisted into the post-war era and, rather than being a unifying experience, the First World War 'accentuated existing class and ideological tensions among women.'

The persistence of pre-war attitudes is a theme examined by Donald Avery in his chapter on ethnic and class relations in wartime western Canada. By looking at the experience of immigrants from enemy countries Avery shows how the war experience combined with prevailing attitudes in the dominant culture to set the context and define the status of these workers in western Canada. 'During the years 1914–19,' he writes, 'individuals and groups were deemed loyal or disloyal, law-abiding or revolutionary, according to how their behaviour conformed to the values and norms of the middle-class Anglo-Canadian community.' Avery takes his study of Anglo-Canadian nativism through the war years into the post-war red scare and the 1919 Winnipeg General Strike and concludes that we 'should not underestimate the extent to which the war itself dramatically turned western Canadian public opinion against enemy aliens.'

Joan Sangster also asks important questions about what the British historian Niall Ferguson has called 'the myth of war enthusiasm,'[8] a theme touched on elsewhere in this book by Terry Copp and in the chapters by Adam Crerar and David MacKenzie. Sangster argues that the idea that working-class women moved into war work for patriotic reasons is largely a myth, however 'resilient,' 'shaped by the inevitable hegemony of those with more power to shape public images, symbols, and consciousness.' Yet there was an outpouring of war support and demonstrations of patriotism on the streets of Toronto and other Canadian cities. By exposing the diversity of attitudes that could be found across the country – from urban middle-class English-Canadians and working-class women to rural Ontarians, Westerners, Acadians, Quebeckers, Newfoundlanders, and others – these chapters help us to understand more clearly how Canadians perceived the war.

The theme of moral regulation is developed by both Sangster and Desmond Morton, in the latter case with respect to the families left behind by the men who went off to fight. The Canadian Patriotic Fund was a testament to the determination to ensure that a quarter-million wives and children would not suffer, but Morton also demonstrates how the system was informed by 'moral and social assumptions' and how these assumptions influenced the process. By the end of the war, Morton concludes, 'thousands of working-class women had come in painful contact with both charity and bureaucracy, and neither experience had been pleasant.'

In his chapter on science and technology, Rod Millard also questions the extent of transformation, as he challenges the myths that 'there was no industrial research in Canada before the First World War, the war forced the government to establish the NRC [National Research Council] in 1916, and the NRC then became the focus of industrial research.' The war helped to change attitudes towards science and enhanced the prestige of the scientists themselves, and the creation of the National Research Council was the 'first attempt to organize science on a national basis,' but it was only after the war that the idea became accepted that industrial research in Canada began with the creation of the NRC. Millard traces the roots of these developments back into the pre-war era. He also discusses the migration of scientists and researchers who were lured to the United States because of the lack of research opportunities in Canada, and he illustrates how this 'brain drain' led to a backlash of 'nationalist indignation' in the scientific community.

In raising this larger issue of the rise of nationalist feelings during the war, Millard draws attention to the lack of opportunity in Canada and, more generally, to anti-Americanism in Canadian society. This topic is directly addressed by Paul Litt, who examines the impact of the war on mass culture and Canadian cultural nationalism. Litt demonstrates how mass culture was used to promote the war effort – to encourage recruitment, to raise funds and sell government bonds, and to publicize the war and mobilize public support. He also explores the complexity of this rising sense of nationalism. Canadians were establishing their own autonomy, politically and culturally, by loosening their ties with Great Britain. At the same time, the experience of the war led many Canadians to question the spread of American popular culture in Canada. 'Canadians are known for their ability to consume American culture,' he writes, 'but the heightened emotions of wartime and the differences in points of view of a belligerent Canada and a neutral United States fomented an unusual cultural indigestion.' The irony was that without an indigenous Canadian popular culture to replace it the indigestion would only get worse: 'If Canada became less British, mass culture and the American values it bore would become relatively more influential.' Despite their best efforts, there was little the cultural nationalists could do to offset the influence of American mass culture.

As mentioned above, two regional chapters, Adam Crerar's on Ontario and David MacKenzie's on the Maritimes and Newfoundland, take as their starting points the patriotic enthusiasm that began the war. Crerar tests the strength of this enthusiasm across the spectrum of Ontario society. The way the people of Ontario responded to the war was 'both breathtaking and sobering,' Crerar explains, but these views were not universally shared, and the depth of support for the war effort varied across the province. Giving particular attention to rural Ontario, Crerar sifts through the different attitudes about the war and reminds us that a common cause did not necessarily produce 'shared purposes,' and that 'patriotism in Ontario took many forms and was, in fact, qualified to varying degrees.' Behind the explosion of patriotic enthusiasm in the cities were rural Ontarians and the thousands of French, German, Ukrainian, and African Ontarians who had their own unique stories; for them the war was 'experienced and imagined on many fronts.' Similarly, MacKenzie examines the diversity within Maritime and Newfoundland society and argues that what the war produced in this region would be characterized more accurately as ambivalence rather than transformation. While the war may have been something of a Canadianizing experience for many Atlantic Canadians, he argues that it also helped to ignite a wave of post-war regional discontent in the Maritimes and nourished a growing sense of independence in New-foundland. Ultimately, both authors question the old stereotypes of 'loyal' Ontario and the 'conservative' Maritimes.

In Part Four the aftermath of the war is examined, and in two very different chapters the authors try to answer the question: What did Canadians want and what did they get out of the war? The standard answers are 'recognition' and '60,000 dead,' and these responses pro-vide the starting point for the chapters by Margaret MacMillan and Jonathan Vance. MacMillan looks at the efforts of the Canadians at the 1919 Paris Peace Conference, and the transformation she considers is the evolution of Canada from colony to nation. For the small Canadian delegation, Paris was like a coming-out party on the international stage, but in an environment where their role would be necessarily 'modest,' status and autonomy became ends in themselves. 'Participation in the peace settlements was something of a false dawn for the dominions,' MacMillan concludes. 'They had made an exceptional effort, but none, not even Canada, had the diplomatic resources to sustain a role in international affairs.'

The 60,000 dead weighed heavily on Borden's mind and affected his conduct in Paris, leading him to demand greater autonomy and greater representation for Canada. It was his way of ensuring that these Cana-dians had not died in vain and giving meaning to the loss of thousands of lives. But if MacMillan focuses on the sense of loss on the national level, Jonathan Vance brings it down to the personal level and examines how individual Canadians across the country dealt with and grieved loss on a scale never before experienced. In a way that resonates in the chapters by English, Copp, Crerar, and others, Vance explores the widely held view that the 'nation itself was raised to a higher level of existence because of its sacrifice in Flanders' and suggests that, regardless of whether this assumption was true or false, the 'belief that their loss had meaning and purpose enabled [Canadians] to cope with grief.' There might be debate about what the war was about, but no one could deny the loss of 60,000 Canadians: 'Providing consolation for that loss, rather than rational explanation for the war as a whole, was the goal of the nation's memory of the war.'

MacMillan and Vance and others examine in one way or another how the war has been remembered. Coming to terms with the war experience – dealing with the loss, grief, absences, political turmoil, and social disruption – contributed to the way the war was perceived at the time and, ultimately, remembered. Running through this memory is the idea of transformation – in the economy, in social relations, in politics, in Canada's international standing and elsewhere. But in the end we are left with a very uneven transformation in Canadian life as a result of the experience of the First World War. If there were a new nationalism and unity, they were accompanied by regionalism and undermined by divisions along linguistic, class, ethnic, and gender lines. Where there was pride in accomplishments – on the battlefield and at home – there was also a profound sense of loss, for loved ones who had died and for a way of life that seemed to have disappeared. Internationally there was the achievement of a new-found sense of independence and status, but this autonomy had to be measured against the growing Americanization of Canadian popular culture. Everywhere there was the perception of great social, political, and economic upheaval, the sense that something important had happened, even when in many ways the fabric of Canadian life remained relatively unchanged.

Perhaps our view of the Great War as a transformative period in Canadian history stems from our desire to see the roots of modern Canadian society in the war; that somehow who we are today and the roots of the problems we face can be seen and understood if we look hard enough, crystallized in one short, purposeful period in the war experience. But it is the historian's duty to look more deeply into the historical record – that careful mixture of character and circumstance – and judge the past and the evidence on their own merits. Did industrialized, urban, modern Canada really emerge from the First World War? Many contributors to this book suggest that we can no longer be certain; any examination of the public support for the war, despite the death, devastation, and grim realities of life at the front, must be measured against the unevenness of that support based on region, ethnicity, gender, and class. The debate over conscription, the outrage over Regulation 17, the efforts towards moral regulation, the rise of political and cultural nationalism, the varying experiences of soldiers, working women, farmers, immigrant workers, widows, scientists, and diplomats, the economic fluctuations and regional variations, and even the language used by political leaders all remind us of the complexity of Canada's experience in the First World War and warn against making broad generalizations about that experience.

Finally, the question is raised of whether it would be more appropriate to approach the First World War not as the start of a new era but as the ending of an old one and, in this way, to view it not as the creative moment of the modern age but rather as the last gasp of Victorian Canada. Jonathan Vance elaborates on the idea: 'Two approaches have dominated the historiography: one looks back at the First World War from the modern age, seeing in it the roots of modernist idioms, cultural forms, and modes of expression; the other looks forward to the war from the Victorian age, emphasizing the persistence of nineteenth-century traditions, values, and sensibilities. This debate has produced an immense literature that has most recently leaned towards situating the war at the end of the age that preceded it rather than at the beginning of the age that followed it.' Perhaps Borden understood as much when he wrote in his diary on 11 November 1918, the day the war ended: 'The world has drifted from its old anchorage, and no man can with certainty prophesy what the outcome will be. I have said that another such war would destroy our civilization. It is a grave question whether this war may not have destroyed much that we regard as necessarily incidental thereto.'[9]

Canadians had no idea of what they were getting themselves into in August 1914. But from that starting point evolved the linguistic tensions, the social and economic dislocation, the unleashing of nationalisms, the political turmoil, and an outpouring of emotions ranging from enthusiasm, patriotism, and determination to resignation, horror, anxiety, and grief. Canada and Canadians may have 'come of age' during the Great War, but if that is the case, then this new-found sense of maturity came at a very high price.

The generation that fought the war has largely passed, but the memory and the myths of that experience remain – to be reconsidered, questioned, and debated. Perhaps the fact that the First World War is now lost to living memory helps to explain our renewed interest in examining and understanding it. Clearly, Canada's war experience still fascinates and appeals to Canadians today, almost a century later, and it undoubtedly will continue to do so for many years to come. The chapters that follow are a reflection of this continuing interest in the history of Canada and the First World War.

## NOTES

1 John Keegan, *The First World War* (New York: Random House, 1998), 9.
2 Robert Craig Brown and Ramsay Cook, *Canada, 1896–1921: A Nation Transformed* (Toronto: McClelland and Stewart, 1974), 1.
3 Michael Howard, *The First World War* (Oxford: Oxford University Press, 2002), v.
4 For example, some recent works specifically focused on the war, by authors other than those in this volume, include Tim Cook, *No Place to Run: The Canadian Corps and Gas Warfare in the First World War* (Vancouver: UBC Press, 1999); Jeffrey A. Keshen, *Propaganda and Censorship during Canada's Great War* (Edmonton: University of Alberta Press, 1996); Susan Mann, ed., *The War Diary of Clare Gass, 1915–1918* (Montreal: McGill-Queen's University Press, 2000); Bill Rawling, *Surviving Trench Warfare: Technology and the Canadian Corps, 1914–1918* (Toronto: University of Toronto Press, 1992); Ian Miller, *Our Glory and Our Grief: Torontonians and the Great War* (Toronto: University of Toronto Press, 2001); and Bill Freeman and Richard Nielson, *Far From Home: Canadians in the First World War* (Toronto: McGraw-Hill Ryerson, 1999).
5 Some recent novels that deal with the First World War and its legacy include Jack Hodgins, *Broken Ground* (Toronto: McClelland and Stewart, 1998); Frances Itani, *Deafening* (Toronto: HarperCollins, 2003); and two novels by Jane Urquhart, *The Underpainter* (Toronto: McClelland and Stewart, 1997) and *The Stone Carvers* (Toronto: McClelland and Stewart, 2001).
6 Robert Craig Brown, *Robert Laird Borden: A Biography*, 2 vols (Toronto: Macmillan, 1975 and 1980).
7 See Robert Craig Brown, '"Whither are we being shoved?" Political Leadership in Canada during World War I,' in *War and Society in North America*, ed. J.L. Granatstein and R.D. Cuff (Toronto: Thomas Nelson and Sons, 1971), 104–19.
8 Niall Ferguson, *The Pity of War* (New York: Basic Books, 1999), 174–211.
9 Borden, quoted in *A Nation Transformed*, 338.

# 1 Craig Brown's Logical Reason

RAMSAY COOK

During the great debate in the 1970s, over the supposed 'Americanization of Canadian universities,' I occasionally thought about my good
friend and colleague, Robert Craig Brown. Had I wanted an example, a
prime, personal example of the academic imperialism of the United
States, Brown could have been it. Back in 1957 when Brown, having just
graduated from the University of Rochester, arrived at the University of
Toronto as the recipient of a Canada Council fellowship, his presence
immediately caused me more than a little inconvenience. A good Methodist, he had demonstrated his theological confusion by applying to
live in Knox College, a bastion of continuing Presbyterianism. For two
years I, a lapsed member of the United Church, had occupied a room on
the first floor of West House in that same residence. I enjoyed life there,
even though the room was somewhat grubby and the meals were
unappetizing. The West House inhabitants were argumentative and
irreverent; some were even known to lubricate their intellectual and
religious life with cheap scotch or even cheaper sherry.

Without warning, in the late summer of 1957 I was informed that I
had been banished from West House to lonely exile in Centre House.
Two things made this news very hard to take. For one thing, West
House, including my room, had been cleaned and painted over the
summer for the first time in years. The cleansing of Centre House had to
wait another year or so. And then the unkindest cut of all: an American,
entering the masters program in history, had been assigned the space
that I, a PhD student in history, had come to call home. The arrival of
Brown, impeccably attired in quasi–Ivy League style, was a dark day
for me. Surely this was a classic example of colonialism. The Canada
Council had invited this newcomer in, paying his way, and the college

authorities uprooted a native so that this foreign agent could live, if not in luxury, then at least in a freshly painted room. In my overcharged imagination I visualized him being served specially prepared shepherd's pie in the dining room! Though I didn't see it clearly at the time, the American academic invasion of Canada was obviously off to a quick start.

Brown, in his courteous and amiable fashion, soon made it plain that he was not the advance guard of the U.S. *Kulturkampf*. He quietly demonstrated that he had come to the University of Toronto with considerable previous knowledge of Canada, learned under the guidance of Mason Wade, who in those days was renowned for having written a book that no English Canadian historian had even attempted, namely, *The French Canadians, 1760–1945* (1955). Moreover, Brown was a Democrat, something not that usual in Livonia, his home town in upstate New York. His attitude towards the Eisenhower administration and the continuing influence of McCarthyism in U.S. public life, an influence that had contributed directly to Herbert Norman's suicide in Cairo in April 1957, proved to be remarkably Canadian. Still, those first years must have been not too easy for Craig, since in Diefenbaker's Canada, partly because of the Norman tragedy, there was more than a little edginess in attitudes towards the United States and Americans. Perhaps that atmosphere – the debate over membership in NORAD, Walter Gordon's dire predictions about the impact of U.S. direct investment, the cancellation of the Avro Arrow, the Cuban missile crisis, and the controversy over nuclear warheads for our Bomarcs – helped to convince Brown that the study of Canada–United States relations could be exciting.[1] For that was his chosen field.

Before selecting a thesis topic, Craig looked over the Department of History with considerable care. He worked with Maurice Careless on Upper Canada, R.M. Saunders on the Enlightenment, Gerald Craig on the United States, and D.J. McDougall on the British Commonwealth. Not every graduate student found Donald McDougall's rigorous seminars a pleasure. This truly amazing, sightless professor (blinded in battle during the Great War, McDougall entered university in 1919 as a severely disadvantaged veteran) insisted that his students use their eyes – and their time – effectively. He could cite reams of documents and passages from books in sometimes unnerving ways in his unending effort to teach students to read with care. But his demand for exactitude and intellectual clarity, when met, was rewarded by generous grades and invitations to his house to listen to Mozart. Brown met the demands, often heard Mozart, and became one of Mr McDougall's regular, paid readers, a privilege this sardonic professor granted to only his best students.

Craig quickly proved that he was up to the demands that the University of Toronto presented in the late 1950s and early 1960s. Donald Creighton, of course, presented the main challenge to all students in modern Canadian history. Following the completion of the central work of his career, the two-volume biography of John A. Macdonald, Creighton's reputation as a scholar and a teacher was at its peak. Graduate students flocked to his seminar, where they discovered his passion for his subject, his close attention to his students' work, and his unpredictable moods. The faint at heart often shrank before this much larger-than-life performer, who sat with his long pale face in his hands or paced nervously around his Flavelle House office interjecting corrections and comments, while a hopeful apprentice historian stammered through a presentation on the 'double shuffle' or the 'Pacific scandal.' Only the truly courageous – or foolhardy – took up the case for Louis Riel. In 1957 Creighton had been especially buoyed up by the recent Diefenbaker victory, the cleansing of the Liberal stables. The hated Liberals, after over two decades of continentalist drift, were gone. The Tories, at last restored, would surely lead Canada and the Commonwealth into a second Elizabethan age. Creighton, too, had come to power. In his presidential address to the Canadian Historical Association in Ottawa in June 1957 he had excoriated the 'Authorized Version' (read 'Liberal') of Canada's history and declared that the true past was yet to be discovered. After a struggle that led to F.H. Underhill's flight from the Toronto department to Laurier House in Ottawa, Creighton obtained the chairmanship. Neither Creighton himself nor his colleagues enjoyed the abbreviated years of his reign.

An American graduate student entered that particular lion's den at his own risk. Or so it might have seemed. Craig Brown took the risk in his stride and found in Creighton what many other serious students discovered: a demanding, opinionated, tolerant, mercurial, generous, encouraging teacher – even a mentor. That Craig was an American apparently made little difference, for he quickly demonstrated that he was a talented, well-trained student with a professional interest in the history of Canada. Moreover, here was a student who understood that presentation, literary style, was essential to the historian's craft. Creighton didn't have to advise Brown (as he often did with his students) to read novels; he already did, including works by American authors whom

Creighton, paradoxically, often admired, though none as much as Arnold Bennett. Like every other Creighton student, Craig had his difficult moments with his master. More than most, doubtless he found Creighton's often colourful diatribes against the United States outrageous. Irritated as he must have been, he kept his peace, as a well brought-up young Yankee was expected to do. He chose to learn the remarkable things Donald Creighton had to teach and to demonstrate that even an American could help to discover a new Canadian past.

What Creighton certainly taught him – or perhaps he only reinforced an already formulated conviction – was that Canada was a nation with its own institutions, public values, cultural traditions, and, perhaps above all, national interests. (Since Creighton had little sympathy for or understanding of the concerns of Canada's French-speaking population, Brown's later, more liberal views on that subject likely originated earlier in Mason Wade's Rochester classroom.) Had he not learned, or shared, Creighton's strongly held beliefs about Canada's national interests, he would certainly have chosen some other supervisor for his doctoral research. His topic, 'Canadian American Relations in the Latter Part of the Nineteenth Century,' fell right into the period and touched on many of the diplomatic incidents about which Donald Creighton had a thorough knowledge.

The originality of Brown's work, published as *Canada's National Policy, 1883–1900: A Study in Canadian-American Relations*, rested on his argument that the diplomacy of these years could best be understood as a logical extension of Macdonald's well-known National Policy measures: the protective tariff, the transcontinental railway, the acquisition of western Canada and the beginning of its settlement. 'The spirit of the National Policy,' he wrote in the introduction to his study, 'went much deeper than railways, immigrants, and tariffs. Beneath these external manifestations was the will to build and maintain a separate Canadian nation on the North American continent.' After more than 400 pages documenting in detail tariff debates and negotiations, fisheries disputes, sealing quarrels, and boundary conflicts involving Canada and the United States, Brown entitled his conclusion, 'An Expression of Canadian National Sentiment.' He summed up his interpretation this way: 'Surprisingly, for a nation so inexperienced and immature in foreign relations, for a nation which remained a 'colonial nation' both in fact and in law, for a nation torn by domestic quarrels between English- and French-speaking Canadians, this policy appeared to be carefully thought out and rooted in the principle of national survival in the future as well as in the present.'[2] Donald Creighton would certainly have been pleased by this conclusion, and his pleasure must have been heightened by the realization that it had been reached by a student from the United States, now a landed immigrant in Canada.

The development of Craig's views about Canada's national interest did not come as a surprise to me. Since those dark days when he had occupied my room at Knox College, a close friendship had grown up between us. As I was nearing the end of my graduate studies, he sometimes asked my advice about courses, professors, research sources, and other necessities of graduate student life. In the autumn of 1958 Donald Creighton was appointed to the Monckton Commission on the Central African Federation, and I received an exceedingly temporary appointment in the Department of History as a replacement. I moved out of Knox and Craig joined me in a basement apartment let to us, probably illegally, by a wonderfully eccentric, hard-drinking, elderly woman, who lived on an affluent street in North Toronto. (She often trapped the squirrels in her garden and drove them to a nearby park where she released them. She regularly expressed astonishment, on her return, that her garden was still filled with squirrels – doubtless the same ones she had transported!) During the subsequent year and a half we both worked very hard preparing for comprehensive exams, writing theses and lectures, and grading papers. Craig cooked, I washed the dishes. We drank beer, listened to music – Craig's classical records – played atrocious tennis, took in an occasional baseball game, manned the mops when the sewers backed up, fought off the odd bat in the middle of the night, and occasionally allowed our unorthodox landlady to ply us with generous amounts of rye whisky. These were good times. My admiration for Craig's discipline, common sense, scholarly devotion, and sense of humour – not to mention his skill in disguising hamburger – convinced me that he would be a talented professional historian and, I hoped, a life-long friend. The rental partnership broke up in the spring of 1960 when Craig and Gail were married. I followed suit a week later. We ushered for each other. The circle of friendship now doubled in size and became permanent. The scholarly partnership would soon develop new dimensions.

Craig never suggested to me that he intended to return to the United States once his graduate work was completed. Probably, like all the rest of us, he was ready to take whatever post came up – and in those years very few did on either side of the border. As things turned out, he was ready for a job at just about the time when Canadian university expansion – both numbers of universities and numbers of students at all levels – got under way. In 1961, his thesis still to be examined, Brown took a position in the Department of History at the recently established University of Calgary. He quickly became a central member of that department, soon taking a weekly trip to the University of Alberta in Edmonton to help out with the graduate program there. Though an easterner, he nevertheless found the informality of western society attractive. The magnificence of Alberta's landscape appealed to both Browns in a very fundamental fashion. The west seemed to suit Craig and not merely because it allowed him to take up trout fishing – an art that included tying his own lures. Its history interested him. Had he resisted the fleshpots of Toronto, to which he returned first temporarily and then permanently beginning in 1964, his historical work might very well have taken a somewhat different direction.

Living in Calgary meant ready access to Banff National Park, and Craig naturally developed an interest in its history. One of his earliest and most original essays was presented at a conference on the national parks system in Canada held in Calgary in October 1968. He entitled the essay 'The Doctrine of Usefulness: Natural Resource and National Park Policy in Canada, 1887–1914.' While the subject was a new one for Craig, and indeed in Canadian historiography, his interpretation was an extension of an argument he had already made. He sketched out and analysed with care the debates surrounding the establishment of Banff, our first national park. His argument was that early parks policy had to be understood in a wider context of natural resource and national development. Parks, though areas for conservation, were similar to mines and timber because they were 'useful' even if only for recreation and revenue generation. Parks policy, like the foreign policy he had studied in his first book, was best understood as an extension of 'the expansionist, exploitative economic programs of the National Policy of the Macdonald Government after 1878 ... the term "wilderness" was scarcely used in discussion of parks policy and then only to suggest a primitive condition demanding "improvement" in order to make a park.'[3] Embedded in this persuasive essay was the potential for a larger study, one that could have encompassed the virtually unexamined work of the Canadian Commission of Conservation, established in 1909, which Brown commented on tentatively in his parks study. But that potential project slid into the background once Brown moved to the University of Toronto in 1964, and he soon found himself being offered other research opportunities.

Craig easily made a place for himself in the Toronto department, where he began as a temporary replacement for Donald Creighton and then stayed. He taught Canadian-American relations, and his interests moved from the late Victorian age into the twentieth century. He was quickly recognized as a conscientious teacher and a demanding scholar and editor. We renewed our old partnership almost at once; he joined me as associate editor of the *Canadian Historical Review* in 1964 and succeeded to the editorship four years later. He applied his admirable editorial talents to a centennial project with J.M.S. Careless, an excellent collection of essays, each covering a decade, entitled *The Canadians, 1867–1967* (1967). His willingness to work with and for others brought all sorts of tasks Craig's way over the years. Together with Sid Wise he published *Canada Views the United States* (1966), a valuable study of Canadian public opinion about the United States. He later wrote a first-class chapter on the second decade of the twentieth century for an innovative textbook, *Twentieth Century Canada* (1983) with J.L. Granatstein and others.

In the mid-1980s he accepted an invitation from Louise Dennys and Malcolm Lester to bring together a group of historians to produce a lavishly illustrated, scholarly history of Canada. The task was a major one, since Craig's goal was not merely to produce a textbook with a great many illustrations and photographs. He understood and told his unruly herd of authors that an 'illustrated history' was one where the text and the illustrations had to be thoroughly integrated, that one without the other could not tell the complete story. *The Illustrated History of Canada* (1987) is easily equal to similar books published elsewhere. (Since I was one of Craig's contributors, my view of the quality of the final product is obviously unbiased.) Most notably, it was the first survey of Canadian history to pay serious attention to the history of Native Peoples before the Europeans arrived. A French edition, in both cloth and paper, found a large francophone audience, while a Spanish version was published in Mexico on the recommendation of Pierre Trudeau. With such a range of editorial experience, it is hardly surprising that Craig was approached by the Champlain Society when a new editor for its prestigious series was needed in 1987.

The extent to which Brown had become a committed and indispensable member of the Canadian historical profession by the end of the 1960s is perhaps best illustrated by a fundamental decision that he made in 1967. After several summers labouring in the collections of the Public Archives of Canada, Craig decided to build a cottage in the

Gatineau. Like many other Canadian historians, to say nothing of Ottawa's politicians and public servants, the Browns realized that there is no place for human life in the heat, humidity, and rumour-mongering that descends on the Nation's Capital during most of July and August, the research months. But the beauty of the Gatineau, mosquitoes and all, the prospect of a swim after a day in the Borden Papers, and some fishing and sailing on weekends offered a compelling alternative to a young historian who had grown up within easy reach of the Finger Lakes in New York State. Another ten years would pass before Craig officially became a Canadian citizen, but the real decision about his future home came with the purchase of a lot sitting high over the shore at Grand Lake. Having reassured Craig that Quebec would almost certainly never separate from Canada, I felt it my duty to act on my beliefs and soon acquired a summer place at a somewhat less grand lake a half hour closer to Ottawa. Our continued friendship and collaboration was ensured. Our kids could play 'Dungeons and Dragons,' learn to sail, and read *Tintin*, while we got on with the serious business of doing Canadian history. Often, though not often enough, Craig would pick me up at the end of my cottage road so that together we could battle our way through menacing gravel trucks, slow-moving tractors, and haying machines on our way to that Canadian scholars' shrine, the Public Archives of Canada.

It may have been on one of those early morning joy rides, with an uncovered gravel truck in front spewing stones at Craig's Volvo and the one in the rear-view mirror creeping closer and closer, that I confessed that I might never finish my volume in the Centennial Series, the one devoted to the 1896–1921 period. My research on the Laurier years approached completion and I had done a great deal on Quebec, French language rights, and the conscription crisis. But that left large holes probably amounting to more than half of the planned book. I had been at it for about five years, my deadline was past, and Professors Morton and Creighton were beginning to ask pointed questions. Would Craig be interested in bailing me out?

Naturally Craig took a little time to think about my proposition. He was already launched on a very important new project – a biography of Sir Robert Borden. It was that work, of course, that made him such an obvious scholar to become my partner. I knew we could work together, not only because of our long friendship, but also because we had often discussed many of the historical issues that my projected book would be expected to cover. He asked some questions about my approach to organizing the book. I told him that my intention was to deviate some-what from the pattern set in the already published volumes of the series. Where those volumes had generally adopted a chronological, narrative approach, I wanted to write a more thematic study, examin-ing some topics that would illustrate the general characteristics of the period. Those were developments that the two of us had often dis-cussed, namely, the gradual emergence of an urban-industrial society in the quarter-century that I had been assigned. There would, of course, be several chronological chapters interspersed among the topical ones, especially those that would carry the political and diplomatic history forward. I was not surprised that Craig readily approved this general approach and immediately offered some suggestions about subjects that might be treated analytically.

Before agreeing to join me, Craig had to convince Henry Borden that this digression would be a valuable stepping-stone towards writing the Borden biography. For my part, Professors Morton and Creighton would have to agree to this new partnership. The latter was easy – anything that might kick-start their delinquent author evoked unrestrained en-thusiasm. Craig's detour also won approval. Then, before he threw me the lifeline, he set one perfectly reasonable condition: the entire final product would be presented as the joint work of the two authors, neither being identified as having written one part or the other. That meant we were entering a genuine partnership, just what I wanted. To seal the deal I proposed listing the authors alphabetically. We then set about finishing the research and writing the book, reviewing each draft chapter together and, with Eleanor Cook's help, bringing an agreed approach and common style to the revised versions. Disagreements were rare and never fundamental; there were a few errors that neither of us caught. The happy memory of writing the final two paragraphs together is still clearly etched in my mind. I can't recall which author came up with the book's subtitle, *A Nation Transformed*, but I do remem-ber the word play it evoked (would it be mistaken for a history of electricity? How about 'A Nation Transpired?' And so on.) The book turned out exactly as intended: a single book by two authors. Craig proposed that we dedicate it to D.J. McDougall, the First World War veteran and teacher we loved and admired and for whom, one day, we would serve as pallbearers. That dedication put a perfect seal on our successful partnership.

Brown had been strategically placed to do me this great favour be-cause, as I mentioned, he had agreed to write a life of Sir Robert Borden.

That, too, was part of his Canadian baptism. Not surprisingly, Henry Borden had first asked Donald Creighton to write the biography of his uncle. Creighton at first had agreed, but for his own reasons he never really got down to work on his new subject, preferring instead to focus his polemical pessimism on the supposed decline and fall of his beloved country. My guess is that Creighton was not attracted to Borden, whose sombre, matter-of-fact temperament contrasted so sharply with the high-spirited, hard-drinking John A.; Borden was simply not Wagnerian enough. So Creighton decided to find someone else to take over his job. His former student and now his colleague, Craig Brown, was his choice. Though neither Craig nor Donald Creighton thought of it this way, Creighton's imprimatur struck me as the equivalent of Canadian citizenship. Creighton's public utterances were increasingly anti-American, yet he willingly recognized that Craig, whatever the land of his birth, was the historian of Canada most likely to present a thoroughly researched, well-written, balanced portrait of the only successful Conservative prime minister since Macdonald. Creighton might also have thought that Brown and Borden had many temperamental similarities: quiet competence, patience, and perseverance. And, underneath their deceptively calm exteriors, the prime minister and the professor were energetic and decisive, capable of both occasional anger and loud laughter. 'Self-control, and patience and courage in the face of adversity, [Borden] had repeatedly observed, were the first steps toward achievement and the fulfilment of duty,'[4] Brown would later write, lines that could have been applied to the biographer himself without any significant alteration.

   *Robert Laird Borden: A Biography*, completed in 1980, remains Brown's major scholarly achievement. It was everything that could be expected of a biographer: exhaustively researched, effectively organized, tightly written, and, above all, very perceptive about the character of a prime minister who had tried his best to reveal as little of himself as possible. Readers of Borden's diaries knew that he entertained strong opinions about the public men of his time. They also knew that in times of stress Borden often suffered from boils and that he loved to play golf. But Brown teased much more out of the documents than the obvious: Borden emerges from this study as a person of ambition as well as conscience, of decisiveness and self-doubt, and of a judicial temperament that might have suited him better for the bench than for politics. 'From his perspective,' Brown concluded in a typically detached way, 'putting the interests of "country above party" had been a consistent principle of his political career.'[5] Hardly the road to long-term political success.

Borden, both in opposition before 1911 and as prime minister for the next decade, led a fractious party that constantly threatened to split apart. He faced caucus revolts and harsh criticism from more successful provincial Conservative party leaders before he finally drove Laurier from office. No problem was more persistent and ultimately more corrosive of Conservative unity than the place of the Quebec members in the party. Given Laurier's domination of Quebec, it is not surprising that Borden had to make do with the threads and patches of Quebec political life. Both the unpredictable Conservative, F.D. Monk, and the predictable nationalist, Henri Bourassa, made life almost unbearable for Borden. Brown's treatment of this subject is truly masterful in its detail and in its detachment: he sympathizes with Borden, whose frustrations were unending, but he also understands the problems faced by Borden's Quebec supporters. The Conservative leader had made a dubious bargain with the Nationalists in 1911, and Brown does his best to follow Borden's efforts, ultimately failed efforts, to make the alliance work.[6] His account of the Regulation XVII/Conscription/Union Government crisis carefully details the reasoning that led Borden to value Canada's war effort above Canada's domestic unity. Borden's limitations are frankly revealed, his strengths underlined. There will almost certainly never be a better, more tempered, critical account of Borden's war leadership than that found in Brown's biography and in a brief, compelling essay entitled '"Whither are we being shoved?" Political Leadership in Canada during World War I.' Who has better summed up Borden's Union Government than Brown did in 1971? 'Union government was the vehicle of both the assets and liabilities of Borden's political leadership. It was a creature of the politics of war. It violated all the canons of traditional political leadership. At its base was no party nor any recognizable traditional constituency support. It substituted a wartime national purpose for a celebration of peacetime national unity. Its foundation was an artificially created 'National' constituency and a singleness of purpose. Most important, its authority was temporary.'[7]

Though Brown recognized that Borden had made wartime decisions that ruptured national unity and led to a collapse of the Union Government, his final judgment on Borden was, characteristically, a balanced one. The rupture of national unity had to be weighed, as Borden himself claimed, against another principle that had guided Brown's assessment of politicians and policies from the time of his earliest writings: the

Soldiers leave by rail: troops off to war, ca. 1914 (City of Toronto Archives, Fonds 1244, Item 814)

national interest. That theme ran like a red thread through the Borden biography, becoming especially evident in the war years. Borden's assessment of the 'national interest' explained his decision to place military victory ahead of national unity in 1917, a Hobson's choice.

Borden's conduct of wartime relations with London provided Brown with the most convincing evidence of Borden's commitment to the national interest. In an essay that he wrote for a book honouring his mentor, Donald Creighton, he offered a subtle revision of the accepted view that Borden's imperial policy had evolved from an 'imperial' to a 'national' focus by the end of the Great War. From the outset, Brown believed, 'Canada's war aims were nationally defined, general, moral and unselfish.'[8] That position underlay both Resolution IX of the Imperial Conference in 1917, with its call for 'continuous consultation' among the members of the empire, and Borden's opposition to the renewal of the Anglo-Japanese Treaty in 1921. He contended that though Borden believed that the interests of Canada and the imperial interests should coincide, the Canadian leader nevertheless insisted that Canada had a right and duty to define its own interests, even if doing so resulted in conflict with Great Britain. The source of potential conflict, Brown explained, was that 'Borden deliberately brought the point of view of North America to the councils of the empire, a point of view that reflected the growing identity of Canadian and American interests.'[9] If there was ambiguity in this formulation – and there was – that ambiguity faithfully reflected the state of the imperial game at the end of the Great War. Brown's achievement was not to erase the ambiguity but rather to make it understandable. With the Borden biography Craig established himself as the leading historian of Canada's role in the First World War.

Craig dedicated the second volume of *Borden* to Donald Creighton, but his detached approach to the life of Sir Robert meant that his study differed markedly from his mentor's unabashedly committed account of Sir John A.'s career. Yet the two scholars shared a common belief in the validity of biography as an approach to understanding the past. 'I think that an Historian's chief interest is in character and circumstance,' Creighton famously remarked. Brown knew that he was writing the Borden biography not only in Creighton's long shadow but also at a time when Canadian historians had begun to argue that the 'life and times' approach had serious limitations. Craig decided to dispute that claim in his presidential address to the Canadian Historical Association in Montreal in the spring of 1980. His presentation deftly surveyed the field of Canadian biography, examining novel approaches and new and old criticisms. As usual, he was both judicious and firm. Biographers too often gave in to the temptation of biased advocacy; social history and social sciences such as psychology could add new insights to historical biography. But in the end, he maintained, biography remained a discrete and essential approach to the past. The biographer's 'obligation remains what it has always been: to disclose with sympathy and candour, and with such literary grace as he can command, as much as he can discover of his subject's private and public life. Without historical biography, there can be no historical "dialectique constant entre l'individu et la société." And that dialectic, after all, is an essential element not just of social history but of all historical inquiry.'[10] Labouring in the presence of Sir Wilfrid and Sir Robert for more than a decade could hardly have suggested any other conclusion. *Robert Laird Borden* illustrated the point and won his colleagues' admiration.

The completion of the Borden biography lifted a heavy responsibility from Craig's shoulders. It had been a long haul, interrupted by his work on *A Nation Transformed*. Observing Craig through those summers in the

Gatineau was a lesson in discipline for all of his friends. Long hours at the Public Archives, when the warm sun and the brisk sailing winds beckoned at Grand Lake, demonstrated his devotion to research and to exploring the undiscovered places in the Canadian past. Few, if any, Canadian scholars could challenge his record of attendance in the Archives reading room overlooking the mighty Ottawa River. Knox College had doubtless prepared him for the Archives cafeteria, where only poutine added variety to a recognizably Presbyterian menu. The copy of the final volume of *Borden* that Craig gave me as a reward for reading his draft manuscript included this amusing but self-revelatory message. 'Now all you will have to read at Tenpenny Lake are thesis drafts,' he wrote in his characteristically neat hand. My translation: '*Borden* is finished at last!'

The two-volume biography completed, Craig, despite his stalwart defence of the genre, didn't look for another major biographical project. He did, however, continue to demonstrate his skills in a series of succinct gems he wrote for the *Dictionary of Canadian Biography / Dictionnaire biographique du Canada*. The Great War continued to fascinate him, especially its impact on Canadian domestic developments. Scientific research – and Craig, perhaps spurred on by his science-educated wife Gail, had a long-held interest in science – had become a 'national interest' during the First World War. Brown's essay on the physicist Sir John McLennan demonstrated once again his capacity to bring together biography, politics, imperial relations and intellectual life. As always, the footnotes demonstrated that Craig wore his scholarship lightly: his research, as always, was resourceful and exhaustive.[11]

While Brown's scholarly work continued in these years, its pace was inevitably slowed by his increasing involvement in the administrative responsibilities that he willingly assumed. His patience, capacity for detailed work, and genuine fascination with university politics and intrigue, made him a natural leader in a variety of jobs. At the University of Toronto he served as associate dean of the graduate school and briefly as acting dean between 1981 and 1984, followed by five years as vice-dean of the Faculty of Arts and Science, 1987–92. The real challenge came in 1992: after having served his department in almost every other capacity he became chair for a five-year period. In his various responsibilities he offered friendly encouragement to his colleagues, who, in turn, recognized his ability and willingness to take the tough decisions that made his superiors look good. This was a part of my friend's life that I admired, because it so clearly demonstrated his strong sense of duty and loyalty to the institution that had given him a home when he came to Canada. It also made me appreciate my own good fortune – and that of others – in having avoided any such responsibilities. Craig was the kind of academic citizen who made the lives of the irresponsible possible.

Craig's administrative talents and his scholarly reputation were widely recognized beyond the University of Toronto. Having served on the Council of the Canadian Historical Association he became president in 1980. In 1984 he was elected a fellow of the Royal Society of Canada. Four years later he became the vice-president of Academy II (Humanities and Social Sciences). The presidency of Academy II followed for a three-year term. Occasionally, the Royal Society does something adventuresome. Craig, along with Professor John Meisel, serving a term as president of the society, took charge of one of those rare initiatives: the Royal Society of Canada – Beijing Academy of Social Sciences study of Canadian democracy. The Canadian team, on which I was an occasional substitute player, hosted their Chinese counterparts in Canada for lectures and discussions and travelled to the Peoples' Republic to continue these exchanges. Other Canadian specialists were recruited to explain to the Chinese researchers the mysteries of bilingualism, elections, federalism, income tax, bankruptcy and labour law, civil society, women's equality rights, and much more. At the final session in Niagara-on-the-Lake (where the capitalist who owned all of the hotels was a Chinese woman from Hong Kong), the Beijing scholars presented papers on Canadian democracy. They seemed to have taken in much of what had been taught. Events proved, however, that even modest hopes that the sterling example of Canadian democracy might change the Peoples' Republic of China were excessively optimistic.

Craig's role in the China project was an essential one. He was its major-domo, planning the session, arranging travel, finding Canadian scholars to participate, engaging in the discussions, eating, even cooking, Chinese food. His superb organizational skills surprised no one. But in one respect a new, if temporary, Craig emerged. Like Cecilia Bartolli, Craig long held to the sensible belief that no place is worth visiting unless it can be reached by land, preferably by train or, in a pinch, by Volvo. Nothing daunted, he and Gail *twice* flew to Beijing, and *twice* returned by air. (Later, trips to Israel and even to Vancouver were safely ventured.) The Chinese scholars quickly recognized Craig as a person they liked and trusted, one who enjoyed bok choy and Beijing duck. The Browns formed friendships that have continued long after the relegation of the China project to the academic filing cabinet. On the Chinese side, the firmness of that friendship has been repeatedly demonstrated during visits to Canada, regular electronic correspondence, and once, when Craig was ailing, by the gift of a dozen capsules of '"Longevity" Ursine Seal Penis Special-Effects tonics.' In generous recognition both of our more than forty years of friendship and of my greater need, I suppose, Craig passed the elixir on to me!

The longevity of our friendship, of course, is not the outcome of any medication, traditional or scientific. As is probably in the nature of friendships among academic people, common scholarly interests are at the centre of it. That is an essential bond. But beyond my admiration for Craig's scholarly performance, his editorial skills, and his outstanding contributions to the Canadian historical and academic community, there is something else, something more personal. He is *the* example that springs to mind when I quote, as I often do, Mavis Gallant's self-evident truth: 'a Canadian is someone who has a logical reason to think he is one.'[12] That logic, I am now convinced, began to take shape long ago in that unfairly acquired, freshly painted room in Knox College.

## NOTES

1 J.L. Granatstein, *Yankee Go Home?* (Toronto: HarperCollins, 1996), chaps 4–8.

2 Robert Craig Brown, *Canada's National Policy 1883–1900: A Study in Canadian-American Relations* (Princeton, N.J.: Princeton University Press, 1964), 12, 402; see also Robert Craig Brown, 'The Nationalism of the National Policy,' in Peter Russell, ed., *Nationalism in Canada* (Toronto: McGraw-Hill, 1966), 155–63.

3 Robert Craig Brown, 'The Doctrine of Usefulness: National Resource and National Park Policy in Canada 1887–1914,' in J.G. Nelson, ed., *Canadian Parks in Perspective* (Montreal: Harvest House, 1969), 58.

4 Robert Craig Brown, *Robert Laird Borden: A Biography*, Vol. II (Toronto: Macmillan, 1980), 208.

5 Ibid., 197.

6 Robert Craig Brown, *Robert Laird Borden: A Biography*, Vol. I (Toronto: Macmillan, 1975), 245–53.

7 Robert Craig Brown, '"Whither are we being pushed?" Political Leadership in Canada during World War I,' in J.L. Granatstein and R.D. Cuff, eds, *War and Society in North America* (Toronto: Thomas Nelson, 1971), 119.

8 Robert Craig Brown, 'Sir Robert Borden, the Great War and Anglo-Canadian Relations,' in John S. Moir, ed., *Character and Circumstance* (Toronto: Macmillan, 1970), 206.

9 Robert Craig Brown, 'Canada in North America,' in John Braeman, Robert H. Bremner, and David Brody, eds, *Twentieth-Century American Foreign Policy* (Columbus: Ohio State University Press, 1971), 359.

10 Robert Craig Brown, 'Biography in Canadian History,' *Historical Papers / Communications Historiques* (1980), 8.

11 Robert Craig Brown, 'The Life of Sir John Cunningham McLennan Ph.D, O.B.E., K.B.E., 1867–1935,' *Physics in Canada / La physique au Canada*, 56, 2 (March/April 2000), 91–102.

12 Mavis Gallant, *Home Truths* (Toronto: McClelland and Stewart, 1981), xiii.

# Part II
# Fighting the War

# 2 The Military Effort, 1914–1918

TERRY COPP

Most of the world remembers the First World War as a time when 'innocent young men, their heads full of high abstractions like Honour, Glory and England ... were slaughtered in stupid battles planned by stupid Generals.'[1] English-speaking Canadians, while generally accepting this view, have supplemented it with an imaginative version of a war in which their soldiers won great victories and forged a new national identity. Both of these approaches have served to promote literary, political, and cultural agendas of such power that empirical studies of what actually happened during the war have had little impact upon the historiography. Recently, a new generation of scholars has challenged this approach, insisting that 'the reality of the war and the society which produced it' are also worthy of study.[2] If historians are to continue to study the past to further understanding of what happened and why it happened that way, they need to remember that the men and women who participated in events like the First World War were not concerned with the views of later generations. The meaning of their war was constantly changing, and since no one knew the outcome or the consequences of decisions which needed to be made, they relied upon the best information available at the time and tried to act in ways that did not violate their shared values. This essay is therefore intended to introduce readers to the events of the war as well as the way historians interpret them.

It is clear, for example, that while Canadians were surprised that the assassination of an Austrian archduke should lead to war, those citizens interested in world affairs had long been aware of the possibility of such a conflict. The enmity between Germany and France, the alliance system, and the increasingly bitter rivalry of the German and British empires were topics of informed discussion throughout most of the decade that preceded the war.[3] The 'naval question,' which along with reciprocity of free trade with the United States, dominated pre-war political debate, sensitized many of those normally indifferent to such topics. Canadians were divided on issues of war and peace and especially divided on military and naval expenditure precisely because they thought they understood what was at stake.

French-Canadian opinion, at least within Quebec, was almost universally opposed to any form of military expenditure which might underwrite Canadian participation in foreign wars. Within English-speaking Canada there were sharp divisions between pro-empire activists, Canadian nationalists, anti-militarists and declared pacifists. While newspapers such as the *Montreal Star* and the Toronto *Mail and Empire* offered strong support for military preparedness, the Toronto *Globe*, the Methodist *Guardian*, and the voice of the western farmer, the *Grain Growers' Guide*, were equally adamant about the dangers of militarism.[4]

Canada's leaders played no part in the decision for war in 1914, and it is literally true that Canada went to war because Britain was at war. This statement, while accurate, does little to help us make sense of the events of August 1914 in Europe or in Canada. To achieve understanding we must answer three different questions: (1) Who was believed to be responsible for the outbreak of war? (2) Why was Britain involved? (3) What kind of war was it going to be? The answers to these questions seemed obvious to informed Canadians. Germany was threatening the peace of Europe and violating Belgian neutrality as part of an attack on France. Britain was defending France against German aggression and coming to the assistance of Belgium. The war was likely to be over by Christmas, after decisive battles between standing armies, but it might last until 1915.

The response of most English-speaking Canadians was predictable. Canada was part of the empire and must actively support the mother country in a just war which Britain had tried to prevent. This view of the origins of the war was dismissed as simplistic in the 1920s, when historians developed a revisionist interpretation which ignored evidence of German intentions. Today, the scholarly consensus presents a picture not very different from the one accepted by Canadians in 1914.[5]

The country's commitment to the war effort was not in doubt, but Canada could not provide any immediate assistance. Wilfrid Laurier's attempt to create a Canadian navy, able to defend Canada's coasts and assist in the protection of imperial sea lanes, ended with his defeat in

1911. The Liberal-controlled Senate then blocked Prime Minister Robert Borden's Naval Aid Bill, which offered direct financial assistance to the Royal Navy. As a result, in 1914 the Royal Canadian Navy possessed one seaworthy, if obsolescent light cruiser, HMCS *Rainbow* and two submarines hastily purchased from the neutral United States by the government of British Columbia.[6]

Canada's regular army of 3,000 all ranks, plus some 70,000 volunteers serving in the militia, constituted a far more considerable force than the navy. Under the energetic if eccentric leadership of Sam Hughes, minister of militia since 1911, fifty-six new armouries and drill halls were built and training camps created or expanded. Hughes is usually remembered for his misguided commitment to the Ross rifle, a Canadian-designed and manufactured weapon, which proved deficient under combat conditions. But if Hughes is to be condemned for his errors of judgment, he must also be remembered for encouraging more realistic training, marksmanship, the acquisition of modern guns for the artillery, and the expansion of the militia.[7]

Whatever view one takes of Hughes, it is evident that no Canadian field force could possibly have gone into action on a European battlefield in 1914. This reality did not deter the minister. On 6 August he sent 226 night telegrams directly to unit commanders of the militia ordering them to interview prospective recruits and wire lists of volunteers for overseas service to Ottawa. Hughes bypassed existing mobilization plans requiring the Canadian Expeditionary Force to assemble at a new, yet to be built, embarkation camp at Valcartier, near Quebec City.

Would the original plan have worked more smoothly? Would a conventionally recruited force of 30,000 men have been ready to leave for England in October? We will never know, but it is impossible not to be impressed with what Hughes and William Price, who created camp Valcartier and organized the embarkation of troops, accomplished in just seven weeks.

Who were the men who volunteered to go to war in 1914? Desmond Morton suggests that, 'for the most part, the crowds of men who jammed into the armouries were neither militia nor Canadian-born.'[8] Most, he argues, were recent British immigrants anxious to return to their homeland in a time of crisis, especially when Canada was deep in a recession which had created large-scale unemployment. The best available statistics suggest that close to 70 per cent of the first contingent 'were British born and bred' though the officer corps was almost exclusively Canadian. Command of the First Division went to a British officer, Lieutenant General Sir Edwin Alderson, but Hughes appointed Canadians to command the brigades, battalions, and artillery regiments. Much the same pattern held for the second contingent: 60 per cent were British born, but their officers were Canadian.[9]

When news of the war reached the colony, Newfoundlanders were still mourning the loss of more than 300 fishermen in a spring blizzard. The response nevertheless was enthusiastic, and in the absence of a recent British immigrant population, recruits were drawn from a cross-section of town and outport communities. Less than 250,000 people lived in Newfoundland in 1914, but thousands volunteered to serve in the Newfoundland Regiment and the Royal Navy.[10] Imperial ties were no doubt basic to this response, but many were drawn to serve by the promise of decent pay and a meaningful role in a war which could not be much more dangerous than the sea.

A recent study of ideas current in Ontario before the war argues that the rush to enlist in 1914 was due to cultural influences which 'worked together to inculcate in young boys the notions of masculinity and militarism that would create soldiers.' War was presented as 'masculine event' and a 'romantic commitment to war had entrenched itself as a pseudo-religion in the province indoctrinating young boys with a glamorized notion of sacrifice.'[11] There may be some limited value in this kind of explanatory framework when we speculate about the motives of those who sought commissions in the expeditionary force, but there is no evidence to indicate that such ideas influenced the relatively small numbers of Ontario-born, ordinary-rank volunteers.

The men who gathered at Valcartier were supposed to be at least five feet, three inches, tall with a chest measurement of thirty-three and a half inches, between eighteen and forty-five years of age, and ready to serve for one year 'or until the war ended if longer than that.' Officers received from $6.50 a day for a lieutenant colonel to $3.60 for a lieutenant. Non-commissioned officers could earn as much as $2.30 a day, while the basic rate for a soldier was $1.10. The Canadian Patriotic Fund, which is the focus of Desmond Morton's chapter, provided additional support for families from private donations. The fund, with chapters across Canada, offered support only after a humiliating investigation of the recipients and then provided assistance on a sliding scale which paralleled the army's rates of pay. A dollar a day was not far below the income of a junior clerk or unskilled labourer and was far above the cash paid to a farm worker. The army was thus an attractive proposition to many single men seeking escape from the dull routines of work or the harsh experience of unemployment. A large number of married men also volunteered, but Sam Hughes, who insisted participation had to be voluntary in every sense of the word, decided that 'no recruit would be accepted against the written protest of his wife or mother.' According to the newspapers 'long lists of men were struck off the rolls' because of this regulation.[12]

As the Canadian Expeditionary Force and the Newfoundland Regiment departed for England, a second contingent, which would become the 2nd Canadian Division, was authorized. This decision (7 October) was made in the context of the German advance on Paris, the dramatic retreat of the British Expeditionary Force from Mons, and the miracle of the Battle of the Marne, which saved France from immediate defeat. If the war was seen as a romantic adventure in early August, by October the harsh reality of high casualties and the prospect of a German victory created a more realistic view.

By October Canadian opinion was also deeply affected by the plight of the Belgian people. Voluntary organizations including farm groups, churches, and ad hoc committees responded with offers of money, food, clothing, and plans to aid Belgian orphans and refugees. This spontaneous outpouring of sympathy preceded the first atrocity stories, which served to further intensify anti-German sentiments and public support for participation in a just war.[13]

The 1st Division arrived in Britain on 14 October and reached its tented camp on Salisbury Plain near Stonehenge just in time for the worst, wettest winter in recent memory. Over the next four months the contingent trained and equipped itself to join the British army in Flanders as a standard infantry division. Major General Alderson, an experienced British officer, was given command. The establishment of 18,000 men included three brigades, each consisting of 130 officers, 4,000 men, and 272 horses. Each brigade contained four infantry battalions of approximately 900 men commanded by a lieutenant colonel. A battalion was made up of four rifle companies, each divided into four platoons. Additional firepower was provided by two sections of two Colt machine guns per battalion. The three divisional artillery brigades, equipped with modern fifteen-pounder field guns, provided the firepower that was supposed to permit troops to assault enemy positions neutralized by shelling.[14]

There is no consensus among historians as to how well prepared the Canadians were when they entered the line in March 1915. Desmond

Second contingent of soldiers from Saskatoon, Saskatchewan, 1915 (National Archives of Canada, PA38523)

Morton describes the Canadians as 'woefully unready.'[15] John Swettenham, whose book *To Seize the Victory*[16] is still a very useful survey of the Canadian military effort, emphasized the problems of the Ross rifle and other difficulties with equipment. Bill Rawling's important study, *Surviving Trench Warfare: Technology and the Canadian Corps, 1914–1918*, reminds us that the Canadian artillery was not able to fire its guns until the end of January 1915 and then was allotted just fifty rounds per battery. 'The gunners,' he writes, 'would have to wait until the move to France to gain any real experience with the tools of their trade.' Rawling concludes that the 1st Division was 'hardly a well-prepared formation,' but notes that trench warfare was new to the 'well-trained professional European armies as well.'[17] In the official history, *Canadian Expeditionary Force, 1914–19*, G.W.L. Nicholson quotes the commander of the British Expeditionary Force, Field Marshal Sir John French, who reported that the Canadians were 'well trained and quite able to take their places in the line.' This is the sort of thing generals are required to say and has little other value.[18]

A recent study of the 4th Infantry Battalion offers a detailed analysis which suggests that the 'mad Fourth' worked hard at a comprehensive training program in both England and Europe. Paired with the Royal Welsh Fusiliers in Belgium, platoons were rotated through the trenches and prepared by repeated exercises in rapid fire, fire control, and close combat drill. When first ordered into action in April 1915, the companies leapfrogged forward in perfect order using fire and movement. They were stopped some 600 yards short of their objective and suffered heavy losses, but their counter-attack towards Mauser Ridge played a significant part in stemming the enemy's initial advance.[19] Further studies at the battalion level are necessary before firm conclusions can be drawn, but it is important to recognize that the events of the war may not lend themselves to simple notions of the transformation of raw recruits into experienced professional soldiers. The reality may well be that no Canadian formation fought a more important or more successful battle than 2nd Ypres.[20]

The German army's experiment with chlorine gas, as a method of breaking the stalemate on the Western Front, has been re-examined by Tim Cook in his book *No Place to Run*.[21] The Canadians were, he reminds us, sent into a salient which 'protruded into the German lines like a rounded tumour, eight miles wide and six miles deep.' The positions they took over from the French covered 4,500 yards north of Gravenstafel Ridge and were overlooked by German observers on Passchendaele Ridge to the east. 'Shells came from everywhere except straight behind us,' one gunner noted in his diary. The Canadians were shocked by the state of the trenches, which resembled muddy holes rather than those created in training.

Eight days after their tour of duty began a period of quiet which had settled over the salient was broken by an intense artillery barrage beginning in the late afternoon. 'Along with the shells came an ominous grey-green cloud four miles long and half a mile deep' which crept upon the 45th Algerian and 87th French divisions. 'One by one the French guns fell silent only to be replaced by screaming choking Algerians running into and past the Canadian lines ... The victims of the gas attack writhed on the ground. Their bodies turned a strange gas-green as they struggled to suck oxygen into their corrupted lungs. The chlorine attacked the bronchial tubes, which caused the membranes to swell into a spongy mass and ever-increasing amounts of fluid to enter from the bloodstream. The swiftly congested lungs failed to take in oxygen, and the victims suffocated as they drowned in their own fluids.'[22] The Canadians were spared all but the edges of the cloud, and it was evident that they would need to launch a counter-attack to check the expected German advance. There was much confusion as well as indecision and moments of panic, but the counter-attacks mounted by the 1st and 3rd brigades that night were carried out with skill and resolution.

Early on the morning of 24 April, as the Canadians and the first British reinforcements struggled to build new defensive positions, a second gas attack began. The 15th and 8th battalions of Canada's 2nd Brigade, holding the original lines in what was now the apex of the salient, saw the gas drifting towards them and urged each other to 'Piss on your handkerchiefs and tie them over your faces.' Urine, the chemistry students in the army recalled, contained ammonia, which might neutralize the chlorine. Cook quotes Major Harold Matthews's vivid memories of the moment. 'It is impossible for me to give a real idea of the terror and horror spread among us by the filthy loathsome pestilence. It was not, I think, the fear of death or anything supernatural, but the great dread that we could not stand the fearful suffocation sufficiently to be each in our proper places and to be able to resist to the uttermost the attack which we felt must follow and so hang on at all costs to the trench we had been ordered to hold.'[23]

Matthews's emphasis on the duty of resisting 'to the uttermost' and fears of failure to do one's duty may strike modern observers as strange, but his contemporaries understood him well enough. Courage and determination were no proof against the full force of the gas, however, and as the Canadians slowly retreated, wounded and severely gassed soldiers were abandoned to become prisoners or to face execution. A new defensive line some 1,000 metres further back was established with the assistance of British troops, and the next day the Germans launched a series of conventional attacks near the village of St Julien, where the famous 'brooding soldier' Canadian war memorial now stands. After the German advance south of the village was halted, General Alderson was ordered to recapture St Julien and 're-establish our trench line as far north as possible.' This absurd order compounded the growing chaos and led to further heavy losses. Stopping the German advance was one thing; retaking ground in a salient valued solely for reasons of Belgian pride and British prestige was quite another. On 26 April yet another attack into the German positions was launched. The Lahore Division of the British Indian Army advanced until gas, used for the first time defensively, broke the impetus of the attack.[24]

The Canadians emerged from the battle with horrendous casualties: over 6,000 men, including 1,410 who became prisoners of war. This casualty rate, 37 per cent of the troops engaged, would never be exceeded, not even at the Somme.[25] The British and Canadian press lauded the Canadian achievement and the enemy acknowledged their 'tenacious determination,' but behind the scenes there were serious conflicts over the conduct of the battle, including sharp criticism of Brigadiers Arthur Currie and R.E.W. Turner. Many Canadian officers were equally unhappy with the performance of senior British commanders.[26] After April 1915 this tension between British and Canadian officers helped to ensure that the 1st Division became the core of Canada's national army rather than an 'imperial' formation drawn from a dominion.

News of the gas attack and the valour of the country's soldiers reached Canada on 24 April before the battle was over. The newspapers reported that Canadian 'gallantry and determination' had saved the situation, but they hinted at heavy losses. The Toronto *News* described the mood: 'Sunday was one of the most anxious days ever experienced in Toronto, and the arrival of the officers' casualty list only served to increase the feeling that a long list including all ranks was inevitable. Crowds scanned the newspaper bulletin boards from the time of arrival of the first lists shortly before noon, until midnight, while hundreds sought information by telephone. Historian Ian Miller, writing of Toronto, describes the dawning awareness that whole battalions had been devastated. At first it was impossible to believe that battalions such as the 15th, made up of men from the city's 48th Highlanders, had been wiped out, and the press assumed that many were prisoners of war. When the full lists were available in early May, the truth was apparent. The 15th Battalion had virtually ceased to exist, and 'half the infantry at the front have been put out of action.'[27] The events of the spring of 1915 transformed the war from a great adventure to a great crusade. A week after the enemy introduced the horrors of gas warfare, the *Lusitania* was torpedoed off the coast of Ireland with a loss of 1,369 civilians, including 150 children. Newspapers across Canada published heart-rending stories about the victims and survivors of the sinking alongside further accounts of the fighting in the Ypres salient. The war was now recognized as a struggle against a brutal, barbaric enemy.

In revisionist accounts of the Great War some writers have sought to minimize German war crimes in 1914–15, but at the time Canadians recognized policies designed to inspire terror for what they were. Recently, historian Jeffrey Keshen has added to the revisionist approach, arguing that Canadians were 'manipulated' by elites and a 'jingoistic press,' which presented 'unrealistically blithe images about trench warfare.'[28] In his study, *Propaganda and Censorship during Canada's Great War*, based on government censorship files, he suggests that Canadians at home were denied the opportunity to learn the realities of war and were force-fed a romantic version of heroic sacrifice.

This view of the home front is contradicted by Ian Miller's detailed study of Toronto in which he cites examples of private letters routinely published in the press describing the war in gruesome detail. This was particularly true after the first gas attack when, to cite just one example, a letter from the front printed in the Toronto *World* informed readers that 'the dead are piled in heaps and the groans of the wounded and dying never leave me. Every night we have to clear the roads of dead in order to get our wagons through. On our way back to base we pick up loads of wounded soldiers and bring them back to the dressing stations.'[29]

The censors could do little to prevent the printing of such letters, and they proved equally unable to control the content of articles on the war. One attempt to stop the publication[30] of Robert W. Service's gritty descriptions of his experiences as an ambulance driver was ignored by editors determined to print front-line reports from the popular author and poet. Service's description of the 'Red Harvest' of the trenches, with its images of 'poor hopeless cripples' and a man who seemed to be 'just one big wound,' left no room for doubt about the ugliness of war.[31] The effect of such accounts was to inspire young Canadians to enlist in a great crusade against an evil enemy.[32] Historians who are uncomfortable with this reality should avoid imposing their own sensitivities on a generation which had few doubts about the importance of the cause they were fighting for.

The Canadians returned to the battlefields of Flanders on 17 May, capturing 'one small orchard and two muddy ditches' at a cost of 2,468 casualties. The capture of the 'Canadian Orchard' was a small part of a major Franco-British offensive which included a futile attempt to seize Vimy Ridge.[33] Overall Allied losses in May and June totalled more than 200,000 men, a clear demonstration that battles could not be won with the weapons available in 1915. The British and French field commanders were convinced that with more and better shells for the artillery, including ones filled with gas, they would break the German defences. Lord Kitchener, who was striving to create a 'New Army' which would place seventy divisions in the field, was less sure. He was preparing for a long war but admitted he had no idea of how it might be won.[34] It is evident that the British generals, like their French and German counterparts, were totally surprised by the harsh realities of trench warfare. They simply had no idea of how to get men across the zones of machine-gun, mortar, and artillery fire to close with the enemy. They were equally unprepared to exploit any breach in their opponent's defensive position if it should occur.

Senior British officers, with a few outstanding exceptions, demonstrated a profound lack of imagination and initiative in the early years of the war. The first suggestions for a tracked armoured vehicle which could overcome barbed wire and cross trenches were made in Britain during the fall of 1914, but the army was uninterested. Instead, experiments were carried out by a 'landships committee' formed by Winston Churchill through his control of naval expenditures. The first such vehicles, known for security reasons as 'tanks,' were ready for use in July 1916 and employed for the first time on 15 September, though another year passed before large numbers were available.[35] Steel helmets, which saved many lives, were issued by the French in early 1915, but British and Canadian troops waited another year before helmets became standard issue. The Germans made extensive use of trench mortars, but it was not until August 1915 that the British War Office authorized the mass production of the British-invented Stokes mortar.[36] The shortage of artillery shells was not resolved until 1916. The public were not aware of these problems, but they were well informed about machine guns, which were said to account for German success in trench warfare.

The machine-gun movement, which became a popular crusade in Britain, was launched in Canada by John C. Eaton of the department store family, who donated $100,000 to purchase armoured cars equipped with Colt machine guns. The concept of motorized armoured machine-gun carriers was an initiative of Raymond Brutinel, a French immigrant to Canada, who organized 'the first motorized armoured unit formed by any country during the war.' Brutinel's 1st Canadian Motor Machine Gun Brigade was reinforced by the batteries created in Canada, though the static conditions on the Western Front provided little opportunity for mobile warfare, and before 1918 the brigade was used primarily in a static fire support role.[37]

Other individuals and associations hastened to offer money for additional machine guns, which were to be provided 'over and above the regular compliment supplied to each battalion.' By the fall of 1915 these private initiatives were halted by Prime Minister Borden's embarrassed announcement that all equipment required by the troops would be paid for out of the 'Canadian Treasury.'[38]

The arrival of the 2nd Canadian Division in England in June 1915 raised an important question about the future of Canadian formations in the British Army. Sam Hughes was determined that they should serve together and proposed the formation of the Canadian Corps. Normally, the composition of a British corps, made up of two or more divisions, varied according to the exigencies of war, but Kitchener agreed that an exception could be made for the Canadians. Alderson was appointed to command the Corps and two Canadian militia officers, Arthur Currie and R.W. Turner, were promoted to command the 1st Division and the 2nd Division, respectively.[39]

Despite the evident stalemate and heavy casualties, Allied generals and their political masters agreed that the war must continue. At the Chantilly conference of July 1915 a decision was reached on a massive Anglo-French offensive to be carried out in the spring of 1916. Preparations, especially the production of enough guns and shells to destroy the enemy's barbed wire and crush his defences, were to be the foundation of an attack they hoped would rupture the enemy front, leading to a mobile war and victory on the field of battle. The same optimism was evident within the German army, where plans for an offensive designed to win the war in 1916 culminated in the attack on the French fortress city of Verdun. The intent was not to capture ground but to bleed the French army and destroy its will to fight.[40]

The Canadians spent a relatively quiet winter, and it was not until spring 1916 that 2nd Division was committed to a major action. Georges Vanier, the future governor general, who was serving with the 22nd Battalion, wrote to his mother describing the emotions he felt when marching through France, 'the country I love so much in order to fight in its defence.'[41] Then, as the French and German armies tried to destroy each other at Verdun, his battalion and the rest of 2nd Division were ordered to take over positions near St Eloi, which a British division had fought to capture and hold. The British had sunk mine shafts under the German lines and set off explosions that wiped out the landmarks and created seven craters, the largest of which was 50 feet deep and 180 feet across. The attempt to relieve that British division in the midst of the battle compounded a bad initial plan, and the Canadians were soon caught up in a disaster which cost the division 1,173 casualties.[42]

The battle of St Eloi led to another crisis in command relationships when the Corps commander sought to dismiss General Turner and one of his brigadiers for alleged incompetence. The new British commander-in-chief, General Sir Douglas Haig, refused to confirm the decision because of 'the danger of a serious feud between the Canadians and the British ... and because in the circumstances of the battle for the craters mistakes are to be expected.'[43] Canadian historians have tended to side with Alderson and condemn Turner, noting that political interference from Hughes and his representative Sir Max Aitken (later Lord Beaverbrook) saved Turner and cost Alderson his job as Corps commander.[44] But the case against Turner is made on Clausewitzian grounds, suggesting that a competent commander is by definition one who reacts properly and masters the situation. If this standard is applied, uniformly few generals on either side make the grade, and we are left with fallible, stubborn, imperfect humans, unable to foresee the future and almost always overwhelmed by the chaos of battle.

The Canadians, now including the 3rd Division, spent the summer of 1916 in familiar positions north of Ypres. The enemy was still able to shell the salient from several directions, making life in the forward lines both miserable and very dangerous. Many Canadian (and British) officers expressed their bitter opposition to orders to hold and attempt to expand the Ypres salient. Sam Hughes, always suspicious of decisions made by British professional soldiers, created a major controversy when he publicly denounced the policy. By the spring of 1916 Hughes had little credibility left, and Borden moved to dismiss his troublesome minister.[45]

The men serving in the front lines knew little of these policy matters, which seemed remote from the soldier's experience of war. The best social history of the Canadian Corps is Desmond Morton's *When Your Number's Up*, which is rich in detail.[46] Morton notes that, except during an attack, battalions spent one week in the forward positions, with companies rotating between the three lines of trenches. Even quiet periods brought a steady drain of casualties from shells, mortars, and enemy sniping, with much heavier losses recorded during raids on the enemy trenches. Tradition has it that the Canadians invented or at least perfected large-scale raids, but this legend like many others requires revision, not to mention a more sophisticated assessment of their value. As Tim Cook has demonstrated, in the raid carried out in March 1917 at

Vimy Ridge, the casualties 'not only temporarily impaired the fighting efficiency of 4th Division, but called into question the whole policy of raiding.'[47]

The war also produced tens of thousands of non-battle casualties, including 7,796 who died of disease or accidental injury.[48] By 1916 the army and its medical officers had begun to recognize and treat 'shell shock' as a traumatic stress disorder of the mind rather than a physiological reaction to explosions. This did not necessarily mean more humane treatment; many medical practitioners believed that nervous soldiers could be made to recover by using electric shock and other methods of forcing a return to duty.[49] It is impossible to determine how many soldiers suffered from or were treated for shell shock, but if the ratio observed in the Second World War applies, the total may have reached 20,000.[50]

In the chapter titled 'Officers and Gentlemen,' Desmond Morton presents a series of anecdotes describing the 'rigid class system' which separated officers from the men in the ranks. All commissioned officers, he notes, had a soldier-servant called a batman, 'from the Hindi word for baggage.' Officers wore a collar and necktie and ate, whenever possible, in an officers' mess rather than lining up to have food ladled into mess tins. Even the most junior officer was better paid than the most experienced soldier and could look forward to the prospect of leave, which was denied to the ranks. Preferential treatment was provided when an officer was recovering from wounds or coping with the trials of the military justice system. 'In return for these privileges,' Morton asks, 'what did officers actually do?' The answer 'at least for regimental officers is that they gave leadership, took responsibility, and set an example, if necessary by dying ... Officers were the first out of the trench in an assault or night patrol and last out in a retreat.'[51] Not every officer was able to lead by example, and Morton presents the view, first argued by Steve Harris in his book *Canadian Brass*, that regimental officers were the weak point in the Canadian Corps.[52] Morton's own evidence is mixed, and a far more systematic study of the performance of junior officers is required before any meaningful conclusions can be drawn.

Much the same problem exists with regard to staff officers, brigadiers, and generals. Canadian historians and journalists have concentrated most of their attention on Arthur Currie, because he assumed command of the Canadian Corps in the aftermath of the successful battle for Vimy Ridge. To the general public Currie remains a heroic figure, but as his biographer Jack Hyatt notes, Currie was a complex man with both strengths and weaknesses. Hyatt reminds us that 'any reasonable judgment of military leadership ... requires a consideration of historical record and context.'[53] It also requires some basis of comparison, and, in the absence of studies of other divisional and corps commanders, conclusions about Currie must be tentative.

For example, we are just beginning to receive balanced assessments of individuals like Major General A.C. Macdonnell, who led 7th Infantry Brigade before his promotion to command the 1st Division. Ian McCulloch, who has studied the operations of 7th Brigade, suggests that Macdonnell was an exceptional officer, who emphasized high training standards 'and the development of a new distinctly Canadian attack doctrine.'[54] Macdonnell's colourful personality and personal bravery won him the nickname 'Batty Mac' and the kind of popularity that Arthur Currie, with his stiff personality, could never achieve. We know little about the other senior officers, all of whom require study.

While the Canadians endured life in the Ypres salient, the British began their major 1916 offensive: the Battle of the Somme. The Somme is now remembered chiefly for the first day, when 21,000 men were killed and 35,000 wounded,[55] the worst single-day disaster in British military history. Canadians did not take part, but the Newfoundland Regiment, part of the British 29th Division, lost 272 men killed and 438 wounded from a strength of 790 men; that is why 1 July is Memorial Day in Newfoundland.[56]

The failure to achieve the hoped-for breakthrough did not mean the battle was over, and the Somme fighting continued throughout the summer. One of the few bright spots was the success of the Royal Flying Corps in winning air superiority over the battlefield. S.F. Wise, who wrote *Canadian Airmen and the First World War*, notes that with new tactics and the concentration of 400 aircraft the RFC was able to dominate the sky, forcing the enemy to find the resources to meet this new threat. Fully 10 per cent of the pilots engaged at the Somme were Canadians who had transferred from the army.[57]

The RFC also played a major role in the new offensive which began on 15 September 1916. The Canadian Corps, three divisions strong, was part of an attack which involved two British armies. The battle of Flers-Courcelette began with the first ever attempt to employ tanks on the battlefield. Haig's decision to use the small number of tanks then available to assist in a set-piece attack was and continues to be criticized,

A Canadian battalion in a bayonet charge on the Somme (Archives of Ontario, C224-0-0-9-18, AO 537)

because it sacrificed the element of surprise.[58] It is evident that Haig believed a breakthrough was still possible in 1916, and he insisted on using whatever was available. The Canadians, attacking astride the Albert-Baupaume road, were supported by two detachments of three tanks each. According to Nicholson, the 'presence of the tanks encouraged many Germans to surrender,' but most were put out of action in the first hours of the battle.[59] The RFC, which attacked the enemy's trenches with machine-gun fire, may well have played a larger role in securing the initial modest gains. Despite improvements in artillery doctrine and a vast increase in the supply of shells, Flers-Courcelette quickly degenerated into an attritional battle which was to cost the Canadians 24,029 casualties. These losses included 1,250 men of the 4th Canadian Division, which fought its first battle in November 1916.

Haig's policy of continuing the Somme battle after it was evident that there was little hope of defeating the enemy in 1916 was bitterly opposed by many British political leaders, including David Lloyd George, who became prime minister in December 1916. Lloyd George's criticisms of Haig and the war of attrition on the Western Front would continue until the armistice, but in the absence of a convincing alternative strategy the British and French armies continued to plan to renew the offensive in 1917.[60]

Lloyd George was anxious to limit the slaughter in the trenches, but he was not prepared to endorse the various peace proposals put forward by American president Woodrow Wilson, the papacy, and the German government.[61] The proposals were widely discussed in Canada, but since it was evident that negotiations were bound to produce a settlement favourable to Germany because of its occupation of important parts of France, most of Belgium, and large areas of the Russian Empire, few Canadians endorsed the idea of an armistice in 1917. As there was no hope of peace on German terms, the Kaiser and his chief advisers decided to employ 'unrestricted submarine warfare' as a means of ending Britain's capacity to continue the war. This policy, implemented in February 1917, led to the sinking of American ships and a declaration of war against Germany by the United States on 6 April 1917.[62]

Allied military commanders remained committed to victory on the Western Front. The British preferred a plan to win control of the Belgian coast but agreed to cooperate with a French proposal for a coordinated Anglo-French attack designed to encircle and destroy large elements of the German army. Before the 'Nivelle offensive,' named for the new French commander Robert Nivelle, began, however, the enemy withdrew its forward defences to a new position known as the Hindenburg Line, some twenty miles to the east. This manoeuvre shortened and strengthened the German lines, destroying what little prospect of success the offensive had promised, but the operation was not cancelled.

The British part in the April offensive, known as the Battle of Arras, included plans for the capture of Vimy Ridge, a feature which dominated the Lens-Douai plain to the east. The Germans did not abandon the ridge when they withdrew to the Hindenburg Line, since the ridge was considered of vital importance and the defences were thought to be impenetrable. The Battle of Arras, like the rest of the Nivelle offensive, yielded little except death and destruction except at Vimy, where the Canadian Corps won an important local victory announced to the world as 'Canada's Easter gift to France.' The success of the Canadian Corps has given rise to a peculiar myth, which relates the capture of

Vimy Ridge to the emergence of Canada as a nation. This is a theme requiring analysis of the construction of post-war memory rather than reflecting the actual events of April 1917.[63]

Canadian historians have also been drawn to the battle for Vimy Ridge when seeking to examine the idea that the Corps was a particularly effective component of the Allied armies. The most systematic study of these issues is Bill Rawling's *Surviving Trench Warfare*, in which he examines the changes in weapons and tactics between 1914 and 1918. Rawling argues that 'each soldier' became 'a specialist with a specific role to play in battle.' The Canadian Corps, he writes, 'moved away from the concept of the citizen-soldier who could ride and shoot to an army of technicians which, even in infantry battalions, specialized in particular aspects of fighting battles.'[64] Rawling believes that the growing sophistication of the Canadian Corps helps to explain the dramatic success at Vimy and in the battles of 1918.

There is much to be learned from this and other explorations of the evolution of tactics, but Vimy was primarily a set-piece battle dominated by artillery. The troops were carefully rehearsed to move quickly to their assigned objectives, relying on 'one heavy gun for every twenty yards of front and a field gun for every ten yards, twice the density available in the Somme battles.'[65] This enormous firepower, most of it British, together with the elaborate counter-battery work of British and Canadian gunners permitted the Corps to move steadily across the sloping, featureless terrain. By early afternoon on 9 April three of the four divisions had reached the crest of the ridge. When Hill 145, the objective of 4th Division, fell three days later, the entire ridge was in Canadian hands. The victory was costly, 3,598 dead and 6,664 wounded,[66] but the attack, Rawling argues, 'ended with a different balance between cost and results.'[67]

After Vimy the Corps commander, Sir Julian Byng, was promoted, and Arthur Currie took over the task of directing what had become Canada's national army. As Jack Hyatt has demonstrated in his biography of Currie, the transition to Corps commander was fraught with personal and political difficulties. To Currie's everlasting credit these issues did not interfere with his leadership of the Corps in action.[68] In August 1917 Currie orchestrated the capture of Hill 70 on the outskirts of Lens and forced the enemy to try to retake it at enormous cost.[69] Many historians regard this action as the outstanding achievement of the Corps.

Currie did his best to prevent the Canadians from being drawn into

General Sir Arthur Currie, commander of the Canadian troops in France, ca. 1918 (Archives of Ontario, C224-0-0-9-51, AO 6547)

the Third Battle of Ypres, known to history as Passchendaele. Even Haig's most ardent defenders are unable to persuade themselves that the continuation of offensive operations in Flanders made sense in the fall of 1917.[70] The original plan, with its promise of an advance to the Belgian coast, may have had some merit, but by October, when the Canadians were sent into action, the battle could be justified only as an effort to pin down and wear out the German army. Attritional warfare is a two-edged sword, however, and British losses at Passchendaele were at least as great as those suffered by the enemy.[71]

Currie protested vigorously against participation in the battle and tried to enlist Prime Minister Borden in the cause. Hyatt suggests that his opposition was overcome only when Haig intervened to personally persuade Currie that Passchendaele must be captured. Because he had great respect for Haig, Currie obeyed, and the Canadians were committed to a battle which has come to symbolize the horrors of the Western Front.

Currie's opposition to Canadian participation at Passchendaele did not mean that he was opposed to Haig's overall strategy of wearing down the enemy by attacking on the Western Front. What Currie and a number of other generals questioned was Haig's stubborn persistence in continuing operations which had little chance of success. At Passchendaele the Canadians did succeed in capturing the ruins of what had once been the village, but the cost of the month's fighting, more than 15,000 casualties, was a price no Canadian thought worth paying.[72] As Third Ypres ended, the first large-scale tank battle in history was fought at nearby Cambrai, and for a brief moment it appeared that the long-sought breakthrough had been achieved. Then the Germans counter-attacked, regaining most of the lost ground. The war would continue into 1918.

At home Canadians reacted to the war news and the endless casualty lists in varying ways. In French-speaking areas of Quebec the war had never seemed of much importance and few young men had volunteered. The exploits of the one French-Canadian battalion, the 22nd, were featured in the daily newspapers, but public opinion remained generally indifferent or hostile to pleas for new recruits. Henri Bourassa and other nationalist leaders demanded redress from the 'Boche' of Ontario, where French-language schools had been abolished, but there is no evidence that reversal of this policy would have altered French-Canadian attitudes towards the war. The Canadian victory at Vimy Ridge had no discernable nation-building impact in Quebec.

The situation was very different in most English-speaking communities.[73] Hundreds of thousands of young men had joined and tens of thousands had been killed or wounded. Winning the war, thereby justifying these sacrifices, was a shared goal which few challenged. When the pool of able-bodied volunteers dried up in late 1916, public opinion favoured conscription long before Prime Minister Borden announced its introduction. The near unanimity of opinion in English-speaking Canada was evident in the 1917 federal election, when most opposition candidates, ostensibly loyal to Wilfrid Laurier and the Liberal Party, campaigned on a win-the-war, pro-conscription platform.[74]

Arthur Currie tried to keep the Canadian Corps out of politics, but the Unionist political managers were determined to use the military vote to influence the outcome in marginal ridings. The manipulations of the soldiers' vote for partisan political purposes should not be allowed to obscure the overwhelming endorsement the men serving overseas gave to the Unionist cause.

The prospect of an Allied victory appeared remote in January 1918. The collapse of czarist Russia and the seizure of power by the Bolsheviks led to negotiations to end the war in the east. Inevitably the peace treaty, signed at Brest-Litovsk, was dictated by Germany and included vast transfers of territory. The German army could now bring large numbers of troops to the Western Front and seek victory on the battlefield before the American Expeditionary Force was ready for combat.[75] The French government and military believed that the best they could hope for was to withstand the expected German attack and prepare to renew the offensive in 1919, relying on the full force of the American army. The British government shared this view, though General Haig insisted that, after defeating a German attack, the Allies could win the war in 1918 by vigorous action.[76]

In 1918 the Canadian Corps played a major role, out of all proportion to its relative size. One reason was the decision to maintain all four Canadian divisions at full strength rather than follow the British example and reduce the number of infantry battalions from twelve to nine. The Canadian Corps found the men it needed not through conscription but as a result of the decision to break up the 5th Division forming in England and use its battalions to reinforce the four divisions in the field. This move allowed the Corps to solve its manpower problems for the spring of 1918, though it was evident that if the war continued, tens of thousands of conscripts would be required. Currie was also responsible for improvements in the training and organization of the Corps, including a reorganization of Bruitnel's machine gunners into a mobile reserve 'mounted in armoured cars and directly under the control of the corps commander.'[77]

Between March and June 1918 the Germans unleashed four major operations, recovering all the ground gained by the Allies since 1914, capturing 250,000 prisoners, and inflicting more than 1 million casualties on the Allied armies.[78] It was all in vain. The German commanders gambled everything on a collapse of Allied morale, but when the offensive ended in July, their armies, overextended and exhausted, faced a powerful and resolute Allied coalition under the command of Marshal Ferdinand Foch.

The Canadian Corps, holding ground well to the north of the main point of the German attack, was initially required to place divisions under British command, but after Currie protested, the Corps was reunited under his control. Although this policy was bitterly resented by the British senior officers, who were fighting a life-and-death struggle with the German army, Currie and Borden were adamant: the Canadians would fight together.[79]

On 8 August 1918 the Corps, deployed alongside Australian, British, and French formations, launched an attack at Amiens which was so successful that it became known as the 'black day' of the German army. S.F. Wise, who is preparing a book-length study of the Amiens battle, emphasizes the effect the Allied advance had on the German high command. 'They had struck,' he writes, 'a crippling blow at the will of the enemy, surely the chief object of strategy.'[80] The offensive soon lost momentum, but this time Haig agreed to break off the action and mount a new attack at Arras to be spearheaded by the Canadians. The period from 8 August to 11 November 1918 became known as the 'Hundred Days,' a period in which the Allied armies made spectacular gains, defeating the German armies in a series of battles which many historians believed determined the outcome of the war.[81] Throughout the Hundred Days the Canadians were in action at Amiens, Drocourt-Quéant, Canal du Nord, Cambrai, Valenciennes, and Mons.[82] The cost of these victories, more than 40,000 casualties,[83] was high, but they were seen as the necessary price of ending the war in 1918. Recently, British military historians have concentrated their research on this period, arguing that too much attention has been paid to the attritional battles of 1916 and 1917. Developing the themes first argued by John Terraine,[84] historians associated with the Imperial War Museum in Great Britain have begun an assessment of every division which fought in the armies of the British Empire. Their preliminary work suggests that many British as well as the Canadian, Australian, and New Zealand divisions were highly effective military organizations before and during the Hundred Days.[85]

Canadian historians have long argued that the Canadian Corps, which was continuously in action during the last months of the war, was instrumental in the Allied victory. This theme has been reinforced by the publication of Shane B. Schreiber's book, *Shock Army of the British Empire*,[86] which portrays the Corps as an exceptionally effective, professional organization capable of sustaining successful operations over a three-month period. A somewhat different approach to the last phase of the war has been offered by University of Calgary historian Tim Travers, who is critical of the strategic and operational doctrines pursued by Haig's armies in 1918.[87] Bill Rawling, who never allows himself to forget the human consequences of military decisions and tactical innovation, provides another kind of balance to the military effectiveness school by analysing casualty rates, which were exceptionally high in 1918.[88]

Canadians were not involved in the negotiations which led to the armistice of 11 November 1918, but it is evident that both Currie and Borden shared the views of British, French, and American diplomats, who were determined, in President Wilson's words, 'to make a renewal of hostilities on the part of Germany impossible.' This meant that Germany would have to surrender more or less unconditionally, and so it proved. Canada's military effort in the First World War allowed the prime minister to insist upon the right to sign the Treaty of Versailles and to secure separate membership in the League of Nations.[89] Canada's new international status was only one sign of the growing sense of nationhood felt by English-speaking Canadians.

The Canadian Corps and the Canadian people had accomplished great things together in what they believed to be a necessary and noble cause. Most Canadians held to this view of their war experience despite the rise of revisionist accounts of the causes of the conflict and efforts by poets, novelists, and historians to portray the Great War as an exercise in futility. When the decision to build a great memorial at Vimy Ridge was made, the purpose was 'to commemorate the heroism ... and the victories of the Canadian soldier.' The memorial was to be dedicated 'to Canada's ideals, to Canada's courage and to Canada's devotion to what the people of the land decreed to be right.'[90] It was this view of the war that sent enthusiastic crowds into the streets when General Haig visited Canada in 1925.[91] It was this memory of the war that sustained the regular army and militia volunteers throughout the years of retrenchment and depression.

## NOTES

1 Samuel Hynes, *A War Imagined: The First World War and English Culture* (London, 1990), ix.
2 Martin Stephan, *The Price of Pity: Poetry, History and the Myth of the Great War* (London, 1996), xv.
3 Ian Miller, 'Our Glory and Our Grief: Toronto and the Great War,' PhD thesis, Wilfrid Laurier University, 1999, 28–53.
4 Newspaper opinion on these and other issues can be found in J. Castell Hopkins, ed., *The Canadian Annual Review of Public Affairs* (Toronto, 1914–18), (hereafter *CAR*), as well as in the newspapers themselves, available on microfilm.
5 A good introduction to the current research may be found in Keith Wilson, ed., *Decisions for War, 1914* (London, 1995).
6 Marc Milner, *Canada's Navy* (Toronto, 1994).
7 The story of Hughes's deeds and misdeeds may be followed in *CAR* and the *Debates* of the House of Commons. See Ronald Haycock, *Sam Hughes: The Public Career of a Controversial Canadian, 1885–1916* (Waterloo, 1986).
8 Desmond Morton, *When Your Number's Up: The Canadian Soldier in the First World War* (Toronto, 1993), 9.
9 *CAR, 1914*, 180.
10 Ibid., 197.
11 Mark Moss, *Manliness and Militarism* (Toronto, 2001), 143.
12 *CAR, 1914*, 182, 227, 190.
13 Evidence for the public commitment to Belgium and its refugees may be found in every Canadian newspaper. See *CAR, 1914*, 228, for a summary.
14 A.J.M. Hyatt, *General Sir Arthur Currie: A Military Biography* (Toronto, 1987), 16.
15 Morton, *When Your Number's Up*, 31.
16 John Swettenham, *To Seize the Victory* (Toronto, 1965).
17 Bill Rawling, *Surviving Trench Warfare: Technology and the Canadian Corps, 1914–1918* (Toronto, 1992), 21, 23.
18 G.W.L. Nicholson, *Canadian Expeditionary Force, 1914–1919* (Ottawa, 1962), 49.

19  Andrew Iarocci, 'The Mad Fourth,' MA thesis, Wilfrid Laurier University, 2001.

20  For the most detailed account of 2nd Ypres see A.F. Duguid, *Official History of the Canadian Forces in the Great War, 1914–1919*, Vol. 1 (Ottawa, 1938). No further volumes were published. See also Daniel G. Dancocks, *Welcome to Flanders Fields, the First Canadian Battle of the Great War: Ypres, 1915* (Toronto: McClelland and Stewart, 1988).

21  Tim Cook, *No Place to Run: The Canadian Corps and Gas Warfare in the First World War* (Vancouver, 1999), 13.

22  Ibid., 21.

23  Ibid., 25, 24.

24  Nicholson, *Canadian Expeditionary Force*, 78, 83–4.

25  Rawling, *Surviving Trench Warfare*, 221.

26  Timothy Travers, 'Currie and 1st Division at Second Ypres, April 1915,' *Canadian Military History* (hereafter *CMH*), 5, 2 (1996), 7–15.

27  Quoted in Miller, 'Our Glory and Our Grief,' 115, 117–18.

28  Jeffrey A. Keshen, *Propaganda and Censorship during Canada's Great War* (Edmonton, 1996) xi–xii.

29  Miller, 'Our Glory and Our Grief,' 131.

30  Keshen, *Propaganda and Censorship*, 29.

31  Toronto *Star*, 14 December 1915.

32  A total of 42,000 men had been accepted for enlistment in the 2nd and 3rd contingents before Second Ypres. A further 35,000 men enlisted immediately after the battle and by the end of 1915 212,000 men were under arms. The Canadian-born proportion of this total was 30 per cent. *CAR 1915*, 208–9.

33  Nicholson, *Canadian Expeditionary Force*, 103.

34  Llewellyn Woodward, *Great Britain and the War of 1914–18* (London, 1967), chap. 4.

35  B.H. Liddel Hart, *The Tanks* (London, 1959), Vol. 1, chap. 2.

36  Woodward, *Great Britain*, 43–4.

37  Cameron Pulsifer, 'Canada's First Armoured Unit,' *CMH*, 10, 1 (2001), 45–57.

38  *CAR, 1915*, 207–11.

39  Nicholson, *Canadian Expeditionary Force*, 114.

40  Ibid., 160–200.

41  Deborah Cowley, ed, *Georges Vanier: Soldier* (Toronto, 2000), 79.

42  Nicholson, *Canadian Expeditionary Force*, 137–45.

43  Quoted in Hyatt, *General Sir Arthur Currie*, 55.

44  See the recent articles, Tim Cook, 'The Blind Leading the Blind: The Battle of the St. Eloi Craters,' *CMH*, 5, 2 (1996), 24–36; and Thomas P. Leppard,

'The Dashing Subaltern: Sir Richard Turner in Retrospect,' *CMH*, 6, 2 (Autumn 1997), 21–8.

45  The events are outlined in *CAR, 1916*, 260–1.

46  See also Tony Ashworth, *Trench Warfare, 1914–1918: The Live and Let Live System* (New York, 1980).

47  Tim Cook, 'A Proper Slaughter: The March 1917 Gas Raid on Vimy,' *CMH*, 8, 2 (1999), 7–24. But see, in the same issue, Andrew Godefroy, 'A Lesson in Success: The Calonne Trench Raid 17 January 1917,' 25–34.

48  Nicholson, *Canadian Expeditionary Force*, 535.

49  Morton, *When Your Number's Up*, 198. See also Thomas E. Brown 'Shell Shock in the Canadian Expeditionary Force 1914–1918,' in C.G. Rolland, ed., *Health Disease and Medicine: Essays in Canadian History* (Hamilton, 1984).

50  Terry Copp and Bill McAndrew, *Battle Exhaustion: Soldiers and Psychiatrists in the Canadian Army, 1939–1945* (Montreal, 1994).

51  Morton, *When Your Number's Up*, 107.

52  Stephen J. Harris, *Canadian Brass: The Making of a Professional Army, 1860–1939* (Toronto 1988), 98.

53  A.M.J. Hyatt, 'The Military Leadership of Sir Arthur Currie,' in Bernd Horn and Stephen Harris, eds, *Warrior Chiefs* (Toronto, 2001), 44.

54  Ian McCulloch, 'Batty Mac: Portrait of a Brigade Commander of the Great War, 1915–1917,' *CMH*, 7, 4 (1998), 22.

55  Woodward, *Great Britain*, 148.

56  Nicholson, *Canadian Expeditionary Force*, 507–9. See also David Facey-Crowther, ed., *Better Than the Best: The Story of the Royal Newfoundland Regiment, 1795–1995* (St John's, 1995).

57  S.F. Wise, *Canadian Airmen and the First World War* (Toronto, 1980). See also Guy Hartcup, *The War of Invention: Scientific Developments, 1914–1918* (London, 1988).

58  Trevor Pidgeon, *The Tanks at Flers* (Cobham, U.K., 1995), 21–30.

59  Nicholson, *Canadian Expeditionary Force*, 169.

60  Ibid., 198.

61  Woodward, *Great Britain*, 227–42.

62  Holger H. Herwig, 'Total Rhetoric, Limited War: Germany's U-boat Campaign, 1917–1918,' in Roger Chickering and Stig Forester, eds, *Great War, Total War* (Cambridge, 2000), 189–206.

63  Jonathan Vance, *Death So Noble: Memory, Meaning and the First World War* (Vancouver, 1997).

64  Rawling, *Surviving Trench Warfare*, 217. For a parallel discussion of British tactical innovation see Paddy Griffith, ed., *British Fighting Methods in the Great War* (London, 1996).

65 Rawling, *Surviving Trench Warfare*, 219.
66 Nicholson, *Canadian Expeditionary Force*, 265.
67 Rawling, *Surviving Trench Warfare*, 219.
68 Hyatt, *General Sir Arthur Currie*, 74–5.
69 Nicholson, *Canadian Expeditionary Force*, 272–97.
70 Robin Prior and Trevor Wilson, *Passchendaele: The Untold Story* (New Haven, Conn., 1996).
71 Hyatt, *General Sir Arthur Currie*, 84–5.
72 Nicholson, *Canadian Expeditionary Force*, 327.
73 See, for example, Leslie Frost, *Fighting Men* (Toronto, 1967).
74 Patrick Ferraro, 'English Canada and the Election of 1917,' MA thesis, McGill University, 1971.
75 Holger H. Herwig, *The First World War: Germany and Austria-Hungary* (New York: 1997), 392–5.
76 Woodward, *Great Britain*, 324.
77 Hyatt, *General Sir Arthur Currie*, 102–3, 102.
78 Ibid., 105–6.
79 Nicholson, *Canadian Expeditionary Force*, 460.
80 S.F. Wise, 'The Black Day of the German Army: Australians and Canadians at Amiens, August 1918,' in Peter Dennis and Jeffrey Grey, eds, *1918: Defining Victory* (Canberra, 1999), 32.
81 G.D. Sheffield, 'The Indispensable Factor: The Performance of British Troops in 1918,' in Dennis and Grey, *1918*, 72–94. For a more critical approach, see Timothy Travers, *How the War Was Won: Command and Technology in the British Army on the Western Front, 1917–1918* (London, 1992).
82 Shane B. Schreiber, *Shock Army of the British Empire: The Canadian Corps in the Last 100 Days of the Great War* (Westport, Conn., 1997).
83 Nicholson, *Canadian Expeditionary Force*, 485–506.
84 John Terrraine, *To Win a War: 1918, the Year of Victory* (London, 1998).
85 John Lee, 'The SHLM Project – Assessing the Battle Performance of British Divisions,' in Paddy Griffith, ed., *British Fighting Methods in the Great War* (London, 1996), 175–181.
86 Schreiber, *Shock Army of the British Empire*.
87 Travers, *How the War Was Won*.
88 Bill Rawling 'A Resource Not to be Squandered: The Canadian Corps on the 1918 Battlefield,' in Dennis and Grey, *1918*, 43–71.
89 Robert Craig Brown, *Robert Laird Borden: A Biography*. Vol. II, *1914–1937* (Toronto, 1980), 155–8.
90 Canada, *House of Commons Debates*, 1922.
91 John Scott, 'Three Cheers for Earl Haig,' *CMH*, 5, 1 (1996), 35–40.

# 3 Conscription in the Great War

J.L. GRANATSTEIN

I have been writing about conscription for more than forty years. I first touched the subject when I did my master's degree at the University of Toronto in 1961–2 and looked at the Conservative Party's misfortunes in the Second World War, misfortunes that arose out of its Great War policies and were compounded thanks to its views on manpower and Quebec in the 1939–45 war. That subject became my doctoral dissertation in 1966 and my first book, *The Politics of Survival: The Conservative Party of Canada, 1939–1945* (1967). From there I went on to write *Canada's War: The Politics of the Mackenzie King Government, 1939–1945* (1975), a study of the King government in the war and one in which I looked closely and very favourably at the way King had finessed the conscription issue so much better than Sir Robert Borden. My next book, with J. Mackay Hitsman, was *Broken Promises: A History of Conscription in Canada* (1977), and here for the first time I went through the manuscript sources on the Great War and, not surprisingly, concluded that I had been right: King had done much better than Borden, conscription was a disastrous issue for national cohesion and, moreover, it had little military impact in either war. I was positively derisory in my comments on the 24,132 conscripts under the Military Service Act (MSA) who had arrived in France by 11 November 1918 and no less so about the 16,000 home defence conscripts sent overseas after the conscription crisis of November 1944. Since more than 600,000 men had enlisted in the army in the Great War and 750,000 in the Second World War, the relatively tiny numbers of conscripts scarcely mattered, or so I believed. 'Conscription has simply not worked in Canada,' I said in the last lines in *Broken Promises*, 'and there seems no reason to believe that it ever will.'[1]

I held this position firmly until, in 1984, I read Denis and Shelagh

Wounded soldiers en route for Blighty, ca. 1918 (Archives of Ontario, C224-0-0-10-7. AO 257)

Whitaker's book *Tug of War*, a study of the First Canadian Army's struggle to clear the Scheldt and open the great port of Antwerp for the Allies' use in the autumn of 1944. A Second World War Royal Hamilton Light Infantry officer and battalion commander of exemplary courage, Denis Whitaker understood, as I had not, that under-strength infantry units were at much greater risk in action. An infantry battalion with a nominal strength of 950 men could lose a third, a half, or even three-quarters of its strength in an afternoon, and every loss of a trained soldier left the unit weakened and its firepower reduced. Casualties fell most heavily on the brave, the section commander who led his men forward, the platoon sergeant who rallied the defence, the company commander who, in desperation, called down artillery fire on his own position. A section of ten could be reduced to five in a moment, but in the next attack a day later that same section ordinarily was expected to cover the same ground as if it were at full strength. Generals almost invariably assigned a battalion of 400 men the same kind of objectives to attack or the same portion of front to defend as they did when it was at or near full strength. With fewer men, the casualties increased as the firepower available in the offence or defence decreased. Unit cohesion, the intangible bonds that make men willing to fight and die for their comrades, also suffered from heavy casualties. Shattered survivors needed time to recover and to mourn.

To keep units up to strength, trained infantry reinforcements were essential. If replacements knew how to operate their weapons effectively and understood the basic principles of section and platoon tactics, they could add to the battalion's power. If they did not, if new men had to be shepherded by soldiers acting as nursemaids and shown what to do, they detracted from that strength and were a danger to themselves and their comrades. Moreover, arriving without the personal ties and loyalties that bound the regiment together, the new men were also friendless, completely lacking the personal support systems that were so essential if soldiers were to fight well. Such networks took time to develop, and if the replacements went into action at once, as they did too often, they did so all but alone. Especially after the losses in Normandy and in the Gothic Line battles in Italy, in the Second World War the army received too many ill-trained or untrained reinforcements and put them into the line at once. More Canadian soldiers died as a result.

The Whitakers' book forced me to rethink my treatment of conscription in the Second World War, obliging me to give the military necessities equal weight in the balance with the political requirements. In *The Generals: The Canadian Army's Senior Commanders in the Second World War* (1993), particularly in the chapter on Generals Maurice Pope and Ken Stuart, I tried to do so.

This brief essay is my attempt to be more even-handed in assessing conscription in the Great War. I admit that the military side of the equation receives its due weight forty years later than it should have. *Mea culpa.*

Recruiting in Canada had slowed after mid-1916 and by the spring of 1917 was running at only 4,000 men per month, far below replacement needs. Many of the volunteers opted for any corps but the infantry, making even those low numbers deceptive. This decline undoubtedly was a reaction to the high rate of casualties and to the gradual drying up of the pool of potential volunteers in English Canada. The British born, the portion of the population that provided a wholly disproportionate percentage of enlistments in the first two years of war, were now

all but depleted. A British War Office study had calculated at the beginning of 1917 that 37.5 per cent of British-born Canadians had enlisted.
Enlistment of the native born of British extraction was 6.1 per cent, and
foreign-born Canadians had sent 6.5 per cent into the military.[2] Those
men who remained out of the army, their lapels regularly pierced with
white feathers by women 'recruiters,' were under strong pressure to
enlist. But the high number of casualties, the long lists of the killed,
wounded, and missing that regularly appeared in the newspapers,
were positive disincentives to joining the army.

At the same time, part of the difficulty was that the government
could not decide if it was better to take a farmer or a tool and die maker
and turn him into a soldier. Where could such a man provide the
greatest service? Even after the National Registration taken at the end
of 1916, even after the passage of the Military Service Act in the next
year, and even after the destructive German offensives of March 1918
led the Borden government in a panic to cancel all the exemptions from
conscription it had issued before and after the December 1917 election,
this same problem existed.[3] The mismanagement of manpower that
had begun with Sam Hughes's first call for men in August 1914 had
never been properly corrected.

In French Canada, where enlistments were low and slow, there was
no shortage of men, only of a willingness to serve overseas. The War
Office study of Canadian manpower calculated that only 1.4 per cent of
French Canadians had joined up, the lowest rate in the white empire.[4]
Whether the secret British calculations were correct is almost immate-
rial. The numbers were known in the broad outline to Canadians, and
the Quebec enlistment failure infuriated many English Canadians, who
could neither appreciate nor understand the numerous and varied
rationalizations produced in Quebec to explain this situation. The truth
of the matter was that just as in English Canada the public pressure on
men was to enlist, in Quebec the pressure was not to enlist. Hume
Wrong, scion of a distinguished Toronto family, who had served overseas in a British regiment until being badly wounded and invalided
home, wrote privately and only half-jokingly in May 1917, 'I would
welcome a little military activity in Quebec. My C.O. and I have arranged a little punitive expedition ... And I should delight in catching
Bourassa and Lavergne [the anti-conscriptionist leaders].'[5] Many in
English Canada shared that view – and they were not joking at all.

While it was primarily the refusal of the vast majority of Quebecois to
enlist that drove the politics of the conscription issue at home, it was

also the unwillingness of fit men in English Canada to serve. The government had tried every expedient to avoid an issue that even the dullest politician could see was bound to be terribly divisive, and not only in Quebec. Farmers, labour, ethnics, and parents of young, fit men – none of them wanted conscription that would take away men who did not want to fight from their jobs and families. On the other hand, those with sons, brothers, and fathers at the front wanted them to receive the fullest support. The manpower issue was a terrible one for politicians and the country.

Because many in the government had believed there was a threat from the 393,000 German-born Canadians and the 130,000 immigrants from the Austro-Hungarian Empire, substantial numbers of troops had been kept at home. The 1916 Prairie Census showed that 7.8 per cent of the west's population were born in enemy territory.[6] Just as worrisome, in the United States German Americans, Irish Americans, or German sympathizers constituted a potential threat of invasion. The Fenian raids were within the living memory of men and women, and some soldiers, like the septuagenarian General W.D. Otter, had had their first taste of war against the Irish Americans fifty years before. The prime minister also worried about 'thugs, gunmen, or other lawless individuals, instigated by German emissaries,' who might carry out sabotage attacks, and he certainly feared raids across the border.[7] These fears kept 16,000 soldiers on guard duty against a threat that had scarcely ever existed, though the government could not ignore it. From October 1915 to September 1916 the government had also directed that a minimum of 50,000 Canadian Expeditionary Force (CEF) volunteers be retained at home on training or other duties to protect against all eventualities.[8]

As casualties mounted overseas, the chief of the General Staff, General Willoughby Gwatkin, looked for ways to replace the volunteers on home defence duties and get them into action. In January 1917, Gwatkin told the militia minister, Sir A.E. Kemp, that there were 62,000 men under arms in Canada, 50,000 of them CEF and 12,000 militia on active service. The response, approved by the cabinet in January and February 1917, was to recruit 50,000 men into a Canadian Defence Force (CDF) for home defence. The CDF began recruiting in March, seeking 'men to volunteer for home defence by joining the active militia. An opportunity is now afforded to those who have been prevented from undertaking Overseas service to join this movement.' The Militia Department proposed that CDF volunteers train with CEF volunteers, and serve at a slightly lower rate of pay and allowances on the same terms – to six months after the end of the war – as CEF recruits. The plan called for all 50,000 to be enrolled in April and to go off to summer camp in May.[9]

With the United States in the war after 6 April, there was no longer even the most remote possibility of a military threat from the south, though the prospect of sabotage (of which there had been almost none in Canada) did remain. Potential CDF recruits could figure this out, and they could also see that there was no need for 50,000 men to be retained in Canada. Most, no doubt, feared that if they joined the Canadian Defence Force they would be converted to the CEF and despatched overseas. As a result, volunteers who might have been eager to do their military service only in Canada stayed away from the CDF in droves. By 25 April fewer than 200 men had signed up. Preordained as it may have been, conscriptionists in the government, the military, the media, and the public viewed the CDF failure as proving that only compulsion could produce men now.[10] In the first month of recruiting for the CDF, coincidentally the month of the great Canadian victory at Vimy, casualties overseas were 23,939; volunteers for the Canadian Expeditionary Force numbered 4,761.[11] Conscription's hour had arrived.

To the surprise of the army leadership, Sir Robert Borden decided to impose conscription on his return from a visit to Britain and France in May. The prime minister had been persuaded by the Allies' grave situation and by the needs of the men at the front, and he was bound and determined to achieve his goal. For the next seven months, during and after the progress of the Military Service Bill through Parliament and through the formation of an almost wholly English-speaking coalition government and a bitter, divisive election in December 1917, conscription dominated the public debate.

Overseas, the soldiers watched and waited, most hoping that conscripts would provide the reinforcements the Corps needed. Lieutenant General Sir Arthur Currie had responded to Borden's congratulatory message on his appointment as Corps commander in June 1917 by saying, 'It is an imperative and urgent necessity that steps be immediately taken to ensure that sufficient drafts of officers and men are sent from Canada to keep the Corps at its full strength.'[12] This message, something that Currie believed to be true, had been read in Parliament during the debate on the Military Service Bill, where it annoyed anticonscriptionists. But during the 1917 election campaign, when the government asked Currie (who many Conservatives knew to have been a Liberal) to issue a message to the troops endorsing the Union Government and conscription, he refused, seeing this request as blatant political interference with his command.

By this point, Currie thought it more important to break up the 21,000-strong 5th Canadian Division, sitting in England under Sam Hughes's son, Major General Garnet Hughes, than to impose conscription, which would take months to produce results. Hughes's division was untouchable so long as his father was minister; after Sam's ouster on 11 November 1916, the government, still fearing his wrath, refused to act to use its men for reinforcements for the four divisions fighting in France. To Currie, it was all politics, damn politics. There were enough men in England to replace the Corps's losses at Passchendaele, add to the strength of infantry battalions, and help to create new machine-gun battalions if only the government had the courage to confront Sam Hughes's malign influence. It did not, so Currie refused the government's request.[13] Arthur Currie was a tough, principled man, and he eventually secured the break-up of Hughes's division and its use as reinforcements for his hard-pressed infantry in February 1918.

Whatever Currie thought of the government and however he himself voted, like English-speaking Canadians at home, his men overwhelmingly cast their ballots for the Union Government and conscription. There was pressure applied to soldiers to vote the right way by some conscriptionist commanding officers, and there were stories of political skullduggery galore. It was nonetheless inescapable that 92 per cent of the military vote went to the victorious Borden, enough to switch fourteen seats from the Liberals to the Union Government.[14]

Conscription duly came into force, and the first 20,000 conscripts began to report for training on 3 January 1918, after the election. Only 1,500 francophones would form part of the first batch of reportees, the government was told, 'owing to the fact that there were very few reports for service there; that the claims for exemption have been generally allowed. And that very few of the appeals, which are very numerous, have been disposed of.'[15] More than nine out of every ten men called for service across the country had sought exemption, and many of those who were refused took to the hills. Many of the exemptions that were granted, not least to farmers who had been guaranteed exemptions just prior to the December 1917 election, were cancelled on 19 April 1918 as the great German offensive terrified the Allies. Borden told a delegation of protesting farmers that the war situation was critical and that the Canadian Corps needed reinforcements. He rejected the argument that he had broken a solemn covenant made during the

Soldiers and conscription graffiti (City of Toronto Archives, Fonds 1244, Item 726)

election: 'Do you imagine for one moment we have not a solemn covenant and a pledge to those men?'[16] In Quebec, where evasion of the Military Service Act (MSA) was greatest, with 18,827 defaulters as against only 27,557 French-speaking men who were taken on strength of the Canadian Expeditionary Force,[17] there were contrary (and foredoomed to failure) pressures to create a francophone brigade out of conscripts and volunteers. Asked his views, Currie duly consulted his commanding officers and then vetoed the idea. None of his battalions would accept so much as a company of French Canadians. 'My own opinion is that they should not be kept separate,' Currie said privately; 'they are Canadians the same as everybody else, and the sooner it is so regarded the better it will be.'[18] The minister of militia and defence, now General S.C. Mewburn, urged the overseas minister to encourage good treatment of francophones in the army. 'I honestly think it would be a good policy to have your officers go out of their way to treat them decently,' he wrote to Sir Edward Kemp in London. 'It will make all the difference in the world.'[19] The 22e Battalion would remain the only French-speaking unit at the front.[20]

At the end of the day, Borden had hoped to generate 100,000 recruits by his conscription legislation, and he achieved this result. Of the 401,000 men called up for service, 99,651 were on strength of the CEF on 11 November 1918, the date of the armistice. Of that number, 47,500 had already proceeded overseas and 24,132 had been taken on strength of units in France.[21]

After almost three years in the trenches, the Canadian Corps was a veteran formation that had benefited greatly from its status as a national contingent, a position helped by the independence Currie had carved out for himself and his men. He saw to it that the Corps stayed together, fought together, and worked together, divisions and brigades learning from each others' successes and the failures of the other formations. Ordinarily, British corps were administrative groupings from which divisions could be plucked at will and assigned to another corps or army. The esprit and nationalism of the Canadians came in substantial part from being together. Very simply, the men of Currie's Corps had come to believe themselves unbeatable. Vimy, Hill 70, and the hell of Passchendaele, terrible in cost though they were, had persuaded the Canadian soldiers that they were special. Most of the men at the front might have been British born, but the war turned them into Canadians, and they genuinely believed they could do what other armies could not, and they were right. That they had more resources was a critical bonus, an extra boost that reinforced the Corps's elan.

The Canadian Corps operated its own training schools and found and organized its own reinforcements by geographical area. British formations, by comparison, had no such independence, their schools being run in common and their casualty replacements drawn from a nation-wide and ever diminishing pool. Faced with a serious manpower shortage after the disastrous Passchendaele battles in the autumn of 1916, the War Office ordered a major reorganization: British divisions were to lose three battalions each, their men being parcelled out to bring the remaining battalions up to strength. British divisional organization by the beginning of 1918, therefore, consisted of three brigades, each with three infantry battalions, a 25 per cent reduction in fighting strength.

In early 1918 the British suggested that the Canadian Corps follow suit. The War Office wanted the Canadian Expeditionary Force to be reshaped into a two-corps army of six divisions. The men could be found, the brass hats suggested, by using the units of the 5th Canadian Division and the three battalions from each of the Corps's four divisions. This reorganization would have given Currie a promotion from lieutenant general to general and many of his officers a jump in rank.

With some difficulty, Currie persuaded the new minister of overseas military forces, Sir A.E. Kemp, to decline the suggestion of a Canadian army. There would be scant gain in fighting effectiveness, he argued, and the 'overhead' – the extra brigade and division staffs plus the additional rear area units an army required to operate in the field – would be high. Moreover, there was the practical problem of a short-age of trained staff officers, a category of officer that took time and experience to produce.[22] The brigadier general, General Staff, at Corps headquarters, Currie's senior operational planner, was British, as were the two next senior staff officers, and the first Canadian GSO I, a divisional senior operational planner, did not take up position until November 1917.[23] 'Unbusinesslike,' Currie called it, cleverly finding precisely the right word to squelch the idea with Kemp, an industrial-ist at home.

Currie's refusal to countenance an expansion of his force – and his own promotion – led Stephen Harris to write, quite properly, that 'there was no finer demonstration of the professional ethos that requires loyalty to service before self.'[24] Under Currie, in fact, the Canadian Corps had become a thoroughly professional army, a fighting force with expertise, a culture of its own, and a sense of responsibility to the nation. As its leader, Currie exemplified the professional nature of his Corps. This professionalism shaped all his actions.

At the same time as Currie flatly refused to conform to the War Office's request that he adopt the British Expeditionary Force's weaken-ing of its own divisions, he insisted on maintaining his four divisions at their strength of almost 22,000 men each. Currie wanted to retain three brigades, each of four battalions, in each of his divisions because he realized that stronger divisions were more effective. In addition, this organization offered a substantial benefit in a brigade attack. The usual two battalions up / two in reserve system meant that the follow-on or counter-attack force in the Canadian Corps was always strong. The reorganized British now had to employ two battalions up / one in reserve, which would weaken every brigade's second effort on the offensive and almost invariably produce higher casualties.

Added to the extra battalion in each Canadian brigade was the simple, but critical, fact that Canadian battalions in early 1918 also had, and continued to have, more men than British battalions, thanks to the reinforcements from the breakup of the 5th Canadian Division in England on 9 February 1918. On that date, Headquarters of the Overseas Military Forces of Canada ordered that eleven battalions of the division provide 100 men each to the Corps's reinforcement pool. The divisional artillery had already been sent to France, two field brigades and four mortar batteries arriving in August 1917. Currie used this extra increment of guns as a floater, serving wherever the situation required. Similarly, the three machine-gun companies and the three companies of divisional engineers went to the front before the breakup of the division. But the 5th Canadian Division's twelve battalions and almost 12,000 infantry were the key. The infantrymen reinforced the units in France; indeed, they permitted an extra 100 men to be added surplus to establishment for each battalion. This increased the fighting strength of the Corps's infantry units by 10 per cent, and it provided enough men to keep most battalions at or near full strength until the heavy casualties of the opening battles of the 'Hundred Days,' which began on 8 August 1918.

Thereafter, a ruthless scouring of men in Britain, rear area units, and hospitals for infantry reinforcements had to suffice until sufficient conscripts from Canada – 'drafted men,' the army preferred to call them – began to arrive in quantity. By the beginning of August and certainly by the Drocourt-Quéant battles at the beginning of September, MSA conscripts provided the great bulk of reinforcements for the Corps at the time it suffered its highest casualties of the war. The 24,132 conscripts who reached the front by 11 November amounted to more men than the 5th Canadian Division had provided – and fortunately they arrived just in time to let the Corps fight its most extraordinary actions and garner its greatest successes of the war. The four divisions in France had averaged just under 22,000 men each at the start of the Hundred Days. By its end, thanks to the Military Service Act conscripts and despite terrifyingly heavy casualties, they still averaged almost 21,000 all ranks, a diminution, but a relatively slight one.

The Canadians' comparatively satisfactory reinforcement situation also meant that the other arms and services of the Corps could have more men, more punch than British formations. British divisions had three engineer field companies and a battalion of pioneers; Canadian divisions had nine field companies and additional pontoon bridging specialists. British divisions had a machine-gun battalion of three companies; Canadian divisions could draw on a machine-gun battalion three times the size, thus providing one automatic weapon for every thirteen men compared with one for every sixty-one men in British divisions. What this meant was that a Canadian division was vastly more potent than a British division and had 50 per cent more infantry.[25] A Canadian division was almost the equivalent in fighting power of a two-division British corps; the Canadian Corps was likely the equivalent of a middle-sized British army in power.

The Canadian Corps headquarters similarly controlled more resources that any British corps: 100 more trucks and a more efficient supply and transport organization, more and better signallers, a better maintenance organization to keep heavy equipment functioning, and, because Currie had kept the 5th Division's field artillery brigades intact, the Corps had an extra artillery increment. Moreover, the general officer commanding the Royal Artillery in the Canadian Corps could control all his artillery, unlike his British counterpart, who was more of an adviser. As a result, Canadian guns could be concentrated more easily, faster, and more effectively. The Canadians also had one heavy trench mortar battery per division; British corps had one battery under command.[26] In effect, the Canadian Corps, with its four large divisions and its extra punch, was easily the most powerful self-contained formation in France. The 5th Canadian Division's men and the MSA conscripts had provided the extra manpower that allowed the Corps this strength, and the luxury of additional firepower and units that were up to establishment allowed the Corps to score the victories that made its role so critical in the last three months of the war.

However, it was a very near thing. The Corps' Hundred Days from 8 August to the Armistice cost 45,835 casualties, almost 20 per cent of the casualties sustained by the Canadian Expeditionary Force over the entire war and, extraordinarily, more than 50 per cent of the strength of the Corps's four divisions and 45 per cent of the Corps's total strength on the opening day of battle. To put these totals in perspective, the casualties of the last hundred days were more than First Canadian Army suffered in the entire campaign in northwest Europe from 6 June 1944 to VE Day eleven months later.[27] Open warfare had proved even more costly than the bloody trench warfare that had preceded it, and by 11 November the Corps's units were almost literally on their last legs.

The MSA conscripts played their part in the final battles. Precisely how many conscripted men saw action remains unclear, and we have no firm sense of whether these unwilling soldiers performed well in action. What we do know is that if the war had continued into 1919, as most Allied government and military leaders expected, the 100,000 conscripts Borden's Military Service Act had raised would certainly have been sufficient to keep the Canadian Corps's divisions up to strength for that year. Politically divisive it most certainly was for a generation and more afterwards, but compulsory service had generated reinforcements when the voluntary system had broken down. Those reinforcements kept units up to strength, allowed the Canadian Corps to function with great effectiveness and efficiency in the final, decisive battles of the Great War, and helped to minimize casualties.

NOTES

1 J.L. Granatstein and J.M. Hitsman, *Broken Promises: A History of Conscription in Canada* (Toronto, 1977), 269.
2 Public Record Office (London) (PRO), Cabinet Records, Cab 32/1, War Cabinet, 23 January 1917, appendix 1.
3 At least this was Newton Rowell's view as late as June 1918. See National Archives of Canada (NAC), Robert Borden Papers, Rowell to Borden, 8 June 1918, ff. 53626ff.
4 PRO, Cabinet Records, Cab 32/1, War Cabinet, 23 January 1917, appendix 1.
5 J.L. Granatstein, *The Ottawa Men: The Civil Service Mandarins, 1935–1957* (Toronto, 1998), 113.
6 J.A. Boudreau, 'Western Canada's "Enemy Aliens" in World War I,' *Alberta History* 12 (Winter 1964), 1.
7 Cited in Michael Boyko, 'The First World War and the Threat of Invasion,' York University, undergraduate paper, 1969, 17.
8 NAC, A.E. Kemp Papers, vol. 71, 'Statement Showing Greatest Number of Guards Employed,' 10 February 1917; vol. 115, 'CEF Strength in Canada.'
9 *The Canadian Annual Review 1917* (Toronto, 1918), 309.
10 Granatstein and Hitsman, *Broken Promises*, 49ff.
11 G.W.L. Nicholson, *Canadian Expeditionary Force, 1914–1919* (Ottawa, 1962), 546.
12 Daniel Dancocks, *Sir Arthur Currie: A Biography* (Toronto, 1985), 122.
13 NAC, Arthur Currie Papers, vol. 2, telegram, 3 December 1917; A.M.J. Hyatt, 'Sir Arthur Currie and Conscription,' *Canadian Historical Review* 50 (September 1969), 292–3.
14 See Granatstein and Hitsman, *Broken Promises*, 80–1; Desmond Morton, 'Polling the Soldier Vote: The Overseas Campaign in the Canadian General Election of 1917,' *Journal of Canadian Studies* 10 (November 1975), 39ff.
15 NAC, Borden Papers, Newcombe to Borden, 19 December 1917, f.53483.

16  Barbara Wilson, ed., *Ontario and the First World War, 1914–1918* (Toronto, 1977), lxiv.
17  NAC, Militia and Defence Records, file GAQ 10–473, Assistant Director of Records to District Officer Commanding, Military District No. 12, 9 March 1928.
18  D.P. Morton, 'The Limits of Loyalty: French Canadian Officers and the First World War,' in E. Denton, ed., *Limits of Loyalty* (Waterloo, 1980), 95–6.
19  NAC, Gen. R.E.W. Turner Papers, Kemp to Turner, 17 June 1918, f. 7051.
20  The 60th Battalion, raised in Quebec and with a substantial proportion of francophones, was in the 9th Brigade until early 1917. Then, because it was having difficulty maintaining its strength, the 60th was dropped from the order of battle and replaced by the 116th, whose commanding officer was a Conservative member of Parliament. See the official explanation in Nicholson, *Canadian Expeditionary Force*, 225.
21  In all, 470,224 soldiers served overseas of which 47 per cent were Canadian born; 194,869 never left Canada of which 61.1 per cent were Canadian-born, a figure that reflects the impact of conscription. See Desmond Morton, *When Your Number's Up: The Canadian Soldier in the First World War* (Toronto, 1993), 278–9.
22  *Report of the Ministry: Overseas Military Forces of Canada 1918* (London, n.d.), 333–4.
23  John A. English, *The Canadian Army and the Normandy Campaign: A Study of Failure in High Command* (New York, 1991), 15.
24  Stephen Harris, *Canadian Brass: The Making of a Professional Army 1860–1939* (Toronto, 1988), 138; Desmond Morton, *A Peculiar Kind of Politics: Canada's Overseas Ministry in the First World War* (Toronto, 1982), 152ff.
25  Nicholson, *Canadian Expeditionary Force*, 382ff.
26  This description is based on the able account in Shane Schreiber, *Shock Army of the British Empire: The Canadian Corps in the Last 100 Days of the Great War* (Westport, Conn., 1997), 19ff.
27  John A. English, *Marching through Chaos: The Descent of Armies in Theory and Practice* (Westport, Conn., 1998), 62–3.

# 4 Political Leadership in the First World War

JOHN ENGLISH

Craig Brown is one of very few Canadian historians to address directly the subject of political leadership, and his analysis of Canadian leadership during the First World War is unsurpassed. In his 1980 article, 'Fishwives, Plutocrats, Sirens and Other Curious Creatures: Questions about Political Leadership in Canada,' Brown stressed that 'perceptions of political leadership are like images in a hall of mirrors. They are partial, shifting, transitory.'[1] Writing at the early dawn of postmodernism and five years after the appearance of Paul Fussell's *The Great War and Modern Memory*, Brown considered the ways in which we construct our memory of what wartime leadership was. In his biography of Sir Robert Borden, of which the second volume was also published in 1980, Brown placed Borden far more at the centre of wartime political leadership than contemporary and historical analyses had suggested. The limits of Borden's choices and the sources of his commitment became much better understood.

Leadership is a rare topic among historians. The best-known recent work is by a political scientist; most titles about leadership are about leadership in business. Leaders, of course, are the elite; and the language of leadership – der Führer, il Duce, Beloved Helmsman – has been academically unfashionable, even risible.[2] The literary memory of the First World War is of leaders disgracefully distant from those who died in the trenches. Fussell wrote in the 1970s that 'one powerful legacy of [British General Douglas] Haig's performance is the conviction among the imaginative and intelligent today of the unredeemable defectiveness of all civil and military leaders.'[3] Failure of leadership in the First World War has remained a dominant theme. Summarizing the twentieth century in the early 1990s, Eric Hobsbawm suggested that the 'great ministers or diplomats of the past' such as Talleyrand or Bismarck would have wondered why their successors had not settled the war before 'it destroyed the world of 1914.'[4] Talleyrand was at the centre of restoring an earlier world after the Napoleonic wars, but the leaders of 1919 neither restored an earlier world nor created a new world based upon collective security and international institutions.

Borden himself left texts that condemned other wartime leaders. He told the Imperial War Cabinet that British war leadership was appalling and that incompetent officers remained while the talented in lower ranks received no recognition, a legacy of aristocratic tradition that amounted 'to scrapping the brains of the nation in the greatest struggle in history.' British Prime Minister David Lloyd George privately agreed with Borden, but such agreement did not cause Borden to relent in his criticisms. In midsummer 1918 Borden turned upon Lloyd George at Sunday tea and said: 'Mr. Prime Minister, I want to tell you that, if ever there is a repetition of the battle of Passchendaele, not a Canadian soldier will leave the shores of Canada as long as the Canadian people entrust the government of their country to my hands.' Nevertheless, Borden expressed no doubts about the war's purposes and criticized those who did. He thought South African Jan Christian Smuts's musings about the need for a peace short of victory were dangerously flawed and believed the German war machine had to be completely smashed. He dissented strongly from American President Woodrow Wilson's view that the dominion prime ministers lacked the will to pursue war to its full end and strongly criticized Wilson's own faint-heartedness.[5]

Hobsbawm and many others, such as British historian Niall Ferguson, have agreed with Smuts's view that war to the 'full end' was 'fatal to us too.'[6] Borden and many other wartime leaders have been easy targets, uttering, as they so often did, phrases about duty, honour, and democracy while the modern age, with its ironic, discontinuous, and anti-traditional ways, was successfully storming the heights of western life. In photographs of wartime and later, Borden seems to belong to an earlier age: he wears Edwardian suits and watch chains and parts his hair in the middle. In his post-war *Letters to Limbo*, a curious set of letters to an imaginary newspaper editor, what Fussell termed the high diction that died in the trenches abounds. Warfare is still strife, actions are still deeds, and the young girls on a Toronto-Ottawa train 'rent the air with instrument and voice, producing a vile cacophony to the vast disturbance and indignation of the other passengers.'[7] In *Letters to Limbo* and elsewhere he extolled the poetic excellence of Audrey

Alexandra Brown and sought to advance her career. Brown was, David Staines writes, 'the last important representative of romantic poetry in Canada, deeply indebted to the English Romantic poets, especially Keats.' Her best-known poem, which Borden deeply admired, was 'Laodamia,' which revealed her attraction to 'a legendary past,' 'colourful descriptions,' 'musical cadences,' and 'ornate' verse. It was a world far from Graves, Sassoon, and Pound, and so was Robert Borden.[8] In his sketch of Canada's 'Bigwigs' in 1934, Charles Vining wrote that Borden was 'an extremely distinguished old gentleman who lives in Ottawa and tries not to notice what is going on there.'[9] The world had seemingly moved beyond him.

Yet, Vining noted, Borden had been the sole allied leader to last through the war and by 1934 had become 'a chief architect of national independence' and, furthermore, 'probably the only Canadian who would be publicly acceptable as Governor-General.'[10] Jonathan Vance's *Death So Noble*, a study of memory and war in Canada, hints why Borden was the only acceptable Canadian governor general in 1934. Canadians in mid-Depression shared a view of the war that was dominated by 'the successful defence of Ypres in 1915, the capture of Vimy Ridge in 1917 ... the triumphant Hundred Days that preceded the Armistice of 1918,' and, above all, by the belief that the war had made the nation. Others, such as Frank Underhill and Will Bird, recalled the generals' stupidities, the divisions between the French and the English, the Military Voters Act, the internment of aliens, and the angry veterans in 1919. Those memories were not shared at memorial services in the interwar years or in myriad other interwar remembrances. Here, one looked to the past to find an example for a better future: 'Painful and costly, the war had nevertheless conferred more than it wrenched away because it took Canada a few steps farther along the road to its destiny. If only everyone would realize this fact, the myth of the war could become a constructive force of unparalleled power. It would create a new nation, pure in its essence and secure from internal divisions.' For those who remembered the war most, Robert Borden represented these memories.[11]

Author of disunity yet creator of independence, an expression of Canadian commitment but the deliverer of the young to slaughter: such contradictory images swirl around Borden and his colleagues. What did leadership mean to Borden in his own times? How has what Brown termed shifting and transitory perception created those images and obscured what Borden and those around him deemed political

Sir Robert Borden, March 1918 (W.I. Topley, National Archives of Canada, PA28128)

leadership to be. Who were leaders and followers? What was the context in which they interacted? Finally, what was the language they shared?

## Leaders and Followers

In analysing the failure of British war leadership, Borden pointed to the distance between leaders and followers. He believed that Canada was different. He even suggested to the Imperial War Cabinet that Canadians should undertake the training of the newly arrived American troops because Canadians, like Americans, did not have an aristocracy that placed birth over merit.[12] He attributed the success of the Canadian Corps to the lack of a professional military caste closely linked with a hereditary elite. Wilson's early use of 'democracy' had resonance for Borden, and he and Loring Christie, his legal and international affairs adviser, wrestled intellectually with the problems of democratic legitimacy and public opinion in Canada and internationally. In this democratic spirit in January 1918 Borden decided that hereditary titles were 'entirely incompatible with our institutions' and told the governor general, the Duke of Devonshire, that they should be abolished.[13] The democratic tide in wartime extended the vote to women for the 1917 election (albeit in a perverse form in the Military Voters and Wartime Elections acts). The Borden government introduced war profit taxes and income taxes on the wealthy. Moreover, there were restrictions on luxuries that sought to assure the appearance of equal sacrifice and obligation. Conscription itself fitted well into equality of sacrifice. The justifications for conscription derived from the age of democratic revolution, the 'people's armies' that fought for democracy in those times, and from Borden's sense of British Canadian democracy. Arthur Currie was no artistocrat but a general for a democratic people's army.

The rhetoric of British Canadian democracy became increasingly majoritarian as the war progressed. When one looks at the character of wartime leadership in Canada, the British-Canadian background of the political leaders of Canada's war effort is striking. Elected in 1911, the Conservative government of Robert Borden concentrated decision-making among a few, partly by choice and partly by circumstance. Although the Conservatives had success in Quebec in the 1911 election, Borden's decision to proceed with the Naval Bill without holding a referendum, as the Quebec nationalistes believed he had promised to do, weakened the francophone voice within the cabinet. By 1913 the cabinet did not have a strong francophone member; by 1 April 1918 francophone representation in the cabinet consisted of one senator, the postmaster general. That senator, Pierre-Edouard Blondin, was one of two Roman Catholics in the cabinet of fourteen. Although women voted in 1917, no woman was elected and none was a member of cabinet. There were no members of German, Ukrainian, Jewish, or Asian origin in the Unionist caucus. The British Protestant Churches – Methodist, Presbyterian, and Anglican – accounted for the religious affiliation of 83 per cent of Unionist members but of only 45 per cent of Canadians. Almost 39 per cent of Canadians were Roman Catholic, but only 3 per cent (five members) of the Union Government caucus were.[14]

There were three Unionist members of German background, but one (W.A. Griesbach) was an Anglican and the others (J.J. Merner and James Bowman) were Methodists. The sole Unionist French Canadian, J.L. Chabot of Ottawa, listed himself as an 'imperialist.'[15] There were 403,417 Canadians who identified themselves as German in the 1911 census, and 44,036 who were 'Austrians,' about 6.2 per cent of the population. In the 1908 federal election, 'Germans' tended to vote Conservative in eastern Canada, although the negative correlation for Germans and Conservative Party support in the west was not strong. In 1917, however, those 'Germans' who could vote went strongly against the Union Government and the Conservative Party bore the animus for several generations. In that election, Brodie and Jenson found that the correlation of party vote and ethnicity was by far the most pronounced in Canadian history, with those of British background overwhelmingly Unionist and those of French background overwhelmingly Liberal.[16] The Canadian government, then, was democratically elected but unrepresentative in character.

In looking at Canada in 1917, one sees a situation similar to modern democracies where government excludes significant minorities, especially when identity questions are fundamental to political definition and discourse. Leadership in a society such as Israel (approximately 18 per cent Arab), Estonia (30 per cent Russian) or Malaysia (32 per cent Chinese) asserts the primacy of the majority because of security, ideological, or religious concerns. Dissident views are reflected in minority legislative factions, but leadership groups tend to be exclusive. Minorities are fragmented while the majority tends to be coherent, especially when challenged. Relationships with minority groups exist but are informal and intermittent. In wartime, the intermittent becomes even more irregular. The focus intensifies on the central purpose, and leadership resides in definition of that purpose. 'Leaders and followers,' James MacGregor Burns writes, 'are locked into relationships that are closely influenced by particular local, parochial, regional, and cultural forces. In the progression of both leaders and followers through stages of needs, values, and morality, leaders find a broadening and deepening base from which they can reach out to widening social collectivities to establish and embrace "higher" values and principles.'[17]

In the winter of 1917 the base was disintegrating for Borden and his government as voluntary recruitment collapsed. The result was a crisis of legitimacy. The first wave of volunteers had been British born; the next wave came overwhelmingly from urban centres, particularly in Ontario, Manitoba, and English Quebec. Recruitment figures were reflected in the Victory Loan Campaigns of 1917–18, in which Ontarians gave over $220 per capita, Manitoba almost $170, but no other province more than $120. As indicated in the *Historical Atlas of Canada*, 'untapped manpower' (eligible male population between eighteen and forty-five) was greater than 50 per cent in all provinces except Manitoba; in Quebec it was over three-quarters of the population.[18] The Census of Canada of 1951 traced where those who had served lived after the wars. Although many veterans did not return to their pre-war homes, the patterns of veteran settlement, a sample of which is shown in table 4.1, are highly revealing.

Canada's wartime leaders knew these numbers well. They knew where they were followed and where they did not lead. Following historians of Victorian Britain, Bruce Curtis has emphasized how fundamental the impact of statistics was upon state formation in Canada in the nineteenth century.[19] Similarly, statistics about enlistment stirred controversy in both wars and shaped leadership perceptions. Reading Robert Borden's diary and correspondence in wartime, one is struck by how much of the rapidly expanded state structure was beyond his purview, how agendas overflowed, how options and different opinions narrowed, and how much numbers came to matter. Following the failure of national registration, which revealed differences among areas and peoples, Borden asked his minister of militia in April about the state of recruitment for the Canadian Expeditionary Force. Edward Kemp replied precisely in numbers that bore enormous political weight: 'voluntary enlistment has about reached its limit. Enlistment overseas for March seven thousand and sixty three ... Thirty five thousand will be shipped during April.' This news came just as 3,598 Canadians died in their magnificent victory at Vimy Ridge. Borden had been in Britain

Table 4.1
Postwar patterns of veteran settlement*

| War | Census subdivision** | Number served | Ethnicity |
|---|---|---|---|
| First World War | Beauce<br>pop. 54,973 | 44 | 99% French |
| | Sherbrooke<br>pop. 62,166 | 476 | 83% French |
| | Wellington<br>pop. 66,930 | 1,653 | 79% British |
| | Russell<br>pop. 17,666 | 97 | 81% French |

*Figures include those who served in non-Canadian forces. Populations are for 1951. Figures for Second World War veterans are proportional to those for First World War veterans.
**Beauce is in rural Quebec and Russell in rural Ontario. Sherbrooke in Quebec and Wellington (Guelph) are urban ridings with smaller cities.
Source: Ninth Census of Canada, 1951, Vol. 1, Population (Ottawa: Queen's Printer, 1953).

since February at the Imperial War Conference, where the sense of crisis was profound and the distance from the complexities of Canadian population and politics great. The numbers and the setting made conscription seemingly unavoidable.[20]

Borden had told Sir Charles Hibbert Tupper in December 1916, after Tupper had encouraged adoption of conscription: 'We have more than two and a half millions of French Canadians in Canada and I realize that the feeling between them and the English people is intensely bitter at present. The vision of the French Canadian is very limited. He is not well informed and he is in a condition of extreme exasperation by reason of fancied wrongs supposed to be inflicted upon his compatriots in other provinces, especially Ontario.'[21] When commitment and service increasingly redefined democratic participation, Kemp's numbers trumped 'two and a half millions.' The passing of the wartime franchise acts and the restructuring of Canadian parties reflected that redefinition. It also drew upon arguments made by women that their war service entitled them to the franchise, upon older arguments in Britain and Canada for the respectability of the 'working man' and their right to the franchise, and on even earlier arguments for recognition of the new bourgeoisie in more effective legislative fora. Democracy was still fresh in 1917, and its novelty made it a pliable substance.

## Context

The First World War was a calamity. In a classic study of calamity and its impact, Piotr Sorokin, who knew war and revolution well, described the various effects of a calamity: decrease in rationality, increased emotionality, and a focus on the calamity that paradoxically makes choices about dealing with it more difficult. Studies of stress have found, most unexpectedly, that when other factors were held constant, 'intellectually stimulating leaders increased the felt stress ... among subordinates.' Such leaders may contribute to stress among followers. Consultation is valued in non-crisis situations but less so in times of crisis.[22]

The 'felt stress' in 1917 was uneven across Canada. In those centres where sons were more often at the front, anger, denial and emotionality were pervasive. In those where enlistment was low, anger was surely present, but its direction was different. In such a setting, consultation becomes difficult and may contribute to stress. In a recent study, Ian Miller strongly argues that the city of Toronto knew well the brutal conditions of war and the possibility that friends and family who enlisted would die. The population of the city was literate; it read its daily newspapers that reported the battles and the deaths in great and grisly detail. Why, Miller asks, did Canada's women and men, well informed of the dangers their relatives and friends faced, intensify their support for the war in 1917?[23] What did stress mean in such a setting?

In 1917 in Toronto the University of Toronto sponsored four lectures on 'The Federation of Canada' given by history Professor George Wrong, editor Sir John Willison, legal scholar Zebulon Lash, and university President Robert Falconer. The occasion was the fiftieth anniversary of Canadian confederation. The lecturers could not imagine their nation's death in that dreadful winter. As Benedict Anderson has observed, a nation's biography is fashioned 'up time,' which is marked by deaths that, 'in a curious inversion of conventional genealogy, start from an originary present.' Thus the Second World War begat the First World War and the ancestor of the State of Israel is the Warsaw uprising. And so the Great War begat Confederation for these Toronto lecturers, and its reality completed Confederation's meaning.

George Wrong's historical work concentrated on French Canada, and his work reflected his experience as a summer sojourner at the elite anglophone resort of Murray Bay, downriver from Quebec. For Wrong, Carl Berger writes, 'all that was admirable and permanent in Quebec society lay in the small rural villages like St Augustin, not in the provincial capital or the burgeoning industrial cities.'[24] These villages had charmed him when he wrote about them in his pre-war historical writings; the charm of their traditional ways faded in wartime. In his 1917 lecture he talked about the physiocrats who taught that nature was all-sufficing. Since 1867 the influence of Darwin had changed minds: 'Society ... does not consist of fixed orders, each content and moving permanently in is own sphere.' He had come to realize, as had others, that 'only that has survived which was in vital harmony with the spirit and conditions of a new society.' Those on the happy Quebec manors, 'a garden of calm delight where all is beautiful,' would pass away in 'the scene of ceaseless struggle in which victory is to the strong.' Strength resided in empire, and Canada must play its full and recognized part. Those who shirked the struggle would not endure: 'our successful men are those who were free to adjust themselves to what they found in the country and to conquer conditions by learning to know them.'[25]

George Wrong's oldest son died at the Somme on Dominion Day 1916. He told his listeners in early 1917 that he despised the word *Dominion* and favoured Kingdom of Canada because 'Kingdom' would express Canada's 'exact relation to the British Crown and also the equality of status with the mother country which it is now so desirable to foster.'[26] Thus, Confederation gained meaning with equality of status. So did his son's death. Another son, Hume, was a lieutenant in the British army. In May 1917 he wrote to his brother, Murray: 'It really looks now as though there was going to be something approaching a rebellion in Quebec. In any case, there is bound to be bloodshed, in rioting if not in organized revolt. I would welcome a little military activity in Quebec. My C.O. and I have arranged a little punitive expedition to consist of a string of cars armoured with boiler plate and armed with Lewis guns. It would be the greatest sport in the world to fight against an enemy which was without artillery or machine-guns. And I should delight in catching Lavergne or Bourassa.'[27] Darwinian struggle rather than the happy Quebec manor was now the crucible of nationhood.

Today, George Wrong told his University of Toronto listeners, we find 'only that has survived which was in vital harmony with the spirit and conditions of a new society.'[28] The isolated villages and priests along the St Lawrence River were to become the detritus of history. Canada's vastness, once to be celebrated, had become its liability. It was 'the penalty of vastness that it is both difficult to create a common public opinion in Canada, and when the opinion exists, difficult so to concentrate it as to make effective at the national capital.' War had remade his past and nation.

Wrong's son had died; his other son also might die. He saw his vision of *bonne entente*, based upon the enduring patterns of the Quebec parish, shatter. The gentle priests had become the disciples of Bourassa. His home province of Ontario disappointed him too. He lamented in 1917 that the 'wealthy class' in Canada had not yet shown 'the taste for country sports,' or 'a vital and intelligent interest in the problems of agriculture and the raising of stock,' as had the 'wealthy class' in Britain. We had learned, he proclaimed, 'that a country of small landowners is very likely not to till its land to advantage.' He had long ago left the small farm, where his father had failed to make a living, and the Elgin County grammar school, where he had learned to read and spell. He had married Edward Blake's daughter, had sent his children to Oxford, where he had once spent some summer months that indelibly marked his own ways. In 'Humewood,' his Jarvis Street mansion, his Scottish maid put on the oil lamp, his students sat at dinner as servants piled up cutlery around them, while he lamented 'the type of speech one [now] hears in law courts and lecture rooms.' Later, he would lie in front of the fire, occasionally taking snuff, and frivolously comment as his wife read Trollope. When his son fell at the Somme, what did he say to his brother from the back concessions whose accent he deplored and whose ways he now despised? What did he say to his wife? He had learned to be costive, to shield emotion, and to pile up cultural capital around his self.[29] The war was peeling away those careful constructions, leaf by leaf.

The British prime minister's brilliant son Raymond Asquith also fell at the Somme. The prime minister had last seen him when he visited the front with Haig, and when they shook hands, Haig noticed that the prime minister trembled. The bad news came after dinner on 15 September. When told, Asquith put his hands over his face and 'walked into an empty room and sat in silence.' When Robert Borden saw Asquith soon after, he was uncharacteristically giddy, and Borden regretted that 'he did not cultivate a greater abstinence in the use of wines.' Asquith wrote long and infatuated letters to Venetia Stanley and Sylvia Henley, which he crammed with state and personal secrets. His 'temperament,' to use a contemporary term, had failed.[30]

Others 'failed,' too. Mackenzie King went to a psychiatrist. Annie Pearson, described by her son Lester as a strong person, was 'broken in spirit' in 1917 and asked her husband to write to the minister of overseas militia to ask that Lester be allowed to return on furlough. Family friend Sam Hughes had granted favours before, but now Hughes was gone, along with 'special favours.' Lester went to Oxford, where he took special training under Robert Graves, although Graves himself collapsed that summer.[31] Hughes became increasingly erratic as he sat on the backbenches. Borden was frequently exhausted and had to drop all activities, even though his doctor told him that he was physically well. When Borden was absent, the stress was evident in the cabinet. Sir Thomas White fretted in the spring of 1917; in early 1918 he told Borden he must resign. Earlier he had been a pillar: 'Borden often came to White's door when he needed a few minutes away from his work. Without asking, White knew what was required. Off the two would go for a brisk walk around the Parliamentary Library. Nothing was said of budgets or soldiers. Instead, the weary politicians exchange recollections of their favourite stanzas of poetry.[32] Anger, stress, fear, and emotionality drove those most affected to fragments of memory and the construction of shells of familiar material. In that construction, Borden was a more appropriate craftsman than other more 'intellectually stimulating' alternatives. His familiarity resassured when assurance was most needed.

## Language

Fussell emphasizes how high diction perished with the battles of the First World War. Rupert Brooke's romantic language and vision died with him, and other warriors, such as Owen and Graves, robbed war of romance, and their words and vision were the rich seeds of modernism. In wartime and, as Vance has shown, in post-war remembrance, Canada's leaders and the soldiers' kin clung to traditional forms of expression. In the cities, the churches, the newspapers, and the memorial services English Canadians read and heard 'familiar stanzas.' There were, of course, the magnificent Christian hymns that called on Christian soldiers to march forward and assured grieving parents that death lacked its sting. When Borden announced that he intended to introduce conscription, he brought a message from the Canadian men in European hospitals, from men 'who have come back from the very valley of the shadow of death. And there was a call to us from those who have

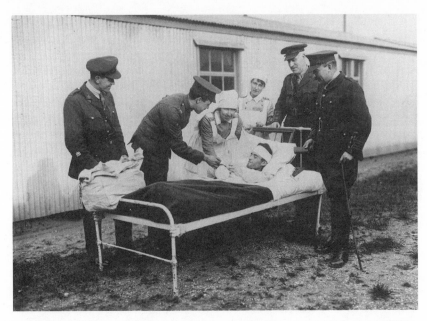

Wounded soldiers voting at a Canadian hospital near Arras, France (William Rider-Rider, National Archives of Canada, PA3488)

passed beyond the shadow into the light of perfect day, a call to us that their sacrifice shall not be in vain.' As in McCrae's 'In Flanders Fields,' Borden asks that we take up the dead soldiers' quarrel with the foe. From their failing hands, the torch must be grasped.

By the 1970s such rhetoric had passed as in a dream, a very bad dream. For Fussell, McCrae's images and words were 'a propaganda argument,' like the rhetoric of the scurrilous patriot, Horatio Bottomley.[33] Isaac Rosenberg's, 'Break of Day in the Trenches,' in Fussell's view the best war poem, also employs the literary traditions of pastoral poetry but looks 'forward' in its informality, insouciant ironic idiom and its 'ordinary' talk.[34] Yet in wartime and post-war remembrance in English Canada, one heard McCrae, not Rosenberg. The language of the conscription debates and of the armistice was never informal and was deliberately distinct from 'ordinary' talk. That language endured into peacetime and even into the next war as not only Churchill drew upon King Hal at Agincourt, but also Mackenzie King based wartime discourse upon Christian image and Victorian rhetoric. Sandra Gwyn, in

*Tapestry of War*, describes how the First World War transformed Canadian lives, but interestingly, she finds that few of her subjects could 'easily have lived in our own times.' The most likely in Gwyn's view was the heroic ambulance driver, Grace MacPherson Livingston. Yet her rebellion lay in her insistence that she march with the men in the post-war Armistice parades where McCrae and the Book of Ecclesiastes shaped the setting.[35]

Language is fundamental to leadership. In his study of the mutiny on the *Bounty*, Greg Dening points out that Bligh was not a violent captain, as myth and film have it. Language was at the centre of Bligh's inability to command and his inability to understand the metaphors of captaincy. Dening argues that 'Bligh's bad language was the ambiguous language of his command. It was bad, not so much because it was intemperate or abusive, but because it was ambiguous, because men could not read in it a right relationship to his authority.'[36] Borden's critics, historians and contemporaries, could point to incidents or facts that illustrated weakness and error, ranging from bad rifles to misspent millions. His language, however, was not ambiguous. It was familiar, and in a setting where so much was unfamiliar and incredible (who in August 1914 would have believed half a million Canadians would fight such a war?), he took from religious and political tradition those images and phrases that his listeners recognized. The language of service was linked to conscription, and a political act that was novel and a war that was incredible were encapsulated within traditional and meaningful frames.

These frames were seen through a glass darkly in Russell and were probably 'bad' in Beauce. Because they were so rich in the detail of British-Canadian Protestantism, the alienation of francophone Canadians from empire and Britishness became deeper. In Wellington County and other British-Canadian fastnesses, the language endured in public and private representations of wartime experience. It became increasingly obsolete in other settings, such as the university classroom and the literary clubs.

## Conclusion

Hew Strachan's recent history of the opening of the First World War has underlined how leaders faced difficult choices and how their responses were largely rational amid a growing sense of calamity. Similarly, George Cassar, in his study of Asquith as a war leader, though recognizing his increasing eccentricity, argues that history has dealt too harshly with his wartime leadership. Forgotten in the criticism of his frivolous letters and leisurely style was the fact that he 'brought the country into the war without civil disturbance or political schism, a feat which in the beginning had seemed impossible.' Moreover, Cassar argues, his 'high statesmanship and imperturbability' inspired confidence when Britons learned in the terrible spring and summer of 1915 that the war's outcome was uncertain.[37]

In the 1930s Borden, as Vining has noted, had become 'a chief architect of national independence,' at a time when that creation was, in various meanings, a potential source of national consensus. When a later generation of Canadian historians turned to the politics of war itself, however, they found in that past the source of disunity. A.M. Willms, in a 1956 article, 'Conscription, 1917: A Brief for the Defence,' did not convince historians writing in the next decades. During the 1960s Quebec moved into the centre of Canadian politics, and Vietnam made any notion of the 'lovely war' of 1914 thoroughly risible. When J.L. Granatstein and J.M. Hitsman, two Canadian military historians, published their extensive study of Canadian conscription in 1977, the year after the election of René Lévesque, they chose as their title and theme 'Broken Promises.' René Lévesque accepted their interpretation in the manifesto he issued for the referendum on separation in 1980 in which the conscription crisis was principal supporting evidence for the argument that Quebec needed independence.[38]

Craig Brown published his second volume of the Borden biography in 1980, and his article on leadership appeared in the same year, when Canada's future seemed so much in doubt. His statement that perceptions of leadership are partial, shifting, and transitory has particular relevance for a twenty-first-century assessment of Borden's leadership. Brown himself shifted the focus with his analysis of war aims, Borden's attachment to the Canadian commitment, and the nature of that commitment as it was understood by the cabinet of the day. He did not excuse the manipulation of the franchise, but he did present the framework within which decisions were made in 1916 and 1917. A sense that those in a later period might see Borden's work differently pervades his analysis. We are now seeing studies of wartime leadership and followership by a generation born after Vietnam and educated after the national crisis of the 1970s. In recent works Jonathan Vance and Ian Miller concentrate upon English Canada and the war and follow paths where the thickets of national and international politics had overgrown direct contact with the experience of wartime leadership. Granatstein, in this volume and elsewhere, has also said that his analysis of conscription in the 1970s reflected those times, particularly the national unity crisis.

In their centenary history of Canada's transformation in the first part of the twentieth century, Brown and Ramsay Cook claimed that the election of 1917 was the greatest triumph of British-Canadian nationalism, but it was its last. British-Canadian nationalism in mid-war was indeed triumphant. Moreover, it was profoundly dangerous in a nation where those of non-British background constituted over 40 per cent of the population and where many of British background themselves did not share the particular expression of British-Canadian nationalism so strongly expressed in English Canada's urban centres. Conscription was a response to a real military need, but even more, it became a symbol of Canadian commitment and a product of the fear, expressed in Wrong's lecture, that Canada was not a nation.

'What If?' has recently fascinated military historians.[39] What would have been the consequences had Borden not introduced conscription in the spring of 1917? Surely the result would have been a sullen majority and a rebellion that stirred even darker forces than those that appeared in the 1917 election. Surely those Toronto boardrooms and private clubs where British-Canadian nationalism flourished would have seen plots to bring in a Canadian Lloyd George to smash the opposition. In Montreal and even Quebec City, where the boardrooms and clubs had few who spoke or understood Quebec's majority language (except the staff and servants), would not the potential for conflict have been so much greater? What would have happened with the Canadian Expeditionary Force if conscription had not been imposed and the Canadian Corps had fallen far below full strength? Hume Wrong ended his vicious dream of machine gunning French Canadians with the comment: 'Still let us hope for peace – and conscription.'[40] What if there had been no conscription? Would Canada have known peace?

The First World War was a calamity that coincided with a period of extraordinary change in North American history. In such times, a leader who seemed stolid, who lacked Lloyd George's oratorical fire, and who lacked partisanship suited Canada well. His language was traditional and his view of war romantic, but these characteristics were shared by most soldiers and their families. A language of modernity would have been alien in Canada. Canada had neither an Easter Rebellion, nor a Khaki election, nor the Black and Tans. Borden managed conscription in a fashion that brought a sense that Canada had paid down the price for equality within the empire. The 'equality of sacrifice,' the compelling and chilling phrase that fuelled the call for conscription, was linked by Borden to the equality of nationhood within empire that made the war seem more of a victory than it really was. In January 1918, a month after the bitterest election in Canadian history, the Quebec legislature rejected a motion calling for Quebec secession. Premier Lomer Gouin, who had strongly opposed the Unionists in 1917, rejected with equal fervour any suggestion of secession. In May 1918 he politely turned down Borden's request that he join his government but accepted Borden's request that Quebec 'be in his charge both provincially and federally' while he was absent in Europe.[41] Both Borden and Gouin knew that the nationalist furies would fade; to sustain them would be fatal.

Historians have seen Borden through the prisms appropriate to the age in which they worked. I have argued that our times are more understanding of the challenge facing him in a period when an increasingly strong-willed majority demanded harsh penalties against those who did not conform. His imperturbability smothered anger, his indecisiveness postponed conflict, and he spoke in a language that resonated with his followers. He too long ignored those who would not follow him, but he concentrated upon controlling the fury of British-Canadian nationalism at its height. It was probably his only choice in his times. That we understand Borden's leadership better is partly the product of our own times but even more the result of Craig Brown's biography, the finest study of Canadian wartime leadership ever written.

NOTES

1 R.C. Brown, 'Fishwives, Plutocrats, Sirens and Other Curious Creatures: Some Questions about Political Leadership in Canada,' in R. Kenneth Carty and W. Peter Ward, eds, *Entering the Eighties: Canada in Crisis* (Toronto: Oxford University Press, 1980), 149–60. See also, R.C. Brown, '"Whither are we being shoved?" Political Leadership in Canada during World War I,' in J.L. Granatstein and R.D. Cuff, eds, *War and Society in North America* (Toronto: Nelson, 1971), 104–19; and R.C. Brown, *Robert Laird Borden: A Biography*, 2 vols (Toronto: Macmillan, 1975, 1980).

2 James MacGregor Burns, *Leadership* (New York: Harper and Row, 1978).

3 Paul Fussell, *The Great War and Modern Memory* (London: Oxford University Press, 1975), 12.

4 Eric Hobsbawm, *The Age of Extremes: The Short Twentieth Century, 1914–1991* (London: Abacus, 1995), 29.

5 National Archives of Canada (NAC), Borden Diary, 14 July 1918. See also Brown, *Borden*, 2: 137–9, 2, 140–1.

6 Niall Ferguson, *The Pity of War: Explaining World War I* (New York: Basic Books, 2000).

7 Fussell, *Great War*, 21–2; Henry Borden, ed., *Letters to Limbo* (Toronto: University of Toronto Press, 1971), 31, letter of 12 May 1933.

8 *Letters to Limbo*, 114, letter of 11 July 1934. David Staines, 'Audrey Alexandra Brown,' in Eugene Benson and William Toye, eds, *Oxford Companion to Canadian Literature*, 2nd ed. (Toronto: Oxford University Press, 1997), 153.

9 R.T.L. [Charles Vining], *Bigwigs: Canadians Wise and Otherwise* (Toronto: Macmillan, 1935), 15.

10 Ibid., 16.

11 Jonathan F. Vance, *Death So Noble: Memory, Meaning, and the First World War* (Vancouver, UBC Press, 1997), 10–11, 266.

12 NAC, Imperial War Cabinet 16, 13 June 1918; Borden Papers, vol. 341.

13 NAC, Borden Papers, diary entries 2 and 15 January 1918. See Brown, *Borden*, 2: 133–4, for an excellent discussion of this issue.

14 Fuller detail on these figures is found in John English, *The Decline of Politics: The Conservatives and the Party System, 1901–1920* (Toronto: University of Toronto Press, 1977), 199–201.

15 Ibid. Interestingly, the largest religious affiliation was Presbyterian (38 per cent), an indication of the presence of the Liberals in the Unionist caucus.

16 See Janine Brodie and Jane Jenson, *Crisis, Challenge and Change: Party and Class in Canada* (Toronto: Methuen, 1980), 96.

17 Burns, *Leadership*, 429.

18 Robert Craig Brown and Donald Loveridge, '"Unrequited Faith": Recruiting and the CEF, 1914–1918,' *Revue internationale d'histoire militaire* 51 (1982), 53–78; Christopher Sharpe, 'The Great War, 1914–1918,' in William Dean, Conrad Heidenreich, Thomas McIlwraith, and John Warkentin, eds, *The Concise Historical Atlas of Canada* (Toronto: University of Toronto Press, 1998), plate 40.

19 Bruce Curtis, *The Politics of Population: State Formation, Statistics, and the Census of the Candas, 1840–1875* (Toronto: University of Toronto Press, 2001).

20 NAC, Kemp Papers, Borden to Kemp, 5 April 1917, Kemp to Borden, 10 April 1917, vol. 53, f.8.

21 NAC, Borden Papers, Borden to Tupper, 2 January 1917, vol. 16.

22 P.A. Sorokin, *Man and Society in Calamity* (New York: Dutton, 1943); and David Hickson and Suan Miller, 'Concepts of Decisions: Making and Implementing Strategic Decisions in Organizations,' in Frank Heller, ed., *Decision-Making and Leadership* (Cambridge: Cambridge University Press, 1992), 134–5.

23 Ian Miller, *Our Glory and Our Grief: Torontonians and the Great War* (Toronto: University of Toronto Press, 2001).

24 Carl Berger, *The Writing of Canadian History: Aspects of English-Canadian Historical Writing: 1900–1970* (Toronto: Oxford University Press, 1976), 17.

25 George Wrong, 'The Creation of the Federal System in Canada,' in *The Federation of Canada* (Toronto: University of Toronto Press, 1917), 34–5.

26 Ibid., 22.

27 Quoted in J.L. Granatstein, *The Ottawa Men: The Civil Service Mandarins, 1935–1917* (Toronto: Oxford University Press, 1982), 113.

28 Wrong, *Federation*, 32.

29 Berger, *Writing of Canadian History*, 8–9; Granatstein, *Ottawa Men*, 110–16; Wrong, *Federation*, 33; Vincent Massey, *What's Past Is Prologue* (Toronto: Macmillan, 1963), 21–2; interview with Paul Martin, May 1979. Martin, a student of Wrong, recalled meeting Wrong's brother in a southwestern Ontario general store in the 1930s. The brother had a Canadian country speech and was an evangelist. An astonished Martin learned quickly that the brothers had little contact.

30 George Cassar, *Asquith as War Leader* (London: Hambleton, 1994), 197. Borden, *Letters to Limbo*, 78–9.

31 E.A. Pearson to Sir George Perley, 6 June 1917. L.B. Pearson Personnel File, Dept. of National Defence, National Archives Record Centre, Job. No. 30; Martin Seymour-Smith, *Robert Graves: The Assault Heroic, 1895–1926* (London: Hutchinson, 1982), chap. 3.

32 Brown, *Borden*, 2: 130.

33 Borden, *Memoirs*, 2:699. Fussell, *Great War*, 249–50.

34 Fussell, *Great War*, 250.

35 Sandra Gwyn, *Tapestry of War: A Private View of Canadians in the Great War* (Toronto: HarperCollins, 1992), 460.

36 Greg Dening, *Mr. Bligh's Bad Language: Passion, Power and Theatre in the Bounty* (Cambridge: Cambridge University Press, 1992), 61.

37 Cassar, *Asquith*, 234.

38 A.M. Willms, 'Conscription 1917: A Brief for the Defence,' *Canadian Historical Review* 37 (1956), 338–56; and J.L. Granatstein and J.M. Hitsman, *Broken Promises: A History of Conscription in Canada* (Toronto: Oxford, 1977).
39 Robert Cowley, ed., *What If?* (New York: Berkley, 2000). The essays on the First World War emphasize the disruption of the times and the unavoidability of war.
40 Quoted in Granatstein, *Ottawa Men*, 113.
41 NAC, Borden Papers, diary entries, 11 May 1918.

# 5 Against Isolationism: Napoléon Belcourt, French Canada, and 'La grande guerre'

## PATRICE A. DUTIL

On 9 December 1914, when it was obvious that the 'war to end all wars' was not going to end as promised by Christmas, an unusual meeting of school trustees took place in Rockland, an Ontario town east of Ottawa in the County of Russell. After the usual shuffle, *retrouvailles*, and handshakes, Napoléon Desrosiers, the chairman of the local separate school board, called the meeting to order and asked the board secretary, a dapper gentleman named J.A. Lombard, if he was ready to proceed. The meeting was packed. People had things to say.

A few people immediately commented about how the European Entente powers had worked 'to establish peace and harmony in and among all classes of the various communities.' The war had broken through barriers, it seemed. One person talked about the British Parliament's recently passed Home Rule Bill for Ireland – which recognized after centuries that the Catholic Irish had rights to particular freedoms. Someone else remarked how France had also recognized inherent rights in annulling the edicts that had expelled religious orders. One speaker even mentioned Russia, the third leg of the Entente, and its pledge to give Poles complete liberty of language and religion.

The situation in Europe touched sensitive chords in the Rockland Separate School Board. At the same time, the board wanted to discuss 'Regulation 17,' a Ministry of Education directive that prohibited teaching in French after grades 1 and 2. The board concluded that the Government of Ontario's actions in suppressing French-language schools did not 'affect the unswerving loyalty of the French Canadian to the British Crown.' Still, it created in their minds 'animosity and discontent' and 'divided energies which should be concentrated on the triumph of a cause dear to all classes, irrespective of race and creed, and hence should, it is earnestly believed, be eliminated for the common good in the present emergency.'

The school board passed motions that encapsulated the discussion and protested the limitations on French in the schools, the discrimination in school inspections, and the suppression of school grants. They signed their petition and Lombard sent it to the Ontario premier, William Henry Hearst. A few weeks later, the premier replied by letter: 'The government appreciates the unity of sentiment existing throughout the British Empire on the subject of the present war and is of opinion that at least one of the reasons for this unanimity is the gratitude felt by every self-governing unit of the Empire toward the Parent State in respecting and guarding the right of each State or province to legislate freely within the limits of its constitution.' Responding to the need to address school rights, the premier could hardly have been colder: 'The Legislature of Ontario unanimously adopted the policy upon which the Regulations governing the English-French schools are based,' the letter continued, 'the Regulations are in accord with the wishes of the people as expressed by their representatives in the Legislature and the Government believes in the best interests of the schools. The Government, therefore, is merely doing its duty in carrying out the school law.'[1]

A few days after the meeting in Rockland, a political rally involving a remarkable cross-section of French Canada's elite, ranging from *nationalistes* such as *Le Devoir* publisher and editor Henri Bourassa and Armand Lavergne and noted Liberals such as Senators Raoul Dandurand, Phillippe Landry, and Napoléon Belcourt, launched a campaign to raise funds for 'les blessés d'Ontario' (the wounded of Ontario), a campaign started by the Association catholique de la jeunesse canadienne-française (ACJC).[2] In the diocese of Sherbrooke, a special collection was promoted by Monseigneur Paul LaRocque; the result was a record-setting windfall of over $2,100.00.[3] Within a year, this campaign would raise over $22,000 (about $330,000 in today's currency).

In the crisis days of 1914, when the issues of participation in the war and school rights at home – the two issues that would dominate the 1914–18 period – had already intermixed, the people of Rockland turned to one man, Senator Napoléon Belcourt.[4] He openly questioned the quality of a country that suppressed minority rights, and he struggled with the issue of Canada's involvement with the Entente. At the same time he was eager, by liberal and Catholic convictions, to see Canada defeat Germany and its allies. He was not an anti-imperialist of the

Henri Bourassa sort, who would argue that Canada had 'no moral or constitutional obligation' in helping the war effort and who equated the Ontario government with the Kaiser's Prussians.[5] As a key player in the political and legal battle over Regulation 17 and in his support for Canada's participation in the war, Belcourt provides a remarkable prism through which French Canada's attitude towards the war can be evaluated.

It was argued, and it seems hardly worth contesting almost 100 years later, that French Canada did not 'do its part' in the war of 1914–18. From the very beginning of the crisis, there have been five essential reasons advanced to explain this reality. The first reason was the arrogant attitude of governments over Regulation 17, which simply sapped the desire to participate and robbed the federal government of any legitimacy in claiming that Canada's fight was to help the oppressed. The second related to the first, in that Regulation 17 fuelled the *nationaliste* anti-imperial campaign. The third was that demographic factors explained the poor numbers: eligible French-Canadian men were more likely to have families to support and work in rural areas in far greater numbers than their anglophone counterparts: in other words, there were fewer available men in Quebec in the seventeen to forty-five age group.[6] The fourth reason was that French Canada did not have a martial strain in its culture: calls to arms simply fell on deaf ears. Finally, observers have long pointed to the bumbling administrative decisions made in Ottawa as the government tried to promote recruitment.[7]

More recently, these positions have been re-examined. Some observers have discounted the importance of Regulation 17 and argued that the 'imperial question' – the issue of Canada's place in the British Empire – was far more significant. Others have argued that the urban/ rural demographic explanation of French-Canadian enrolments was hardly distinctive in that Canadian-born English speakers in similar situations were scarcely more likely to sign up.[8] Although the absence of a militaristic culture in French Canada is undeniable, some historians have picked up on the fact that the anti-imperialist message of Henri Bourassa was not foreign to Canadians, particularly those recent immigrants from areas other than Britain. In other words, anti-imperialism was hardly an exclusive French-Canadian position. Finally, the almost anti-French-Canadian administrative aspects of the military, both before and during the war, have been explored.

Napoléon Belcourt's experience as a Franco-Ontarian, Quebecker, and Canadian provides a captivating perspective on French Canada's war: contrary to the *nationalistes*, who could easily undermine a national war effort by pointing to the inequities in Ontario, Belcourt – the top defender of Franco-Ontarians – argued in favour of the war effort. Belcourt's experience points to an underestimated factor in explaining French Canada's reaction to the war: its isolationism. Belcourt feared isolationism for many reasons. He argued as passionately against isolationism in world affairs, against isolationism towards Britain, and against Quebec's growing isolationism within Canada as he did against the forced isolation of Ontario's French-speaking minority. Even though it has been a constant in the French-Canadian outlook or *mentalité*, this attitude, surprisingly, has not been clearly identified as part of the fabric of French-Canadian ideology.[9]

Belcourt knew that any effort to encourage a broadly 'national' participation was unlikely to yield results while English Canada was brazenly redefining the rights of citizenship: indeed, the actions over Regulation 17 and over conscription threatened to deepen French Canada's isolationism. With two issues intimately linked in a manner that he did not like, Belcourt was eager to see the schools situation in Ontario resolved and a consensus on the degree of Canada's enlistment effort because he saw both questions tearing at the Canadian fabric.

Napoléon Belcourt was the son of Ferdinand Belcourt, businessman and member of Parliament for Trois-Rivières, and Marie Anne Clair. The Belcourt ancestors had settled in the Batiscan area in 1675, but the Belcourts were in Toronto in the summer of 1860, preparing for a parliamentary session. Mme Belcourt delivered her child in the capital city of the day while her husband attended to politics (the capital shifted between Canada East and Canada West in those years). All his life, Belcourt would joke that 'he had taken his precautions' by being born in Toronto on 15 September 1860.

Young Napoléon did not grow up in Ontario. He attended the Séminaire St-Joseph in Trois-Rivières, falling under the influence of Monseigneur Laflèche.[10] He then attended law school at Laval, graduating summa cum laude in 1882. Called to the Quebec Bar in that year, he was drawn to the province of his birth and established an office in Ottawa two years later. 'He was my companion at the university,' Senator Raoul Dandurand recalled, 'and we were both called to the Bar of Montreal at about the same time. I can still see him coming in to tell me he had decided to establish himself on the Ontario side of the Ottawa River, in a community where, although some lawyers from

Napoléon Antoine Belcourt, n.d. (photographer unknown. Collection of Marc L. Belcourt)

across the river had offices there; no French lawyer had ever practiced at the bar.'[11] He married Hectorine Shehyn in January 1889, the daughter of Quebec Senator Joseph Shehyn, and they had three daughters, Virginie Béatrice (1890–1966), Gabrielle (1892–1986), and Jeanne (1894–1963). Hectorine died in 1901 and on 19 January 1903 Belcourt married Mary Margaret Haycock. Together they had three sons, Jean Wilfrid (1904–85), Paul Lafontaine (1906–79), Victor Philippe (1908–65), and a daughter who died within the year of her birth in 1912.[12]

Although a busy family man, Napoléon Belcourt proved a remarkable convener. His homes, first at 489 Wilbrod and then at 27 Gouldburne, and his offices in the National Bank Building at 18 Rideau Street (across from the Chateau Laurier) and later in the Castle Building at 53 Queen Street were important gathering points for Catholic, francophone, and political circles in Ottawa.[13] Belcourt wasted no time in following the family tradition of active involvement in politics. An early supporter of Wilfrid Laurier, he first ran (at age thirty) in the federal election of 1891 in the city of Ottawa, but he was defeated. He tried again in 1896 and was elected in the majority that carried the Liberals to power. He was re-elected in 1900 and 1904. In 1904 he was named speaker of the House, a post he held for three sessions. In 1907 Laurier named him to the Senate. According to his friend C.B. Sissons, the noted Victoria College (University of Toronto) historian, Belcourt was 'tall and spare, with the dignity befitting a former Speaker.'[14] Omer Héroux called him a 'noble nature.'[15] Another observer, remembering him as 'pale,' added: 'While he seemed aloof, his passion for work was such that he could not refuse a favour, an undertaking or a plea.' Belcourt was a dour, private man. 'He was ailing all his life,' remembered his friend Dandurand, 'haemorrhages laid him low, and often he faced death.' Another friend said he had 'a great "team spirit" and the virtues of humility, of cooperation and of confidence that it entails.'[16]

Impeccably bilingual, Belcourt was acutely sensitive to the English–French dichotomy in Canada and the Irish–French schism in Catholicism. He first married the daughter of an Irish Catholic, then the daughter of a Protestant, but he 'had been compelled to insist on the use of French at table, lest in the Ottawa *milieu* they [the family] should lose their mother-tongue.'[17] In an article entitled 'Canadian National Unity' published in the *Westminster* in 1907, he complained that little progress had been made in 'fostering a national spirit' and argued that the 'slow development in every branch of human industry, the tardy material progress, the consequent exodus of one-third of our population to the

United States ... were not calculated to awaken a vigorous Canadian patriotism.' Yet he seemed optimistic about relations between religions in Canada: 'The spirit and objective of Confederation can be summarized in two words: "cooperation and solidarity."'[18]

He could be harshly critical. Canada's politics, for instance, were a problem, Belcourt said, because the elite shirked the duties of citizenship and left 'to the less enlightened classes the task of municipal and legislative representation and government.' In many ways he was a traditional Liberal. 'The best government is the one that governs least,' he argued; 'it would be a good thing to remind those gentlemen of the need for a greater individualism and of a greater spirit of private enterprise.'[19]

In terms of Canada's presence in the British Empire or in international events Belcourt was something of an internationalist, like other Quebec political leaders such as Raoul Dandurand, Rodolphe Lemieux (Laurier's able Quebec deputies), and, to a certain degree, even Sir Wilfrid himself. 'Canada is the last hope of democracy,' he said. 'The eyes of the whole civilized world are upon Canada, and its attempt to create and maintain an ideal democratic polity will be watched with the keenest interest. Failure to rise to the opportunity will deserve and no doubt receive universal condemnation. Canada owes it to herself and to the world, and to the cause of democracy as well, and especially to her future generations, to assure in her land of "milk and honey" democracy's ultimate triumph.'[20]

Together, they faced the wrath of Henri Bourassa, the grandson of Louis-Joseph Papineau, who since the Boer War had distinguished himself in pleading against Canadian involvement in British affairs and in favour of cutting the imperial tie. It would be difficult to exaggerate the vilification of Bourassa in English Canada during the war years, particularly as he sharpened his opposition to the war effort from the middle of 1915 on.[21] He was denounced as a German spy, a traitor, and a criminal by some of the prominent men of his day. He often faced police harassment and threats to his life. Bourassa, nonetheless, never failed to speak in English Canada to make his views better known. His searing editorials on the empire and against Canadian imperialists in Le Devoir were collected in a series of pamphlets and books, many of them published for the English-speaking market.[22]

Inspired by Bourassa's views, many have generalized Quebec's attitude as 'anti-imperialist and nationalist.' A closer reading of the situation leads me to the conviction that there was a deeper and more meaningful ideology at play. Repeated appeals by the French-Canadian elite – politicians, bishops, business people, some union leaders, eminent journalists – to come to the aid of Catholics, of the French, or of the Belgians equally fell on deaf ears. French Canadians, for the most part, did not want to see their youth squandered in the muddy battlefields of Europe. 'Isolationism,' which has seldom been used to define a position in Canada[23] and has been employed with so little precision even in the United States, can explain the position of most French Canadians towards the First World War. 'Isolationism' as one historian described it, 'is an attitude, policy, doctrine, or position opposed to the commitment of American force outside the Western Hemisphere, except in the rarest and briefest instances. The essence of isolationism is refusal to commit force beyond hemispheric bounds, or absolute avoidance of overseas military alliances. Rejection of forceful commitments beyond the hemisphere is the point on which all have agreed.'[24] This definition – easily applied to Quebec – could also be applied to many parts of Canada in the early twentieth century.

Isolationism in Quebec and in French Canada was tested during the Boer War and in the Naval Bill debates of 1909–10, but it most clearly emerged during the First World War. Bourassa's version struck a chord in many levels of French Canada's leadership and in the wider population, but it would be a mistake to argue that he applied the concepts to French Canada on his own. In fact, it was espoused by a wide variety of people who had different reasons for arguing that Canada should not involve itself in defending the Triple Entente powers. In the United States, Senator Robert A. Taft famously commented that the label 'isolationist' was given to 'anyone who opposed the policy of the moment.' The same could be said of Quebec isolationists, who, like their American cousins, continually denied that they were isolationists.[25]

The isolationist debate in the United States was very similar to the Quebec experience in other ways. The *Chicago Tribune*, for example, proudly referred to isolationists as 'nationalists.' In both cases, there was a factor of geographic and demographic concentration. In the United States, isolationism was explained by pointing to ethnic, geographic, and economic realities and was found to be prevalent in German and Irish minorities scattered in the United States.[26] Voters in the mid-west, notably German- and Scandinavian-American Lutherans, were noticeably isolationist and their influence was felt in Washington.[27] Although rooted deeply in the mid-west, isolationists such as Senators Robert La Follette of Wisconsin and George W. Norris of

Nebraska proved sufficiently influential to divide many political parties and help to delay American entry in the war until 1917. They would argue that to involve the United States in the European war would imperil democracy at home and would thus be a denial of the very raison d'être of the United States. 'As Americans, they [French Canadians] deny any close relationship with either France or Europe,' André Siegfried, the noted French sociologist, pointedly observed in the 1930s.[28]

Belcourt, holding a view that rejected isolationism and allowed for Canadian involvement in the world, sincerely attempted to justify a presence in a war. Against the likes of Bourassa, he would argue that French Canadians 'never sought or even contemplated the severance of the British tie.' For Belcourt, the link to Britain and its political traditions was central to the Canadian compact and thus worthy of defence. Belcourt would insist that Canadians needed the protection of the British Crown and should defend it, militarily if need be, until a reasonable accommodation could be arranged between English- and French-speaking peoples in Canada. The battle over Regulation 17 proved the truth of this assertion.

### Significance of Regulation 17

The debates on this issue had been burning for over two years by the time war was declared against the Kaiser.[29] Sensing the growing importance of the Franco-Ontarian community, and urged by Irish Catholics, the Government of Ontario asked its chief inspector of public and separate schools to investigate the quality of education in the Ottawa valley in 1908. He reported that the quality of teaching in the French-speaking schools (known as 'bilingual schools' or 'English-French schools' because English had a major presence) was poor. The reaction among francophones in the Ottawa region was swift. On 24 January 1909, 100 people from Ottawa met and supported idea of a conference that could unite disparate forces.[30] The event took place a year later (both Prime Minister Wilfrid Laurier and Leader of the Opposition Robert Borden attended) and a new organization was created, the Association Canadienne-française d'éducation de l'Ontario (ACFEO). Napoléon Belcourt was elected the first president in January 1910. He would occupy his position for two years, until a member of the Conservative Party would be chosen in order to curry favour with governments both in Ontario and in Ottawa. At the time Belcourt assumed his post, French Canadians constituted fully 8 per cent of the population of

Ontario, up from 2 per cent at Confederation. According to the census of 1911, there were 202,422 francophones in the province. In 1909, however, the ecclesiastical census of the province reported 247,000 French Canadians. The net effect was that 250,000 was the figure often cited in newspapers and speeches.[31]

The ACFEO lost little time in bringing to light the weakness of Franco-Ontarian representation in the political and judicial arena and submitted to Prime Minister Laurier a long list of inequities, in terms of judges named to the bench and senators, in comparison with Irish Catholics in Ontario (who were fewer – between 175,000 and 200,000), or the English minority in Quebec.[32] The petitioners argued that the weak representation constituted a 'grave injustice.' They maintained early that, because of their weak representation in Parliament, they had to be compensated with effective representation in the courts in order to protect their rights.

Events proved them prescient. In March 1911 Howard Ferguson, the future Ontario minister of education and premier, introduced in the legislature a motion asserting that 'no language other than English should be used as a medium of instruction' in any school in Ontario.[33] Acting on the report of its chief inspector, the Ontario government adopted Regulation 17 in June 1912 (it would be amended in 1913 and made law in 1915).[34] Essentially, it outlawed the creation of new bilingual schools, limited teaching in the French language to the first two years of school, imposed the teaching of English from the very first grade, required that all teachers be qualified to teach in English, and limited the use of French as a language of communication. To enforce these new regulations, the government announced that the schools would be monitored by both a French-speaking and an English-speaking superintendent. 'Circular of Instructions, 17' was, according to Premier James Whitney, designed to improve the instruction in French-language schools. It quickly assumed a far greater importance than a routine administrative standard. Francophones saw nothing less than the hand of state-ordered assimilation.[35]

Regulation 17 was enforced by a rule that any school that failed to comply would forfeit support from public funds and that its teachers would be liable to suspension or cancellation of their certificates. From the beginning, the Ottawa Separate School Board, two-thirds of whose trustees were francophones, refused to enforce Regulation 17. The first appeals were political. With weak representation in the Ontario cabinet, leaders of the ACFEO sought help from Ottawa. The new prime minister, Robert Borden, was asked to invoke federal powers to suppress the Ontario law. He refused, but in the fall of 1912 Borden wrote to Whitney to express his concerns. Whitney responded that this issue came under provincial jurisdiction.[36] In the face of such obstinacy, Franco-Ontarians organized themselves, helped in no small part by funding received from Quebec sources. In 1913 they launched *Le Droit*, a French-language daily, and it proved an effective mouthpiece. It supported the Ottawa Separate School Board and cemented support for its actions as it continued to refuse to comply with the hated language rules. It is worth noting that the Société Saint-Jean-Baptiste in Montreal, led by Olivar Asselin, raised $12,600 (over $200,000 in today's currency) for the ACFEO through their « Le sou de la pensée française » campaign. In total, the ACFEO received $15,400 (over $244,000 in today's currency) from Quebec sources between 1910 and 1913.[37]

Belcourt, like others, hoped that the provincial elections in Ontario in June 1914 might have helped to cool the situation in Ontario. The governing Conservative Party, still led by Whitney, pledged full endorsement of Regulation 17, while the Liberals, led by Newton Rowell, remained surprisingly vague and non-committal.[38] The Conservative Party was returned to power, but the Franco-Ontarian Tories who had supported the Regulations were defeated.

A few weeks after the election, the Ottawa Separate School Board closed its schools, asserting that it could no longer pay its teachers without the support of the provincial government. By September 1914, with the war in Europe now fully engaged and politicians of all stripes in Canada pledging their support to the Triple Entente, 8,000 students in Ottawa were without teachers. Led by Samuel Genest, the French majority sought a city by-law allowing it to issue debentures to raise money for new schools to be operated independently of the Department of Education's rulings. R. Mackell, one of the minority school board members, asked for an injunction against the board's decision to close the schools to prevent it from borrowing or paying staff while refusing to comply with Regulation 17. The Ontario Supreme Court ordered the board to reopen its doors and to employ only qualified teachers. Premier Whitney died a few days later and was replaced by William Hearst, who in that October placed the Ottawa Separate School Board under trusteeship. Although the issue had been festering since 1912, there was now a legal point on which Franco-Ontarians could seek redress in the courts, since the political apparatus had completely failed to respond to their demands for justice.

Belcourt leaped at the opportunity to use this case as a platform to argue against the root cause of the action, Regulation 17. Representing the Ottawa Separate School Board, he launched a suit against Mackell and argued the case in early November 1914 before Mr Justice Lennox, an individual Belcourt later described as 'an ignorant and narrow-minded fanatic.'[39] The timing could hardly have been worse for the war effort. English Canada was demanding a national effort to support the British Empire while at the same time denying francophones in Ontario the right to an education in their own language. In late November 1914 the Ontario Supreme Court ruled in favour of Mackell, finding the board guilty of disobeying the laws of the province. Henri Bourassa denounced the 'Prussians of Ontario.' Soon the Quebec government, which had kept quiet about the sister province's affairs, adopted a legislative resolution on 13 January 1915 in which it unanimously deplored the controversy and asserted that the legislators of Ontario were deficient in their understanding and application of traditional British principles.

Belcourt appealed the Lennox decision in the winter of 1915 to the Appellate Division of the Supreme Court of Ontario. Chief Justice Clute had listened to the crown's arguments for two days, and Belcourt was looking forward to pleading in favour of recovering the monies of the Ottawa board taken by the commission and not returned. Belcourt had not stood before the court for ten minutes before Mr Justice Clute said, 'in a bare-faced exhibition of bigotry and boorishness,' that no argument could be made that would 'impress him.' Belcourt was allowed to continue only when another judge protested, saying that he was very anxious to hear the argument.[40] Not surprisingly, the Appellate Court found against the Ottawa Separate School Board in July 1915.

Before the courts, as much as before the Senate or before the public, Belcourt argued against the letter and the spirit of the law on three fronts, and his positions inspired a similar line of argument across the country. First, he maintained that Regulation 17 was effectively removing rights already acquired in the school regulations devised in Canada West by Egerton Ryerson and supported by Oliver Mowat.[41] He pointedly did not use the argument that French was guaranteed in the constitution because there simply was no provision for it. Technically, he argued, the separate school law, unlike the public schools law, did not prescribe the use of the English language, indicating that the framers of the legislation had no intention of ever limiting the use of French. He argued, moreover, that Regulation 17 was inconsistent with the requirements of section 93 of the British North America (BNA) Act, which granted the provinces the right to legislate exclusively in the area of education, providing that the rights of denominational schools were not affected. In essence, he maintained that learning in French in Ontario was a right that 'once granted, is not susceptible of being withdrawn. If withdrawn, as is clearly sought to be done by Regulation 17, the Courts in their ordinary inherent jurisdiction have the power and duty to determine that Regulation 17 is *ultra vires* of the Legislature.' Outside the court, and not without some bitterness, Belcourt blamed the negotiators of the 1867 pact for the predicament of Franco-Ontarians. 'I always believed that the leaders of Lower Canada had completely lost sight and prudence in not demanding a clear and explicit recognition of our religious and linguistic rights,' he told Henri Bourassa.[42]

Second, he argued that the usage of French, and by implication the right to be instructed in it, constituted a natural right. In court, he pointed out that Regulation 17 'constitutes the only attempt ever made in the British Empire to deprive British subjects of the use of their mother tongue.'[43] Outside the court, he was more eloquent: 'Far from affecting our duty or hiding our devotion to the British Crown and British institutions,' he argued, 'the free use of our mother tongue, with the recognition of our laws and our institutions, has been the pure source whence we drew the will, the courage, and the valour which enabled us more than once to save this country for the Empire. Had the French language not been made equal before the law in the past, I would not hesitate to say that to-day it would be an act of simple justice, and of profound political wisdom to recognize it as such.'[44]

Belcourt's argument had a more legalistic aspect on the issue of taxpayers' rights. He claimed that the taxpayers who funded the separate school system had a right 'similar to other rights of property' to determine how funds would be spent. 'Regulation 17,' he asserted, violated 'natural law and natural justice' because it sought to take away the right to have one's own money, paid in by way of school taxes, applied in accordance with one's own wishes. While Belcourt was willing to recognize that the Department of Education did have rights to oversee the schooling taking place in the province, he argued that it was a shared duty, the result of a shared funding. Stated otherwise, the government could not deprive the ratepayers of the use or control of the taxes contributed by them to their school boards for educational purposes.[45] Outside the court, Belcourt called into question the unequal funding of separate and public schools, particularly the diversion of taxes paid by semi-public, industrial, financial, and commercial corporations to public schools, not to separate schools. Belcourt, utterly beside himself, was defiant:

> And, as if this weren't enough, it is now threatened that if the French-speaking Canadians in Ontario persist – and there can be no doubt that they will – in their present attitude that the French language shall, in certain well defined parts of the province, be the vehicle of instruction, the whole of their school tax contributions will be diverted to the use of the public schools, and they shall, furthermore, be deprived of the schools built and paid for and supported out of their own moneys. The majority may possibly – though it is very doubtful – so ordain; but who will say that such would not constitute a flagrant and intolerable denial of justice? ... Not only have the educational authorities in that province passed sentence of death upon the French language in the schools, but they have committed the execution of this sentence to the bilingual teachers who will be required to strangle French speech and French thought. And to make sure that death will ensue, the government has appointed supervising inspectors who know nothing of the French language to supervise the gruesome task. Why not suppress the name as well as the thing itself?[46]

Belcourt's third key argument was that Regulation 17 was, 'educationally speaking, an absurdity.' He described the educational reach of the regulation as 'manifestly a pedagogical heresy' and 'utter nonsense,' in that students would have to be taught subjects in a language that they could not understand. Outside the court, he protested that that Franco-Ontarians hardly deserved such treatment. Education was a key promise for a better future, and government efforts to stifle the learning initiative were counterproductive. Franco-Ontarians were aiding the development and prosperity of Ontario; they lived in peace and harmony with their neighbours and did not deserve discriminatory practices.[47]

Every court of the Province of Ontario rejected Belcourt's arguments. As news of court decisions unfailingly disappointed and the obstinacy of Queen's Park proved unshakable, the schools in the shadow of Parliament Hill in Ottawa rapidly became ethnic battlegrounds. Father Charles Charlebois, *curé* of Sainte-Famille parish and the guiding spirit of the resistance in Ottawa, considered that perhaps having a friend inside the governing Tory party might be an asset to the movement. He sent a long, hand-written letter to Senator Phillippe Landry in January

1915, asking him to assume the presidency of the ACFEO. Landry, an old ultramontane Tory and speaker of the Senate, accepted the offer a month later and promptly drafted a letter to the Ontario premier that again linked the war and Ontario's educational battle: 'Should not the entente cordiale which today united the English and the French on the battlefields of Europe be able to bring together in our own country the descendants of those two great nations?'[48] Hearst never responded, leaving the courts to answer.

The controversy caught fire in March 1915, when the Ontario government effectively declared 190 schools in the province ineligible for grants. It then secured passage of a bill empowering it to set up a commission to take over the duties of the Ottawa Separate School Board; in July it abolished the Ottawa Separate School Commission and named a three-person commission (one of whom would be French speaking) to manage the schools. Despite Sir Wilfrid Laurier's urgings, the Liberal opposition led by Rowell supported the bill. Suddenly, the issue was spilling far beyond the boundaries of Ontario's Queen's Park and onto Parliament Hill, Quebec, and Rome.

In June 1915 bishops and archbishops in French Canada sent a petition to Pope Benedict XV, telling him that the French language was a 'rampart' against the mixed marriages deplored by the Holy See. Their argument was that the battle against Orangeism in Ontario had to be successful; otherwise, the Protestant forces would exert themselves against Catholicism in other provinces. The petition also asked him to put pressure on the Canadian political system, because under Regulation 17 Catholic schools would fall within the inspectorate of Protestants, which 'places them at the mercy of an enemy of their traditions and beliefs.'[49] Mgr Latulippe, the Bishop of Haileybury, travelled to Rome to explain the situation and returned in October 1915. At that point, Phillippe Landry urged Cardinal Bégin of Quebec City to go to Rome to direct 'the battle that must begin before the roman congregations ... Only your Éminence can bring us victory.'[50]

As the school year began in September 1915, two teachers (the Desloges sisters) were fired. In protest, they occupied the Guigues School and declared that they were no longer working for the Separate School Board. Defended in the streets by angry parents, they had created their own institution on board property and refused the inspection of the government. When in the same fall the Supreme Court of Ontario sustained the validity of Regulation 17, Belcourt decided to take the case to the Judicial Committee of the Privy Council in London. 'The

French and Catholic minority in Canada has better chances of obtaining justice from the privy council than it does from the Supreme Court,' he told his colleague Aimé Geoffrion. 'Having seen these English speaking judges in the Supreme Court up close for over 25 years, I can say that all of them, almost without exception, held views that were passably narrow and an invincible prejudice against us. I can't help having more confidence for our cause in front of the Privy Council than the Supreme Court when it comes to minority rights.'[51] Belcourt hoped for a political solution; the procedural delays created by Government of Ontario lawyers in *Mackell v. Trustees* showed that a quick solution was not forthcoming.[52]

The decision of the Ontario Supreme Court galvanized Franco-Ontarian efforts. Belcourt, never content to limit his presence to the courtroom, also took to the streets. In the winter of 1916 he started a campaign to encourage Ottawa taxpayers not to pay their school taxes. His efforts were supported by a strike of bilingual teachers[53] and by a march of 5,000 French Canadians to Parliament Hill, asking for federal intervention. A handful of representatives met with Prime Minister Borden, but without success.[54] At the same time, the Quebec legislature passed a bill authorizing municipalities in Quebec to make contributions towards the financing of 'bilingual agitation' in Ontario. Wilfrid Laurier, who had been fairly quiet on the issue, grew indignant. Not surprisingly, he invoked many of the arguments Belcourt had rehearsed since the beginning of the crisis. He vented his spleen on Stewart Lyon, editor of the putatively Liberal *Globe*, and accused him of not living up to the principles of Blake and Mowat. 'The whole situation is one which is very clear and which can be easily settled upon the lines of Liberalism, as it was forty years ago by the Mowat government,' he told Lyon; 'it was then agreed, and everybody accepted, that every child in Ontario should receive an English education but that parents of French origin should also have the right, in addition, to have their children taught in their own language. Who can object to this? Is there a Liberal who is not ready to stand for this reasonable position? I confess to you that I am disturbed by the present attitude of your paper. I am not disposed for my part to yield neither to the extremists of Nationalism nor to the extremists of Toryism.'[55] Laurier also dissected the issue in what he called a 'too prolonged correspondence' with Newton Rowell, the Ontario Liberal leader, in the spring of 1916. Laurier was despondent: 'Henceforth, the Orange doctrine is to prevail – that the English language only is to be taught in the schools. That seems to me absolutely tyrannical.' By mid-May, Laurier had concluded that the 'line of cleavage' separating him and Rowell was now 'final and beyond redemption.' He told Rowell, 'I write with a heavy heart. The party has not advanced; it has sorely retrograded, abandoning position after position before the heavy onslaughts of Toryism.'[56]

Events proved even harder to bear for Laurier that spring, when the Liberal government in Manitoba rescinded the clause in the School Act that gave the parents of ten children the right to request bilingual instruction.

It would take time for the case to make its way to the Judicial Committee of the Privy Council in London, and action was required immediately. The Liberals, led by Laurier himself, pressed Borden to work against the Ontario school regulations. Laurier drafted a motion, along with Rodolphe Lemieux, Laurent-Olivier David, and Paul-Emile Lamarche, a nationalist MP who was rapidly developing ties with the Laurier camp. On 9 May 1916 Ernest Lapointe tabled the motion in the Commons, resolving 'that this house, especially at this time of universal sacrifice and anxiety, when all energies should be concentrated on winning the war, while fully recognizing the principle for provincial rights and the necessity of every child being given a thorough English education, respectfully suggest to the Legislative Assembly of Ontario the wisdom of making it clear that the privilege for the children of French parentage being taught in their mother tongue be not interfered with.'[57] The Lapointe motion, which was clear in not requesting that the federal government use its powers of disallowance, was debated, but it was rejected by 107 votes to 60. Although seven French-speaking members elected under the Conservative-Nationalist banner voted in favour, the French-speaking ministers in Borden's cabinet voted against the motion, claiming that the symbolism of castigating provincial legislation was ruinous to confederation. The vote was predetermined but could only depress Laurier further: eleven western members and one Ontario member of his own caucus voted against the Lapointe resolution.

Ten days later the French-speaking ministers in Borden's cabinet, led by Esioff-Léon Patenaude, drafted a memorandum asking that the federal government intervene before the Judicial Committee of the Privy Council in Great Britain and threatened to resign if no action was taken. Borden refused to acquiesce to the demand.[58] In protest, the now seventy-year-old Conservative Senator Philippe Landry quit the speaker's chair of the Senate in order to dedicate himself entirely to the Franco-Ontarian battle, and he campaigned across Quebec to raise awareness of what was happening in Ontario. Landry drafted a revealing *aide-mémoire* of arguments regarding the struggle against Regulation 17, part of which concerned 'national honour': 'A people that finds itself faced with an unjust and merciless aggressor has the honorable duty to resist to the last. This is our case in Ontario. We are in the same situation as the Belgians and the French. A people owe it to its honour to reject national insults. Regulation 17 holds many screaming ones: a) It places our language below that of German. b) It places us as stewards of the state like simple savages with its double inspectorate. The struggle has so long been engaged that we cannot abandon it without national disgrace. We have burned our bridges.'[59] Without a doubt, his greatest success occurred when he accompanied Belcourt to a rally of 10,000 people at the Parc Lafontaine in Montreal on 19 June 1916 and gave a thundering speech denouncing the school regulations. Belcourt then left for Europe, to argue the case before the Privy Council and to visit the front.

In London, Belcourt repeated many of the same arguments he had used in the past, but added a few extra notions. He held that section 133 of the BNA Act implied the right to teach French where francophones requested it. 'I presented this argument to the judicial council by saying that in order to fully and freely exercise their rights as citizens as conferred by the Confederation Act, as much to defend and protect himself, his belongings and his freedom, and also to fulfill his fair share of duties, every citizen must have the right to use his mother tongue,' he told Bourassa. 'That is why it is necessary to recognize the right to French-language education for those whose mother tongue is French. Section 133, by decreeing that both English and French are official languages, implies that there is a right to education in the French tongue.'[60] Belcourt went further. He argued that Regulation 17 had caused real harm to the French Catholic minority in Ontario in terms of religious freedom. He argued that the objective of section 93 was to perpetuate religious rights legally established at the time of Confederation. In Ontario, laws passed in 1863 authorized the building of Catholic schools and ensured rights to taxes in order to maintain them. By removing the right to learn in French, Regulation 17 was in effect denying the right to a religious education. Hopeful that the justice that had eluded Franco-Ontarians at home could be found in the Parliament of the mother country, Belcourt ended his argument before the Privy Council and proceeded to a fact-finding tour of the Western Front (see below).

While the battle of the Somme raged, Franco-Ontarians awaited the judgment of the high London tribunal, as well as some sort of pronouncement from Rome. The Holy See responded on 27 October 1916. In his Encyclical Letter Benedict XV refused to take sides between the Irish and the French-speaking Catholics of Ontario and instead limited its verdict to a call for calm and unity. Two weeks later, the Privy Council in London rendered its decision. It found Regulation 17 intra vires, but declared ultra vires the takeover of the Ottawa Separate School Board. For Belcourt, there was finally some vindication. By finding that the provincial government had no right to take over schools, the Privy Council effectively gave the school board the tools to continue its fight. 'In other words,' he told Henri Bourassa, 'if the government had been able to put its hand on our schools and control them, it also had the right to impose Regulation 17 ... The Privy Council declared *ultra vires* the takeover of our schools. Otherwise, I must repeat, the minority would have been rendered impotent.'[61]

The Privy Council and pontifical decisions effectively ended the legal fight over Regulation 17, but it did not take away any of the bitterness. Indeed, the Hearst government in Ontario passed new legislation to strike down school boards that did not comply with the government and insisted that new settlers in Northern Ontario sign agreements not to educate their children in French. As Belcourt noted, the Ontario government 'did not try at any time to settle the question ... [and] did not want the question to be settled,' simply because it perceived it as an issue on which it could hold onto power.[62] The greater significance of Regulation 17, however, was its effect on French Canada at large. The monthly magazine L'Action Française was launched in 1917; its primary focus would be language rights in Canada. Belcourt and Landry had also alerted all the francophone communities in the land to their difficulties, and their mailboxes were consistently replenished with encouraging correspondence and petitions from across the country.

The high points in the battle over Regulation 17 paralleled almost exactly the cruellest losses of life on the battlefields of Europe. As tempers flared in Canada over the rights of citizenship of the French minority, the mounting casualties intensified the cry for more support of the war effort. The fight between English and French now would take place over the enlistment of soldiers for the war effort, a battle that would further bruise an already demoralized French-Canadian population.

## The Enlistment Issue

Did French Canadians refuse to fight? Yes, and no. Although no records of language spoken were kept by the military, it is commonly asserted that roughly 62,000 French Canadians enlisted in some way in the war effort (about 620,000 men in Canada were enlisted in total). By the end of the war, it is estimated that there were 35,000 French-speaking men from all parts of Canada in uniform. Although French-speaking soldiers would be deployed in other units (one historian estimated that 62 per cent of Quebec's infantry volunteers joined English-speaking battalions),[63] fourteen explicitly French-Canadian battalions were created during the war (identified on their cap badge as *Bataillon Canadien-français* or *Bataillon Outremer*): eleven from Quebec, one from Alberta (the 233ième *Nord-Ouest*), one from New Brunswick (the 165ième *Acadien*), and one from eastern Ontario (the 230ième *voltigeurs Canadiens-français*).[64] Still, only three of the fourteen French-speaking battalions, the 22nd, 41st, and 69th, were recruited to strength (1,100 men). Many soldiers were decorated for their valour. Clearly, French Canadians fought in the war.

Placed in perspective (about 30 per cent of the Canadian population was French Canadian), however, it is evident that the effort was relatively light. On a province-by-province basis, Quebec ranked at the bottom by every measure. Far fewer eligible men (15.3 per cent) in Quebec volunteered for the war effort than the Canadian average (31.4 per cent).[65] It must also be remembered that 18 per cent of Quebec's population at that time was English speaking; Quebec figures therefore must not be interpreted as solely 'French speaking.' Conscription eventually had to be used to increase enlistments, and Quebec supplied more conscripts as part of its contribution (34.1 per cent) than the Canadian average (20.5 per cent). In terms of men who actually served overseas, Quebec had the lowest ranking at 14.4 per cent (the next lowest was Saskatchewan at 21 per cent). By one calculation, French-Canadian participation was 'the lowest rate in the white Empire.'[66]

If isolationism was widely held in French Canada, it did have its limits. It was, as in the United States, an 'ideology under stress.'[67] The political leadership in Quebec never argued against the war effort and did support it in many ways. The Catholic Church, at the height of its influence in Quebec, supported war against Germany and its allies, but there is little doubt that there was dissension among the bishops and among local priests, close to the people, who were not partisans of the call for enlistment.[68]

Indeed, many French Canadians spoke in support of Great Britain and France in the late summer and early fall of 1914.[69] Parliament met in a special session on 18 August, and all the bills dealing with the war were passed without a dissenting vote.[70] Henri Bourassa's first editorial in *Le Devoir* of 29 August defined the *nationaliste* position. On 8 September he asserted that aid to the empire was as critical as it was natural.[71] Church pronouncements in favour of war first appeared on 23 September 1914. At the same time, Médéric Martin, mayor of Montreal, announced that employees of the city mobilized by Belgium or France would continue to receive their salaries. The Montreal chapter of the Canadian Patriotic Fund was launched with panache with Mgr Bruchési, the archbishop of Montreal, and Mayor Martin present. The efforts were directed by the English-speaking elites of Montreal, but the fund's direction and management were held as exemplary of an '*entente cordiale*' in September 1914.[72]

There were surprisingly few elected politicians who spoke out against enlistment. Rodolphe Lemieux, for example, was unforgiving in his intense criticism of Sam Hughes, but he supported the war effort and encouraged enlistment nonetheless. Indeed, his own son would soon enlist.[73] Senator Belcourt was no exception in his eloquence. 'Enlist, my young compatriots!' he urged a large crowd assembled in Montreal's Sohmer Park in October 1914. 'If we have to send two or five or ten French-Canadian regiments, we'll know how to find them,' he continued. 'Is it not because the sacred cause of freedom for all is in imminent peril that the real civilization is threatened to its very root? I know that you do not love war any more than I do. We Canadians are a pacifist race. For over one hundred years we have lived in complete peace and we appreciate its worth to the degree where we will make all the necessary sacrifices to ensure its survival here and its return elsewhere. Our pacifist spirit must not compel us to become doctrinaire pacifists.' His argument was liberal. Canada had to fight to affirm the right to live, to defend liberty, honour, the solidarity of civilized peoples, to avenge the outrages and the national insults, and to protect the weak from the brute: 'Canada, no more than other civilized nations, has no right to remain a silent witness to the terrible and barbaric drama that is being played out on the bloodied and devastated fields of Belgium and France. England may be next; perhaps even Canada. Hence our duty is clear. It is urgent, it is immediate, and it will only be accomplished when we will have exhausted – if we must – all our resources of men and money ... French Canadians are not going to negotiate their share of sacrifices; they never had, they never will. Their devotion to the empire is as total as every resource at their disposal. It is clear now that the war will be long and that it will bring incalculable and terrible losses and sacrifices.'[74]

Belcourt's assurance that French Canada would not 'negotiate' its participation was exaggerated. 'The pity of it is,' the writer Elizabeth Armstrong would write twenty-five years later, 'that the government never took full advantage of this French Canadian ardour of 1914.'[75] In the 1st Division that went to France, only one company was French speaking. Of the 36,267 men who formed the first contingent of the Canadian Expeditionary Force, 1,245 (3.4 per cent) were listed as 'French-Canadian.'[76] The only senior French-Canadian officer was Lieutenant-Colonel H.A. Panet of the Royal Canadian Horse Artillery, a division that proved its valour at the second battle of Ypres, barely a few weeks after landing in Europe.

The weak French-Canadian presence could easily be explained by the reality that the military life was not seen as particularly attractive or worth pursuing. In 1912 only 27 of a total of 254 officers of the Canadian army were French Canadian.[77] Given this tradition, the early news on enlistment was not surprising and tested the most entrepreneurial spirits. Arthur Mignault, a Montreal doctor, singularly rose to the challenge and did so brilliantly.[78] He put up $50,000 ($793,836 in today's currency) to raise a regiment, soon called the Royal 22nd (or, as they would be nicknamed in English, the Van Doos). It would take Mignault and others almost six months to bring the corps to capacity (many recruits decided to desert), so that it could make the trip overseas, but he did attract honourable men, not the least of whom were Georges Vanier and Thomas Tremblay. Mignault also established a French-Canadian hospital, General Hospital No. 8, at St-Cloud, near Paris.

On the whole, however, Ottawa's recruitment policy of relying on local initiative to create military units while keeping central control on deployment did not work well in French Canada.[79] Apart from Dr Mignault, few wealthy or entrepreneurial French Canadians showed an inclination to find recruits, and civilian recruitment associations that were effective in English Canada simply did not work effectively in Quebec or in French Canada generally.[80] J.L. Granatstein and J.M. Hitsman have demonstrated that, in terms of administrative designs, the Canadian militia was 'structured to be unattractive to French Canadians.'[81] Sam Hughes and his lieutenants consistently proved insensitive to the need for ensuring some form of homogeneity within ranks. This negligence had multiple effects. First, it clearly discouraged enlistment. What point could there be in joining the ranks with a few neighbourhood chums when chances were likely that one would be thrown into battle with people who did not share – or respect, it must be said – one's language and culture? Hughes, and the politicians in cabinet he reported to, simply were blind to the racialism of their own society, a concept that was hardly foreign to them, since it extended into the burgeoning world of professional hockey. Indeed, four years before the war started, a rule had been adopted in order to guarantee a team of recognizably French-Canadian players: no National Hockey Association club could hire a French-Canadian player unless the *Canadien* had given its approval. In 1912 the practice was relaxed somewhat so as to allow each team a complement of two French-Canadian players, while the *Canadien* was allowed two English-Canadian players. Surely, Hughes and his advisers could have absorbed a lesson on how French Canadians prized recognizably francophone undertakings.[82]

Other efforts to mount regiments tell a story of frustration, incompetence, and negligence. The second attempt to form a regiment of French Canadians, the 42nd, failed quickly. The 41st Battalion was too beset by corrupt and incompetent leadership to be sent abroad.[83] The 57th Battalion also collapsed and most of its soldiers were transferred to the hapless 41st or to the 22nd. Efforts to raise the 69th Battalion to capacity failed but did furnish the 22nd with more troops. The 167th was raised to capacity but was squandered by the incompetence of its leader, Colonel Onésime Readman. The 206th, led by a close friend of the Tory government, Tancrède Pagnuelo, would become an even worse embarrassment. The 165th Battalion, which was raised in Acadia, was dissolved upon its arrival in England, and its soldiers were scattered in English battalions. Against all odds, in the poisoned atmosphere of the winter of 1916 a battalion of Franco-Ontarians was created in eastern Ontario, but it, too, would serve only to replenish depleted units. Efforts at enlistment failed generally and, as Desmond Morton has observed, efforts to recruit suitable officers did no better.[84] In the end, although thirteen distinctively French-Canadian battalions had been created (most not near half capacity) by the summer of 1916, the military had clearly failed to mount an effective recruitment campaign.

There were fine opportunities. The fiery *nationaliste* and francophile Olivar Asselin, for example, initiated the 163rd battalion at the end of

November 1915.[85] It was brought to battle strength by May 1916, only to be sent to Bermuda. It finally reached Europe in November 1916, but there was broken up to provide reinforcements. Asselin would serve briefly as a platoon commander in the 22nd, but he was then redeployed to reinforce an English-speaking unit. Asselin's abilities were simply squandered. The management of recruitment by Ottawa consistently undermined efforts on the ground. The federal government's inability to identify and capitalize on war heroes revealed an overwhelming indifference to propaganda needs. Olivar Asselin was one of the most recognizable figures in Quebec and a *nationaliste* who argued for participation. That his battalion was never used as a unit, but only exploited for reinforcements, was a colossal error.[86]

Ottawa's insensitivity to the need to routinely create role models in French Canada resulted in an impressive list of screw-ups. Remarkably, three of the six French-Canadian officers in the French-speaking company of the legendary first CEF division that went to Europe would eventually become lieutenant colonels, yet in the assessment of one historian, 'most were fated to return to Quebec for the humiliating struggle to recruit compatriots for the front.'[87] Major general Oscar Pelletier, who commanded a great deal of respect, was placed in charge of an outlook post on the island of Anticosti. François-Louis Lessard, the only French-speaking general in the army and a personable character, was made inspector general of troops in eastern Canada.[88] Colonel J.P. Landry, son of the senator and speaker of the Senate and the highest-ranking militia officer before the war, was finally given command of the 5th Brigade of the 2nd Division in 1915, but his commission was revoked. He was perhaps too inexperienced to lead men into battle, but the implication stung. 'His father, Senator Philippe Landry, had taken command of the Franco-Ontarian resistance to Regulation 17,' notes Desmond Morton. 'Sam Hughes had struck back.'[89] Not surprisingly, the dream of a French-Canadian brigade would never materialize.

The gripping story of French-Canadian courage in the trenches of Europe belonged to the 22nd Regiment. But even the 22nd, part of the 5th Infantry Brigade of the 2nd Division, was poorly used. Almost 5,000 men served in the 22nd Battalion, most of them volunteers. The average age of the soldiers was twenty-four and for the officers twenty-seven. More than 1,100 of them died; a few thousand more suffered injuries. It was a unit that had more than its share of morale problems, and, in the absence of a steady leadership during extended periods, discipline problems were grave. Five men in the 22nd were executed, the most by far of any battalion. Indeed, 28 per cent of soldiers executed by the Canadian army were French Canadian, clearly a disproportionate number.

The soul of the 22nd was Thomas Tremblay, who was second in command in March 1915 when the unit was sent to Europe. Georges Vanier (who would become the first French-Canadian governor general) called Tremblay 'the greatest French Canadian soldier since Salaberry,' a man who was 'just and severe,' but who 'despised danger; his men knew – and you can't trick a soldier – that he had no fear, eager to do himself what he asked of others.'[90] The 22nd showed it could fight when Tremblay led them. In the first days of January 1916 Tremblay – not even thirty years old – assumed command of the unit. In that month, Vanier and four men destroyed a German nest in a daring mission. Tremblay would eventually lead a three-day drive at Courcelette (where every officer was injured or killed) and in the Regina Trench in the fall of that year. Earl Haig, the British field marshall, described the Courcelette battle as 'the most effective blow yet delivered against the enemy by the British Army.'[91] But the rewards for Tremblay's courage were slight. When the 5th Brigade needed a new commander, Thomas Tremblay was overlooked, although he was more experienced and more decorated than the other candidate. He would eventually command, but only three months before the end of the war. Sadly, Tremblay would be forgotten by his countrymen.[92]

Ottawa proved unable or unwilling to use the stories of French-Canadian courage at the front to encourage enlistment. Two years into the war, the 22nd was still the only French-Canadian battalion at the front, since the 41st, the 57th, and the 69th had been broken up and dispersed as reinforcements in the ranks of the 22nd. In July 1916 officers of the 206th Battalion were blamed for serious disciplinary problems and were sent home. Given the abundance of bad news, the press and the politicians in English Canada were increasingly critical of the poor recruitment effort in French Canada. Rodolphe Lemieux responded in the House of Commons that, by his count, there were between 8,000 and 9,000 French Canadians in the ranks of the infantry battalions in Canada and overseas by the middle of 1916. When French Canadians in other branches of the service or in English-speaking units were included, it was calculated that approximately 12,000 francophones were active in the military.[93]

The bitterness and confusion around enlistment poisoned efforts to improve the situation. In the summer of 1916 Talbot Papineau took his cousin Henri Bourassa to task for discouraging enlistment in a series of published letters, but to little effect.[94] Talbot Papineau himself would eventually die at the front. All the same, the noisy exchange revealed the tension of the situation. In November 1916 Arthur Mignault was asked to head a commission to reorganize the recruiting of French Canadians in Canada, but nothing substantive resulted.

Belcourt personally would discover the conditions of the front in the summer of 1916. After he made his arguments against Regulation 17 before the Judicial Committee of the Privy Council, he joined a delegation of thirty-three parliamentary representatives from the British Empire on a fact-finding tour of the front. They were received and entertained by the king and queen, the president of the French Republic, and the prime ministers of Britain and France and members of their cabinets. He left with 'impressions of the deepest kind which can never be forgotten or duplicated.' He visited the French and British fronts: the Somme, Picardie, and the Grand Fleet in the North Sea. He saw Compiègne, Aisne, Péronne, and then Ypres. He met the 22nd and he was touched: 'May I say here that never was I more proud of my French blood and that my compatriots were represented in the battle line, as they are in many other places, by such brave fellows that they were taking their full share of the sacrifices and would in good time be entitled to their share in the ultimate triumph.' His description of the troops was positive: 'Nowhere can you find a more robust and healthier looking lot of men and in better spirits, all conscious of the great task entrusted to them, individually and collectively, imbued with the calm resolve to give up their lives if necessary, for the sake of Canada, the Allies and democratic ideals.' Belcourt's rhetoric was again decidedly, if sentimentally, liberal: 'the tie which so closely unites and binds the Allies is the bond of a common sentiment, of common ideas of right and justice ... It is the struggle of might against right; it is the fate of democracy which is being decided on the battlefields of Europe. And to me it is quite inconceivable that it can be God's will to allow democracy to perish, because the very faith which is common to all the allies and democracy itself, rests upon common ideas of equal liberty, of common brotherhood.'[95]

Belcourt did not hesitate to share his impressions upon his return to Canada. 'I broke down and could not restrain the tears,' he said; 'my heart bled at the sight of such suffering and anguish and I uttered the most earnest prayer of my life that this horrible butchery, this devilish slaughter and carnage might then end. My pacifist instincts, my abhorrence of this ceaseless torrent of horrors got the better of my judgment and I prayed for peace, for immediate peace.' Yet he did not hesitate to link his emotions with the need for Canada and the United States to end their isolationism:

> I wholly fail to understand how anyone, with anything like an adequate conception of the rights of man, of human justice, of the solidarity of men and nations to another one, can fail to grasp the supreme duty of the hour, can hesitate to proffer whatever aid or assistance may be in his power, to help avenge an outraged humanity and destroy the colossal scourge of Prussian piracy and bloodshed, so long as so elaborately designed and prepared, so wickedly and brutally inflicted on innocent Belgium, Serbia and France.
>
> ...
>
> Neutrality in certain parts of the world may be explainable, but I feel quite sure that there is a certain democratic nation which will ultimately be driven to the inevitable, if tardy, conviction that mere money making is after all but a very poor, indeed a very miserable compensation for the loss of national prestige, national honour, caused by neglecting or ignoring international modern solidarity, the solidarity of civilized mankind.[96]

Belcourt was proud to speak both English and French in Europe. The high point of the visit for him was the occasion of a speech he gave in Paris, in response to the welcoming words of the French president. Raoul Dandurand later recalled 'They chose him as their spokesman at the Elysée, Paris, before the President of the French Republic, who has since remarked more than once that Senator Belcourt's speech was one to be long remembered.'[97] For Belcourt, it was remarkable that a speech in French was made, 'on the soil of France, at the one and only real international function during the visit and at one of its most solemn and inspiring moments.'[98]

Belcourt left Europe as the battle entered its bloodiest phase in August 1916. As the war dragged into 1917, statistics painted a picture that only invited comparisons. Up to the end of April 1917 a total of 14,100 French Canadians had enlisted – 8,200 from Quebec, meaning that 42 per cent of enrolees came from outside Quebec. In comparison, according to Sessional Paper 143B, 125,245 native-born, English-speaking Canadians had enlisted in the Canadian Expeditionary Force, and 155,095 British subjects born outside Canada had also done so.[99] In other words, less than 5.1 per cent of enlisted men were French speaking.

To force enlistment, the Borden government passed the Military Service Act on 24 July 1917, requiring all men between the ages of twenty and thirty-five without families to support to register. In Quebec, many hostile demonstrations erupted, but by Thanksgiving of that year the first conscripts were called to report, exemption tribunals were organized, and men were summoned for duty by mid-November. By the end of the year, 117,000 men from Quebec had reported and all but 2,000 asked to be excused from serving. Every student from Laval University appeared before the tribunal armed with a letter from his school asking that he be exempted.

It was in this heavy atmosphere of forced enlistment that the Union Government was created and that the long-delayed election of 17 December 1917 was held. In Quebec, the campaign would serve to show how unpopular the Borden government had become. Bourassa (a supporter of Borden in 1911) now endorsed the Laurier Liberals. Quebec was united as never before in its rejection of the war and the attitude of the Union Government towards Regulation 17. Quebec voted overwhelmingly (72 per cent) against the government; indeed, seventeen ridings were won by acclamation. Only three ridings, strongly anglophone, voted Union. In the Maritimes, as in Ontario, the Liberals lost many ridings but inevitably held those that had strong French-speaking populations. The verdict crystallized the reality of a clash between English and French and, increasingly, of French Canada's isolation from the rest of the country. In the final days of the year, Joseph Francoeur tabled a motion in the Quebec legislature: 'This house is of the opinion that the province of Quebec would be disposed to accept the breaking of the Confederation pact of 1867 if, in the other provinces, it is believed that she is an obstacle to the union, progress and development of Canada.' The motion was debated in late January 1918 but was not voted on.

Conscription thus became commonplace in neighbourhoods and towns that had vehemently opposed it. When called to report during the winter of 1918, Quebeckers protested angrily, and protests came to a head in Quebec City during the Easter weekend at the end of March. Provoked by insensitive gestures and forced enlistments, leaderless and disorganized crowds sometimes 15,000 strong gathered in front of the recruitment office. In response, the military set up a barricade of sorts at the intersection of St-Vallier and St-Joseph Boulevards, and reinforcements from Toronto were brought in to secure the peace. Riots were finally squelched when five men were shot and killed. The shots that

Anti-conscription parade at Victoria Square, Montreal, Quebec, 24 May 1917
(National Archives of Canada, C6859)

rang out in that wet, early spring only confirmed that the gulf that
separated English and French Canadians seemed unbridgeable.[100]

As the German offensive in the summer of 1918 took its toll, more
and more French-Canadian men were marched to war. In the end,
27,557 would be drafted (about 23 per cent of the conscripted corps).[101]
The news from the front hit hard among the Liberal leadership. Rodolphe
Lemieux lost a son in late August 1918.[102] Six months later, on 24 March
1919, he nonetheless introduced a motion for amnesty for conscientious
objectors: 'That, in the opinion of this House, amnesty should now be
granted to religious conscientious objectors to military service,' even
though very few men claimed conscientious objector status in Quebec.[103]

## Rebuilding Bridges

Napoléon Belcourt would spend his post-war years (he died of a stroke
on 7 August 1932) trying to harmonize the discordant voices in Canada's

politics. Like many Liberals, Belcourt was disillusioned by the war effort.[104] After the disappointing decision of the Privy Council, the battle to save Ontario's French-language schools would have to stay political, outside the courts. Belcourt was again named president of the ACFEO in 1921, a post he would hold until 1930. A war that many thought could unite French and English Canadians had proved everything to the contrary.[105]

From his unique perspective, Belcourt was worried that Quebec – already isolated from international events – was now isolating itself within Canada, and he dedicated much of the rest of his life to building bridges between English and French Canadians. He supported the *Bonne entente* movement's attempt to find the common elements of Canada's two founding peoples and thus to try to reconstruct the connections necessary for a healthy confederation, and through it he met English-Canadian intellectuals he would enlist in the crusade against Regulation 17. Leaders of the *Bonne entente* introduced him to C.B. Sissons, who would write an eloquent protest against the education laws of Ontario in 1917.[106] In 1918, on the heels of the conscription crisis, William Henry Moore published *The Clash! A Study of Nationalities.*[107] Belcourt, who considered it 'a really marvellous book' because it confirmed his view that English and French Canadians were growing dangerously apart, sent 200 copies to France and Britain with a personal letter to each recipient. Belcourt also worked with key Toronto intellectuals to found the Unity League.[108] As he would boldly state a few years later, 'French Canadian nationality is not fanciful dream or mere hope. It is a reality living and capable of indefinite survival. ... French Canadians ... have the right to expect and to receive the complete recognition and the treatment due to a full partner in good standing in the Confederation partnership.'[109] He restated his argument:

> The covenant or deed which gave life to the Canadian federation, and upon which it must now and ever depend, constitutes nothing more and nothing less than a partnership agreement, without limit of time ... All the members of the national firm put all their respective assets and *all their goodwill* into common pool, to be administered for the advancement and prosperity of each and all, every one reserving to itself autonomous control over its own local concerns, with mutual guarantees, and under their protection of the King and Parliament of the United Kingdom. It is the traditional and universally recognised rule concerning all partnerships that partners shall render to one another from time to time a true

and faithful account of the doings of the partnership. The application of the rule becomes especially necessary, or, at all events, very desirable, whenever anyone or more of the partners exhibit symptoms of disaffection or disappointment. It would be idle or worse for anyone in Canada to deny that for some time past such symptoms have been and are still here only too much in evidence.[110]

Belcourt never abandoned the crusade against Regulation 17 and continued to argue that the right to schooling was tied to the right of free speech. He was an active member of the Unity League and missed no opportunity to participate in the halting, if renewed, dialogue between English and French. As he told the Student Christian Movement Conference at Convocation Hall, University of Toronto, in late December 1922: 'For more than a century and a half the French of Canada have tenaciously insisted upon and persisted in the maintenance and preservation of their religious beliefs and practices, their linguistic rights and privileges, their customs, habits and usages and traditions. They have accepted and loyally performed their obligations to the Crown and their duties of citizenship. They secured responsible Government for Canada and twice at least saved Canada for the Empire.' Acknowledging that, in the sensitive post-war years, his message of reconciliation might be difficult to accept, Belcourt asked for an understanding of French Canadians: 'Let us not forget that everyone individually contributes to the prosperity, solidarity and progress of the Dominion, that each is entitled to equal right and equal consideration, each owing allegiance to the whole. Our motto ought to be "All for each and each for all." Canadian national unity is today the paramount need of Canada. We shall never obtain it, or preserve it unless we practice that which it has been my great privilege to, very inadequately but most sincerely and earnestly, preach.'[111]

Belcourt also worked closely with the Irish-Catholic leadership in Ontario to heal the wounds of Regulation 17.[112] In his encouraged state, he considered that the resolution of the issue would play a critical role in bridging the chasm between Quebec and the rest of Canada. Upon Howard Ferguson's accession to the premiership in 1924, he wrote to William Moore, 'the Premier is responsible for Regulation 17; I have not lost hope that he will after all feel inclined to do justice.'[113] Events would prove him right. Conceding that the Ontario government's actions in education had been a total disaster, Howard Ferguson, the same man who had sharpened the claws of Regulation 17 in 1912, repealed the measure in 1927.

Belcourt also maintained a vibrant dialogue with the *nationalistes* in Quebec, who in turn on 24 May 1924 awarded him the only 'Grand Prix d'*Action française*' they would ever grant. A medal was struck in his honour, and it was dedicated as a recognition of 'the most fecund and meritorious act in defense of the French soul in America.' Belcourt attended the induction in the Parc Lafontaine with his family as well as his brothers and sisters and heard the Chanoine Groulx heap praise on him. In his typically modest way, Belcourt accepted the prize by acknowledging that 'it is to the Ontario minority that your congratulations are principally addressed.'[114] Armand Lavergne offered his congratulations and thanks *comme Canadien* a few days later from his office in Quebec City.

There were many images of French Canada during the Great War that would endure, many that would fade. People would remember tales of men hiding in the woods for fear of conscription; of Rodolphe Lemieux, losing his son at the front, comforted by Sir Wilfrid; the unbound courage of Georges Vanier; the passion of Henri Bourassa; the public service of Arthur Mignault; the brave leadership of Lieutenant Colonel Thomas Tremblay; ordinary soldiers like Private Paul-Adrien Lambert, who enlisted in the 22nd as quickly as he could and so honoured himself and his company in combat that he was awarded the most esteemed Distinguished Conduct Medal. There also were victims, such as Honoré Bergeron, a forty-eight-year-old card-carrying carpenter and father of six, killed in the streets of Old Quebec, not far from his home, for protesting conscription.

Not least were the evenings of debate of the Separate School Board in Rockland and in many other places in Ontario, where the issues that bitterly divided Canadians were discussed. That image probably captured the true flavour of the experience of French Canada and the war of 1914–18, because it symbolized the impotence of the minority and the arrogant disregard of the Tory party, both in Ontario and in Ottawa. Robert Craig Brown, Borden's biographer, argued that Borden's stand on Regulation 17 was correct.[115] While it did have some legal basis, Borden's position was to do nothing about an issue that enraged a good portion of the French-Canadian elite. The government's stance on conscription and on 'national unity' was nothing but a sad mockery. Borden could have done more politically, short of disallowing provincial legislation, something even Laurier did not counsel. Evidently, shoring up support in Ontario on education matters was more important than a broad Canadian consensus on war aims. The Conservative party paid a high price: it destroyed its legitimacy with French Canadians (although there were some moments in 1930, 1958, and 1988) and forever changed the political landscape in this country. By being able to count on consistent support in Quebec, eastern Ontario, and *Acadie*, the Liberal Party would dominate Canada for the rest of the century, while the debate over Regulation 17 animated the *nationaliste* element far more, and far longer, than the conscription crisis. For years Lionel Groulx and the contributors to *L'Action française* would comment on the episode and its meaning.[116]

Among the images of the war is a picture of the tall, spare Napoléon Belcourt, eager to argue for reconciliation and for understanding between those who wanted war and those who did not and between those who wished to redefine the rights of citizenship by removing educational rights and those who saw in that act of bad faith the denial that Canada was a country worth preserving. Belcourt and those of his ilk quietly provided the glue that ultimately held the country together. He spoke to English and to French; he spoke his truth to friendly crowds and to hostile audiences also. He did not wish for war and had no coin for those who wanted to force men to the front. But he saw the suffering in Europe and encouraged enlistment. In all cases, Belcourt argued for the minority and, ironically perhaps, pleaded against isolationism of all sorts. Above all, he had the nerve to put things in perspective: 'How trivial, by comparison at least, are our domestic quarrels and conflicts; that French and English in Canada, as in France, can and should be brothers, real brothers; that only a thorough union of 'piouspious' and 'tommies' can vanquish the Germans, so Canada can live and prosper only by a real union, a cordial entente between English and French, by their sharing fully and constantly a common purpose, a common ambition and a common effort.'[117] It was a view he did not hesitate to share with Henri Bourassa: 'Like you, I see that we can hope – and no one wishes for it more than me – that with time, patience and experience we can create a common mentality that will allow us to establish a solid, cosmopolitan federation which will be united and harmonious, even if it brings together disparate elements. But that day appears far away.'[118]

French Canada was as much changed by the politics of 1914–18 as English Canada, but in a different way. After the war, two clearly competing visions of French Canada emerged. The first vision was a notion that the French fact outside Quebec was a reality under siege and that new action had to be taken to preserve the vitality of those minorities. The second was that Quebec was isolated in the face of English Canada's growing sense of power. The debates took on a new immediacy with the events of the war; no longer could positions be defended by invoking the events of the distant past. French Canada emerged fragmented from the war and, after Laurier's death in 1919, without a uniting figure. Napoléon Belcourt and his friend Henri Bourassa would continue to share optimism for Canada, while Lionel Groulx and his young followers deepened their doubts.

NOTES

I am grateful to Drs Roger Hall (University of Western Ontario), Nelson Michaud (Université Laval), Paul Litt (Carleton University), and Ramsay Cook for their comments on an earlier draft of this chapter and to the Archives Deschâtelets, Ottawa, for permission to use its papers.

1 Archives Deschâtelets (AD), Ottawa, Philippe Landry Papers, Note from Alexandre Grenon to anonymous 'Monsieur,' February 1915. The petition and the Hearst response are enclosed, HH7062.L35R8; extract taken from the petition.

2 Ibid., George Baril to Landry, 2 décembre 1914, HH7062.L35R2. Archbishop Bruchési's speech can be found in the same file. Cardinal Bégin's most interesting letter of support to Archbishop Bruchési is also included in the file. See also Robert Rumilly, *Histoire de la province de Québec* (Montreal, n.d.), 12: 104.

3 Pierre Savard, 'Relations avec le Québec,' in Cornelius Jaenen ed., *Les Franco-ontariens* (Ottawa, 1993), 236.

4 As his colleague Senator Raoul Dandurand explained years later, 'when Regulation 17 ... was enacted in the province of Ontario, Senator Belcourt became the leader of his compatriots,' *Senate Hansard*, 12 October 1932, 5; Robert Craig Brown and Ramsay Cook qualify Belcourt as 'The Franco-Ontarian Leader' in *Canada, 1896–1921: A Nation Transformed* (Toronto, 1974), 255.

5 René Durocher, 'Henri Bourassa, les évêques et la guerre de 1914–18,' in *Historical Papers / Communications historiques* (1971), 251.

6 See J.L. Granatstein and J.M. Hitsman, *Broken Promises: A History of Conscription in Canada* (Toronto, 1977), 29.

7 Oscar D. Skelton noted: 'There was among French-Canadians a real if usually passive loyalty to the British Crown; there could not be anything of the personal interest of the newcomer from the British Isles, nor the racial sympathy of the men of British descent and British traditions.' See

his *Life and Letters of Sir Wilfrid Laurier* (Toronto, 1965), 2: 166. Laurier was among the first to blame the rural nature of Quebec and the Nationalists for poor enlistments (ibid., 168). See also Jacques Michel, *La participation des Canadiens-français à la grande guerre* (Montreal, 1938) for a detailed rationale for the weak participation. A more recent recapitulation of the issue is Robert Comeau, 'Opposition à la conscription au Québec' in Roch Legault and Jean Lamarre, eds, *La première guerre mondiale et le Canada : contributions socio-militaires québécoises* (Montreal, 1999).

8  See, for example C.A. Sharpe, 'Enlistment in the Canadian Expeditionary Force 1914–1918: A Regional Analysis,' *Journal of Canadian Studies* 18, 4 (Winter 1983–4), 21.

9  Interestingly, Mason Wade, an American, did make the link, but he did not discuss it; see *Les Canadiens-français de 1760 à nos jours*, Paris, 1963), 2: 53. See also Comeau, 'Opposition à la conscription,' 109. Some have linked Bourassa with the ideology of pacifism, but although pacifism is a close cousin of isolationism (Belcourt would identify himself as a pacifist on occasion), they are not the same. See Denis Monière, *Le développement des idéologies au Québec* (Montreal, 1977), 241. Certainly, studies of pacifism in Canada have given the impression that pacifism was non-existent in Quebec; see Thomas P. Socknat, *Witness against War: Pacifism in Canada, 1900–1945* (Toronto, 1987).

10  See Omer Héroux, 'Belcourt et la crise scolaire ontarienne,' *Le Droit*, 25 July 1957.

11  *Senate Hansard*, 12 October 1932, 5.

12  I am grateful to Mr Marc Belcourt of Montreal (Napoléon Belcourt's grandson) for these details.

13  The temptation to draw a parallel between Belcourt and Jules de Lantagnac, Lionel Groulx's protagonist in *L'appel de la race*, published in 1922 under a pseudonym, is difficult to resist (the novel was subsequently translated as *The Iron Wedge*). Louvigny de Montigny, an Ottawa journalist and civil servant, quickly brought the parallel to light, though Groulx denied it. Groulx, who genuinely admired the senator, worked diligently to ensure that the *Action française* award its first (and only) decoration to Belcourt. *L'appel de la race* told the story of a lawyer practising in Ottawa (corner of Sparks and Elgin Streets), born in 1871. Like Belcourt, he was a friend of the Oblate order and lived on Wilbrod Street, near Sir Wilfrid. Well-known citizens, such as Samuel Genest and Landry, figured prominently in the book – the only one who does not is Belcourt himself. Lantagnac graduates from McGill University and basically abandons his French heritage as much as the language. He marries an Anglican girl

(who converts, of course, to Catholicism), like Belcourt, and has two girls (Nellie and Virginia) and two boys (Wolfred and William) (Belcourt had three of each). Lantagnac is converted to the cause of language and is elected in 1917 for the riding of Russell to defend the cause of Franco-Ontarians. 'Ontario is the first buttress of Quebec,' wrote Groulx (50). In almost every detail, Lantagnac is a replica of Belcourt. See also Michel Bock, '"Le Québec a charge d'âmes" : L'Action Française de Montréal et les minorités françaises (1917–1928),' Revue d'histoire de l'Amérique française 54, 3 (Winter 2001), 371. Michel Gaulin's 'Introduction' to a reprinted The Iron Wedge (Carleton University Press, 1986) is of interest, but it does not make the link with Belcourt.

14 C.B. Sissons, Nil alienum: The Memoirs of C.B. Sissons (Toronto, 1964), 235.

15 See Omer Héroux's obituary for Belcourt in Le Ralliement (Septembre-Octobre 1932), 215–16.

16 AD, N.A. Belcourt Papers, Anonymous, 'M. N-A Belcourt' (Notes for a parish bulletin notice or sermon?), 23 January 1933, HH 6024.B42 R3. The English is my translation.

17 Sissons, Memoirs, 236.

18 AD, Belcourt Papers, N.A. Belcourt, 'L'Unité nationale au Canada' (Ottawa, 1908); speech delivered in July 1907. Published as 'Canadian National Unity,' Westminster, September 1907, 9–10.

19 Ibid., 9–10, 11. For a perspective on the radical element of the Liberal party in Quebec that was also taking on the corruption at the municipal level see Patrice Dutil, Devil's Advocate: Godfroy Langlois and the Politics of Liberal Progressivism in Quebec in the Laurier Era (Montreal, 1994).

20 Belcourt, 'Canadian National Unity,' 5.

21 See Durocher, 'Henri Bourassa,' for a description of Bourassa's evolution on the issue.

22 Among them were The Foreign Policy of Great Britain (1914); The Duty of Canada at the Present Hour (1914); La langue française au Canada (1915); Canadian Nationalism and the War (1916); Le Devoir et la guerre, le conflit des races (1916); Hier, aujourd'hui, demain (1916); Independence or Imperial Partnerships? (1916); La conscription (1917); L'emprunt de la victoire (1917); L'intervention américaine (1917); Que devons-nous à l'Angleterre (1917); and, presciently, La prochaine guerre impériale. En serons-nous? (1920).

23 For an interesting discussion of the application of a tradition of isolationism to Canadian foreign policy today see Jean-François Rioux and Robin Hay, 'Canadian Foreign Policy: From Internationalism to Isolationism?' Discussion Paper No. 16, Norman Patterson School of International Affairs, Carleton University, 1997.

24 John Milton Cooper Jr, *The Vanity of Power: American Isolationism and the First World War* (Westport, Conn. 1969), 2.

25 Justus D. Doenecke, *Not to the Swift: The Old Isolationists in the Cold War Era* (Lewisburg, Pa., 1979), 12.

26 See Robert H. Zieger, *America's Great War: World War I and the American Experience* (New York, 2000); Robert H. Ferrell, *Woodrow Wilson and World War I* (New York, 1985); Ross Gregory, *The Origins of American Interventionism in the First World War* (New York, 1971); Daniel M. Smith, *The Great Departure: The United States and World War I* (New York, 1965).

27 See the discussion of the various interpretations in Cooper, *Vanity of Power*, 250–3.

28 André Siegfried, *Canada: An International Power*, 2nd ed. (London, 1947), 217. The book was originally published in French under the title *Le Canada, puissance internationale* in 1936.

29 For Elizabeth Armstrong, Regulation 17 was the single greatest factor that slowed the war effort in Canada; see *The Crisis of Quebec, 1914–1918*, Carleton Library Series (Toronto, 1974). H.B. Neatby called Regulation 17 'the most important factor' in undermining the French Canadian participation in the war effort; see *Laurier and a Liberal Quebec* (Toronto, 1973), 222. John Dafoe suggested that the 'movement against Ontario was Nationalist in its spirit, its inspiration, and its direction. Side by side with it went a Nationalist agitation of ever increasing boldness against the war'; see *Laurier: A Study in Canadian Politics* (Toronto, 1968 re-ed.), 95. The grip of Regulation 17 was obvious in generations to come. Fernand Dumont raises it in his introduction to Jean Provencher's book about the deaths of Quebeckers who dared to protest conscription; see *Québec sous la loi des mesures de guerre, 1918* (Montreal, 1971). Granatstein and Hitsman agree that 'with great force and great effect, Bourassa carried the attack against the Ontario government's policy on bilingual schools and linked this issue to the war'; see *Broken Promises*, 31. A recent observer has dissented from this position. See René Castonguay, *Le chevalier du roi : Rodolphe Lemieux et le parti libéral, 1866–1937* (Quebec, 2000), 155.

30 See Marilyn Barber, 'The Ontario Bilingual Schools Issue,' in Robert Craig Brown, ed., *Minorities, Schools and Politics* (Toronto, 1969). Barber seems perplexed by the action, and argues that the creation provoked Regulation 17: 'Their intention was not to *defend* their rights but to *extend* their rights, not only to protect existing rights but also to secure additional ones' (74; italics in original). See also Peter Oliver, *G. Howard Ferguson: Ontario Tory* (Toronto, 1977), 41–3.

31 Barber, 'Ontario Bilingual Schools Issue,' 66. Historians have examined the

'creation' of the Franco-Ontarian 'nation' and support Belcourt's notion that Franco-Ontarians constituted a people. See Chad Gaffield, *Language, Schooling, and Cultural Conflict: The Origins of the French-Language Controversy in Ontario* (Montreal, 1987), and Gaétan Gervais, 'L'Ontario français (1821–1910),' in Cornelius Jaenen, ed., *Les Franco-ontariens* (Ottawa, 1993), 113. See also David Welch. 'The Social Construction of Franco-Ontarian Interests towards French Language Schooling,' PhD thesis, University of Toronto, 1988.

32 National Archives of Canada (NAC), Wilfrid Laurier Papers, Reel C896, six-page Petition to Laurier, 26 November 1910, signed by Belcourt, president, and C.A. Séguin, secretary.

33 Cited by Margaret Prang, 'Clerics, Politicians and the Bilingual Schools Issue in Ontario, 1910–1917,' in Brown, *Minorities, Schools and Politics*, 88.

34 The inspiration and events around Regulation 17 are varied and have been discussed at length in C.B. Sissons, *Bilingual Schools in Canada* (London, 1917); George Weir, *The Separate School Question in Canada* (Toronto, 1934); Franklin A. Walker, *Catholic Education and Politics in Upper Canada* (Toronto, 1955), and *Catholic Education and Politics in Ontario* (Toronto, 1964); Lionel Groulx, *Les écoles des minorités*, vol. 2 of *L'enseignement français au Canada* (Montreal, 1933); Barber, 'Ontario Bilingual Schools Issue; Prang, 'Clerics, Politicians and the Bilingual Schools Issue in Ontario'; Robert Choquette, *Langue et religion : histoire des conflits anglo-français en Ontario*, 2nd ed. (Ottawa, 1980); Arthur Godbout, *Nos écoles franco-ontariennes : Histoire des écoles de langue française dans l'Ontario des origines du système scolaire de 1841 jusqu'à nos jours* (Ottawa, 1980); Nelson Michaud, 'Les écoles d'Ontario ou le dilemme des conservateurs québécois : confrontation des principes nationalistes et de la réalité politique,' *Revue d'histoire de l'Amérique française* 49, 3 (Winter 1996), 395–417.

35 See Charles W. Humphries, *'Honest Enough to be Bold': The Life and Times of Sir James Pliny Whitney* (Toronto, 1985), 202.

36 Robert Craig Brown, *Robert Laird Borden: A Biography*, Vol. 1, *1854–1914* (Toronto. 1975), 246.

37 Choquette, *Langue et religion*, 181.

38 Dafoe offers a view on Laurier and the Franco Ontarians: 'They were, he said, politically powerless and leaderless; the provincial Liberal leaders, who should have been their champions, had abandoned them; the obligation rested upon him to come to their rescue' (Dafoe, *Laurier*, 98).

39 AD, Belcourt Papers, Belcourt to Omer Héroux, 16 April 1920, HH6017B42M39.

40 Ibid., Belcourt to Burke, 10 October 1918, HH6017B42M 10.

41 Egerton Ryerson argued: 'As the French is the recognized language in the country as well as the English, it is quite proper and lawful for the trustees to allow both languages to be taught in their school to children whose parents may desire them to learn both' (Gaffield, *Language*, 11). In his first chapter Gaffield discusses at length the Ryerson attitude.

42 AD, Belcourt Papers, 'Argument of the Hon. N.A. Belcourt, K.C., on behalf of the Board,' 6; see also 13–15. Belcourt to Bourassa, 12 January 1928, HH6012.B42C 106 (my translation).

43 Ibid., 'Argument of the Hon. N.A. Belcourt, K.C., on behalf of the Board,' 11.

44 Text reprinted in N.A. Belcourt, 'French in Ontario,' pamphlet reproduced from an article in *University Magazine*, December 1912, 9.

45 AD, Belcourt Papers, 'Argument of the Hon. N.A. Belcourt, K.C., on behalf of the Board,' 9, 10.

46 Belcourt, 'French in Ontario,' 6.

47 Napoléon Belcourt, 'The French Canadians Outside Quebec,' *Annals of the American Academy of Political and Social Science* (May 1923), 7.

48 AD, Philippe Landry Papers, Charlebois to Landry, 26 January 1915, HH 7062.L35R7; Landry to W.H. Hearst, 4 June 1915, HH 7062.L35R31.

49 AD, Belcourt Papers, 'A sa Sainteté Benoit XV,' June 1915, HH6012.B42C109.

50 AD, Philippe Landry Papers, Landry to Begin, 1 October 1915, HH7062.L 35R 82 (my translation).

51 AD, Belcourt Papers, Belcourt to Aimé Geoffrion, 17 April 1913, HH 6017.B42L 1 (my translation); see also Belcourt to Eugène Lafleur, 14 May 1913, HH6017.B42L2.

52 AD, Philippe Landry Papers, Belcourt to Landry, 21 December 1915, HH7062.L335R 103 (my translation).

53 See Centre de recherche en civilisation canadienne-française, Université d'Ottawa, Fonds Association Canadienne Française de l'Ontario, file C2/209/17 for a series of petitions.

54 See Robert Craig Brown, *Robert Laird Borden: A Biography*, Vol. 2, *1914–1937* (Toronto, 1980), 51–2.

55 NAC, Laurier Papers, C908, Letter to Stewart Lyon, 29 February 1916.

56 The letters are conveniently reprinted in Oscar D. Skelton, *Life and Letters of Sir Wilfrid Laurier*. Vol. 2, Carleton Library Series (Toronto, 1965), 171–3.

57 See Paul Bernier, *Ernest Lapointe : Député de Kamouraska, 1904–1919* (La Pocatière, 1979) 122–33.

58 See Nelson Michaud, *L'énigme du Sphinx : regards sur la vie politique d'un nationaliste : 1910–1926* (Sainte-Foy, 1998), 48–51; Brown, *Borden*, 2: 52.

59  AD, Philippe Landry Papers, 'Quelques Motifs de Continuer la Résistance au Règlement XVII,' n.d. (1916?), HH7062L35R (my translation).
60  AD, Belcourt Papers, Belcourt to Bourassa, 12 January 1928, HH6012.B42C 106 (my translation).
61  For background on Rome's decision, see John Zucchi, *The View from Rome: Archbishop Stagni's 1915 Reports on the Ontario School Question* (Montreal, 2002).
62  Cited in Oliver, *G. Howard Ferguson*, 79.
63  Desmond Morton, *When Your Number's Up: The Canadian Soldier in the First World War* (Toronto, 1993), 61.
64  Cited in Sharpe, 'Enlistment,' 29.
65  See Sharpe's 'revised data,' which make clear distinctions of eligibility, (ibid., see chart on 20).
66  Granatstein and Hitsman, *Broken Promises*, 62. The authors cite cabinet documents.
67  See Doenecke, *Not to the Swift*.
68  See Durocher, 'Henri Bourassa,' 248–75.
69  See Elizabeth Armstrong, *Crisis of Quebec*, 57. It is also worth noting that Gustave Franck, a leader among unionized workers, insisted on participation in the war and later openly supported conscription. Franck was born in Belgium. See Eric Leroux, *Gustave Franck : figure marquante du syndicalisme et précurseur de la FTQ* (Montreal, 1999).
70  'In fact Sir Wilfrid Laurier, the leader of the Liberal opposition, had to insist at one time that the government measures be at least read, not merely passed without any discussion whatsoever. On the Liberal as much as on the Conservative side of the House of Commons, it seemed to be the consensus of opinion that the government should be given carte blanche to help with the war' (Armstrong, *Crisis of Quebec*, 64).
71  Cited in ibid., 77.
72  Desmond Morton, 'Entente Cordiale? La section montréalaise du fonds patriotique canadien, 1914–1923 : Le bénévolat de guerre à Montréal,' *Revue d'histoire de l'Amérique française* 53, 2 (Autumn 1999), 215.
73  Castonguay, *Le chevalier du roi*, 147.
74  AD, Belcourt Papers, Discours, Parc Sohmer, October 1914, 1, 2, 3.
75  Armstrong, *Crisis of Quebec*, 79.
76  Granatstein and Hitsman, *Broken Promises*, 123.
77  Desmond Morton, 'French Canada and War: The Military Background to the Conscription Crisis of 1917,' in J.L. Granatstein and R.D. Cuff, eds, *War and Society in North America* (Toronto, 1971), 93.

78  See Pierre Vennat, *Les poilus québécois de 1914–1918 : histoire des militaires canadiens-français de la première guerre mondiale* (Montreal, 1999), 29–41.
79  Of note is Niall Ferguson's confirmation that men put up with inhumane conditions and kept fighting because they 'stuck by their pals or mates'; see *The Pity of War* (London, 1999), chap. 12.
80  See R. Matthew Bray, '"Fighting as an ally": The English-Canadian Patriotic Response to the Great War,' *Canadian Historical Review* 61, 2 (1980), 152.
81  Granatstein and Hitsman, *Broken Promises*, 24.
82  When Jack Laviolette indicated that he was forming the Montreal *Canadien* Hockey team in late 1909, an understanding was reached among the various franchises of the National Hockey Association that no French-Canadian players would be hired until Laviolette had completed his roster. League officials contested the practice. See *La Presse*, 11 November 1910.
83  See Morton, 'The Limits of Loyalty: French Canadian Officers and the First World War,' in Edgar Denton III, ed. *Limits of Loyalty* (Kitchener, 1980) 92; Vennat, *Les poilus québécois*, 163–9.
84  Morton, 'Limits of Loyalty,' 83.
85  See *Le Devoir*, 22 January 1916.
86  See Vennat, *Les poilus québécois*, 297–305.
87  See Morton, 'Limits of Loyalty,' 89.
88  Jean-Pierre Gagnon, *Le 22ième bataillon (canadien-français), 1914–1919 : Étude socio-militaire* (Quebec, 1986), 382.
89  See Morton, 'Limits of Loyalty,' 90.
90  Cited in Gagnon, *Le 22ième bataillon*, 302–4.
91  See Robert Speaight, *Vanier: Soldier, Diplomat and Governor General: A Biography* (Toronto, 1970), 59. Vanier was on leave while the battle of Courcelette raged and apparently always regretted not being a part of it. The battle is described in Vennat, *Les poilus québécois*, 271–83.
92  The memory of the Great War in Quebec is untilled territory. See Jonathan F. Vance, *Death So Noble: Memory, Meaning, and the First World War* (Vancouver, 1997), 259–60.
93  Armstrong, *Crisis of Quebec*, 129.
94  For more detail on Talbot Papineau, see Sandra Gwyn, *Tapestry of War* (Toronto, 1992).
95  N.A. Belcourt, *The Effort of the Entente*, address delivered before the Canadian Club and the Women's Canadian Club of Ottawa, 10 November 1916, published as a pamphlet, 1, 12, 13.
96  Ibid., 10.
97  *Senate Hansard*, 12 October 1932, 5.

98  AD, Belcourt Papers, Belcourt to Howard d'Egville, 28 February 1917, HH6017.B42L3.

99  Cited in Granatstein and Hitsman, *Broken Promises*, 28.

100 See Jean Provencher, *Quebec sous la loi des mesures de guerre, 1918* (Montreal, 1971).

101 Granatstein and Hitsman, *Broken Promises*, 97–8.

102 Castonguay, *Le chevalier du roi*, 169.

103 Socknat, *Witness against War*, 87, 81.

104 Stuart I. Rochester, *American Liberal Disillusionment in the Wake of World War I* (Pittsburgh, 1977) is interesting in this regard.

105 Brown and Cook highlight the hopes for unity in *Canada, 1896–1921*, 250–1.

106 Sissons, *Memoirs*, 232.

107 Toronto, 1918.

108 Interestingly, Margaret Prang has written that 'Senator Landry and the members of the French-Canadian Education Association were not devotees of the Bonne Entente' ('Clerics, Politicians,' 110).

109 Hon. Napoléon Belcourt, *Canada, A Bilingual Nation?* speech (n.d.? 1923), published as a pamphlet, 4. See also AD, Belcourt Papers, Belcourt, *Quebec and the Dominion* (n.d., 1921?), HH 6021 B42R 30.

110 Belcourt, *Canada, A Bilingual Nation?* 1.

111 Ibid., 6, 9. See also Napoléon Belcourt, 'The French Canadians Outside Quebec,' *Annals of the American Academy of Political and Social Science* (May 1923), 12.

112 See Oliver, *G. Howard Ferguson*, 332–8.

113 AD, Belcourt Papers, Belcourt to William Moore, 5 July 1923, HH6017 .42L23. See also Belcourt to John Godfrey, 30 June 1923, HH6017.B421.

114 Undated, untitled speech, but very clearly Belcourt's acceptance speech at the Parc Lafontaine. I am grateful to Marc Belcourt for sharing this document with me. It has been sent to the curators of the Belcourt Papers.

115 Brown, *Borden*, Vol. II, 54.

116 A measure of the concerns of the *Action française* confirms that Regulation 17 would remain the key focus of this influential journal. See Michel Bock, '"Le Québec a charge d'âmes" : L'*Action Française* de Montréal et les minorités françaises (1917–1928),' *Revue d'histoire de l'Amérique française* 54, 3 (Winter 2001), 370.

117 Belcourt, *Effort of the Entente*, 6.

118 AD, Belcourt Papers, Belcourt to Bourassa, 12 January 1928, HH6012.B42C 106, (my translation).

# 6 The Economic Impact of the Great War

DOUGLAS MCCALLA

In this essay I come to the question of the war and the economy from the perspective of a research program that revisits the larger narrative of Canadian economic history. A theme of that larger project, which the war nicely illustrates, is the power of established stories and images, which dominate understanding long after research has called them deeply into question. Such stories are most clearly visible in surveys, introductory texts, and popular accounts, but are also the explicit or implicit context for much specialized research. Even criticism, by reaffirming the importance of familiar themes, can reinforce them. That suggests the need to retell the story on a different basis altogether.

## The Shape of the Story

An event as vast as the Great War had profound implications for every aspect of participating societies, their economies very much included. So it is no surprise that Kenneth Norrie, Douglas Owram, and Herbert Emery conclude the chapter on the war in their standard text in Canadian economic history by emphasizing that 'the war brought important changes in the Canadian economy, changes that would last long beyond the war itself.' Many of those changes are captured in the image of a wartime 'boom economy' – a period of 'hectic prosperity' and immense industrial development.[1] During the war, Craig Brown and Ramsay Cook write, 'Canadian industrial plants were vastly expanded and even then stretched to their limits'[2] Summing up an era dominated by war, Pierre Berton writes, 'The change was spectacular. In a half century [from 1899 to 1953], we were transformed from an agricultural nation ... to an industrial economy with a bedrock of natural resources.'[3]

If industry is the most prominent theme, it is not the only one. The war has been understood to have had many economic consequences, including changing 'a *laissez-faire* style of economic life ... almost beyond recognition';[4] 'accentuat[ing] the distinctiveness of the prairie region' and its 'lack of economic diversification';[5] developing 'new technologies' that were subsequently 'applied to domestic uses';[6] 'strengthening ... economic links between Canada and the US';[7] 'accelerat[ing] ... the movement of people from rural areas to cities';[8] and significantly affecting many other patterns of work, notably for women. For example, in the book accompanying the television series, *Canada: A People's History*, the authors write: 'Tens of thousands of women had taken the place of men in factories, banks, and offices ... they were the ones making the economy work and manufacturing the weapons and munitions.'[9]

The war's economic importance is reinforced because it is a historical dividing line, a turning point around which our entire narrative is organized. Many specialized studies begin or end with it, and it is a common break point in the internal structures of works that span it.[10] Many of the latter include passages such as the following, from *Canadian Women: A History*: 'By the end of World War I a full-blown industrial society had emerged.'[11] Such phrasing seems to make the war important in Canadian industrial development, although in the authors' larger discussion it is recognized that the rhythm and chronology of industrialization actually had little to do with the war.

There have been challenges to this dominant impression, notably by Michael Bliss. His work on wartime munitions production underpins most textbook discussions of the war economy, yet in his own survey of business history, *Northern Enterprise*, he comments only that 'in some ways the war was good for some kinds of business.'[12] Similarly, in his study of Ontario workers during the war, James Naylor observes of the war economy that it 'had a widely uneven impact on different trades and localities.'[13] That tone, rather more common now, after a generation of research on class, regional, and gender themes has highlighted the divisiveness of the war, is captured also by Alvin Finkel and Margaret Conrad in their widely used introductory textbook, in which they argue that the war 'fail[ed] to usher in a major transformation in society.' Nevertheless, they still present the war as 'the catalyst for many changes, the most enduring of which was the enhanced role of the federal government in the lives of all Canadians.' They also stress industrialization, writing that 'Canada's productive capacity received a tremendous boost during the First World War. Although it did not change the direction of the Canadian economy in any major way, the war sped Canadians a little faster down the road to industrial maturity.'[14]

As all the writers recognize, when the war broke out, the Canadian economy was in a deepening recession, and some of what looks like wartime growth represented no more than a rebound. By the end of 1915 it was realized that this would not be a short war, and the strains of sustaining a growing army and increasing war production were becoming evident. Whatever the pressures, few can have imagined that war conditions would be permanent. Even though the war ran for three more gruelling years, it was not a long period in which to effect fundamental structural changes.

## The War Economy in Long-Term Perspective

Most of the authors quoted are well aware of long-run trends. Yet their questions, the organization of their narratives, and their language reinforce a story of dramatic change in a short time. A case in point is Norrie, Owram, and Emery's text, whose section on 'the long-run economic and social consequences of the war' addresses 'three long-run effects' – industrial development, regional inequities, and implications for western agriculture – that it shows were not consequences at all.[15] Rather, they were trends and processes that were already well established before 1914 and that would have continued even had the war not intervened. Much the same point can be made of many of the themes of the standard war narrative, as can be seen in selected information on some principal trends (table 6.1). Some data are available on an annual basis and others only at intervals. Of the latter, information drawn from the decennial census misses the war altogether.[16] In interpreting series that fluctuated cyclically, it is important to note that the trade cycle was approaching a peak when the pre-war census was taken in 1911 and was at the low point of a trough when the next census was taken in 1921. Evidence from 1926, after the economy had rebounded, helps to compensate for such variations.

Although the sacrifices and readjustments of outputs and consumption of wartime make it imperfect as a representation of living standards then, real growth in Gross National Product per capita is still the single best measure of economic growth (table 6.1, col. 1).[17] From this perspective, the war looks more like a complex cyclical episode than a fundamental moment in the longer-term growth of the economy. In real

Table 6.1
Some Main War-Era Trends

| | Real GNP per capita (1900 $) (1) | Agriculture in GNP Per cent (2) | Manufacturing in GNP Per cent (3) | Iron and steel in manufacturing Per cent (4) | Women gainfully occupied (000) (5) | Women's share of labour force Per cent (6) | Improved acres prairie farms (000,000) (7) | Urban share of population Per cent (8) | Federal government spending in GNP Per cent (9) |
|---|---|---|---|---|---|---|---|---|---|
| 1881 | 121 | 35 | 22 | 15 | | | | 26 | 5.7 |
| 1891 | 140 | 28 | 25 | 14 | 196 | 12 | 1.4 | 32 | 5.4 |
| 1901 | 182 | 25 | 21 | 12 | 239 | 13 | 5.6 | 37 | 5.7 |
| 1911 | 246 | 21 | 21 | 17 | 367 | 13 | 23.0 | 45 | 5.8 |
| 1916 | 273 | 24 | 20 | 19 | | | 34.3 | | 13.6 |
| 1921 | 203 | 16 | 22 | 14 | 490 | 15 | 44.9 | 50 | 8.8 |
| 1926 | 276 | 17 | 20 | 14 | | | 49.2 | | 6.3 |
| 1931 | | | | | 666 | 17 | 59.7 | 54 1941 definition | |
| | Urquhart Table 1.6 | Urquhart Table 1.1 | Urquhart Table 1.1 | Urquhart Table 1.12 | HSC D86, D88 | | HSC M41-43 | HSC A1, A68 | Gillespie Table B-1 |

Note: Leacy, Historical Statistics of Canada, D120, 123 gives a higher estimate for women, based on labour force concept: 1901 and 1911, 15 per cent; 1921, 17 per cent; 1931, 19 per cent.

Sources: M.C. Urquhart, Gross National Product, Canada, 1870–1926: The Derivation of the Estimates (Montreal and Kingston: McGill-Queen's University Press, 1993); Leacy, Historical Statistics of Canada; W. Irwin Gillespie, Tax, Borrow & Spend: Financing Federal Spending in Canada 1867–1990 (Ottawa: Carleton University Press, 1991).

terms (expressed in 1900 dollars), GNP per capita had doubled from $121 to $246 between 1881 and 1911 (and would reach its pre-war peak in 1913 at $259). As we would expect from the story of high wartime outputs, it reached a new high of $273 in 1916 (and a wartime peak, not shown in the table, of $282 in 1917). Of course we cannot know what the pattern would have been had there been no war, but it gives some context to these numbers to note that the wartime peak was only 9 per cent higher than the level of 1913, making the rate of increase during the war no faster than in the pre-war decade. After 1917 real GNP per capita fell sharply, to a trough of $203 in 1921; that figure , however, was still higher than in any year before 1905. By 1926 it had regained its wartime level.

In 1881 agriculture had accounted for 35 per cent of GNP and manu-facturing for 22 per cent (table 6.1, cols 2 and 3). Three decades later, and after the settlement of the prairies, an entire new agricultural region, agriculture's share had fallen to 21 per cent. The war briefly reversed this trend, but by 1921 agriculture's share of GNP had fallen to just one-sixth. Through the same period, manufacturing varied be-tween one-fifth and one-quarter of GNP. Within manufacturing, iron and steel products, at the peak of wartime output, accounted for almost one-fifth of manufacturing value-added (col. 4). This is in keeping with the standard war story, but with 17 per cent of industrial value-added in 1911, this was already the country's leading industrial sector in the decade before the war. At its wartime peak, iron and steel accounted for about 4 per cent of total GNP. That was a large contribution for a single industry, but even then, other industries accounted for more than 80 per cent of industrial value-added.[18] After the war, the share of iron and steel products returned to its normal long-term range, at 14 per cent of the manufacturing sector in 1921 and 1926. That is, wartime production reflected this sector's peacetime importance and somewhat extended it temporarily, rather than being a fundamental industrial transformation.

With the exception of shells and other munitions, most of what Canada produced during the war was what it could already produce.[19] And shells would not be needed after 1918. If the war left genuine, long-term technological gains, they must have been mainly in enhanced industrial capacity for precision work, which could be transferred to other sectors if warranted. But such skills already existed before the war and could have been further developed without munitions work; certainly the technologies to which they might be applied in the 1920s were develop-

ing before 1914. Motor vehicles are an obvious example: vehicle regis-
trations were growing before the war and continued to do so even
during the war. This was the basis for their sustained expansion afterwards. Much the same could be said of electricals, the telephone, pulp
and paper, farm mechanization, and other growth areas of the 1920s.[20]
In a number of these technologies American companies played a strategic role. Their prominence in Canada was due not to the war but to the
evolution of the structure of American business, already well under
way before 1914.

Because they figure so prominently in many accounts of the war
economy, it is important to discuss women's role, although the topic is
more fully addressed by Joan Sangster in this volume. In 1891, 1901,
and 1911 about one 'gainfully occupied' worker in eight was female
(table 6.1, col. 6). In 1921 women represented 15 per cent of the work
force and in 1931 they constituted 17 per cent. Thus, the war era was
indeed associated with a growing trend for women to be part of the
paid workforce. In terms of the actual work they did, both before and
after the war, most of the women worked in clearly gendered sectors.
One of these was clerical work, whose rapid growth is sometimes
presented as a consequence of wartime replacement of men by women.
Women did indeed replace men, but here, too, the war simply continued a pre-war trend.[21] More commonly, as we have seen, the story has
stressed women's unconventional work in the war economy, notably in
munitions, where it has been estimated that up to 35,000 women were
involved.[22] That figure comes from sources unlikely to have underestimated; even if accurate, it needs to be put in context. For example, it
was less than 10 per cent of the number of women in the 'gainfully
occupied' labour force in 1911; just 7 per cent of the 490,000 such
women in 1921; only slightly over 1 per cent of the whole workforce in
either year; and less than 2 per cent of all women aged fifteen and over
in Canada in 1911.[23] Only a tiny minority of working women were
employed in unconventional work, such as the munitions industry, and
then only for a short period, at most two years. However emphasized in
propaganda at the time and in our subsequent narrative, they were a
very small part of the stories of women in the workforce, women in the
war, and the wartime economy itself.[24]

The argument that the future of the prairies was distorted by the war
depended in part on the war's failure to foster industrialization (and a
mixed-farming economy) in the west that was most unlikely to occur.
For prairie agriculture, the story is that the war prompted undue spe-

cialization in grains, encouraged expansion onto inappropriate and marginal lands, and lured farmers unwisely into debt to finance their expansion and into neglect of long-term best-practice techniques for short-term gain. But in most respects the war did no more than extend a process already well under way. Thus, the improved acreage in prairie farms quadrupled in each of the two pre-war decades, to reach 23 million acres by 1911 (table 6.1, col. 7). In each of the next five-year intervals another 11 million acres were added to the total, bringing it to about 45 million acres by 1921. Although some of the extension may have been to marginal lands or may have been achieved at undue cost, the process of expansion was by no means over in 1921. Indeed, another 15 million acres were added to the stock of improved land by 1931, and that still did not end farm expansion.[25] Equally, about the same proportion of that improved land (around 50 per cent) was seeded in wheat in both 1911 and 1921[26] – not out of line for a newly opened, rapidly expanding region. The sharply etched agrarian and regional political protests of the immediate post-war era are evidence of war-induced economic discontent, but that discontent was already emerging strongly in the pre-war period. That is, the war reinforced trends; it did not initiate them.

In the agrarian politics of the post-war period, urbanization was often denounced – and sometimes related to the war. The war, in fact, coincided with what seemed a major threshold in urbanization, since the 1921 census recorded that half the population now lived in urban places.[27] The figures in table 6.1 (col. 8) are based on the 1941 definition of urban, which included all incorporated villages, towns, and cities. But no matter what definition is used, the trend was the same, and it had begun long before the war. Indeed, urban centres were so much a part of western development that the huge wave of prairie settlement after 1900 actually accelerated the trend.

Thus far we have considered long-term trends for which there is little or no need to invoke the war. By contrast, the war did sharply increase the share of the federal government in the economy. Throughout the period to 1911 federal spending was equal to somewhat over 5 per cent of GNP (table 6.1, col. 9). By 1916 that figure had jumped to 13.6 per cent, and in 1918 it peaked at 16 per cent. This was a huge change. But even with a new level of federal debt, the government quickly reduced its spending after the war, getting back almost to traditional levels by 1926. The standard story also stresses government's efforts to regulate the economy, some more effective than others; almost none lasted much beyond the war. One wartime innovation that did live on was the tax on income, albeit at a level that exempted most Canadians. Otherwise, the transformation the war had brought in the federal government's place in the economy was largely reversed in the post-war period.[28] On the other hand, the memory of intervention remained.

## Prices and the World Economy

As wartime scarcity and wartime finance began to have their impact during 1915, prices rose. Accelerating inflation led countries to try various measures of price and wage controls and rationing, but with at best partial and limited effectiveness; prices continued to rise anyway. By 1917 prices in Britain had more than doubled from pre-war levels; Canadian and American prices rose less but in almost parallel fashion, even before the United States entered the war (see figure 6.1 for wholesale price indexes).[29] In the pre-war decade, Canadian prices had risen considerably, but the wartime inflation was on another scale altogether, one unknown in Canada since the mid-1850s. Although rising prices have been part of the Canadian story of the Great War, their implications have not always been explored, and it is not always evident that the process was universal.[30] Discussions can readily leave the impression that the problem could have been prevented by different Canadian policies; for example, this is a clear implication of some accounts of the Canadian government's approach to war finance. During the war, discussions often focused on the malign figure of the profiteer, caricatured in innumerable cartoons.[31] Echoes can be found in later historical accounts, despite the fact that a process this universal and of this magnitude was obviously not attributable to the behaviour of specific individuals or groups.

Inflation affected every aspect of economic life, threatening established understandings of values and relationships among them. The insecurity that resulted was pervasive. Even those whose wartime circumstances allowed their incomes to keep pace with rising costs cannot have been sure that they would continue to do so. In the arguments over wartime sacrifices and choices, existing social fault lines – such as cleavages of class, interest, and region – were sharply highlighted. But the war did not create those divisions.

Among the losers, in one common argument, were Canadian farmers, whose prices were among the first to be subject to control during the war.[32] This is especially the case for western grain farmers, who are

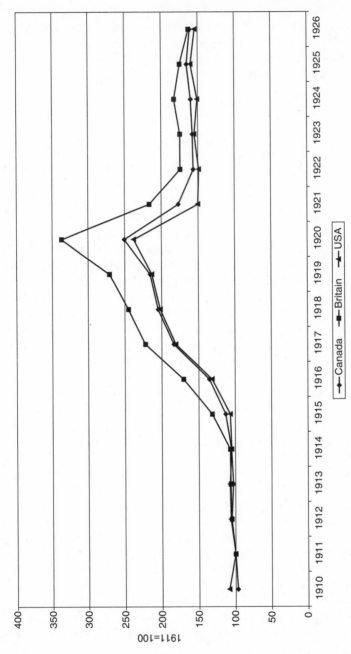

Figure 6.1. Wholesale Prices in Three Countries

*Sources:* Leacy, *Historical Statistics of Canada*, K33; B.R. Mitchell with Phyllis Deane, *Abstract of British Historical Statistics* (Cambridge: Cambridge University Press, 1962), 476–7; *Historical Statistics of the United States*, Bicentennial ed. (Washington, D.C., 1976), E23

seen as having borrowed too much, on the expectation of continuing high prices, and thus as having locked themselves into debts that would be very hard to repay at the lower price levels of the 1920s. Ironically, farmers seem to have felt that the marketing processes established during the war were worth preserving or recreating.

Both the controls and the buffetings that ordinary people experienced in attempting to keep up might be resisted and resented, but to a degree they could also be understood and accepted as part of winning the war.[33] What was much harder to accept was that prices continued to rise after the war, not peaking until 1920. Post-war inflation was clearly a consequence of the war, yet it is important to distinguish between the direct processes involved in fighting and winning a war and the subsequent processes of making peace and reconstructing the economy. After 1920 prices fell quickly, but in 1926 they still were 50 per cent higher than before the war. As Bliss's careful comment on the war's effects on business, quoted earlier, suggests, who won and who lost from such precipitous inflation and deflation is less clear than some discussions would suggest; it is by no means clear how far anyone could reliably have discounted all these trends in a way that would ensure strong net gains at each stage. Most obviously, those who borrowed early and paid back in inflated money might have come out ahead if the assets so acquired continued to produce a high enough rate of return once the war was over. In the whole economy, however, such gains were offset by equal and opposite real losses to lenders. In that some of these lenders ultimately were not within the Canadian economy, there may have been some net gain to Canada from the process.

Another implication of wartime inflation is that expressions of current values encountered in the sources at the end of the war are vastly higher than at the beginning. If not carefully discounted, they make wartime growth seem much larger than it was in real terms, and deflating values in the midst of such a rapid and massive disruption is an uncertain process with necessarily arbitrary elements.

The story of prices is a reminder that Canada participated in the culture and institutions of the world economy through flows of goods, capital, credit, people, and information. Both before and after the war, the international reference points for the Canadian economy were Britain and the United States, although the relative balance between them had continued to shift towards the latter. Indeed, one of the war's most profound long-term economic impacts was the fundamental disruption of the London-centred international financial system by which the world settled accounts.[34] During the 1920s states and bankers sought to rebuild what the war had destroyed or to build a new international system; that they ultimately failed had much to do with the depth and severity of the ensuing Great Depression.

## Conclusion

Summing up recent historiography on the war and the international economy, Chris Wrigley writes, 'While it can be acknowledged as a truth that the First World War was a turning point in the history of the international economy, the nature of its impact remains complex and debatable. The effect of the war itself is often difficult to disentangle from other developments. Where the war clearly did have an impact, it could nevertheless be the case that the change would have taken place without it.'[35] In essence, in this chapter I seek to make the same case in a specifically Canadian context. The argument is that in the standard Canadian story, major structural changes, long in the making and unlikely to have been any different without the war, are routinely associated with and even attributed to the war. Yet the war did not affect in any fundamental way trends in the structure of the economy and the business system, the prime new technologies, or the dominant urban patterns. Nor did the war economy change any of the fundamental class, regional, gender, interest, and other lines of Canadian society. All of these elements of the story of the war's impact thus have the story backward: they actually reflect what the Canadian economy had become by 1914.[36]

Why have we told ourselves otherwise? In essence, historians have followed a political narrative first shaped by actors at the time as they sought to make sense of the events in which they were caught up.[37] Once established, periodization, like other kinds of categorization, deeply influences what we can think. Historians have contributed also through their professional attachment to change, often stylized in dramatic terms and organized around turning points – that is, brief moments of actual or potential transformation and even revolution. For textbooks, we can attribute some of the responsibility to the need to use existing secondary material and to fit into established courses and boundaries. Some texts are more effective than others at catching the nuances of recent Canadian literature, with its emphasis on variation and quite specific experiences. Yet even in adding these stories, they cannot avoid reinforcing the main narrative, by emphasis, by pictures, and by not dis-

Munitions factory, ca. 1915 (City of Toronto Archives, Fonds 1244, Item 850)

cussing some of the key elements at all. It is common, for example, to rely on pictures, such as those of women munitions workers, whose existence is a function of the wartime propaganda machinery.[38] By contrast, there are no pictures of financial processes and other abstract systems.

The scale of the war, its terrible carnage, and the magnitude of its consequences for the old political order in Europe called deeply into question many basic assumptions about order – political, moral, social, intellectual, and economic. The emergence of a communist regime in Russia was only the most visible evidence of the process. Established understandings of the economic order were, of course, debated throughout the western world. This process had an institutional parallel in the disruption of older patterns of organizing world trade and the settlement of transactions. As the failure of post-war efforts to restore that system suggests, part of the story was really about the peace, a fact that is also evident in the graph of prices, which surged after the war. This is a story that goes back to Keynes and other critics of the post-war processes of re-establishment. Telling it in the Canadian context requires addressing whether Canada had much, if any, autonomy within or influence on the larger macroeconomic processes that shaped it. Another essential issue is what Canadians themselves understood those processes to be and how that affected their decisions. Furthermore, the story of the Canadian economy and the war should begin with a clearer sense of the structure of the economy in 1914. Already a balanced industrial economy, more complex than the traditional story has tended to imply, it was adaptable enough both to send a rapidly expanding contingent overseas and to increase outputs. Its responsiveness and flexibility would be as tested by the return of peace as it had been by the shocks of the war. For the war itself, and its aftermath, the dominant image must be disruption, not transformation.[39]

## NOTES

It is a pleasure to be able to contribute to a work honouring Craig Brown. As the editor of the first paper I ever submitted to a scholarly journal, he applied his superb editorial skills with a generosity and constructive spirit that were enormously encouraging. In any editing I have undertaken, it is those high standards that I have sought to meet. This paper forms part of a research program undertaken during a Killam Research Fellowship, awarded by the Canada Council, and continued with the support of the Canada Research Chairs program. I am deeply grateful to both. An earlier draft was presented to a colloquium of the History Department at Trent University; my thanks to colleagues for being a sympathetic audience and for their challenging questions. It is not their responsibility that I still do not have answers for many of them.

1 Kenneth Norrie, Douglas Owram, and J.C. Herbert Emery, *A History of the Canadian Economy*, 3rd ed. (Scarborough: Thomson/Nelson, 2002), 282, 279. See also Robert Bothwell, Ian Drummond, and John English, *Canada, 1900–1945* (Toronto: University of Toronto Press, 1987), 169.
2 Robert Craig Brown and Ramsay Cook, *Canada 1896–1921: A Nation Transformed* (Toronto: McClelland and Stewart, 1974), 234.
3 Pierre Berton, *Marching As to War: Canada's Turbulent Years, 1899–1953* (Toronto: Doubleday Canada, 2001), 1. This understanding of the Canadian socio-economic context also informs Berton's 'stereotype' of Canadian soldiers; see Desmond Morton, *When Your Number's Up: The Canadian Soldier in the First World War* (Toronto: Random House, 1993), 277–8.

4 Brown and Cook, *Canada, 1896–1921*, 249.

5 Gerald Friesen, *The Canadian Prairies: A History* (Toronto: University of Toronto Press, 1984), 349. See also John Herd Thompson, *The Harvests of War: The Prairie West, 1914–1918* (Toronto: McClelland and Stewart, 1978), 71–2.

6 Alison Prentice et al., *Canadian Women: A History*, 2nd ed. (Toronto: Harcourt Brace Canada, 1996), 283.

7 Graham D. Taylor and Peter A. Baskerville, *A Concise History of Business in Canada* (Toronto: Oxford University Press, 1994), 390. A similar view is expressed in Don Gillmor, Achille Michaud, and Pierre Turgeon, *Canada: A People's History*, (Toronto: McClelland and Stewart, 2001), 2: 131.

8 Alvin Finkel and Margaret Conrad, *History of the Canadian Peoples*, 3rd ed. (Toronto: Addison Wesley Longman, 2001), 2:209.

9 Gillmor, Michaud, and Turgeon, *Canada: A People's History*, 2:101.

10 For example, see S.N. Broadberry and N.F.R. Crafts, eds, *Britain in the International Economy, 1870–1939* (Cambridge: Cambridge University Press, 1992). Although its title suggests that the book covers the whole period, all but one of the essays end in 1914 or begin after the war.

11 Prentice et al., *Canadian Women*, 112.

12 Michael Bliss, *Northern Enterprise: Five Centuries of Canadian Business* (Toronto: McClelland and Stewart, 1987), 374.

13 James Naylor, *The New Democracy: Challenging the Social Order in Industrial Ontario, 1914–25* (Toronto: University of Toronto Press, 1991), 41.

14 Finkel and Conrad, *History of the Canadian Peoples*, vol. 2, quotes at 201, 208, and 185–6.

15 *History of the Canadian Economy*, 277. Friesen, quoted earlier, also goes on to show why the west was developing as it was.

16 In addition to the main census, there was a prairie census in 1916 and an annual postal census of manufactures. More and better annual data were also beginning to be produced by Canada's growing statistical system.

17 For a discussion of the standard of living question in wartime, see Jay Winter, 'Paris, London, Berlin: Capital Cities at War' in Jay Winter and Jean-Louis Robert, eds, *Capital Cities at War: Paris, London, Berlin 1914–1919* (Cambridge: Cambridge University Press, 1997), 10–13.

18 In terms of employment, iron and steel at its peak in 1917 accounted for over 11 per cent of the 675,000 jobs in industry. See *The Canada Year Book 1921* (Ottawa: King's Printer, 1922), 365.

19 See for example, Ian M. Drummond, *Progress without Planning: The Economic History of Ontario from Confederation to the Second World War* (Toronto: University of Toronto Press, 1987), 149–50 and table 9.1, 410. In this book,

see also Kris Inwood, 'The Iron and Steel Industry,' 201 and tables 11.3, 11.4, 416–18; and Tom Traves, 'The Development of the Ontario Automobile Industry to 1939,' 208–15 and table 12.4, 422.

20  In the case of farm mechanization, a common war story has the federal government attempting to foster the adoption of tractors, although there is nothing to suggest that the program had anything to do with the rate of adoption of tractors by farmers. For this story, see Finkel and Conrad, *History of the Canadian People*, 186; Brown and Cook, *Canada, 1896–1921*, 238. Norrie, Owram, and Emery (*History of the Canadian Economy*, 276) show in their war chapter a picture of a custom threshing outfit, yet such mechanized operations were not specifically or uniquely associated with the war. See Cecilia Danysk, *Hired Hands: Labour and the Development of Prairie Agriculture, 1880–1930* (Toronto: McClelland and Stewart, 1995), 94.

21  F.H. Leacy, ed., *Historical Statistics of Canada*, 2nd ed. (Ottawa: Statistics Canada, 1983), D10 to D85. See also note to table 6.1. For trends in office work, see Graham S. Lowe, *Women in the Administrative Revolution* (Toronto: University of Toronto Press, 1987), 49.

22  David Carnegie, *The History of Munitions Supply in Canada, 1914–1918* (London: Longmans, Green, 1925), 254. The actual passage reads '35,000 women, it is estimated, helped to produce munitions in Canada during the war.'

23  It was equivalent to less than 6 per cent of the 600,000 men (or about 16 per cent of the c. 220,000 men with 'industrial' occupations) who joined the Canadian Expeditionary Force during the course of the war. For these numbers, see Morton, *When Your Number's Up*, 277–9.

24  For context on the biases in the historiography of women and war, see Colin Coates and Cecilia Morgan, *Heroines and History: Representations of Madeleine de Verchères and Laura Secord* (Toronto: University of Toronto Press, 2002).

25  By 1971, when the series in *Historical Statistics of Canada* ends, there were over 80 million improved acres of land in prairie farm holdings.

26  See *Handbook of Agricultural Statistics, Part 1 – Field Crops 1908–63* (Ottawa: Dominion Bureau of Statistics, 1964), 17–19.

27  Cf. Gillmor, Michaud, and Turgeon, *Canada: A People's History*, Vol. 2, 132.

28  On British parallels, see Kathleen Burk, 'Editor's Introduction,' in K. Burk, ed., *War and the State: The Transformation of British Government, 1914–1919* (London: George Allen & Unwin, 1982), 4–6.

29  There were equivalent patterns in other price series and other countries, with some variation in amplitudes. See Chris Wrigley, 'The War and the International Economy,' in Chris Wrigley, ed., *The First World War and the*

*International Economy* (Cheltenham, U.K.: Edward Elgar, 2000), 18. Of seventeen countries listed in his table 1.5, only Spain, Australia, New Zealand, India, and the United States had lower peaks than Canada. Most other European countries for which there are data had more severe inflation than the United Kingdom. See also the discussion in Bothwell, Drummond, and English, *Canada, 1900–1945*, 181–2.

30  The best textbook account is in Bothwell, Drummond, and English, *Canada, 1900–1945*, 181–2. Much is made of inflation in Prentice et al., *Canadian Women*, but the presentation is confusing and lacks proportion, for example, in speaking of 'high prices for the necessities of life' (231) in 1914–15.

31  Jean-Louis Robert, 'The Image of the Profiteer,' in *Capital Cities at War*, 104–32.

32  See, for example, R.T. Naylor, 'The Canadian State, the Accumulation of Capital, and the Great War,' *Journal of Canadian Studies* 16, 3 and 4 (Fall-Winter 1981), 39.

33  See Ian Hugh Maclean Miller, *Our Glory and Our Grief: Torontonians and the Great War* (Toronto: University of Toronto Press, 2002), 13.

34  See Norrie, Owram, and Emery, *History of the Canadian Economy*, 262–3.

35  Wrigley, 'The War and the International Economy,' 25.

36  For a similar emphasis, see Bill Albert, *South America and the First World War: The Impact of the War on Brazil, Argentina, Peru and Chile* (Cambridge: Cambridge University Press, 1988), 2.

37  See, for example, the discussion of sources in Miller, *Our Glory and Our Grief*, 205–8.

38  See, for example, the images of women workers in munitions in Norrie, Owram, and Emery, *History of the Canadian Economy*, 273; Gillmor, Michaud, and Turgeon, *Canada: A People's History*, 117; Brown and Cook, *Canada, 1896–1921*, illustrations section after 274; and Peter A. Baskerville, *Ontario: Image, Identity, and Power* (Toronto: Oxford University Press, 2002), 165.

39  See the account of much earlier wars in Louise Dechêne, *Le partage des subsistances au Canada sous le régime français* (Montreal: Boreal, 1994).

# Part III
# The War at Home

# 7 Mobilizing Women for War

JOAN SANGSTER

There is not one thing heroic about this work. To set free
a man to fight. To make the bombs that kill him ...
Why men would keep this from us, I fail to understand. A job
is not romance ...

Betsy Struthers, 'The Bullet Factory'

This poetic rendition of women munitions workers during the First World War[1] was penned in the 1980s, reflecting more recent feminist aversion to the violent machinery of war as well as a healthy scepticism that women doing the drudgery of men's work was automatically a sign of progress. A diametrically different portrayal appeared in the official history of munitions manufacture in Canada, written by an army colonel just after the war. In the few paragraphs on women in this long tribute to contracts, technology, and war, the author recounts a story to characterize the 'development of [women workers'] moral sense without which the memory of the struggle would be sordid.' A woman making fuses is 'stunned' to hear that her son has just been killed at the front, but she refuses to go home and grieve as others urge her to do. Instead, she 'set her face like flint and worked harder than ever' as a means of asserting her patriotic duty to avenge her son.[2] One lesson conveyed – that women took up factory war work for patriotic reasons – remained fixed in many historical accounts for years to come and sometimes even reappears in popular culture today.[3]

It is hardly surprising that these versions of women and the First World War, distinguished by form, presentation, time period, and ideology, vary so dramatically. What is of interest is why and how such reconstructions of the memory of war make their way into our historical writing and everyday consciousness. Interpretations of women and war – even apparently fictional ones – rest in part on events, documents, and actual living people, but each is also the product of interpretation, engagement, and sensibility, or in other words, the product of history. In this chapter I explore the mobilization of Canadian women during the First World War, giving fresh attention to how and why the memory of war has changed over time. Although there is strong evidence that the war did not result in significant shifts in gender and social structures, the wartime crisis remains a useful means of exploring these shifting historical interpretations, as well as the resilience of gender ideologies, class differences, and social tensions in Canadian society.

Many explorations of the two world wars in North America and Britain over the last twenty years have been focused on the 'watershed question,'[4] asking if changes in work, culture, family, and state provision during wartime effected meaningful and long-lasting changes in women's lives. This is a legitimate question, especially given the emphasis in war writing on querying transformations in politics, *men's* consciousness, and modern culture, but it is nonetheless difficult to measure the war as an engine of 'progress' for all Canadian women because of the immense contradictions that wartime mobilization produced. Although it is a much-repeated truism in feminist writing that women's experiences are marked by differences as much as commonality, it is certainly worth repeating with regard to social class and ethnicity in the context of the Great War. While working-class women were perceived by the state as potential factory fodder, middle-class women were more often courted as political allies. While the latter often portrayed the war as a pathway to political and social 'regeneration,' the former became the very real, repressive targets of anxieties and fears concerning moral 'degeneration.' Ethnicity further cross-cut these divisions, with white, British-born and Anglo women more likely to embrace the war effort, while women from so-called enemy-alien nations faced marginalization and, for some, the agony of internment of male family members.[5] While conscription and trench warfare seemed to impose the ultimate gender demarcation in experience, separating women and men into the two solitudes of the home front and the war front, in fact the Great War accentuated class differences so decidedly that home front women also appeared to inhabit two – or more – solitudes by 1919.

## Memory and Historical Interpretation

In his impressive exploration of memory and the First World War, Jonathan Vance argues that, by the interwar period, certain hegemonic interpretations of the war had already come to dominate history, politics, and culture. Even writers apparently critiquing the war often unintentionally reinforced these notions of the war as a well-intentioned crusade for democracy; as a homogenizing, unifying event; and as the stimulus to the creation of a new nation and indeed of a new Canadian manhood.[6] War mobilization, the state, and gender ideology, as feminist historians have also argued, were interconnected in important ways. The dominant iconography during the First World War revealed man as the 'just warrior' and woman as the moral mother, sacrificing her sons to the cause.[7] Indeed, this was one of the images used by Nellie McClung in *Next of Kin*, her 1917 book portraying the war as a regenerating 'comeback of the soul.'[8] The related theme of men's honourable protection of women and family was utilized in recruiting, symbolized in the government's poster 'Hun or Home?' by an ogre-like German enemy threatening a defenceless mother holding a baby.[9] Although other versions of manhood and war were voiced by some dissident socialists, pacifists, and feminists, these definitions were beleaguered and marginalized.[10]

Even as the war was being fought, Canadian women were creating their own historical version of the war, often drawing on these same images and justifications in order to place themselves strategically within, rather than marginal to, the nation. Women as sacrificing mothers was a key theme in such writing, but so, too, was women as nation builders. Anglo-saxon, middle-class, professional, and politically astute women used the organ of the National Council of Women, *Women's Century*, to promote their view that the war would inevitably prove their worth as citizens and lead to a new era described in no less than millenarian rhetoric. British and Canadian women, they claimed, were creating a new 'soul' of the nation, contributing to a 'nobler conception of the state,' and participating in a 'peaceful revolution' for women.[11] The Canadian 'nation' they extolled, of course, was constructed in the image of their own racial, ethnic, and cultured personas. At the Women's War Conference called in 1918 by the government, these same women asserted their historical significance by representing themselves as the 'Mothers of Consolidation,' walking in the footsteps of other state-builders, the Fathers of Confederation: 'We are looking forward to a period of reconstruction ... As those who fifty years ago gathered together on behalf of their country were known as the "Fathers of Confederation" so these women will be known as the Mothers of Consolidation.'[12]

Labour newspapers also advanced a watershed theory of the war before it was even over. The *Industrial Banner* argued that the war was both creating a vital 'new nation' and that labour could never return to its former view of women: 'there will be [a] new status that woman-hood will occupy ... Things will never revert back to where they were prior to the outbreak of hostilities. That is clearly impossible for wom-anhood is facing an altogether different horizon, when larger and still greater opportunities open out before the sex.'[13] Even some socialists opposed to the war portrayed it as a great divide, arguing that the suffering and exploitation associated with war-making would lead to the radicalization of working-class women in the future.

The notions that war altered women's political claim to citizenship, led to more acceptance of working women, and undermined 'Victorian' sexual and social mores thus emerged in the interwar years as some-thing of historical wisdom. Although historians would later marshal evidence to argue that changing sexual mores were evident in the earlier years of the twentieth century, those people who lived through the war insisted that it not only 'shot religion high, wide and hand-some,' but also transformed sexual morality, in part because the young were less worried about their 'virtue' when death could claim soldiers so quickly. Oral history reveals the power of this image. The war, concluded one man, occasioned a 'letdown in moral and conduct and dress,' so much so that by the 1920s 'there was a lot of horseplay, immorality ... girls were more permissive, and the men more daring.'[14] It is possible that the way in which historical memory is created and an interviewee's cognizance of the centrality of this dramatic world event became an understandable hook on which to hang more slowly evolv-ing social changes.

As Cynthia Commachio points out, a defining cultural marker of the 'flaming youth' in the 1920s was their claim to be completely different *from* pre-war youth; their increased social freedom and embrace of consumer culture was self-consciously promoted as a reaction *to* the war. In popular memory, in other words, the war became a key refer-ence point to explain longer-term shifts in gender relations of the early twentieth century. This theme was often relayed through the popular press. In 'The Challenge of Freedom,' appearing in *Chatelaine* in 1929, the author takes as her basic starting point the assumption that a new 'freedom, social political and economic' had been granted to women after the war. During the war, said politician Irene Parlby, women were needed to 'carry on the work when men were overseas,' and they both exhibited a new sense of service and secured new recognition for their work. An illustration for the article showed nurses aiding injured soldiers, making the point that 'during the war, with the courage of an altered status and freedom, women gave "till it hurt."'[15]

In contrast, a controversial Canadian film of the 1920s, *Carry On, Sergeant!* suggested that the cultural images of femininity had not been transformed during the war. Filmed in 'Hollywood North,' and intended to provide a truly Canadian war story, the film emphasized the heroism of serviceman Jim McKay and his struggle overseas to stay dedicated to the pure and true wife at home, in the face of the aggressive temptation posed by a French *estaminet* girl, Marthe, who relentlessly pursues him. Jim eventually gives in to her advances, only to die on the battlefront, at least redeemed for his sexual sins and disloyalty to his wife by dying for his country. The film offered a traditional, dichtomized view of good versus evil women; moreover, the mere *presence* of the sexual theme was seen as controversial when the film made its debut.[16]

While many war novels were primarily concerned with the traumatic effects of warfare upon Canadian manhood, authors did deal, tangentially, with women. Some authors reproduced the image of the suffering, sacrificing mother, like the Icelandic mother portrayed in Laura Salverson's *Viking Heart*, who loses her beloved son to the war.[17] Novels also portrayed the war as the pressure cooker that produced a new woman and new gender roles. In Hugh MacLennan's *Barometer Rising*, the hero's love interest, Penny, not only worked as a ship designer (a highly unlikely occupation if there ever was one) but gave birth to his child before they married. Her unusual occupation, her intellectual stature, and her refusal to completely abandon her child in shame left no doubt that she represented a clear break with Edwardian womanhood.[18] Likewise, in Douglas Durkin's *The Magpie*, the returned veteran, Craig, interacted with three important women in his life, one of whom finds her political voice in the aftermath of her own husband's death at the front, for she comes to see the war as a callous, greedy exercise in power by the ruling elite. She subsequently becomes an outspoken pacifist and socialist, living with a man who is a labour organizer. Even Craig's wife, who proves to be selfish, materialistic, and apolitical, secures her new amusements in the country club, cocktails, and adultery, surely something of a departure from past norms. Craig's ultimate love choice is an accomplished sculptor who finds her artistic voice abroad after working as a nurse in the war.[19]

The notion of a new woman, born of wartime exigencies, was not simply a creation of masculine authors. Georgina Sime, an upper-middle-class Scottish emigrant to Canada and short-story writer, also portrayed the war as a turning point, creating 'new freedom' for working women. In 'Munitions,' a piece in her collection, Sister Women, she explored the thoughts of a young domestic turned munitions worker as she rode the streetcar to work one day. The protagonist, Bertha, is literally 'liberated' from her safe, boring, and stultifying work as a maid when she takes on munitions work at the urging of a fellow servant. Sime uses the spring-time weather as a metaphor for Bertha's regeneration: 'the sense of freedom! The joy of being done with cap and gown. The feeling that you could draw your breath– speak as you liked – wear overalls like men – curse if you liked.' While Sime's story replays some of the stock themes of middle-class women's organizations – that munitions work, despite the drudgery involved, would offer women new opportunities – it did convey a less negative view of working-class women. The munitions women's loud behaviour, bawdiness, and sexualized humour on the streetcar are portrayed not as immoral but rather as good-natured camaraderie.[20]

The resilient equation of the war with new social and political roles for women was in part shaped by Canada's close cultural connections to Britain. British novels, newspapers, and immigrants created a path of communication between the two countries, and the British war experience was thus extrapolated to Canada. Commentaries and studies of British women war workers were plentiful, also claiming a 'renaissance' in women's work and status.[21] Even in a recent, 1990s Canadian film on women in the First World War, And We Knew How to Dance, this connection is used: footage of British militant suffragettes (including one throwing herself under the King's horse) and possibly footage of British munitions workers are integrated. By interviewing women whose memories stress women's non-traditional work and the granting of equality, the filmmakers dramatically and visually reproduce for a contemporary audience the image of the war as a significant break-through for Canadian women.

The image of the war as political turning point for women was occasionally queried in the interwar period by feminists disappointed with women's apparent abandonment of reform and their return to 'partyism.'[22] More recently, historians have also questioned the notion that it was the war that led directly to enhanced political equality.[23] However, one can forgive the women at the time for their claims to the contrary, since there was the *appearance* of a more direct connection. Well-organized, publicly vocal, middle-class women continually promoted the talents of the 'new woman' that war had uncovered; their urgent calls for increasing substitution of women in non-traditional 'men's work' underscored their faith that the war would usher in new equality for women – though ironically, they were building a case for *their* campaign on the arduous labour of working-class women.[24]

The view of the war as a wake-up call for politicians who rewarded loyal women with the vote remained so tenacious that it affected succeeding generations of historians. Certainly, women's pro-war loyalty had much to do with Borden's Wartime Elections Act, a 'gerrymandering' ploy used to secure the votes of pro-war women, as Robert Craig Brown frankly notes.[25] But according to historian Catherine Cleverdon (whose book appeared in 1950), even the subsequent, wider granting of suffrage in 1918 was largely due to the war. Her interpretation may have been shaped by images of the more recently fought Second World War; it did not question the claims of suffragists themselves that the war was a 'lever' that forced 'women's body and soul' into the political arena, and as a consequence, the 'ballot' was handed to her after little struggle.[26]

This argument was eventually challenged by some feminist historians in the 1970s and 1980s, whose critical analysis of the class and race ideology of mainstream suffragists suggested that the war provided male elites with 'an excuse' more than a reason to grant the vote.[27] As a more critical feminist history emerged, the popular image of the First World War as a watershed that 'drastically changed the role of Canadian women in the workforce,' was also questioned, a theme confirmed by subsequent studies of the resilient gender inequalities faced by working women in the 1920s.[28] Our reinterpretations, however, have also left us, ironically, in the position of countering the lingering memory of war in women's oral histories that remain, still, constructed around the war as a life-changing watershed in their lives.

**Mobilizing Women for Work**

Since the idea that women's work was transformed during the First World War has been central to the memory of war, we should examine

Canadian sisters looking around the ruins of their quarters, which were struck by a bomb, 3rd Canadian Stationary Hospital, ca. 1918 (Archives of Ontario, C224-0-0-10-48, AO 3928)

the issue of the mobilization of women's wage labour for war. Nowhere is the historical evidence more problematic, for every statistic on women's work, as Deborah Thom argues for the British experience, is suffused with ideology. Statistics showing women's massive entrance into men's jobs and munitions in particular were used at the time to promote further use of female labour, to reassure the public that the government labour plan was succeeding, and even to convince women themselves that work was available. For example, the claim by the Canadian government's Imperial Munitions Board that 35,000 women were working in munitions in 1917 is highly unlikely, compared with other Montreal and Ontario factory employment numbers.[29]

Photographs are also an intriguingly deceptive source. We are well acquainted with popular images of women making large shells, perhaps dressed in unconventional trousers or overalls, handling machinery and metals coded at the time as masculine. In both Britain and Canada, the government issued a special book of photographs (and in

Canada a film) exhibiting this work in order to entice other employers to take on female labour.[30] But how representative were such photographs when the majority of working women remained in domestic and other factory employment, and when the largest female incursion into male jobs may have been in clerical work? Not only were munitions photos intended as a labour recruiting tool; they have also remained seared on the public memory, because they were more interesting, unusual, and, at the time, even exotic, given women's costume of bandanas and bloomers.[31] Feminist historians, too, have often utilized pictures of women's 'non-traditional' work as a means of representing war work, reflecting our own understandable fascination with the malleability of the sexual division of labour.[32]

In Ontario, where probably around 60 per cent of munitions work was located, the provincial government was also able more accurately to track women seeking out munitions work, since the advent of war coincided with the development of new state-run employment bureaux (including separate women's departments), conscious of their record-keeping role; in some cities, the government admitted, people assumed the bureaux were only *for* the recruitment of war workers.[33] Even in Ontario, bureaucrats sometimes declared that 'many' women were flooding into munitions, but added that they did not have the exact statistics on hand.[34] Moreover, it is crucial to remember that, outside central Canada, war work was sparse: according to one estimate in 1916, only 1 per cent of war contracts were being filled in the west and 4 per cent in the Maritimes.[35] Women's work encompassed very different problems in these regions; in the last year of the war, for instance, Saskatchewan women's groups were still desperately pressing all levels of government to find ways to encourage women to take up domestic positions in rural areas.[36]

At the beginning of the war general unemployment ravaged most of the country. The crisis was so severe that Vancouver middle-class women's groups held emergency mass meetings to raise funds and devise means to deal with poverty-stricken 'unemployed girls.' Through 1915 young women were still being forced into service when they wanted factory work; shelters were being sought for the 'casual poor'; and some female occupations reported that there was a 25 to 30 per cent shortage of jobs for women seeking work.[37] An Ontario government inquiry into unemployment published in 1916 was surprised not at women's presence in the workforce, but only at the massive numbers – as many 8–10,000 – who were jobless. In response, officials could only muster the unimaginative recommendation that women have better vocational training, at home and institutionally, primarily for domestic service, since 'any woman who is a competent house worker need not fear unemployment.'[38] In fact, the National Council of Women (NCW) repeated this suggestion throughout the war, concerned as it was with the shortage of maids. Will it become so desperate that families will have to 'move into hotels' as was the case in the United States, worried NCW leader Constance Hamilton, revealing her rather privileged view of the world.[39] Recovery in central Canada was not evident until 1916, as women filled clerical positions or found work on war contracts; in the west, bereft of such wartime welfare for business, unemployment plagued some cities well into 1917.

The substitution of women for men was not a significant political issue until later in 1916, when Joseph Flavelle, in charge of the Imperial Munitions Board (IMB), persuaded Borden and the cabinet to create a special labour portfolio in the IMB, to which he appointed one of his eager political protégés, Ontario MPP Mark Irish. Irish made the introduction of female labour into munitions one of his major priorities; he publicized the issue, circulated the British and Canadian books on women in munitions, tried to work closely with provincial governments to faciliate the use of female munitions workers, and lobbied manufacturers heavily, sometimes enticing them with the suggestion that women would be a more malleable, less militant workforce. He also appointed two female 'welfare supervisors,' both eminently respectable women, to offer advice to and supervision of the new female workforce.[40]

There is no doubt that Irish faced some opposition, a fact he was careful to note in *his* retrospective view of his accomplishments. Employers were sometimes reluctant to hire women for non-traditional jobs, not always because they feared women's lack of skill or strength but because they did not see the expense involved as justifying the outlay for new facilities such as restrooms and lunchrooms. In 1917, for instance, when some manufacturers perceived a coming downturn in contracts, they resisted hiring women, grumbled Irish, because they did not want to make the expensive 'alterations' necessary; they were looking for the largest return on their cash in a short period of time. Similarly, expense was a concern in the internal government debate about hiring women in an explosives plant in Trenton. While one reason was the protective fear of the effects that dangerous chemical work might have on women's health, in the list of four reasons given number one was that the 'large expenditure of money' needed to create facilities for women did not make the substitution 'economic' enough.[41] Perhaps their decision was fortunate, since on Thanksgiving Day 1918 the plant exploded, levelling half the enterprise and resulting in an exodus of refugees from the town.[42]

It was not simply that employers feared unsettling the gendered division of labour; occasionally, they saw some *working-class* women as unsuitable. The company used to hire female inspectors complained initially that 'common factory girls' could not or would not do the job well, because they were less committed to the war, while more dedicated, middle-class women 'would not go down to factory districts and work in close contact with an ordinary class of labour.' This executive was soon proved wrong: a newspaper article trumpeting the availability of inspection work encouraged two well-educated Peterborough women to write to the prime minister asking for jobs in Toronto, and their successful plan to flee sedate Peterborough reminds us that women did utilize the war as an opportunity for escape or adventure.[43]

Irish faced other obstacles. In order to persuade women that night shifts posed no dangers to women trying to get to work, the chief press censor agreed to suppress reports of 'women being interfered with on the streets,' and some provincial governments altered legal prohibitions on women's night work. The Ontario government partially relaxed its night work rules for war work, but rejected attempts by some factory owners eager to do likewise in their workplaces.[44] The Quebec government, less enthusiastic about the war, refused Irish's overtures concerning night work and adhered rigidly to other limitations on women's factory work, much to the annoyance of Irish and the IMB. Irish understandably had more success with patriotic, English middle-class women who set up YWCA-sponsored canteens for factory women. These examples suggest that the federal government's attitude towards female labour was as much pragmatic and cost conscious as it was protective. Similarly, an Ontario government study arguing for a nine-hour day for women used munitions workers to make the point that reasonable hours would 'eliminate fatigue' and mistakes and also lead to 'maximum output.'[45]

The philosophy of the IMB concerning the use of female labour was multifaceted. Although both Irish and Flavelle perceived that filling labour shortages was the key issue, Irish also believed that by substituting women, men not only would be released for service, but would be literally edged out. The use of female labour was thus a subtle recruiting tool for the army. Not all government leaders agreed; the future prime minister, R.B. Bennett, complained to Irish that the established gendered division of labour, if not gender peace, would be upset, and according to Irish, Bennett actively discouraged Winnipeg women from working in industry or farm production: '[Bennett claims] the employment of women will create a female industrial army doing the work of men at a low wage, which, when the overseas force returns, will be opposed by a male army of unemployed ... women once engaged in factory work will never give it up.'[46]

If the state's response to female wage earners was shaped by economic and pragmatic issues as well as army recruiting concerns, what was women's response to the publicized claim that new, non-traditional jobs were available for them? The answers were ambiguous. In Montreal, Nancy Christie shows, these jobs were not necessarily easy to fill, and the Women's War Registry recommended situating middle-class women in them so that they would *not* 'compete with returned soldiers.'[47] In Toronto and other centres, women reportedly lined up for munitions work; in one year, over 6,000 women applied for munitions jobs, although only 2,000 were placed. Women's responses, in other words, were part of a continuing tradition of working-class women moving from one job to another in search of more hospitable working conditions and better pay. With 'tales of fortunes' to be made in munitions, working-class women were just as likely as anyone else to want a share.[48] The fact that munitions work was sought after also led to ethnocentric cries to keep 'foreigners' and 'aliens' out – indeed, for Irish this issue was just as explosive as female labour, judging by the hostile letters to the IMB about 'aliens' securing placement in war industry.

Women accustomed to factory work may have been less intimidated by the sight of machinery than IMB publicity and articles written by middle-class women suggested. A 1918 Ontario study of applicants for munitions work ascertained that the vast majority were single women of Canadian or British descent between twenty and thirty years of age, and, significantly, over 50 per cent hailed from other factory or domestic work. Far fewer were from the professions or had been 'leisured' (a category that may have designated homemakers). In Ontario and Montreal, as many as one-third (a fairly high percentage) were married women, suggesting that working-class wives were also trying to bolster the family economy when jobs were temporarily plentiful.[49]

The questions of how skilled this work was and also how women perceived their own labour are difficult to ascertain. The label given to women's munitions work, namely, 'diluted' labour, was also suffused with ideology. If dilution meant taking a skilled job and breaking it down into unskilled parts, this was not an accurate description of all female positions; rather, it simply reflected a value judgment about *women* doing the work! Some of the jobs, assembling fuses and shells, for instance, simply directly substituted female for 'unskilled' male labour. Ironically some of these repetitive tasks, such as operating punch presses, would later be dominated by females in the mass production consumer and electrical industries that flourished after the war. It may be, as Thom suggests for Britain, that there were fewer technological shifts in women's work than we imagine – 'the innovation was more in the telling of the tale and in the management of people.'[50]

It is true that, by war's end, a small number of women had tasted male work for the first time as they operated elevators, lathes, or milled tools. The *Labour Gazette* carefully plotted these changes across the country, noting when women were used by piano manufacturing firms in Toronto, as bus conductors in Halifax, or in the rail yards in Fort William. However, these instances were relatively rare, so that in late 1918 it was recorded that the substitution that was 'commonplace' in Britain was yet in an 'experimental stage' in Canada.[51] Rarity made it all the more newsworthy. In Kingston a newspaper columnist entertained his readers with a treatise about women tram conductors: Would their morals be compromised, could they handle it physically? How would customers react? he asked at great length.[52]

One of the most detailed studies of women's work, a survey of industrial occupations in Montreal conducted by Enid Price, located a small number of women in railway shops and new industrial positions for women in about half of the metal-working plants doing munitions work, but only one plant claimed that women were paid 'at the same rate as men.' Usually, substantial differentials existed in women's and men's pay rates; moreover, munitions provided men, proportionately more than women, with the majority of jobs.[53] There was little change in rubber, garment, and other factories where women were already a presence, but more noticeable substitution in clerical occupations, such as banking, where wartime labour shortages and the substantial use of female labour not only accelerated a trend towards 'feminization' already in motion, but caused 'enduring' changes to the nature of clerical work.[54] Even if employers were eager to hire women, telling Price that females 'did routine work better than men,' they did not abandon their gendered understanding of why and how women worked. The problem with women, bankers intoned, was that they did not see earning as lifelong, they would not do overtime, and if 'a better position is offered they leave without scruples,' a sign, apparently, not of entrepreneurship but of 'disloyalty.'[55] Unfortunately, this rare wartime survey drew its information from clerical and managerial staff, *not* from workers; also, it was sponsored by a business-dominated organization, though one with prominent liberal feminists involved, as an aid to understanding 'what may be achieved in industry with the increased volume of industrial output by unity of purpose and effort.'[56] It, too, in other words, was shaped by ideological suppositions concerning women and work.

Aside from the inflated numbers of women workers, one of the enduring munitions myths was that many women who did not need paid employment took this work for patriotic reasons. Indeed, in *And We Knew How to Dance*, one informant says, 'there was everything from poor beggars to society women. We had them getting brought down to work in their chauffeured limousines.'[57] Some women may have perceived their work to be both necessary and patriotic, but there is not clear evidence of chauffeured limousines transporting grande dames to the production lines. This myth was seldom promoted in the labour press, more concerned with issues of wages and working conditions and with scoring a political point about class exploitation. In 1915 the *Industrial Banner* published an exposé of women's exploitation by peace activist Laura Hughes, who, like many middle-class women before her, went 'undercover' to discover life as a real 'worker.' Hughes reported on bad ventilation, crowded rooms, and poor pay for unending piecework at the Simpson's knitting mill that supplied underwear for government contracts.[58] Later *Banner* editorials complained that men and women were being mercilessly exploited in munitions as the owners accrued great profits, 'taking it out of the hides of their working men and women and working girls by reducing their wages and in some instances increasing their hours of labour as well.'[59]

Ignoring government pleas not to interrupt war production, women workers also protested, even walked off the job, if they were aggrieved, though press censorship may have kept some protests hidden from public scrutiny.[60] Hamilton women munitions inspectors threatened to strike in 1917 when faced with wage reductions for incoming workers, and a conflict was narrowly avoided. In the same year, a group of women approached the *Toronto Star* in order to gain publicity for their grievances. 'They are killing us off as fast as they are killing men at the trenches,' the deputation of six complained with considerable dramatic effect. They cited the case of a fellow worker who supposedly had dropped dead in the streetcar (though she had heart trouble) as well as two others whose fatigue had led to tragic consequences. Twelve-hour shifts, night work, a six-day week, and difficult working conditions were described by the 'girls,' who claimed that they had just refused to work a fourteen-hour shift and, as a result, had been told to leave.[61] Oral recollections also relay a less than romantic picture of munitions work. One woman working on shells remembers her factory as 'all these avenues and avenues of clanking, grinding, crashing machines ... the machinery was all open. The one thing that they were terrified of was the belts and our hair ... and [to the back of us] was a blasting furnace so if there ever was a fire, nothing could have saved us.'[62]

One of the most telling indicators of gender relations during the war was the attitude of organized labour to the very limited incursion of women into non-traditional jobs. Early skirmishes between unions and employers primarily concerned fair-wage clauses in munitions contracts or the prospect of registration as a feared precursor to conscription.[63] Nonetheless, women doing men's work at lower pay, as well as the de-skilling of work, had always been a perceived threat for organized labour, raising the spectre of a downward pressure on male wages; labour activists warned that capitalists would never easily relinquish their 'stranglehold on [cheaper] labour.' Inevitably, then, there were tensions from the shop floor relayed to the political realm: Irish dealt with rumours of a protest by male tram conductors in Toronto over the introduction of women, and when a few women were hired into Montreal railway shops, male workers as far away as Winnipeg were mobilized, 'incensed' as they were by the threat of 'dilution.'[64] Nationally, the Trades and Labour Congress (TLC) also became agitated. Their 1917 meeting called for the unionization of women in order to stem their 'exploitation' and their threat to male wages; in 1918 they again urged the government to 'protect' those women replacing men with better working conditions, though they were also adamant that female labour should not be used before all male labour was exhausted. A more positive strategy was the TLC's recommendation, endorsed by many labour papers, for equal pay.[65] Such pronoucements were in keeping with pre-war ideals; the labour movement, indeed many socialists, embraced the ideal of a family wage with a male breadwinner, seeing the employment of children and wives as a sign of exploitation, not liberation.

As the economy recovered by 1916–17, more women organized, and more went on strike in 'traditional' areas of female work. Like men, women embraced unions, even in the public sector for the first time, as a means of protecting their meagre earnings from inflation and protesting intensified work regimes. Judging by the number of strikes involving women, argues Linda Kealey, the period from 1915–20 saw sharp increases in women's union activism.[66] From small-town telephone operators to urban laundry workers, women were showing new interest in the power unions might offer them, dispelling any notion that they were too timid to strike. In Vancouver, a bewildered man was astonished when irate female laundry workers climbed on his car and told him to take his shirts elsewhere.[67]

Labour struggles during the war thus reflected some masculine ambivalence about female labour but also the rising tide of working-class – especially rank-and-file – militancy. Where women and men shared workplaces, they sometimes struck together, though they seldom questioned the gendered division of labour within the plant. This was the case in a Victoria munitions strike of 1917, sparked by the dismissal of an elected committee-man by a manager determined not to recognize any union group other than that of his skilled mechanics. Other male and female workers in the plant were determined to secure some union representation as well. Moreover, strikers did not rise to the bait when the general manager made the potentially divisive argument that he had been told by the IMB to 'replace as many men as possible with women.' Nor was it only in munitions, or in mixed-gender workplaces, that women's militancy occurred. In a strike of candy makers in Winnipeg the next year, the predominantly female workforce complained that some were working 'large machinery, replacing men who went to the front' for paltry wages of $9.00 a week. It was not the crossover into male jobs that was the issue, but the low wages, wildly fluctuating hours offered, and 'petty persecutions' by foremen and *forewomen* (the latter 'to our shame' said organizer and socialist Helen Armstrong) that motivated the demand for unionization.[68]

It is true that, when all the unskilled in a workplace were women, the skilled men might well abandon them. This was the case in an Ottawa strike of women press feeders who could not persuade the male plate printers to support them when they walked out and attempted to unionize. The girls claimed a fellow worker had been fired for merely 'laughing' on the line; management labelled it rampant 'insubordination' and proceeded to hire replacements. By 1919 the strike became a contested issue within labour's ranks as the Trades and Labour Congress and its local allies offered no aid to the union, urging the women to return to work. According to one male militant, one disreputable trade union leader was letting his daughter cross the picket line! There is no 'pep' in the TLC anymore, charged a male supporter of the women strikers, indicating that the issue was not only one of gender or unskilled/skilled divisions; rather, radicals also saw this as proof of a sedate, accommodating union bureaucracy.[69]

What is most revealing about all the wartime strikes is that *almost none* was fought over equal pay or dilution issues. One exception was a Toronto strike of aeroplane assemblers in which 600 men and 100 women struck over wages, overtime, and reinstatement of a fired unionist. The union wanted women to be paid the same rate as machinists and toolmakers when they 'were doing the same work,' and it argued strongly to have women's rates raised, especially in jobs they shared with men. While labour portrayed the skilled men as chivalrous, claiming the machinists had 'nothing to gain but are out to support those lower down,' their support for equal pay and better female rates was accompanied by the usual fears that female labour would diminish men's earning power or their access to jobs. The labour men, reported the press, said women were 'not indicating if they would return to domestic life after the war, and if it came to laying off a man or woman, the employers had to take a stand.' There was no mistaking what unionists wanted this to be: 'we have nothing against the employment of women ... what we do claim is that returned soldiers whom the firm apparently will not employ on this work, could do the work and if women are employed then they should be paid the same rate of wages as men.'[70] This strike, however, was an exception to a more general pattern of men and women accepting a gendered division of labour but arguing collectively and militantly for the improvement of this entire structure for all working people.

The concentration of the press on women in munitions was parallelled by their fascination with women farm workers. By 1917 many levels of government were frantic to find people to harvest crops, also important to the war effort. In eastern Ontario, farm labour was so scarce that the respectables overseeing the farm recruiting urged that a woman recently convicted of wearing male attire have her federal sentence suspended so that she could join the ranks of rural labour. Why should someone be sent to a federal prison for donning men's clothes, they mused, when she could be out doing the work of a man?[71] Farm labour shortages were also a problem in the prairie west, where women were sought after as domestic and general hands.

The most visible historical records, again, often stress women's incursion into untraditional labour and the recruitment of patriotic, Anglo-Saxon, middle-class girls to join the ranks of the 'farmerettes.' Official pictures published by the Ontario government, for instance, showed women beside large trucks and tractors, in rustic hats and even bloomers, posing with the tools of their trade, often smiling for the camera. Newspapers, still entranced with the notion of 'inverted roles,' in this case cultured, urban females joining the ranks of rustic, rougher labour, gave the campaign considerable publicity. Like Mark Irish, the government claimed its recruitment project was initially opposed by reluctant farmers and growers, but with some prodding and after a summer of work, they realized how useful women were, leading to new acceptance of female labour and higher food production. Within this major recruitment, however, a gendered division of labour remained intact: men were used for harvesting, girls and women for 'lighter' work, such as fruit picking, which, as a participant at the Women's War Conference noted, had always been female work. Moreover, the actual numbers of 'farmerettes,' especially urban women with no connection to farms, were smaller than other groups. The Ontario government first targeted high school boys in 1917, adding girls when the latter pushed to be included, and in the following year male harvesters numbered 6,000, high school boys 8,000, and the fruit pickers campaign placed only 1,200 women.[72]

As with the mobilization of munitions labour, the question was not so much that women were doing forms of work unknown to female labour, but that growers were reluctant to provide the economic outlay – such as housing – for this temporary workforce. As Margaret Kechnie points out, the recruitment of college girls for farm work by well-placed women reformers, in cooperation with the Ontario government, was not without its wrinkles. Despite the attempts of the YWCA to set up supervised camps for the girls, amenities were rustic – worse, wages were so low that there were rumours of a berry pickers' strike in 1917.[73] Bad weather, uncertain harvests, costs of food and board caused discontent, and the next year, notwithstanding the intervention of the NCW to improve the situation,[74] the number of college girls declined, while high school girls, especially those raised on farms, predominated.

The farmerettes were not simply overwhelmed by the difficulties of making a decent wage through such hard, hot labour. As Kechnie relates, using the diary of one University of Toronto student, they also looked down on their rural counterparts, who were seen as common and coarse.[75] Some farmerettes also saw the regular farm workers as immoral. Indeed, a major theme running through the recruitment of farm and urban labour was the belief that women's morals needed extra protection, endangered as they were by war conditions. The war was certainly not a homogenizing and unifying experience for one middle-class woman who went to pick fruit, only to complain bitterly to the government that her fellow female pickers were predominantly low-class, immoral, and sexually depraved. In her lengthly report on the flax pickers, Miss Taylor claimed there were constant 'moral irregularities,' largely because the flax-milling company refused to pay for matrons from the YWCA or the Woman's Christian Temperance Union (WCTU).

The girls, she wrote, had 'rough house dances every night in the barn,' entertained men in their tents, and displayed absolutely no sense of modesty, doing their washing 'half dressed' near country roads where anybody could look on. Their tents were like pig stys, with 'half washed underwear hanging on the trees.' 'It smelt like a choir of negroes,' she wrote, with a racist flourish. The so-called camp captain in charge, she continued with disgust, was an 'elocutionist from Toronto [who] smoked cigarettes and painted herself,' and who introduced a camp doctor who supposedly gave 'certain pills to girls who had made the mistake of indiscretion.' The few college girls stuck together, appalled as things 'degenerated,' and even some decent girls were 'ruined.' The worst part, she concluded, was that these lower-class girls dared to call themselves 'patriotic,' a label she clearly thought should be reserved for the decent, sexually moral, and upright women of Canada.[76]

### Mobilizing Morality for War

Miss Taylor's apocalyptic version of things falling apart reflected a strong concern voiced by various religious and reform organizations that the wartime emergency also required the vigilant protection of the family and morality, including sexual purity. Because the war emergency unleashed strong anxieties about sexual laxity and non-conformity, mobilizing morality for war was just as important in the minds of many as mobilizing the raw power of labour for war production.

On the one hand, morality was associated with patriotism, loyalty to the empire, and the defence of Anglo-Saxon values in the face of the

'Teutonic aggressors.' Women who supported the war portrayed it as a just crusade; the national regeneration that they claimed the war would bring *was* moral regeneration. This was epitomized in the WCTU's successful campaign against alcohol, deemed by the WCTU an even greater 'scourge than war ... or German bullets.'[77] The morality of patriotism was lived out by many women in voluntary work. Women raised hundreds of thousands of dollars through imperialist organizations like the Imperial Order Daughters of the Empire (IODE) or through the Red Cross; in 1914 alone the IODE contributed to the construction of a naval ship, a hospital wing, and many ambulances. As well as mobilizing their considerable financial power, these women gave unpaid, volunteer labour to the registration of citizens; to organizations like the Canadian Patriotic Fund; to the production of clothes, bandages, and other goods for the military; and to thrift campaigns. Some of these efforts clearly crossed class lines, drawing in white, Anglo, working-class women. Perhaps most important, these women became political allies for those waging the war. They aided recruiting efforts, declaring from public platforms that only the selfish women would 'hold back their husbands, fathers and brothers,'[78] while also publicly repudiating feminist pacifists, castigating them mildly as naive and misguided or more forcefully as 'dupes' of the enemy.[79]

The moral endorsement of prominent women was highly sought after by the ruling elite, hence Borden's attempts to secure Nellie McClung's support for the Wartime Elections Act. The government's Women's War Conference of 1918 represented a prime example of this mutually sought-after alliance. The attendance list was a who's who of important farm and reform groups, though labour women, as well as those from non-Anglo communities, including Québécoise women, were noticeably absent. Delegates passed resolutions ranging from the control of food production and conservation to prohibition and industrial activity. They were most profuse in their thanks to the government for 'taking them into their confidence' and for placing one woman on the Registration Board. An NCW article even urged the government to consult with an appointed, *not elected*, 'advisory board of women ... with [a] strong magnetic woman [Emily Murphy] at the helm.[80] Eager to assert their new political respectability, they also demanded reforms such as equal pay and a new federal children's bureau.

It is hard to escape the conclusion, however, that the government got the better end of this political alliance. When the war ended, there was no children's bureau; moreover, equal pay had never been a remote possibility in the government's labour strategy, which had not even sanctioned 'fair wage' clauses in its munitions contracts. When women took seriously the government's rhetoric about their new importance, lobbying in 1919 for a female delegate at the Versailles Peace Conference, Borden's private response was revealing: 'I cannot see any possible advantage in selecting representatives from [the women's] societies mentioned. ... I do not know of any work they could do if they came ... I should prefer ... not to take any action.'[81]

The absence of labour and non-Anglo women at the 1918 conference was a stark reminder that the women's movement was not unified during the war. Indeed, some working-class women used the labour press as a vehicle to critique the prosecution of war, while the most radical socialist women challenged the war itself, indicting capitalism and militarism as the root causes of the unnecessary conflict.[82] Linking ethnicity and class in their critiques, socialists like the fiery Helen Armstrong mounted a courageous critique of the government's nativist internment policies, pointing to their cruel consequences for the 'starving' women and children of internees.[83]

These ethnic and class tensions and the very different conceptions of morality that shaped working-class and middle-class women's sensibilities about war were manifested in other contexts, too. The hiring of women of 'good pedigree' as munitions 'welfare supervisors' reflected the understanding by government officials that women with high moral standards were needed to oversee working women's less certain morals in a rough, masculine, working environment. This was made clear in 1918, when the Air Force wanted to use the services of the IMB welfare supervisor Mrs Fenton (who had actually been laid off) to oversee women in its employment, and the IMB agreed in order to prevent the taint of sexual immorality and the 'cesspit' of 'public scandal' from touching the Air Force.[84]

The perceived influx of women into new and masculine employments – even if it was very exaggerated – accentuated the anxieties of middle-class reformers about the sexual morality of working-class women. In *Women's Century*, a prominent reformer explained with an anecdote. She was sitting on the streetcar, listening to girls from the factories, whose 'careless, reckless' approach to life and love indicated little respect for the 'sanctity of marriage.' These girls, living in a 'feverish state of unnatural excitement and unrest all day' and in the 'darkened gloom' of sensational movies at night were disturbing enough, but her second example was worse. A young woman, ostentatiously dressed in her new-found wealth, sat with her silk blouse unbuttoned, flirting with a young soldier. The only thing worse than her shockingly loose morals was her 'designedly wicked ... foolish temptation' of this fine 'specimen of young manhood.' Similar concerns, of course, resulted in the creation of 'hostess houses' by the YWCA near military camps both to protect soldiers from predatory prostitutes and to keep young women from endangering their sexual virtue. 'Girls and Khaki' were a potentially lethal combination warned many writers; the 'glamour of a uniform' might lead to women's easy abandonment of morality.[85]

Social workers and reformers repeatedly voiced their fear that delinquency and family upheaval might result when the patriarchal authority of men was transferred to the battlefront, though it was primarily working-class families that came under their critical view. Concerns about the morality of working-class wives also characterized the state and charitable aid (intended primarily to aid enlistment) provided for dependent wives of soldiers. The Canadian Patriotic Fund (CPF), Nancy Christie argues, reinforced at its 'very basis the preservation of class boundaries,' while simultaneously acting to 'morally regulate' women, through their 'family visits' inspecting women's spending, behaviour and morals.[86] CPF visitors had to ascertain if women were 'worthy of assistance,' properly searching for wage work to supplement their allowance, eschewing 'wastefulness, luxuries and recklessness.'[87] That this regulation was resented was evident not only in some oral recollections, but also in the more politicized columns of labour papers. In 1917 the *Industrial Banner* cautioned soldiers' wives to beware of the 'leading ladies,' who would call and pretend interest in their welfare when they were interested only in securing their vote. These women are the wives of men making fortunes, while we suffer, scrape by and serve overseas, the same people who moralistically inspect your Patriotic Fund spending, claiming '[you] were not conducting yourself in a manner becoming a lady,' daring to 'go out to the movies rather than scrubbing floors.'[88]

The war thus engendered a rhetoric of regeneration, but also heightened anxieties about degeneration. Nor was existing legislation on morality perceived to be adequate. In 1918 the federal government pushed through a criminal code amendment making it a crime to have a home 'unfit for a child' because of the parents' 'sexual immorality, habitual drunkenness or any other form of vice.' A few years after the war, prominent lawyer and child-saver W.L. Scott explained that he had drafted the bill for the government because it was found that there were 'many instances' where the father went to the front and the mother and some 'scoundrel' then 'lived in adultery' to the 'great detriment of the child's morals,' though the problem of adultery was not confined to these families.[89] Similarly worded legislation in Ontario was used to prosecute parental neglect and 'immorality,' sometimes even women who 'deserted' homes they claimed were violent.[90] Debating the bill in 1918, some parliamentarians noted that the bill reflected the intensified moralism of the war atmosphere, and they worried its vague scope would lead to 'mischevious' and 'extreme' prosecutions. It nonetheless became law, and its use in the next decades, particularly against working-class and poor families, confirmed some of these fears.[91]

This was simultaneously a period of intense legal prosecution of sexual 'immorality,' especially the sale of sex. In 1918 a federal bill was enacted to criminalize those who falsely registered as man and wife in hotels and boarding houses, and the age of consent for girls was raised. As a response to the highly organized social purity campaigns, prostitution laws were extended in 1913 and 1915, creating new offences such as living off the avails of prostitution and tightening offences such as procuring. Public investment in the idea that white slavery and prostitution threatened both the home and young innocent women resulted in increased policing; in the first two years of the war, John McLaren notes, the conviction rate for bawdy-house arrests across Canada was two to three times what it had been in the early years of the century.[92]

NCW and WCTU women clearly saw the war as the vehicle for needed purification, ridding Canada of alcohol, prostitution, venereal disease, and immorality. This campaign was sometimes described in eugenic and ethnocentric language, stressing the value of Anglo-Saxon culture and the need to limit reproduction of the eugenically 'unfit.' Wartime pressures also led to more public discussion of venereal disease, and under pressure from medical, reform, and military forces, provinces took action through Public Health Acts, while tough, even draconian, controls were implemented through the new federal Venereal Diseases Act of 1918, a measure applauded by those women who feared VD as a scourge against womanhood.[93] These anti-VD campaigns, however, were also shaped by class assumptions. Just after the federal VD law was passed, Mark Irish suggested to Flavelle that more anti-VD education needed to be done in 'large industrial works,' such as munitions, for 'both men and women of the lower order grades of life recognize only one penalty as arising from sexual intercourse, namely pregnancy,' while the greater evil, VD, was little understood by 'these workers.' Although he saw this VD issue as a 'sidelight' to his major task of dilution, Irish equated such moral education directly with the work of the female welfare supervisor, Mrs Fenton, who had supposedly dealt with a number of 'unfortunate' cases of moral downfall.[94] It is not surprising that, even after the war, those women most likely to be incarcerated in reformatories under the VD act were poor, working-class women.

The anti-VD campaign was linked to another moral project of the war years, namely, the creation of voluntary female police patrols, whose job was to 'rescue' women by policing urban spaces and preventing – or directly halting – sexual immorality. Responding to the ongoing lobbying of middle-class reformers, police matrons had been hired in some Canadian cities, but the war 'brought to a climax' an intense campaign to integrate women into policing, though primarily in a separate sphere dealing with domestic and moral issues. Drawing on the model of British patrols, the NCW repeatedly extolled their value as a protective measure against VD and to stop the 'charity girl, patriotic prostitute and incorrigible girl from becoming a professional prostitute.'[95] The patrols suggested that the moral problem of the day was not only sex for sale but sex given away, reflecting the increasing promiscuity of women. As the Toronto police chief grumbled during the war, prosecutions of 'houses of ill fame' had declined, but this decrease did not 'necessarily indicate the morality of the city had improved, but merely that sexual intercourse is indulged in other ways in other places beyond the reach of the police.'[96] In 1918 voluntary female patrols were set up in Toronto and Hamilton, and Montreal hired its first policewomen, whose work, as Tamara Myers shows, was hampered in part because the working-class women they patrolled sometimes resented this moral surveillance and intervention.[97] As in Britain, the means for 'women to move into an area of masculine authority' was accomplished by co-optation into police ideology and culture, and the exercising of arbitrary power *over* other women.[98]

The mobilization of morality for war therefore had both coercive and class-specific consequences, whatever the good intentions proclaimed by those doing the moralizing. Some working-class families, embracing the dominant notions of sexual respectability, were disturbed by their daughters' apparent embrace of 'immmorality' during the war and endorsed this coercion. In one court case, 'Katie,' a young woman from small-town Ontario, ran away to Toronto and was charged with vagrancy; she was then sent to the reformatory to be treated for VD. Even after release, she wanted to stay in Toronto, to the consternation of her guardian siblings. Her brother, serving overseas, intervened, writing that he wanted her 'in an institution until he [came] home to look after her and take charge.' The one advantage of the war for some incarcerated women was the difficulty of deportation; when a recent Welsh immigrant working in munitions was sentenced to the same reformatory, she escaped deportation because no ship could be found to take her home.[99]

There is also some evidence that the women and their families who were accused of immorality either resented the notion that their class position made them less respectable or embraced different standards of dress, dating, and sexual and familial mores that challenged the values of middle-class sobriety and sexual purity. Soldiers might also defend their partners against the moral approbation of the legal authorities. When one soldier's wife was charged with performing an illegal abortion on a friend, she was incarcerated, only to give birth herself to an illegitimate child. The reformatory superintendent and the local Children's Aid Society differed over whether the child should be adopted as soon as possible or the woman should be 'compelled to nurse it as long as possible' (probably to atone for her shame), but both agreed she had to admit her 'improper actions' and hope that her husband would 'protect' her when he returned. However, it 'appears from his letters,' said the superintendent with some surprise, 'that he will forgive her.' A younger woman, arrested on street-walking charges and sent to the reformatory, secured even more adamant support from her soldier fiancé, who wrote to the superintendent from a nearby military hospital, begging to see his 'Violet,' at least once a month. 'I looked into this matter and I don't think Violet is so bad as things look, therefore I'm going to stand by her. And I will tell the world I'm going to marry her as soon as she gets out,' he declared.[100] His loyalty, especially given the charge, may have been somewhat unusual, but it does suggest that the moral surveillance of women so keenly embraced by some reformers during the war did not meet with the approval of those women and their families most likely to fall under the gaze of roving morality patrols.

**Mobilizing Women for the Mathers Commission**

In 1918 the Ontario government prepared public circulars encouraging women to leave war-related jobs. Yet, there is little evidence that they were actually disseminated widely – probably because the number of women who had occupied 'men's' jobs during the war had never been large. The greater historical value of these documents lies in their articulation of the prevailing gender ideology, promoted by the state but with a broader resonance as well. Sustaining the image of the patriotic war worker, the circulars declared that many women had worked as a patriotic 'duty' or because they found it 'interesting,' and now some did not want to 'give this up and go back to housekeeping.' The problem was to be solved, however, by employers who appealed to women's patriotic deference to the soldier's need to support his family and reminded women that this work was not their *right*. The publicity left the door open for women 'who needed to work' to continue to do so, but not in the jobs that men claimed as theirs.[101]

The gender conflict that some, like R.B. Bennett, had feared, however, did not preoccupy the state in the aftermath of war as much as the class and ethnic divisions. Tensions – between men and women, within families separated by war – undoubtedly existed in the wake of a perceived blurring of traditional gender roles, and perhaps they were negotiated by the emphatic post-war assertion of an ideology of separate spheres.[102] However, the more visible political fallout from the war was articulated in the conflicts that erupted as part of the country's 'workers' revolt' and the state's anti-ethnic Red Scare. As labour historians have argued, this revolt was already evident during the war, but it erupted with full force in 1919.[103] Before 1919 women had already taken sides. When Borden was asked by military figures to offer some recognition to the pro-war Women's Volunteer Reserve in Winnipeg, he was reassured that 'these were a good class of women' because during the recent civic strike they had acted as strike-breakers, taking over telephone operators' jobs.[104] A year later, women would again be sharply divided during the strike, highlighting divisions in no way limited to the west. In Ontario, there emerged a new political organization of women from trade unions, union auxiliaries, and label leagues, quite self-consciously forming their 'own national council of women' distinct from the NCW, and in the Maritimes previously unorganized women wage-earners in textiles, candy-making, and service work took an active part in the 1919 labour revolt.[105]

This was not the historical version of war that many feminists had carefully crafted. Nellie McClung's *Next of Kin* and the NCW's *Women's Century* claimed that war had created a new sisterhood, drawing women together, erasing artificial differences of wealth and status.[106] Yet evidence suggests otherwise. The women who testified before the federal Mathers Royal Commission on Industrial Relations in 1918 and 1919 were more concerned with a 'living wage' than moral regeneration; they spoke of the material struggles of homemakers who could not support their families on soldiers' pensions, of rising food prices, and of women's marginal wages. Working-class children, testified Calgarian Mary Corse, were forced into early work, denied an education, let alone the 'better things in life, like music.' 'If I go to the corner with a tin cup and beg for some bread for my children, I am arrested as a vagrant,' she continued; 'another woman can stand on the corner with her furs, boots and corsage bouquet and collect nickels for the veteran ... and she is commended for her petty little scheme. Those are inequalities.'[107]

As a reflection of working-class views, this historical source also is problematic, since the hearings attracted the politicized, vocal, and socialist-minded women. Nonetheless, their angry indictment of capitalism and their passionate commitment to social transformation indicate how the war crisis might accentuate class differences or speed the radicalization of some women. The one middle-class reformer who testified, Rose Henderson, provided a symbol of political change. A well-educated probation officer with the Montreal Juvenile Court, Henderson declared in *Women's Century* in 1918 that labour and capital should seek a rapprochement for the good of humanity, but by the time she testified in 1919, Henderson had cast her lot with working-class and socialist organizations, perhaps losing her job because of these allegiances. When urged by the Mathers Commission to comment on the alien 'problem,' she responded with the radical quip, 'there is no alien in my vocabulary.' Nor were her other demands mild: 'remove the profiteers ... abolish child labour ... nationalize [medicine]' she declared. 'The real revolutionist' at this moment, she told the commission men, perhaps thinking of her own transformation, 'is the woman.'[108]

Rose Henderson's call to socialist arms has not been the dominant historical view of Canadian women and the First World War. The myth of unity, patriotism, and homogeneity, as Vance points out, was remarkably resilient in the interwar period, an observation that extends to much feminist writing as well. In part, the unfolding myth of the war as an engine of progress and a positive watershed for women was shaped by the inevitable hegemony of those with more power to shape public images, symbols, and consciousness; this patriotic memory of war was certainly actively promoted by some elites in the face of evidence of post-war class conflict.[109] As Veronica Strong-Boag perceptively notes, the post-war political realignment revealed that Canadian society could 'benefit its elite and reward the women as well as the men – though not to the same extent.'[110] At the same time, the positive image of the war was probably integrated into popular consciousness because it offered comfort in the face of loss and, for women, eager anticipation of increasing gender equality and progress.

Critical reappraisals of the war have not upheld this image of progress, especially for women workers – though it is entirely possible that a future generation of feminist historians will challenge *our* definitions of 'progress.' Working-class women experienced not massive shifts in the technology of work, but an acceleration of existing trends, such as the feminization of clerical work. The ideal of a male breadwinner and dependent family persisted in post-war social welfare policy, and both work and family were affected by heightened moral and sexual anxieties unleashed by the war, with working-class women those most often targeted as potential dangers to the sexual status quo. The war also accentuated existing class and ideological tensions among women, stimulating the autonomous political organizing of socialist, labour, and pacifist women. The memory of war for these women was summed up in *The Magpie* by Jeannette, the woman radicalized by the war. 'The soul of the world' she told her friend Craig 'was lost' in the mud of France and it was up to the women to retrieve it. From the 'bitterest depths of her heart' she announced that the world needed to be 'turned upside down,' with the 'pampered daughters' of the rich forced to work for starvation wages: 'My only hope now is that those who are down now may have a chance to get up and enjoy the pleasures of life before the end comes.'[111]

NOTES

1 Betsy Struthers, 'The Bullet Factory,' *Censored Letters* (Oakville: Mosaic Press, 1984).
2 David Carnegie, *The History of Munitions Supply in Canada* (London: Longmans, Green, 1925), 257.
3 This is relayed through interviews in the recent documentary film, *And We Knew How to Dance: Women and World War I*, directed and researched by Maureen Judge (Ottawa: National Film Board of Canada, 1993).
4 Joan Scott, 'Rewriting History,'*in Behind the Lines: Gender and the Two World Wars*, ed. Margaret Higonnet et al. (New Haven, Conn.: Yale University Press, 1987), 23.

5 This complexity, for instance, was evident in the English-language labour press; some papers announced their support for the lofty aims of the war, even if they condemned its method of prosecution, particularly the conscription of men, but not wealth. The majority of the 8,579 internees were Ukrainians. See Peter Melnyck, 'The Internment of Ukrainians in Canada,' and Donald Avery, 'Ethnic and Class Tensions in Canada, 1918–20,' in Frances Swyripa and John H. Thompson, eds, *Loyalties in Conflict: Ukrainians in Canada During the Great War* (Edmonton: Canadian Institute of Ukrainian Studies, 1983), 1, 77–99; Gregory S. Kealey, 'State Repression of Labour and the Left in Canada: 1914–20: The Impact of the First World War,' *Canadian Historical Review* 73, 3 (1992), 281–314. Owing to a lack of access to non-English language sources, I have concentrated more on class than on ethnicity in this chapter, but there is ample evidence that ethnicity and culture were also major dividing points for women – with the best documented being French/English divisions.

6 Vance, *Death So Noble: Memory, Meaning and the First World War* (Vancouver: UBC Press 1997).

7 Francis Early, *A World without War: How U.S. Feminists and Pacifists Resisted World War I* (Syracuse: Syracuse University Press, 1997), 91–2.

8 Nellie McClung, *Next of Kin: Those Who Wait and Wonder* (Toronto: T. Allen, 1917), 62.

9 The poster is reproduced in Desmond Morton and Cheryl Smith, 'Fuel for the Home Fires: The Patriotic Fund, 1914–18,' *The Beaver* 75, 4 (1995), 12–19.

10 Early, *A World without War*. On gender and war see also Cynthia Enloe, *Does Khaki Become You? The Militarisation of Women's Lives* (London: Pluto Press, 1983).

11 *Women's Century* (hereafter *WC*) August 1916.

12 *Globe and Mail*, 28 February 1918.

13 *Industrial Banner* (hereafter *IB*), 26 November 1915; 17 September 1915.

14 Interviews with Margaret Hand, Martha Davidson, and Jake Foran, in Daphne Read, ed., *The Great War and Canadian Society: An Oral History* (Toronto: New Hogtown Press, 1978), 217, 188, 213.

15 Parlby's concern was that a younger generation, less interested in public service than in simple rebellion, did not understand what to do with their 'new freedom.' C.B. Robertson, 'The Challenge of Freedom,' *Chatelaine*, November 1929, 10; for similar concerns, see A.N. Plumptre, 'What Shall We Do with "Our" Flappers?' *Maclean's*, 1 June 1922, 64–6.

16 *Globe and Mail*, 13 November 1928. Both R.B. Bennett and Arthur Meighen loaned (and lost) money to the company for this nationalist endeavour. See Peter Morris, *Embattled Shadows: A History of Canadian Cinema, 1895–*

*1939* (Montreal: McGill-Queen's University Press, 1978), 72. My thanks to
Cathy Yager for these references.

17 Salverson, *Viking Heart* (New York, 1923). Even still, as Jonathan Vance
points out in *Death So Noble*, her sacrifice helped to underscore the image
of a new nation in which the immigrant son was one with the native-born
son.

18 MacLennan, *Barometer Rising* (Toronto: McClelland and Stewart, 1958).

19 Durkin wrote *The Magpie* in New York City in the bohemian 1920s, of
course, which may explain why these characters appeared so unconventional (Toronto: University of Toronto Press, 1974).

20 J.G. Sime, 'Munitions!' in *Sister Women* (London, 1919); reprinted in
Sandra Campbell and Lorraine McMullen, eds, *New Women: Short Stories
by Canadian Women, 1900–1919* (Ottawa: University of Ottawa Press, 1991),
332. As Campbell points out, Sime's more candid and 'liberal' views on
sexuality distinguished her from other middle-class feminist writers at the
time.

21 I. Andrews, *Economic Effects of the War on Women and Children in Great
Britain* (New York: Oxford University Press, 1923), 174.

22 Anne Anderson Perry, 'Is Women's Suffrage a Fizzle?' *Maclean's*, 1 February 1928, 5–7.

23 Over the last thirty years, historical writing has reflected the wider concerns of Canadian feminist enquiry. Authors first explored wage labour
and politics, drawing on both Marxist and feminist analyses, proceeded to
questions of social welfare, and have alluded more recently to culture or
enquiries into wartime moral regulation, though studies stressing ethnicity
and race are less prevalent. For one of the first reinterpretations of the war
see Ceta Ramkhalawansingh, 'Women during the Great War,' in Janice
Acton et al., eds, *Women at Work: Ontario, 1880–1930* (Toronto: Women's
Press, 1974), 261–309. On politics, see Carol Bacchi, *Liberation Deferred? The
Ideas of the English-Canadian Suffragists* (Toronto: University of Toronto
Press, 1983). For a different view that stresses the importance of the war
for women's suffrage, see John Herd Thompson, *The Harvests of War: The
Prairie West, 1914–18* (Toronto: McClelland and Stewart, 1978). In later
works pacifism and socialist women have been explored: Barbara Roberts,
*A Reconstructed World: A Feminist Biography of Gertrude Richardson* (Montreal: McGill-Queen's University Press, 1996); Thomas Socknat, *Witness
against War: Pacifism in Canada, 1900–45* (Toronto: University of Toronto
Press, 1987); Linda Kealey, *Enlisting Women for the Cause: Women, Labour
and the Left in Canada, 1890–1920* (Toronto: University of Toronto Press,
1998). Social welfare has been examined by Margaret McCallum, 'Assis-

tance to Veterans and their Dependants, Steps on the Way to an Administrative State,' in Wesley Pue and Barry Wright, eds, *Canadian Perspectives on Law and Society: Issues in Legal History* (Ottawa: Carleton University Press, 1988), 157–77; Nancy Christie, *Engendering the State: Family, Work, and Welfare in Canada* (Toronto: University of Toronto Press, 2000), chap. 2. Regulation has been analysed by Tamara Myers, 'Women Patrolling Women: A Patrol Woman in Montreal in the 1910s,' *Journal of the Canadian Historical Association* 4 (1993), 229–45.

24  The claim on the part of many patriotic women that they had abandoned the suffrage cause for the duration was not entirely true. Some pro-war suffragists like the NEFU did halt their open campaigning, but their pens did not stop for a minute, and every column, speech, and recruiting opportunity they could, they reminded men that they were now proving their loyalty to the state – a clear plea for the vote.

25  Robert Craig Brown, *Robert Laird Borden: A Biography*, Vol. 2, *1914–37* (Toronto: Macmillan, 1980), 100.

26  Cleverdon, *The Women's Suffrage Movement in Canada* (Toronto: University of Toronto Press, 1974), 7. For quotes see Rose Henderson in *WC*, Jan. 1919.

27  Bacchi, '*Liberation Deferred?*'; Brian Tennyson, 'Premier Hearst, the War and Votes for Women,' *Ontario History* 57, 3 (1965), 115–21.

28  Ramkhalawansingh, 'Women During the Great War,' 74, 261; Veronica Strong-Boag, *The New Day Recalled: Lives of Girls and Women in English Canada, 1919–39* (Toronto: Copp Clark, 1988).

29  This number does not make sense in comparison with numbers given by the Trades and Labour Branch of the Ontario government, Enid Price's study of Montreal discussed below, or even the *Canadian Annual Review*.

30  Canada, Imperial Munitions Board, *Women in the Production of Munitions in Canada* (Ottawa: Imperial Munitions Board, 1916).

31  For this argument relating to Britain, see Deborah Thom, *Nice Girls and Rude Girls: Women Workers in World War I* (London: I.B. Tauris, 1998), 87–90.

32  Feminist iconography has drawn on images of women's non-traditional work, such as that of the later Rosie the Riveter. Another example is the poster (showing an Asian woman driving a tractor) that I prepared with Kate McPherson for the book, Bettina Bradbury et al., eds, *Teaching Women's History, Challenges and Solutions* (Edmonton: University of Athabasca Press, 1995).

33  Archives of Ontario (AO) Dept of Labour Records, RG 7, Box 1, file 7-12-0-28, 'Employment Bureaux.'

34  AO, RG 7, Box 1, 7-12-0-10, letter of 'Women's Department' to Mrs Plumptre, 27 June 1918.

35 *Canadian Annual Review of Public Affairs, 1916* (Toronto: Annual Review Co., 1914–18).
36 Christine Smillie, 'The Invisible Workforce: Working Women in Saskatchewan from 1905 to World War II,' *Saskatchewan History* 39, 2 (Spring 1986), 62–79.
37 *Labour Gazette*, October 1914, 468; April 1915, 1,296; December 1914, 676; February 1915, 1,181.
38 Ontario. Sessional Papers (SP), Report of the Ontario Commission on Unemployment, 1916, 63.
39 *WC*, December 1915.
40 While this measure was portrayed as protective and kind, the British example suggests that welfare supervisors also played a disciplinary role; see Thom, *Nice Girls*.
41 National Archives of Canada (NAC), Joseph Flavelle Papers (FP), MG 30 A16, vol. 11, Mark Irish to Flavelle, 21 January 1918.
42 *Daily Ontario*, 15 October 1918, *Globe and Mail*, 15–16 October, 1918. The press reports indicate that Chinese labourers had been hired at the plant. Despite massive damage, no one was killed.
43 Borden aided their search. NAC, Robert L. Borden Papers (BP), reel 4399, 118744–5, 18 June 1916.
44 AO, RG 7, Box 1, file 7-12-0-23, letter to Premier Hearst, 30 May 1918, from a Goodyear executive also wanting night regulations for his factory relaxed. Dr Riddell, of the Trades and Labour Branch, was not sympathetic.
45 AO, RG 7,Box 1, file 7-12-0-16, 'Hours of Work.' In Toronto, for example, 64 per cent of munitions workers worked forty-five hours or less and 25 per cent worked forty-five to fifty-five hours.
46 For the first charge see NAC, FP, 38, 'Irish, 1918–19,' Report upon Labour Conditions in Winnipeg, 7 March 1917; second quote, 38, 'Mark Irish, 1915–17,' Irish to Flavelle, 18 October 1916.
47 Christie, *Engendering the State*, 87.
48 Ontario, SP, 'Report of the Trades and Labour Branch, 1918,' 12, 9.
49 Ibid., 12–13. Of the Hamilton women 14 per cent were 'leisured,' but it is unclear what that term meant – did they not have a previous job or were they homemakers?
50 Thom, *Nice Girls*, 90.
51 *Labour Gazette*, September 1918, 690.
52 *Kingston British Daily Whig*, 24 August 1918, quoted in Barbara Wilson, ed., *Ontario and the First World War, 1914–18, A Collection of Documents* (Toronto: Champlain Society, 1977), 141–4.
53 Price, 'Changes in the Industrial Occupations of Women in the Environ-

ment of Montreal during the Period of the War, 1914–18,' MA thesis, McGill University, 1919. At most, women constituted 35 per cent of manual workers in these Montreal plants in 1917, but in 1918 about 21 per cent. There was a lot of fluctuation over time in such munitions work. By 1918, at the Women's War Conference, one politician claimed the numbers of women in munitions had been reduced to 5,000, and women spoke of unemployment in some cities.

54 Graham Lowe, 'Women, Work and the Office: The Feminization of Clerical Occupations in Canada, 1901–31,' in Veronica Strong-Boag and Anita Clair Fellman, eds, *Rethinking Canada: The Promise of Women's History* (Toronto: Oxford University Press, 1997), 259.

55 Price, *Changes*, 73.

56 Her work was completed for the Women's Department of the Canadian Reconstruction Association, though also submitted for an MA thesis. It appears that Stephen Leacock was on her examining committee.

57 She added that the society women 'didn't last long.' *And We Knew How to Dance*.

58 *IB* 26 November 1915. In 1917 employees were locked out when they tried to organize. See NAC, RG 27 Strikes and Lockouts Files (SL), vol. 305, file 37.

59 *IB*, 17 Sept 1915.

60 The 1916 Hamilton munitions strike, for example, was kept largely out of the press. On press censorship see Jeffrey Keshen, *Propaganda and Censorship during Canada's Great War* (Edmonton: University of Alberta Press, 1997).

61 They were later referred to Irish, who left no record of his interview with them, though he sometimes did intervene with employers to try to mediate such situations: *Toronto Star*, 27 July 1917. This article was read into *Hansard*, 2 August 1917.

62 Interview with Elaine Nelson, in Read, *The Great War*, 154–6.

63 Myer Siemiatycki, 'Labour Contained: The Defeat of a Rank and File Workers Movement in Canada, 1914–20,' PhD thesis, York University, 1986, chap. 4.

64 *Winnipeg Voice*, 17 August 1917; 15 December 1916. In the latter issue it was also stated that railway men were 'up in arms.'

65 *Labour Gazette*, October 1918, 833.

66 Kealey, *Enlisting Women*, 175. Kealey notes that the number of disputes between 1915 and 1920 was equal to the number of disputes from 1890 to 1914.

67 By 1918 there were a number of telephone operator strikes as men and

women in the public sector organized for the first time. The Vancouver laundry strike was so serious that the local labour council debated having a sympathetic strike to aid the workers. Some women faced charges in court after the car incident. NAC, RG 27 SL, vol. 309, files 158 and 159; vol. 309, file 182.

68  NAC, RG 27, SL, vol. 306, file 59; see also a common front of sugar refinery workers in Victoria, vol. 305, file 21; vol. 310, file 48.

69  Ibid., vol. 308, file 71.

70  Ibid., vol. 308, file 84.

71  AO, RG 7, Box. 1, file 7–12–0–22, 'Organization of Resources Committee.' It was noted in a resolution that since 'Venus Cote had been committed to the penitentiary for wearing male attire,' they would ask the minister of justice to 'institute an inquiry,' and if this was the only offence, the sentence 'should not be imposed when there is a call for women to take the place of men.'

72  Ontario, SP, Trades and Labour Branch Report, 1918. The Ontario government was even willing to use 'delinquent' boys from industrial school who redeemed themselves by becoming 'soldiers of the soil' for a summer.

73  Kechnie, '"This is not a paying job": The Farmerette Movement in Ontario during the Great War,' paper presented at the Canadian Historical Association, Ottawa 1993, 15.

74  The National Council of Women urged the Ontario government to intervene, mediate with the employers for the 'welfare of the women.' After the war, though, the NCW did not support a minimum wage for domestic and farm workers. AO, RG 7, file 7-12-0-9, 'Employment: farm and domestic labour, 1918–19,' Constance Hamilton to Dr Riddell, 20 Sept. 1918.

75  Kechnie, '"This is not a paying job."

76  AO, RG 7, Box 1, file 7-12-0-10. Report of Miss Taylor, 13 September 1918.

77  The war provided fertile conditions for the triumph of prohibition. Thompson, *The Harvests of War*; WC, March 1915.

78  *Canadian Annual Review*, 1915, 331. On recruiting see Paul Maroney, '"The Great Adventure": The Context and Ideology of Recruiting in Ontario, 1914–17,' *Canadian Historical Review* 77, 1 (1996), 95–6.

79  *Canadian Annual Review*, 1915, 332.

80  WC, May 1918.

81  NAC, BP, reel c4417, 137730.

82  On women and peace during the war see Roberts, *A Reconstructed World*.

83  Kealey, *Enlisting Women*, 215.

84 NAC, FP, 38, 'Mark Irish, 1918–19': 'Mrs. Wiseman was the daughter of late Sir William Wiseman,' and Mary Fenton, the widow of a Toronto doctor; Irish to Flavelle, 14 January 1918 and 18 September 1918.

85 WC, August, 1918; April, 1918.

86 Christie, Engendering the State, 66, 73.

87 Hamilton Public Library, microfilm 32, 'The Canadian Patriotic Fund: Its Objects, Methods and Policy,' 2nd ed., 19 May 1916; circular of 15 March 1916. My thanks to Carolyn Gray for lending me these notes on the Patriotic Fund. Nellie McClung, in Next of Kin, also uses the example of a wife 'wasting' CPF funds.

88 IB, 7 December 1917; see also IB, 21 September 1917.

89 W.L. Scott, The Juvenile Court in Law (Ottawa: Canadian Welfare Council, 1941), 56. When the law was later challenged, Scott said that he drafted it during the war after hearing from the Ottawa Childrens Aid Society. NAC, Canadian Council on Social Development Papers, MG 28 I 10, vol. 31, file 151, W.L. Scott to Mr Justice Orde, 6 January 1932.

90 Ontario, Statutes of Ontario, 1914, An Act for the Protection of Neglected and Dependent Children, chap. 231, 2(h). For cases of women prosecuted under such circumstances during the war see AO, RG 20-50, Andrew Mercer Reformatory for Females, case files 4673, 4685.

91 House of Commons Debates, 29 April 1918, 1,704–5.

92 John McLaren, 'Chasing the Social Evil: Moral Fervour and the Evolution of Canada's Prostitution Laws, 1867–1917,' Canadian Journal of Law and Society 1 (1986), 150. See also James Snell, 'The White Life for Two: The Defence of Marriage and Sexual Morality in Canada,' Histoire Sociale / Social History 31 (May 1983), 111–28.

93 On Venereal disease see Jay Cassel, The Secret Plague: Venereal Disease in Canada, 1838–1939 (Toronto: University of Toronto Press, 1987); Suzanne Buckley and J. Dickin McGinnis, 'Venereal Disease and Public Health Reform in Canada,' Canadian Historical Review 63 (1982); WC, March 1918 and Oct. 1918.

94 NAC, FP, 38, 'Irish 1918–19,' Irish to Flavelle, 3 April 1918.

95 WC, October 1918.

96 Quoted in McLaren, 'Chasing the Social Evil,' 151.

97 Myers, 'Women Patrolling Women.'

98 The war was probably more central to the creation of female police in Britain. For two views of British patrols see Lucy Bland, 'In the Name of Protection: The Policy of Women in the First World War,' in Julia Brophy and Carol Smart, eds, Women-in-Law: Explorations in Law, Family

*and Sexuality* (London: Routledge and Kegan Paul, 1985), 23–49; Phillipa Levine, 'Walking the Streets in a Way No Decent Woman Should: Police in World War I,' *Journal of Modern History* 66 (1994), 34–78. On similar war-time 'social hysteria' and moral surveillance in the United States see Mary Odem, *Delinquent Daughters: Protecting and Policing Adolescent Female Sexuality in the United States, 1885–1920* (Chapel Hill: University of North Carolina Press, 1995), 126–7.

99  AO, Mercer case files 4863 and 4672. Her charge was theft, indicating that wages in munitions could not be that good.

100  AO, Mercer case file 4839.

101  AO, RG 7, Box 1, file 7-12-0-11.

102  British writers have explored this issue more fully, referring to the 're-pressed anger' of some returning men, sometimes directed towards women. Whether we can simply extrapolate this theme to Canada without more research is open to question. For two British views see Eric Leed, *No Man's Land Combat and Identity in World War I* (Cambridge: Cambridge University Press, 1979); Susan Kingsley Kent, 'The Politics of Sexual Difference: World War I and the Demise of British Feminism,' *Journal of British Studies* 27 (1988), 232–53.

103  Craig Heron and Myer Siemiatycki, 'The Great War, the State, and Working-Class Canada,' in C. Heron, ed., *The Workers' Revolt in Canada, 1917–1925* (Toronto: University of Toronto Press, 1998), 11–42.

104  NAC, BP, 136863, 5 June 1918.

105  Ontario labour women formed the United Women's Educational Association of Ontario, but there also emerged separate women's Independent Labour parties and a Women's Labour League in Toronto. See James Naylor, *The New Democracy: Challenging the Industrial Order in Industrial Ontario* (Toronto: University of Toronto Press, 1991); and on the Maritimes, Ian McKay and Suzanne Morton, 'The Maritimes: Expanding the Circle of Resistance,' in Heron, *Workers' Revolt*, 57.

106  *WC*, Jan. 1916. This magazine also took up the campaign against labour radicals and the 'red spectre' of Bolshevism; *WC*, February 1918.

107  NAC, Royal Commission on Industrial Relations (Mathers Commission) M1980, Corse testimony, 635, 876.

108  *WC*, August 1918; NAC, Mathers Commission, M6425, Henderson testimony, 4047–57. On Henderson see Kealey, *Enlisting Women*, and on her later years, Joan Sangster, *Dreams of Equality: Women on the Canadian Left, 1920–60* (Toronto: McClelland and Stewart, 1989).

109  Tom Mitchell, 'The Manufacture of Souls of Good Quality: Winnipeg's 1919 National Conference on Canadian Citizenship, English-Canadian

Nationalism and the New Order after the Great War,' *Journal of Canadian Studies* 31, 4 (1996–7), 5–28.

110 Strong-Boag, 'The Roots of Modern Canadian Feminism: The National Council of Women,' in B. Hodgins and R. Page, eds, *Canadian History since Confederation* (Georgetown, Ont.: Irwin Dorsey, 1979), 406.

111 Durkin, *The Magpie*, 99, 167–8.

# 8 Supporting Soldiers' Families: Separation Allowance, Assigned Pay, and the Unexpected

DESMOND MORTON

During the First World War, more than a fifth of the 619,586 men who joined the Canadian Expeditionary Force (CEF) were married. Others left orphaned children, elderly parents, and other dependants.[1] A few left families to rejoin other armies – British, French, Belgian, Serbian, Italian, even Russian – in which they had reserve obligations. Still others slipped back to Germany or the Austro-Hungarian Empire.

In earlier wars, soldiers' families were often among the sad detritus of a campaign: women and children abandoned to the charity of family and friends, or camp followers at the mercy of weather or the fortunes of armies. The nineteenth-century advent of mass citizen armies and a Victorian determination to remedy evils ensured that by 1914, while soldiers' families might suffer, they would not generally be neglected. Morale at the front and civil order behind the lines depended on an adequate response to an obvious need. In Canada, soldiers' families would inspire the largest single charity Canadians had yet created, the Canadian Patriotic Fund (CPF). In a celebratory memoir, some recent papers, and a master's thesis the role of the 'Patriotic' has been explored.[2] The focus on the fund during the First World War obscures the fact that the Canadian state and soldiers themselves were larger sources of financial support to most military families than the CPF. Indeed, the fund and the Militia Department were administrative partners in regulating and informing a system that was always complicated by moral and social assumptions as well as by the vagaries of human behaviour.

By creating a separate and ostensibly private organization to assist in meeting the needs of its soldiers' families, Sir Robert Borden's Conservative government relieved itself of both expense and a sensitive responsibility. Headed by a Conservative MP who professed to speak for the fund's largest donors, the 'Patriotic' exercised a powerful influence on the living standards and regulation of soldiers' families, favouring some over others, disciplining those who deviated from its norms, and shaping the behaviour of women who found themselves, in their husbands' absence, subject to social engineering.

When the government accepted an obligation to offer additional support to a soldier's dependants, who should qualify? A widowed mother was an obvious beneficiary, but what about an elderly and invalid father or a sister of working age who had depended on her brother to save her from the labour market? In peacetime, a soldier was treated as a marginal member of society. How far could that status improve when he risked his life for king and country? What about women the British army already described as 'unmarried wives'? No law compelled a man to support a woman who was neither a faithful wife nor a mother. Was a government that compelled a husband to contribute half his pay for her benefit also obliged to be his agent in protecting his interests and those of his children?

At dawn on 4 August 1914 Canadians found themselves officially at war with Germany. During the three previous days, hundreds of French and Belgian reservists had reported for duty, and a voluntary organization to care for their families had begun to take shape in Montreal's French-speaking community.[3] Within days of the outbreak, concern for soldiers' families became a Canada-wide concern. By war's end in June 1919, 619,636 men and women had been enrolled in the Canadian Expeditionary Force and 425,821 had been sent overseas, far from those who depended on them for income support. Among them were 88,347 married men. Other soldiers were the sole support of elderly parents or younger siblings. The 3,776 widowers included many with dependent children.[4]

In 1914 Canada had inherited some practices and precedents for the problems of soldiers' families, but they were known to only a minority of the few Canadians who had involved themselves with the pre-war militia and Canada's tiny permanent force. During his two weeks of annual camp, a militia private enjoyed 'rations and quarters' – the traditional camp fare of beef stew and fresh bread, a leaky tent and threadbare army blankets – and earned between 50 and 75 cents a day during the camp, depending on his length of service and musketry skill. Permanent-force soldiers earned less, though they could depend on barracks and meals during the winter, while unskilled labouring men experienced high unemployment and short commons. If such soldiers intended to marry, the *King's Regulations and Orders for the Canadian Militia* required him to obtain his commanding officer's permission. The commanding officer ascertained that the soldier was financially able to support a wife, and that 'the woman is a desirable character.'[5] The wife of an approved marriage was included in the 'married roll' and became eligible for married quarters – two or more rooms in barracks, depending on rank, family size, and availability – or a small allowance 'in lieu.'[6] The family was entitled to quarters or the allowance even if the soldier-husband was absent on duty. The regulations restricted the permissible 'married establishment' of a unit to 12 per cent of its total strength until 1914. To encourage 'steadier' old soldiers, the regulations were then changed to allow the inclusion of all senior non-commissioned officers on the 'married roll,' but only 8 per cent of lower ranks.[7]

Until the 1900s civilians administered the militia's stores and finances. 'Departmentalization' began in 1900 with an Army Medical Corps and Army Service Corps. In September 1905 civilian clerks were transferred to a Corps of Military Staff Clerks, composed of non-commissioned officers familiar with regulations and routine. A Canadian Army Pay Corps (CAPC) followed sixteen months later, in ten detachments located wherever permanent force units were stationed. In August 1914 the entire corps consisted of fifteen officers.[8] A peacetime militia unit appointed its own paymaster, often a local bookkeeper or accountant who accepted an honorary commission in return for a few days of preparing the pay list after the annual training camp. Few militia paymasters could easily abandon their civilian careers in 1914; even fewer would bring extensive knowledge of militia regulations. However, Canada's pre-war mobilization plan provided for units to recruit and organize in their home districts: the CAPC would collect and train unit paymasters and pay sergeants, so that when the expeditionary force mustered at Valcartier or Petawawa, pay staff would rejoin their units, ready to exploit their new expertise in military regulations, forms, and jargon. It was not perfect, but no one had a better idea.

Within hours of the British declaration of war, the minister of militia, Colonel Sam Hughes, had scrapped the mobilization plan and despatched telegrams to militia colonels to bring hosts of volunteers to Valcartier, the new militia camp outside Quebec City. Officials struggled to catch up. In further telegrams he explained that soldiers were to be enlisted from 12 August at militia rates of active service pay. Local contingents made their way by rail to Valcartier, where, in an atmosphere of high enthusiasm and administrative chaos, they were formed and reformed into artillery brigades, cavalry regiments, artillery batteries, and, ultimately, seventeen infantry battalions, not to mention the other elements of a standard British-style infantry division. On 22 September the volunteers formally switched from the militia to the Canadian Expeditionary Force (CEF).

Material considerations weighed lightly on most of the men who crowded armouries and recruiting centres in the hot August days. Canada was in the grip of a severe depression, and many volunteers had been unemployed. Seventy per cent were British born, many of them recent arrivals. Joining the CEF, cynics claimed, guaranteed a cheap passage home to England and away from signs warning: 'No English need apply.' Most volunteers, and ideally almost all of them, would have been carefree bachelors, with siblings enough at home to support infirm and indigent parents and other family members. In camp, men with money to spend found clusters of makeshift shops selling food, soft drinks, socks, sweaters, and anything else a soldier might want, short of liquor. A devout prohibitionist, conscious that wives and mothers were worried about the moral health of lonely sons and husbands, Colonel Hughes kept the vast camp dry, though Quebec City's bars and taverns were close at hand for those permitted to go on leave. By 3 September CEF pay scales were set. For a single man, with 'all found,' they were generous. A soldier was also assured that he could assign up to four-fifths of his monthly pay to relatives.[9]

Colonel Hughes's call had included married men. The force badly needed trained and experienced officers and non-commissioned officers, and British-trained veterans to stiffen the ranks. Some officers moved their families to the city to enjoy their last few days together. Hughes, a committed feminist and brother of one of Canada's leading proponents of female suffrage, insisted that any married volunteer must have his wife's written permission to enlist.[10] Before the contingent sailed on 1 October no less than seven officers and 372 other ranks were sent home after a parent or wife protested. Others, to avoid such a humiliating fate, forgot to report their wedded state.[11]

By no means all wives got their husbands back. Mrs Gerald Wharton was stranded in Buffalo on 9 August after a fight with her husband: 'I told him I would be better off without him for I worked most of the time to support my child and I think you will agree that I am better off without him but I do not think that he should go free and me be tied

Table 8.1
The Marital Condition of the CEF

| Status | Married | Single | Widower | Total |
|---|---|---|---|---|
| *Outside Canada* | | | | |
| Officer | 7,375 | 15,353 | 118 | 22,843 |
| N/S | 42 | 2,354 | 15 | 3,643 |
| Other ranks | 80,930 | 314,762 | 3,643 | 399,335 |
| Total | 88,347 | 332,466 | 3,776 | 424,589 |
| *Inside Canada* | | | | |
| Officer | 1,718 | 1,590 | 15 | 3,323 |
| N/S | 5 | 436 | 2 | 443 |
| Other ranks | 36,000 | 153,280 | 2,001 | 191,281 |
| Total | 37,723 | 155,306 | 2,018 | 195,047 |
| *Total* | | | | |
| Officers | 9,093 | 16,940 | 133 | 26,166 |
| N/S | 47 | 2,790 | 17 | 2,854 |
| Other ranks | 116,930 | 468,042 | 5,644 | 590,616 |
| Total | 126,070 | 487,722 | 5,794 | 619,586 |

*Source*: NAC, Duguid Papers, vol. 1.

down to work to keep myself and his child as well as mine.'[12] Mrs Roy Hunter of Kamloops said goodbye to her husband, who ostensibly left to join the First Contingent. Mr Hunter kept on travelling. His wife appealed in vain to the army.[13] Mrs Harry Mortimer also got little satisfaction when she saw a picture of her husband with the Canadian Engineers. She insisted that Harry was thirty-five, had married her in 1907, and had left her with three children, but Harry's brother insisted that the soldier was only twenty-three. 'So what do you expect four people to starve since my husband enlisted' demanded Mrs Mortimer, 'and if I don't get anything out of this I will publish it in the Papers showing where the public money is going to.'[14]

Soldiers and their families were early objects of concern. Hardly had the war begun than prominent citizens in most Canadian communities had met to consider what could be done for them. Confident that the war could last for only a few months, federal, provincial, and many municipal governments, railways, banks, and other major employers promised volunteers that their civilian wages would continue 'for the duration' and their jobs would be available on their return. On 18 August a meeting was formally convened in Ottawa by the governor general, the Duke of Connaught, to revive the Canadian Patriotic Fund, used in previous wars to meet a variety of needs, from pensions and medical treatments to a medal for the War of 1812. This time, as designed by Herbert Ames, Conservative M.P. for Montreal-St-Antoine, wealthy heir of a large manufacturing business, and an amateur social observer, the 'Patriotic' would serve only the needs of soldiers' families. When the war emergency session of Parliament met on 21 August, legislation for the fund was the second order of business. On 25 August the duke became president and Ames the honorary secretary and de facto manager.[15]

The government recognized that it could not lay the whole burden of family support on charity. Two precedents were available: families of permanent force soldiers continued to enjoy quarters and subsistence or the financial equivalent, and the British announced a separation allowance of 15 shillings a week to soldiers' families.[16] On 4 September 1914 the cabinet approved a similar 'separation allowance' (SA) for families of CEF members. At rates ranging from $20.00 for the wife of a private and $25.00 for a sergeant's wife to a maximum of $60.00 a month for a lieutenant colonel's lady, separation allowance would be paid monthly. To avoid overpaying those who continued to collect wages from a peacetime employer, it was stated that other income 'may be deducted.'[17]

By early September, a private's wife was assured of half her husband's pay (if he bothered to assign it), $20.00 in separation allowance, plus whatever the Patriotic Fund might grant her and her children. Though the CPF insisted that its branches were autonomous, its national officers soon agreed on a maximum scale, depending on the number of children, that limited a family to $30.00 a month in eastern Canada and $40.00 a month in the west. The Montreal branch decided that a woman needed $30.00 per month to live, a child from ten to fifteen years needed $7.50, from five to ten, $4.50, and under five only $3.00. A mother with a child in each age group needed $45.00 a month. With $20.00 of separation allowance and no other earnings, she would receive $25.00 per month from the fund (assigned pay would be ignored). A British reservist's wife, with only $5.00 from her husband and British SA of $16.68 for herself and a child, needed $27.90.[18] The benefits might seem meagre to a middle-class family, but a working-class mother who had lived through two years of economic hard times would feel well off. As Private Frank Maheux of the 21st Battalion assured his 'poor Angeline,' it was more than the $22.00 he would have sent home from a logging camp.[19]

Women hold bazaars for war aid, ca. 1914–16 (City of Toronto Archives, Fonds 1244, Item 872)

But what if the money did not come? Across Canada, local Patriotic Fund committees took weeks to organize and even longer to gather funds and distribute them. The Montreal branch, Ames's model for the CPF, accumulated 125 requests by 24 August, but its week-long 'Lightning Campaign' took until mid-September to organize.[20] Meanwhile, months passed without separation allowance cheques. Wives were obliged to fend off landlords, extend their 'tick' at the local grocery store, and drain away their scarce savings.

What had gone wrong? Simply put, Colonel Hughes had derailed the Pay Corps's plan to train wartime staff. When Lieutenant Colonel W.R. Ward, four CAPC officers, and seven military clerks reached Valcartier in late August, they found a military chaos. Without formed units, no one could appoint paymasters, much less begin the documentation on which pay and allowances were based. Once a unit's commanding officer was approved by Hughes, he might find a paymaster – sometimes an officer unfitted for more demanding work – and a staff that reflected the CEF's low level of literacy and bureaucratic experience. Even after units were authorized, their composition kept changing. Soldiers remustered, officers were promoted and demoted, and infantry battalions were switched from eight companies to four companies and back again. Officers ambitious enough to start documentation merely had to do the work over again.

The challenge of arranging assigned pay (AP) or approving SA was too complex for Valcartier. Was it a task for a soldier's unit, for headquarters in Ottawa, or for some authority in between? If a soldier died or deserted, his pay ended, but what if his family continued to receive cheques? Who would recover the public funds? One theme was clear from the flood of administrative directives: a paymaster or commanding officer who authorized an improper payment would pay for it from his own pocket – and worse. All rules encouraged caution. All that Ward and his CAPC officers could manage was to pay all soldiers up to 21 September, the date when they became part of the CEF. When the First Contingent left for England at the end of September, confessed the author of the *Official History*: '[a]ssignments of pay to families or relatives and establishment of claims to separation allowance were matters which in the majority of cases were still unsettled.' Not until December 1914 were SA cheques worth $61,815 put in the mail.[21]

Though Ward implored his novice paymasters to complete documentation during the two-week voyage to England, even with calm weather some of his subordinates proved unequal to the task. 'It is terribly discouraging to me to realize that all the work I have done in the last few months and one's best efforts are defeated by the neglect of other people.'[22] Ward spent his own voyage compiling a set of financial instructions for the CEF, spelling out duties of paymasters, rates of pay, and accounting procedures. This material was rushed into print in England as the first stage of training the pay organization. The work continued in England, initially in clear, pleasant weather, then under the endless, cold, driving rains that marked the CEF's first winter. Attestation papers were barely complete and verified before the Canadians left for France at the end of February 1915. Only then could he withdraw unit pay sergeants for training.[23] Captain C.M. Ingalls, a CAPC officer and twenty-three-year militia veteran, crossed on the *Franconia* to find himself and six clerks in a fourteen-square-foot hut on Salisbury Plain, with the task of creating 33,000 pay accounts for the First Contingent. He insisted on moving to a large attic in Salisbury and finally set up an office in London. There he wrestled with record-keeping for a force that included 287 Smiths, many of them named John. To help, he was sent five officers who knew nothing of accounting and a civilian accountant who, he complained, 'could not and would not interpret military regulations.'[24] By August 1915 the Canadian Pay and Record office in London had grown to 740 personnel with fourteen branches, including distinct Separation Allowance and Assigned Pay branches. Divided that month, the separate Pay and Records offices had grown by September 1916 to a combined strength of 2,841 soldiers and civilians.[25]

Only in 1917 was any of this explained to Canadians. In 1914 Valcartier was described as a model, and no one was allowed to know that the professionals might have handled matters better. The plight of penniless wives and mothers was no fit counterpoint for the national patriotic chorus. Few editors were eager to rain on any parades. Northern Ontario's *Haileyburian* was an exception, praising the Patriotic Fund but denouncing Militia Department red tape. One wife in the Ontario mining community had burned her furniture for heat; another was in an asylum and her four children were scattered.[26] In Cape Breton, the former mayor of Glace Bay made it his patriotic duty to visit soldiers' wives and report their grievances to the Militia Department by collect telegram until he was commanded to stop.[27]

Nor did all the fault lie with the CAPC. John Clovis Martin enlisted as a widower and assigned his pay to another woman. The real Mrs Martin wanted it back. Howard Ferry's mother demanded his support, but it took weeks to locate which battalion Ferry had joined. Wesley Peters left his child with a woman when he joined the First Contingent. 'This man is an Indian,' a CPF investigator scornfully reported, 'and, evidently, he did not know enough to apply for any allowance for his mother.'[28]

Recruiting for a Second Contingent began in October. Early in November, the Militia Department tried to avoid administrative delays by sending an immediate $20 payment whenever a separation card had been received, regardless of rank.[29] Wives entitled to more soon expressed their grievances, but a final settlement of arrears was possible only in January 1915.[30] A flood of correspondence developed over early discharges, changes of address and rank, and proof of identity for foreign-born recruits. 'Do not pay Separation Allowance to wives of Russians,' commanded J.W. Borden, the accountant and paymaster general, 'unless proof of marriage is produced.'[31]

Separation allowance had been launched with a brief order-in-council. It did not stay simple. Acting for an absent Colonel Hughes in October, Sir James Lougheed reported the plight of widows 'whose sons were sole support and went to the front.' His cabinet colleagues dutifully agreed that 'families be considered to include such.' A month's reflection also convinced ministers that, except for pay from the federal or provincial governments, 'other income' should not be deducted.[32] Private employers were unlikely to continue their generosity if it was penalized.

Harried officials who devised the separation allowance had little idea of the complexity of family relations in 1914. Initially, Militia Department officials refused to countenance common-law relationships and demanded documented proof of marriage. Widowers were allowed SA for their children but only if the latter were obviously too young for employment (initially under fourteen for boys and sixteen for girls, raised in 1915 to fifteen and seventeen, respectively) and if they had a defined guardian. Divorce in 1914 was scarce and costly, but separations were more common. Could a soldier apply for SA to meet his support payments? Militia Department lawyers approved – if the payments were court ordered. A widowed mother's sole support must be unmarried – one man might support two parts of a family, but not with SA – and the widow must indeed be solely dependent on the soldier. Receiving support from other siblings disqualified the applicant; a certificate from a clergyman or the local Patriotic Fund committee was required to establish the facts. Anyone collecting a regular salary from federal or provincial governments and all members of the permanent force were denied separation allowance. 'Applications for the allowance from parties who do not come under the above provisions cannot be considered.'[33]

Since the war did not end by Christmas, soldiers considered marriage. Could they then apply for separation allowance? Appalled at the spiralling costs and duration of the conflict, the government's answer would have been a blunt no. SA had been devised for men who were married when they enlisted. But was it wise to do anything to discourage recruiting? Was it fair? Ministers were reminded that 'the sudden call for volunteers' had separated couples who might well have exchanged promises to marry. A new order-in-council allowed marriages for men who applied at the moment of enlistment and who were recommended by their new officer commanding, 'but if not married within twenty days hereafter, the permission [would] be cancelled.'[34]

As the separation allowance system grew more refined, the Militia Department had to define a wife or, in some cases, more than one of them in ways that fitted nine provincial legal systems. In November 1915 officials granting separation allowance were provided with a definition in which the ingenuity of several lawyers was apparent: 'For the purpose of the provision of Separation Allowance, "wife" means the woman who was married to the officer or the soldier in question under the laws of the country in which the marriage was solemnised and who has not been separated from her husband by a judicial decree or "separation from bed or board" or some similar decree parting her from her husband's home and children, but where a wife so separated is entitled either by the agreement or by an order of a competent course to alimony, such wife shall be entitled to the extent of such payments or alimony, to the separation allowance.'[35]

Family support, public or private, was exclusively for women and children. Men could look after themselves. Or could they? Mr and Mrs John Grant of Sault Ste-Marie had two sons at the front. He had been paralysed since 1902; his wife, a nurse, cared for him and supported her family by taking in boarders. On 22 May 1915 she suddenly died, leaving her husband penniless and alone. Surely, claimed the local M.P., this was a case for separation allowance. So it might be, agreed J.W. Borden, but it was August before the Treasury Board soundly concluded: 'that instead of dealing with the individual case it would be preferable to have submitted for consideration a general recommendation dealing with cases of this character.' By then, the problem was theoretical: 'As both Mr. & Mrs. Grant have died of want since this case was submitted to Treasury Board,' J.W. Borden minuted: 'there is no need for an O/C now.'[36]

The Grant tragedy should have been the kind of problem the CPF could solve, and officials like Herbert Ames stressed its flexible generosity. In practice, since the fund gathered contributions raised by its branches and then reimbursed branches for approved expenditures, the CPF's rules were as firm as any government bureaucracy. Its donor base ranged from workers giving a day's pay each month to the multimillionaires who regularly took Montreal and Toronto campaigns 'over the top,' but Ames cheerfully invoked them all to influence government policy in ways he and his colleagues approved.

Assigned pay was an early example. By 'assigning' pay to a beneficiary, a soldier supported his family directly. The British required a pay assignment as a precondition for separation allowance. An intermittent libertarian, Colonel Hughes was not inclined to interfere with a soldier's freedom to spend his pay. Neither was the Department of Justice. Its advisers found no legal authority to interfere with a man's right to dispose of his earnings; a man was surely the best judge of his family's circumstances.[37] Those responsible for the Patriotic Fund saw the issue differently. Soldiers who spent all their pay and left their families to depend entirely on separation allowance and the CPF burdened the fund more than those who accepted their 'manly' responsibility. Not only was such an arrangement inequitable between married soldiers, the fund's own donors would rebel at the cost of keeping a feckless soldier's family in decent circumstances.[38] From England, Colonel Ward added his support: 'a large number of men,' he claimed, 'have never ... made any effort at all to provide for their families ... The main trouble is due to the excessive amount of money the men are receiving. I may say that Lord Kitchener is quite annoyed to think that our men are getting 4/6 a day and separation allowance for their families as against the fighting "Thomas Atkins" who is willing to serve his country in the new Army for 1/ a day.'[39]

After a brief campaign concerted by the newly knighted Sir Herbert Ames, the Patriotic Fund prevailed. On 23 January 1915 an order-in-council commanded that, barring special circumstances argued by the soldier, half the pay of non-commissioned ranks in receipt of separation allowance would be assigned to their dependant as of 1 April.[40] For its part, the CPF agreed not to consider assigned pay in assessing the allowance levels for soldiers' dependants. The fiction that the assignment was purely a soldier's choice would be sustained, and his money would be available to pay down debts or develop a post-war nest egg. The CPF's insistence that a private's wife must now count on her assigned pay, however, hints that the principle was fictitious for the fund, too.

From the outset, the Patriotic Fund administrators worked closely with the Militia Department. Local branches had access to military nominal rolls as an aid in identifying eligible families.[41] While the fund could pay an income supplement to any military dependants it judged to be in need of it, receipt of SA soon became a necessary qualification. The CEF's records were needed to protect the fund against fraudulent claims from families whose breadwinner had been discharged, had deserted the CEF, or had never even joined up. At the same time, the CEF denied any influence on the fund. 'This is a civilian association run by a civilian committee,' Major General Logie, commanding in central Ontario, assured a desperate petitioner, and she must make her own approach, perhaps through the Toronto and York County Patriotic Fund Association.[42]

In Montreal, Miss Helen Reid, director of social work for St John's Ambulance became convenor of the women's auxiliary of the powerful local branch of the CPF. The fund, she insisted, had a 'Third Responsibility.' In addition to raising and spending money on soldiers' families, it must provide advice and practical assistance.[43] Part of that responsibility was her 'black book' of wives who had disgraced the cause. One was Margaret Curran, who left Montreal for Toronto owing rent and without informing the branch. Since Mrs Curran seemed 'a very respectable looking woman,' Martha Fennix, Reid's Toronto counterpart, demanded more details. 'Our further investigation,' Reid reported, 'shows that she left Montreal in the night, owing money to her Landlord, Grocer, Sewing Machine agent, and Gas Company, and in fact to nearly everyone she had had anything to do with.' Even Curran's German mother, who had showed up in Montreal, was astonished by her flit. 'Mrs. Curran cannot be believed,' Reid concluded, 'and should be kept under the most strict supervision, not only on account of her German origin, but on account of her character.'[44]

Handling local enquiries and investigations for the SA administrators was a logical extension of a local committee's oversight of its charges. Support from the fund depended on home visits, initially by male members of the branch donations committee, then increasingly by their wives and daughters. Employing what was unmistakably a means test, they were on the watch for extravagance – a telephone, a piano purchased by instalment, perhaps only a new hat.[45] Fund representatives also investigated reports of adultery, drunkenness, and child abuse and neglect, and their advice was sufficient to suspend or cancel separation allowance, though it was left to the soldier, after receiving the reports, to decide whether to alter his pay assignment.[46]

The CPF was not organized everywhere, nor was it the sole source of advice. The province of Manitoba and some smaller cities insisted on a completely autonomous organization. Outside Montreal, Quebec City, and the Eastern Townships, little organization could be found in Quebec, and business was done informally, sometimes by the deputy minister, Sir Eugène Fiset. The mayor of St-Moïse and Father J.V. Beaulieu combined to persuade Fiset to compel Private Belliveau to support his widowed mother. When the widow Précille Chartrand complained that she had never seen the $45 per month her son had been promised on her behalf when he joined the 22nd Battalion, Fiset personally sent her a claims card for her curé to sign. Lt-Col. Émile Rioux asked 'mon cher Fiset' to send him the cheque he had negotiated for Mme Amédée Gagnon; for otherwise he would never be paid. She lived in the country and could come in and collect. Fiset obliged.[47] When the Hon. A.E.

Kemp, MP for Toronto-East, replaced Hughes as minister in November 1916, he accepted the back-channel influence of A.H. Birmingham, Liberal-Conservative organizer for Ontario. True, Mrs Ellen Johnston had received SA from two of her soldier-sons when a son still at home could support her, but she had sent three boys to the front, Birmingham argued, and she was a faithful member of the Loyal Orange Lodge, as were all her sons. Similar consideration was owed to the widow of a former employee of Kemp's old firm, the Sheet Metal Company.

By the spring of 1915 the pay system seemed to be working for both CEF contingents. By the end of March 1915, Duguid reports, members of the CEF had earned $6,896,290.40 and paid $1,255,372.70 in assignments to families and relatives. Despite the dominance of the British born, $916,154.31, or three-quarters of the money, went back to Canada.[48] New battalions organizing in Canada had the benefit of experience.

Most cases were straightforward enough. Frank Amato joined the 180th Overseas Battalion in October 1916, shortly before it went overseas, leaving his wife, Mary, and five children, age eight years to eighteen months, at 68 Mansfield Avenue in Toronto. His mother Angeline, a widow, had other sons to support her. His colonel signed the application and both AP and SA were established by mid-November.[49] Edith Pearl Carey of Kingston should have had no complaints, since her husband, a former CPR trainman, continued to receive his railway pay after enlistment and she received separation allowance. Yet she was annoyed that because of her CPR income, the CPF cut her off.[50] Other women discovered that army discipline affected them, too. The army took six months to explain to a seventy-year-old British Columbia mother that her son's assigned pay had stopped after a court martial sentenced him to fifteen months' imprisonment with hard labour for being 'drunk on the line of march.' Bleak poverty added to her shame and disgrace.[51] Blanche Cushman pleaded in vain for news of Private Fuisse, a Second Contingent soldier who had 'left me his unmarried wife and baby, 3 months old, and both homeless and penniless ... He has never tried to deny the baby which is a beautiful child and his image a baby girl.'[52]

Serious administrative problems continued for many soldiers' families. In Canada, the CEF continued to expand under the newly promoted and knighted Major General Sir Sam Hughes. His freehand style allowed scores and soon hundreds of colonels to recruit battalions in cities, towns, counties, and districts, sometimes under the aegis of an existing militia regiment but increasingly whenever a veteran politician or business leader claimed the right to test his popularity. In a society as unmilitary as Canada, the approach had its merits, but the price was continued chaos.

Inexperienced colonels gave administration a low priority, reproducing some of the chaos of Valcartier. Recruits spent as much as a year in Canada, often billeted in their own homes and raising issues of why separation allowance should be paid to families that saw a lot of them. A typical battalion, according to a pay official, had 50,000 documents; all should have been checked and most were not. New regulations and last-minute scrambles for recruits meant that many units still left Canada with incomplete records. Men who deserted or who were left behind as sick were easily reported as having gone overseas and months followed before the records were corrected. Confusion was compounded when battalions were broken up to provide reinforcements for units in France.[53]

Lost, incomplete, and confused records victimized families in Canada. Every MP had examples of families left destitute because separation allowances and assigned pay never arrived, claimed E.M. MacDonald, a Liberal MP from Cape Breton: 'How can you expect enthusiasm among the plain people of the country when you have cases like this right under their noses?' As a government member, Herbert Ames downplayed the problem, but, as the leading official of the CPF, he insisted that the CPF was the chief alleviating force and blamed paymasters and soldiers themselves for failing to fill out the necessary forms: 'Where avoidable mistakes occur, as they do occur sometimes, and when it is brought to the attention of one of our branches that a woman is not getting her assigned pay or separation allowance, through some reason not explained, she need not suffer, because the Patriotic Fund will give her all the money she needs until the rectification is made.'[54] 'Don't be a bit backward about going after the Patriotic & get all you can,' Ernest Hamilton commanded from England to his wife, Sara.[55] Another man with two children claimed to have done better from the Toronto & York. Yet how many women would care to argue with Helen Reid or one of her minions?

CEF growth added to the burden – and the importance – of the Patriotic Fund. According to Ames, 30,000 families had benefited from the Patriotic Fund by 1916, and the number had doubled by the summer of that year. Whatever the local evidence, Ames continued to insist that the Fund had a flexibility no government could match. In a favourite illustration, he explained to Parliament in 1916: 'If a millionaire and his coachman enlist as privates in the same regiment, each gets $1.10 a day and the wife of each gets $20 a month. In the case of the millionaire's wife, $20 a month is a mere incident to her; she has no need of it at all. In the case of the coachman's wife, provided she has a family of four or five children, she cannot subsist on $20 a month. Consequently the Patriotic fund comes along and says "How much is needed for you and your children to live decently and comfortably?" The Patriotic Fund brings that $20 up to the sum necessary to enable that family to live as a soldier's family should live.'[56]

He also insisted that the fund was the perfect answer to calls to increase separation allowances. By sparing taxpayers the enormous expense of raising everyone's SA when, by CPF standards, only some families urgently needed more money, the fund delivered a substantial benefit to taxpayers while encouraging Canadians to demonstrate their generosity.[57] Local branches also put pressure on the government to tighten up payments. The CPF soon discovered that militia records could not always be relied upon to keep track of significant numbers of deserters and deadbeats. The secretary of the Brantford branch of the CPF urged that Walter Jackson of the 198th Battalion be sent overseas or released. He had a large family and a sick wife, and 'He has, to our knowledge, served in at least three different Battalions, and we understand has made the boast that he will never go Overseas to fight.'[58] Fund officials urged that separation allowance not be paid until soldiers had definitely left Canada, and on 24 January 1916 the Militia Department agreed. Agnes Georgeson was one of the early victims. Her husband wanted to switch battalions and took poor advice, getting a discharge before he joined the other unit. Immediately, his family lost all support until the new unit left Canada, leaving Mrs Georgeson and her three children to live on air. Since unemployment had driven her husband to enlist, she had no savings. 'I can't rest I am just worried to death thinking about the whole business,' she told her husband's colonel. 'For pity's sake try and help us someway out of the difficulty.'[59] It took three months and a host of letters, all acknowledging the urgent need, before Mrs Georgeson escaped her difficulty. Another change proposed in the summer of 1916 arose when CPF officials noted that an orphan's pension was only $12.00 a month, while the same child could claim SA of $20.00, the same rate as a mother received. The change was contested, since it threatened to subject an officer's child to the same rate as that of a private's offspring.[60]

The CPF helped to aggravate a larger inequality. At the outbreak of war, thousands of militia had been deployed to protect the coasts, canals, and other sites deemed vulnerable to sabotage by Germans, Austrians, or even Fenians. By 1915 Home Defence service was obviously more boring than dangerous and perhaps was no longer necessary, but local voters and contractors helped to persuade the government to keep 9,000 soldiers guarding forts, canal locks, and internment camps. Their families felt the brunt of public disdain as well as financial hardship, but citing its donors' opinions, the Patriotic Fund refused to help. By 1916, as inflation sent prices soaring, military pay was inadequate, whether the man earning it was at Ypres or Esquimalt, but home defence soldiers received lower rates of pay and subsistence allowance, and their families were excluded from any CPF bounty.[61]

Anne Failes, whose husband served on the Welland Canal Force, reported that she paid $10.00 for rent, $10.00 for groceries, $5.00 for gas and fuel, $3.50 for clothes and boots, $2.50 for meat and $2.00 each for milk, school books, and an allowance to her aged parents, leaving nothing for a doctor or medicine if any of her four children became sick. Neither her advocacy nor that of Major General Logie, nor a petition from Mrs A.W. Matsell and six other soldiers' wives in Calgary made any difference.[62] Private W.R. Duke, who guarded German internees at Kapuskasing, might as well have been in France so far as his family in New Liskeard was concerned. He earned $300.00 a year less than a CEF soldier, and his wife had to leave their three children and go to Haileybury to find work. 'Now is it fair,' she asked the prime minister, 'that a Government should place parents in such a position that both had to be away from their home and family and no one to train the children for proper citizens of Canada?'[63] A desperate Katie Dickinson, with five sick children and mounting medical debts, pleaded that her husband be sent overseas: he 'could fill a needy corner at the "Front" if he only had the chance, & then his family could be placed out of reach of want.' She got her wish.[64]

Initially the councils of the Patriotic Fund were divided by arguments over Home Defence families. Halifax, Vancouver, and other communities that supplied most of the troops favoured involvement; large inland cities that supplied the bulk of the funds did not. The big cities prevailed, since, as Ames explained to the minister, 'contributions would dry up immediately' if anything was diverted to families of home-defence troops.[65] Resentment at 'shirkers' dodging German bullets found an echo in CPF advice and the government's response. On the eve of the 1917 election, A.G. McCurdy, the Union candidate in Halifax and Kemp's parliamentary secretary, reported a touching meeting with a woman and her four children who had been turned into the street. The rate had to go up, 'otherwise very many of the wives and families of the home defence men will be subject to poor relief and I hate that and you know how the men will hate it.' A week later, the government finally set pay and allowances for home defence troops at the CEF level.[66] The Patriotic Fund did not revise its policy.

As the war dragged on, complications in the administration of separation allowances grew. In October 1916 in a report to cabinet it was acknowledged that 'quite a large number of soldiers having two wives have come to light.' Most were wives married in England and abandoned when the soldier emigrated to Canada and attracted another mate. Some Canadians took on an extra wife while in Britain. On New Year's Day 1916 Mrs Alex S. Seeley of Manchester demanded that the Militia Department track down her husband, who, she learned, had another wife in Canada. Indeed, she may have suspected it: 'when he married me i asked him if he weren't a married man and he told me that he was not a married man but if he was a married man he would soon do away with her an come back to me in england.' Now she wanted the Militia Department 'to hunt him up and make him support his child.'[67] An 'Old Original' from the 8th Battalion, Corporal Seeley now claimed Mrs V. Seeley of Renfrew, Ontario, as his wife. He himself had been discharged as 'medically unfit (hysteria)' in April 1916.[68]

Unlike the Canadians, the British Army had accepted common-law marriages, and some of the common-sense advantages were apparent when the bigamy issue emerged. While a British soldier could support the wife who supported him when he enlisted, Canadian law required that only the first wife be supported. In most cases, that left the Canadian wife and offspring destitute, since cancellation of her separation allowance also cancelled her 'Patriotic.' Faced with these facts, the cabinet obligingly adopted British practice: PC 2615 redefined a soldier's wife as 'the woman who has been dependent on him for her maintenance, and who has been supported regularly by him, on a bona fide permanent domestic bases for at least two years prior to his enlistment.'[69] The reaction was mixed. Helen Reid and other leading women in the Patriotic Fund administration exploded with indignation: the order 'countenances bigamy, non-support and desertion, and thereby imperils the greatest asset of the state and society – viz the family and the home.' It would turn Canada into a 'happy hunting ground' and worse than a Turkish harem where 'all wives and children were provided for.' Armed with the British precedent and careful wording to meet the requirement of Quebec law, the cabinet was unmoved.[70]

Once enlisted, of course, regulations had made it clear since 1915 that soldiers had no business getting married. Political jealousy helped to make trouble for Sergeant W.H. Sharpe, a former Toronto civic employee, when he married Alma Freed in 1916, more than a year after he had described her as his wife in his enlistment papers. Since she had already borne him a son, PC 2615 helped to guide the official reaction: he had only regularized the status of his 'unmarried wife.'[71] That argument would not help Doris Green, who had married Private W.H. Simpson, an orderly at the Ontario Military Hospital at Orpington in Surrey, and who by 1917 was pregnant. Since there was no question of a pre-war engagement, there was no case for SA. Her indignant brother took advantage of Sir Robert Borden's well-publicized presence in Britain and wrote directly to Canada's prime minister to denounce the injustice: 'The practical outcome seems to be that Canada is to secure marriages and healthy human propagation "on the cheap" as our vernacular has it.' After three years of war, did Canada assume 'that these young soldiers will remain chaste and sterile during the lustiest years of their manhood?' Canada's official response was that soldiers had repeatedly been reminded of the rules and that whatever inducements the men themselves might have offered had utterly no backing from the Canadian authorities.[72]

With thousands of Canadian men spending months and even years in England, marriage was a serious issue. Major General Sir John Wallace Carson, the Montreal mining magnate whom Sir Sam Hughes had appointed as his agent in Britain, deplored saddling Canada with expensive, $20.00-a-month allowances because soft-hearted colonels had yielded to any excuse for marriage. 'There is no doubt at all but that we are being "soaked" with many men that are getting married.' To cure the problem, Carson assigned one of his many surplus colonels, H.A.C. Machin, a future director of the Military Service Act, to put a stop to it.[73]

Sir Sam Hughes's influence in England was undercut in September 1916 after Borden appointed his friend Sir George Perley, Canada's high commissioner in London, to a new portfolio as minister of the overseas military forces of Canada (OMFC). It ended entirely when Sir Edward Kemp replaced him as minister of militia in November. Among the least of Perley's inherited problems was a claim for separation allowance from one of the ministry's chief clerks, W.O.1 G.B. Goodall, a stalwart character who had already earned the Meritorious Service

Medal. After two years of engagement, Goodall had married his be-
trothed only to be denied privileges less respectable soldiers enjoyed.
A gentle spirit with a powerful wife, Perley urged his colleague Sir
Edward Kemp to reconsider the issue. Women like Mrs Goodall or Mrs
Green would be entitled to a widow's pension if their husband died,
and 'in practically every case these English wives will ultimately become residents of Canada and mothers of Canadian children.'[74] In July
Perley's advice became an order-in-council: soldiers overseas could
now marry with a commanding officer's consent and a clergyman's
certificate of good character: 'should there be any suspicion that she is
not "a proper person to receive the allowance," a pay officer would
investigate.'[75]

During 1916 a major component of CEF enlistment was older soldiers
recruited in special battalions for the Canadian Forestry Corps and the
Canadian Railway Troops. Because they worked far from the front lines
and usually qualified for working pay, railway and forestry troops
found almost as little sympathy from the Patriotic Fund as Home
Defence soldiers. The fund's assistant secretary, Philip Morris, insisted
that such troops must include working pay in calculating their AP.
Their family income would thus include both the AP and the SA, and
the fund would have to spend little or nothing on them. The donors, as
usual, would insist on it! J.W. Borden, as paymaster general, hardly
made a strong case for the railway and forestry troops by claiming that
'dependents are sometimes inclined to spend money too freely, thus
leaving the soldier himself without anything on his return home.'[76]

Until 1917 generosity to dependants, if often more theoretical than
real, was crucial to voluntary recruiting. Women had been identified
early as crucial influences on a man's decision to enlist. Lavish claims
for the generosity of the separation allowance and the flexible compas-
sion of the Patriotic Fund helped men to join up with a clear conscience.
Their families would be well cared for. Though the government was
slow to notice, however, voluntary recruiting for CEF infantry had
virtually dried up in the late summer of 1916. By the winter of 1917 the
government came face to face with the dilemma of imposing conscription or reducing its fighting strength on the Western Front. To do so
when Russia was collapsing and the French army had mutinied after
the disastrous offensive on the Chemin des Dames was unthinkable for
Sir Robert Borden. The Military Service Act, introduced in June 1917,
meant that henceforth most CEF volunteers and virtually all conscripts
would be single.

Packaging at the Women's Canadian Club, Ottawa, September 1918 (W.J. Topley, National Archives of Canada, PA800010)

Conscription had another consequence. As the country divided, it grew steadily more difficult for the Patriotic Fund to contemplate serious fundraising. Though Montreal's March 1917 campaign broke all records, it could not be repeated.[77] By 1918, as Morris admitted in his history of the fund, parts of British Columbia were distinctly inhospitable.[78] Earlier oversubscriptions and tight-fisted management meant that a crisis was postponed. Indeed, when the war ended on 11 November 1918, two years earlier than feared, the CPF emerged with an embarrassing surplus.

New ministers in Ottawa and London and a harsher edge to Canada's war effort encouraged tighter control of military manpower and more efficient administration. By the end of 1916 the Separation Allowance and Assigned Pay Branch had grown into an impressive bureaucracy. In January 1916 the branch held 65,100 separation allowance accounts. Growth that year was spectacular: by year-end, the department claimed 231,518 SA and AP accounts. In a single month, when twenty battalions left for overseas, the branch had to add 32,267 accounts.[79] Each AP and

SA account required a ledger page and a monthly cheque to the correct address to recipients who were often semi-literate and who seldom grasped the importance of regimental numbers in military filing systems. Defective systems allowed cheques to keep flowing to families of men who had deserted, perhaps to re-enlist under an assumed name. Others may have been honourably discharged, but a crucial document had been lost.

In March 1917 Major Ingalls, who had developed the Canadian Pay and Records offices in London, returned to Ottawa to oversee the SA and AP Branch, an operation that had grown in a year from 1,000 to 13,500 square feet of space and from 189 to 2,055 ledgers.[80] Ingalls inherited a staff of 494 men and 131 women, working at lower salaries than their counterparts in the nearby Imperial Munitions Board. Among his tasks was recruiting women and urging able-bodied male employees to enlist. Permitted to move his branch to a larger building, he installed time clocks and acquired forty-six cheque-writing machines, six scriptographs to sign them, and two mimeographs to produce forms. In the summer of 1917 he hired ninety-two women to consolidate AP and SA accounts in a single ledger. They needed forty-six days. By the end of the summer, the machinery allowed him to send out 250,000 cheques as fast as the post office could handle them.[81]

Ingalls also found himself blamed for everyone else's negligence, insouciance, and greed, from lazy paymasters to dishonest clients. Soldiers told families of promotions before they were promulgated. Deserted wives claimed separation allowance from Ingalls's branch and husbands disowned them there. It was Ingalls who heard from widows, abandoned after a 'sole support' son insisted on switching his assigned pay to a newly married wife. His office was the target for any of the 10,000 SA or AP beneficiaries in the Ottawa area who dropped in on his branch to demand service. He reported 'the persistent manner in which women write for cheques before they are due.' Until he moved his operation, Ingalls even lacked a private room to meet his visitors.[82] Fed up with investigative delays and inconsistencies, the Militia Department backed the SA Branch with its own Appeals Board and a staff of 'lady investigators.' In February 1917 the cabinet approved the Board of Review, consisting of two experienced lawyers and the CPF's assistant secretary, Philip Morris. The chairman was a Nova Scotia lawyer and veteran, Major J.W. Margeson. Within a year, the new board had reviewed 40,000 files and ruled on 28,000 of them.[83] Investigators, usually from the local CPF branch, tracked down overpayments to families of deserters, checked out 'sole support' claims from widows, and sent a Mrs Diprose to Carleton county jail for six months for pretending to be a Mrs Jones for the sake of her SA.[84] Another investigator, May Morris, played a more positive role in investigating a Toronto widow's claim that one of her soldier-sons was her 'sole support.' The father of H.W. and H.T. Smith was a messenger for the Bank of Commerce when he died in 1914, leaving nothing for his widow and four children. The bank provided a three-year annuity, the widow's two sons enlisted, and each assigned $20.00 to support their mother and her mother. The elder son's request for SA was refused, partly because the Smiths' clergyman did not know that the bank annuity had expired, and partly because the Toronto CPF believed that a fifteen-year-old son should have gone to work to support his mother. May Morris got justice done.[85]

Tightening up was predictably unpopular. T.S. Ewart, a Winnipeg lawyer, complained that Margeson's board had cut off a widow who had lost a son at Ypres because her other son had survived as a prisoner of war. Surely she could write to him, a Militia Department official insisted, and demand a larger assignment.[86] Another Winnipeg law firm considered a message from Ingalls to their client to be 'so grossly impudent and impertinent that it is difficult to reply to it at all.' The client, Mrs Carey, had two sons at the front and her late husband, assumed to be well off, in fact had died penniless. The eldest son, who was expected by the AP Branch to support her, was well known to be an invalid. Ingalls was unrepentant. Mrs Carey needed a certificate from the CPF or a clergyman, like everyone else. With so many improper applicants, 'great care was needed.'[87]

Recovering overpayments to families after death or discharge could be sensitive. Often a death notice failed to reach Ottawa in time to stop the monthly cheques; in other cases, it took months to collect a man's personal effects and to finalize his estate. Reclaiming a few hundred dollars from a widow or a bereaved mother was not easy. Other ranks soon gained an officer's privilege of a full month's pay after death. An order-in-council in February allowed widows to receive their SA and AP as a gratuity until their pension was formally granted.[88] While Ingalls agreed to be judicious about the dead, he was convinced that when families improperly collected SA during a soldier's three months of post-discharge pay, they did it 'with a full knowledge that they were taking money that was not due to them.'[89]

Overpayments helped to justify the first increase in separation allowance since the war began. When surplus battalions were broken up overseas, scores of sergeants lost their stripes and their families lost $5.00 of their separation allowance. Promotions and reversions forced Ingalls's branch to make up underpayments and recover overpayments, often just before the man regained his rank.[90] His answer was to standardize all SA at $25.00, an act approved by the government for December 1917, just before soldiers' wives and mothers exercised the special franchise granted them by the Wartime Elections Act. Continuing inflation justified a second increase, in September 1918, to $30.[91]

A little smugly, Ingalls reported his branch's policy of stopping SA, usually on CPF advice, 'for the reason that the wives of the soldiers have become immoral or something like that.' Whatever most MPs felt, he provoked outrage from R.B. Bennett, a former Alberta Conservative leader and future prime minister: 'By what right do you stop payment because someone tells you that she has become immoral?' shouted Bennett. 'I want to know that!' Ingalls fumbled: he had only acted on instructions; he was new to the job; he had righted some injustices, but 'in the larger part of the cases,' he insisted, the grounds were sound. Bennett was not mollified. When a man assigned $20.00 a month to his wife, did that mean 'that the Government of Canada becomes the censor of her morals?' No, quibbled Ingalls, the assigned pay was never stopped, only the SA. Finally, the committee chairman intervened to rescue him in the name of conventional morality: 'I would not say that the Government becomes the censor of [a wife's] morals. When the soldier goes to the front, he leaves his wife and family, usually, in trust to the Government and the Patriotic Fund. Now if that woman becomes immoral and forgets the care of her children, and becomes a drunkard and those children are likely to starve or run wild, the country owes an obligation to the children as well as the wife.'[92]

Apart from the Patriotic Fund's Helen Reid and her counterparts in other branches, family support issues were largely determined by men. Even Reid, sufficiently powerful to be added to the CPF's national committee at the end of the war, always reported to the Montreal branch through Clarence Smith, a former executive of Ames's family shoe business. If not entirely missing from the record, the beneficiaries of the family support programs are very largely silent. They certainly had grievances. Allowances that may have seemed generous to a working-class family in 1914, steadily lost value when inflation hit in 1916. By the war's end, consumer costs had risen 46 per cent.[93] Even early in the war, the gap between the Department of Labour's cost of living figures and the amount the Patriotic Fund considered sufficient was far

Table 8.2
Cost of Living and Soldiers' Family Benefits, 1915

| Province | Family* | Adjusted** | CPF + SA*** | Difference |
|---|---|---|---|---|
| PEI | $47.06 | $35.81 | $31.20 | −$4.61 |
| NS | 50.94 | 38.44 | 35.00 | −3.44 |
| NB | 51.86 | 38.51 | 35.32 | −3.19 |
| QC | 51.20 | 37.00 | 36.30 | −0.70 |
| ON | 46.97 | 37.92 | 37.22 | −0.70 |
| MB | 58.15 | 48.15 | 43.60 | −4.55 |
| SK | 63.04 | 51.34 | 42.73 | −8.66 |
| AB South | 61.76 | 45.26 | 37.30 | −7.96 |
| AB North | 61.76 | 43.61 | 45.51 | +1.90 |
| BC | 63.00 | 53.45 | 39.79 | −13.66 |

* Cost of living figures for food, fuel, and rent for a family of five.
** Adjusted for missing father.
*** SA of $20.00 plus CPF assistance for a family of five.
Source: NAC, Duguid Papers, vol. 1.

higher in the west than the east, and it grew with inflation (see table 8.2) fund officials argued that eastern donors heavily subsidized the western provinces, and allowances in the west were at least $10.00 higher than in the east, but soldiers' wives in Calgary or Vancouver compared themselves with their neighbours, not with their counterparts in Toronto or Halifax.

'The Patriotic Fund,' as E.W. Nesbitt, M.P., explained, 'is ... looked upon to a great extent as a charity, there is no getting over it,' and its stigma was everywhere, from means tests by middle-class wives and daughters with their own grievance over the wartime dearth of maids and charwomen, to newspaper complaints about alleged extravagance by soldiers' wives.[94] Soldiers might urge their wives to demand their rights from 'The Patriotic,' but little in the socialization of Canadian working-class women gave them the courage or the knowledge to do so.[95] Even separation allowance depended on applications by a husband or son, mediated by a highly fallible bureaucracy that stretched from behind the lines in France through Ottawa to an overstretched postal system.

SA recipients could organize in support of a higher rate, but it was not easy. The Soldiers' Wives Leagues formed during the South African War were now dominated by the wives of senior militia officers with patriotism, not feminism or maternity, on their minds.[96] As part of her 'Third Responsibility,' Helen Reid encouraged groups of wives to meet for lectures on infant care and to practise motherly crafts, but the auspices were not encouraging for grievances.[97] During the war, the National Council of Women recorded several 'Next-of-Kin' Associations for soldiers' wives, but most proved quarrelsome and short lived.

Alberta was a leading example. In Calgary, Jean McWilliam, a pre-war Scottish immigrant and wife of a British reservist, worked as a cleaning woman and police matron to support herself and her two children. She saved enough to buy a boarding house and found the energy to organize a Next-of-Kin Association with help from local socialists. Arguments for higher allowances were mixed with demands for limits on profits, higher taxes for the rich, and equal pensions regardless of rank. She also wanted free vocational education for soldiers' children and internment of unemployed enemy aliens. The Calgary group soon confronted a similar association from Edmonton, organized by officers' wives. When the two organizations struggled for the right to be incorporated by the province, the Edmonton women gained support from Roberta McAdams, a nursing sister with strong Tory credentials, elected by Alberta soldiers overseas. Alberta's *Non-Partisan* upheld the Calgary women as 'a working-class organization with the proletarian outlook' and denounced the Edmontonians as 'ultra-patriots,' but the Edmonton group prospered.[98] It reported 300 members at monthly meetings in 1918–19 and a provincial grant that allowed them to run a home for forty children. Its activities, concludes Linda Kealey, 'were probably more typical of Next-of-Kin Associations.'[99]

Even the wives of ordinary soldiers could not always count on the left. Winnipeg's Women's Labour League was sympathetic but robustly denied official support for higher allowances, since its responsibility was to 'working girls and women' and because contradictory statements suggested that the wives did not 'know their own minds.'[100] On the other hand, Mrs J.C. Kemp seems to have organized her Vancouver's Soldiers' and Sailors' Wives Association by walking the political tightrope, including Sir Charles Hibbert Tupper and Charles Macdonald in her organizing meeting and including jobs as fruit pickers in her program as well as higher allowances, pensions equalization, and demanding immediate conscription to 'help our boys end this war.' In the fall, Mrs Kemp was reported as surviving a split, because her critic, Mrs Fink 'did not offer the suggestion politely.'[101]

By the war's end, Canada's was a seriously stressed country, profoundly divided by class, region, and the raw wound of imposing conscription on Quebec. Most of the lines of fracture were reflected in

Table 8.3
International Rates of Separation Allowance and
CPF, 1918

| Family State | Canada* | Great Britain | Australia | United States |
|---|---|---|---|---|
| Wife | $30.00 | $9.00 | $10.00 | $15.00 |
| Wife and 1 child | 40.00 | 16.00 | 13.00 | 25.00 |
| Wife and 2 child | 43.00 | 21.00 | 16.00 | 32.50 |
| Wife and 3 child | 47.00 | 24.00 | 19.00 | 37.50 |
| 1 child | 25.00 | 7.00 | – | 5.00 |
| 4 children | 30.00 | 25.00 | – | 30.00 |
| Widowed mother | 35.00 | 9.00 | 10.00 | 10.00 |

* Canadian separation allowance: $25.00.
Source: Special Committee on Pensions, 1918, 185.

the families of soldiers and those who had undertaken to care for their needs. Exhausted by his wartime services to the Patriotic Fund, Ames left to join the staff of the new League of Nations, leaving his role in the fund to W.F. Nickle, outspoken Conservative MP for Kingston. Ideally, in the eyes of its managers, the fund would have ended with the war, but its staff and its surplus compelled it to continue social service to families whose soldiers had abandoned them and as reluctant administrators of Ottawa's post-war emergency relief for unemployed veterans.

For a debt-ridden government, the cost of separation allowance became an added reason for the Militia Department to speed the return and demobilization of married soldiers. Some 38,000 women and children returned as 'dependants,' almost all from Great Britain. Soldiers with wives and families in England joined them at Buxton and travelled on 'family ships' to Saint John.[102] Since 4 August 1914 about 20,000 Canadian women had become war widows.[103] Since 1916 their financial fate had rested with a three-member Board of Pension Commissioners, chosen for its immunity to pressure and dedication to strict regulations. The board wrestled with many of the complexities the separation allowance administrators had faced and came to similar conclusions.[104] Like the war itself, Canadian demobilization was completed earlier than most experts and administrators had predicted.[105] By August 1919, 97 per cent of the CEF had returned from overseas.

Neither the war nor its conclusion left happy memories. Thousands of working-class women had come in painful contact with both charity and bureaucracy, and neither experience had been pleasant. If men believed that their families would be fairly treated in their absence overseas, they often returned to find them living in the shabbiest house on the street. Even with helpful neighbours, few women could maintain a farm, and those who tried business sometimes fell foul of the CPF or licensing authorities. Some women, as the CPF boasted, used natural frugality, good luck, a steady income, and the fund's oversight to pay off debts, establish savings, and lay a foundation for a prosperous postwar farm or small business. Others had little to show for years of loneliness, anxiety, and struggle but a semi-stranger with bad habits and painful memories, trying to resume his place at the head of the family. Others discovered premature widowhood and continued dependence on suspicious bureaucrats from the Pension Board.

More valuable, if only potentially, was an accumulation of experience and knowledge about a lot of Canadian families. Enough had been learned about the Patriotic Fund that, when war returned in 1939, its revival seems barely to have been considered. Instead, families subsisted on a more generous version of the separation allowance and appealed, in their crises, to an Ottawa-based board or its local agents, usually from the Canadian Red Cross.[106]

Family life, as usual, continued as well as it could.

## NOTES

This article evolved as part of my preparation for a book, entitled *Fight or Pay*, on the families of Canadian soldiers in the First World War. It reflects contributions from many colleagues and students, including Barbara Wilson, Cheryl Smith, Adrian Lomaga, Tanya Gogan, Ulric Shannon, Jenny Clayton, and Gibran van Ert. However, it also reflects the leadership and example of Craig Brown, my colleague and friend over many years and my inspiration in addressing innumerable questions about Canada and its Great War.

1  National Archives of Canada (NAC), MG 30, A.F. Duguid Papers, statistical records for the Official History of the Canadian Expeditionary Force. Using needle-sorting equipment, Duguid's staff identified 9,093 officers, 47 nursing sisters, and 116,930 other ranks as married members among the 619,586 who served in the CEF in 1914–19.

2  See Philip H. Morris, ed., *The Canadian Patriotic Fund: A Record of Its Activities from 1914 to 1919* (Ottawa: n.p. [1920]); also W.F. Nichols, *Canadian Patriotic Fund: A Record of Its Activities from 1919 to 1924*, 2nd Report (n.p., n.d.).

Articles include Margaret McCallum, 'Assistance to Veterans and Their Dependents: Steps on the Way to the Administrative State,' in W. Wesley Pue and Barry Wright, eds, *Canadian Perspectives on Law and Society: Issues in Legal History* (Ottawa: Carleton University Press, 1988), 157 et seq.; Desmond Morton and Cheryl Smith, '"Fuel for the Home Fires": The Patriotic Fund, 1914–1918,' *Beaver* 74, 4 (1995), 12–19; Charles Humphries, 'Keeping the Home Fires Burning: British Columbia Women and the First World War,' unpublished paper presented to the Canadian Historical Association conference, Charlottetown, 31 May 1992; and David Laurier Bernard, 'Philanthropy vs the Welfare State: Great Britain's and Canada's Response to Military Dependants in the Great War,' Master's thesis, University of Guelph, 4 September 1992.

3 See Desmond Morton, 'Entente Cordiale? La section montréalaise du Fonds patriotique canadien, 1914–1923 : le bénévolat de guerre à Mont-réal,' *Revue d'histoire de l'Amérique française* 53, 2 (1999), 208–11.

4 Statistics have been compiled from charts prepared for A.F. Duguid's unpublished second volume of his *Official History of the Canadian Forces in the Great War: General Series* (Ottawa: King's Printer). See NAC, Duguid Papers, vol. 1.

5 *The King's Regulations and Orders for the Canadian Militia*, 1910 (with amend-ments), 139, s. 832. Officers met a more demanding standard, having to demonstrate that their 'means are such as will enable him to maintain himself and family in a manner befitting his position as an officer'; s. 830 (2). The Canadian regulations were a close-to-literal copy of the British regulations.

6 Married quarters were provided with a ration of coal or wood and marked a Victorian-era advance from an era when a soldier's wife set up house-keeping behind a blanket at the end of her husband's barrack room. See W.D. Otter, *The Guide: A Manual for the Canadian Militia (Infantry)* ... (Toronto: Copp Clark, 1913).

7 Ibid., 140–1; ss. 832–3, 844; *Handbook of the Land Forces of British Dominions,. Colonies and Protectorates (Other than India)*, Part I, *The Dominion of Canada* (London: His Majesty's Stationery Office, 1911), 118–22, 126–31. The Canadian regulations virtually echoed the British model, with changes to reflect the local currency.

8 Canada, *Militia List*, August 1914, 119.

9 CEF rates of pay were higher than for the peacetime militia or the perma-nent corps: a dollar a day for a private, plus ten cents a day of 'field allowance'; a sergeant collected a total of $1.50 a day and a lieutenant, $2.60. Officers collected $150.00 in 'outfit allowance' to buy uniforms and

camp equipment. 'Working Pay' for farriers, cooks, butchers, bakers, wheelers, and other scarce trades ranged from $0.50 to $1.00 a day. On separation allowance and assignments, see Duguid, *Official History*, 57; see PC 2254, 3 September 1914 in appendix, 91, 61–2.

10 James L. Hughes, inspector of schools for Toronto and Colonel Hughes's elder brother, had espoused votes for women, equal pay for women teachers, compulsory cadet training for both sexes, and the principles of the Loyal Orange Lodge since the early 1880s.

11 Duguid, *Official History*, appendix 94, 62. This was the second largest category, after the 5 officers and 2,159 other ranks sent home for medical reasons and ahead of the 13 officers and 269 other ranks who asked to be released. Colonel W.R. Ward, the CEF's chief paymaster, suggested that the large number of subsequent claims for separation allowance grew out of concealment of marriage. NAC, Ward to J.W. Borden, Accountant and Paymaster General, 4 November 1914, RG 24, vol. 1271, HQ 593-2-35.

12 NAC, Mrs Wharton to Militia Department, 5 December 1914, RG 24, vol. 1271, HQ 893-2-35.

13 NAC, Henry T. Denison to Col. A. LeRoy, 12 September 1914; note on memo from OC, 6th Field Company, CE, RG 24, vol. 4656, f. 99–88 vol. 1; Humphries, 'Home Fires,' 7.

14 NAC, Charles E. Roland, Manitoba Patriotic Fund to Militia Department, 26 February 1915; Mrs Harry Mortimer to Officer of Pay, 31 May 1915, RG 24, vol. 1234, HQ 593-1-12.

15 See 'A Bill to Incorporate the Canadian Patriotic Fund' Bill No. 7, Special Session, 21 August 1914. Ames was the author of *The City below the Hill* (Toronto: University of Toronto Press, 1972 [reprint]), and the CPF presented an opportunity to test many of his ideas about reforming the poor.

16 For the importance of the precedent for Canada see NAC, Canadian Patriotic Fund circular 4, C.A. McGrath Papers, vol. 2, 4.

17 NAC, Report of 27 August 1914; PC 2266, 4 September 1914.

18 Canadian Patriotic Fund Circular No. 2, MG 28 I, 5, vol. 1. On British and Allied reservists, see Duguid, *Official History*, 1: 61–2. British SA was based on the number of children. A French reservist received 35 cents per day from France and from the French consul; outside the CPF, Belgian families depended on local charity (see ibid.). The CPF maintained families of British and French reservists on the same basis as CEF families. When Italy joined the Allies, families of Italian reservists received support at a much lower level. See Morris, *Canadian Patriotic Fund*, 7, 29–32, 339.

19 Desmond Morton, 'A Canadian Soldier in the First World War: Sergeant François-Xavier Maheux,' *Canadian Military History* 1, 1–2 (1992), 80;

Morton and Smith, '"Fuel for the Home Fires,"' 15. (As the correspondence reveals, Maheux was not forthcoming with assigned pay until he left Canada in June 1915, and his wife was obliged to use his assignment to pay off his old debts.)

20  See Morton, 'Entente Cordiale?' 218–19.

21  Duguid, *Official History*, appendix 230, 163.

22  NAC, Ward to Borden, 4 November 1914, RG 24, vol. 1271, HQ 593-2-35.

23  NAC, Ward to J.M. Borden, Accountant and Paymaster-General, 4 November 1914, RG 24, vol. 1271, HQ 593-2-35. See also Duguid, *Official History*, Appendix 230, 163.

24  Ingalls testimony in 'Proceedings of the Special Committee on Returned Men, 1917,' in Canada, *Sessional Papers* (Ottawa, 1917) (hereafter 'Returned Men, 1917'), 1125.

25  Duguid, *Official History*, appendix 124, 164.

26  NAC, *Haileyburian*, 30 March 1915, cited in RG 24, vol. 1235, HG 593-1-13.

27  NAC, Memorandum re John C. Douglas, RG 24, vol. 1235, HG 593-1-12.

28  Morton and Smith, 'Fuel for the Home Fires,' 13.

29  NAC, Memorandum, n.d., RG 24, vol. 1343, HQ 593-3-22.

30  Among the complaints was one from the adjutant of the 24th Battalion on behalf of Mrs J.A. Gunn, the wife of his commanding officer. See NAC, Capt. Gerald Furlong to A&PMG, 26 December 1914, RG 24, vol. 1343, HQ 593-3-22.

31  NAC, Borden to Ward, 4 January 1915, RG 24, vol. 1271, HG 593-1-35, vol. 3. See also the Stalker case: Fiset to the British Consul-General at San Francisco, 26 March 1918, vol. 1234, HG 593-1-12.

32  NAC, Report of 7 October 1914 to PC 2553, 10 October 1914.

33  NAC, PC 2266, 4 September 1914, set out the initial terms and rates for separation allowance in a single page. For comparison after three years, see Militia and Defence Regulations Governing Separation Allowance, 1 September 1917, under PC 2375. RG 24, vol. 1252, HG 593-1-82.

34  NAC, PC 193, 28 January 1915.

35  NAC, PC, 2605, 26 November 1915, amending PC 2266, 27 August 1915; cited in Morton and Smith, 'Fuel for the Home Fires,' 15.

36  NAC, J.W. Borden minute to: Treasury Board to General Fiset, 10 August 1915, RG 24, vol. 1234, HG 593-1-12. The order was passed, and in January 1916 James Stevens, paralysed from the waist down, expressed his gratitude for $120 in SA; NAC, Kemp Papers, Stevens to Edward Kemp, 12 January 1916, vol. 34, f. 1198.

37  NAC, E.L. Newcombe to Eugene Fiset, 5 December 1914 and Fiset to

Newcombe, 8 December 1914, citing Article 986 of the Royal Warrant, ss. 144, 145, The Militia Act, RG 24, vol. 1271, HG 593-1-35.

38 NAC, see Ames to Hughes, 18 November 1914, RG 24, vol. 1271, HQ 593-2-35; Hughes to Ames, 4 December 1914; Canadian Patriotic Fund circular no. 2, [October, 1915] MG 28, I, 5, vol. 1.

39 NAC, Ward-Fiset, January 1915, RG 24, vol. 1271, HQ, 593-2-35.

40 Report of 18 January 1915, reflecting British and Patriotic Fund pressure, and PC 1148, 23 January 1915.

41 NAC, John D. Adams, Toronto and York Patriotic Fund Association to OC, Military Police, Exhibition Park, 21 November 1914; S.P. Shantz to Major-General F.L. Lessard, 25 November 1914, RG 24, vol. 4285, 34-1-10, vol. 2.

42 NAC, Major-General Logie to Mrs S.H. Raun, 30 August 1916, RG 35, vol. 4286, 34-1-10, vol. 2.

43 NAC, On Reid, see Morton, 'Entente Cordiale,' 218–19, 223, 226–9; *Women's Century*, 4, 8 (1917); Charlotte Whitton, 'Helen Richmond Young Reid,' *Canadian Welfare*, 17, 3 (1 July 1941), 13.

44 NAC, RG 24 vol. 4285, 34-1-10, vol. 1, Helen R.Y. Reid to Miss Fennix, 27 November 1915.

45 Morton and Smith, 'Fuel for the Home Fires,' 17; Morton, 'Entente Cordiale,' 224–9.

46 Ingalls testimony, 'Returned Men, 1917,' 1162.

47 NAC, Mayor Morin and Fr J.V. Beaulieu to Fiset, 2 December 1916; la veuve Victorin Lussier to Fiset, 24 November 1916; Fiset to Lussier, 29 December 1916; Col. Émile Rioux to Fiset, 15 May 1916; RG 24, vol. 1234, HG 593-1-12.

48 Duguid, *Official History*, 164.

49 See NAC, 862019 Amato, Frank, RG 24, vol. 960, HQ 54-21-23-53.

50 Queen's University Archives, Bradshaw to T.S. Munro, 2 April 1917, Title XI Frontenac County Records, Visitors' Record Cards, 1915–1919, cited in Bernard, 'Philanthropy vs the Welfare State,' 66.

51 NAC, Frank Beard to DOC, MD 11, 28 November 1916; Capt. the Rev. J.H. Hooper to OC 6 Field Company, CE, 9 December 1916, RG 24, vol. 4664, f. 99-1, vol. 2.

52 NAC, Blanche Cushman to Col. W.A. Logie, 14 May 1915, RG 24, vol. 4285, 34-1-10, vol. 1.

53 Ingalls testimony, 'Returned Men, 1917,' 1164. Ingalls cited the 257th Railway Construction Battalion, whose swift mobilization brought its colonel great praise. Troop trains reached Halifax with only half an hour to embark – and 3,300 signatures needed from 1,100 men. The pay official

had to sail to England to get his job done. Its predecessor, the 256th Battalion, embarked without sending in a single card for assigned pay or separation allowance. The Pay Office got the blame for the ensuing delays.

54 E.M. MacDonald, *House of Commons Debates*, 1 February 1917, 383, 383–4.
55 Hamilton Papers (in possession of the author), Hamilton to Sara, 30 October 1917.
56 Canada, *House of Commons Debates*, 29 February 1916, 1256. Ames liked the image enough to repeat it before the Special Committee on Returned Men on 5 April 1917. See 'Returned Men, 1917, 151.
57 See Ames, in Canada, *House of Commons Debates*, 29 February 1916, 1256.
58 NAC, RT. Watt to General Logie, GOC, MD 2, 30 September 1916, RG 24, vol. 4286, 34-1-10 vol. 2.
59 NAC, Agnes Georgeson to Lt-Col. J.W. Warden, 102nd Battalion, 17 March 1916, RG24, vol. 4656, f. 990-88, vol. 3; cited in Humphries, 'Home Fires,' 4–5.
60 NAC, PC 1997, 28 August 1916. For discussion see RG 24, vol. 1234, HG 593-1-12.
61 Mrs Dora Horwood, whose husband had joined the Permanent Force, complained that she had to raise her four children on his $40.00 allotment, while a neighbour got $52.00 to raise three children. Manitoba's Patriotic Fund stated and restated the rules. Manitoba Provincial Archives, P 189, f. 3 Edith Rogers Papers, f. S.D.W.F. Horwood, 1917–1928.
62 NAC, Mrs E.J. Failes to General Logie, 5 June 1917, and memorandum, GOC MD 2 to Militia Council, 28 June 1917; Mrs H.M. Humly to Minister of Militia, 31 January 1917; Petition from seven wives of members of 14 Company, CASC, MT Section, RG 24, vol. 1252, HG 593-1-82.
63 NAC, Mrs W.R. Duke to Borden, n.d. [October 1917] RG 24, vol. 922, HQ 54-21-23-8.
64 NAC, Katie F. Dickinson to Col. J.H. Duff Stewart, 16 July 1916, RG 24, vol. 4652, f. 99–36 v. 1. See Humphries, 'Home Fires,' 8.
65 NAC, Ames to Hughes, 1 December 1914, RG 24, vol. 1271, HQ 593-2-35.
66 NAC, McCurdy to J.W. Borden (A&PMG) 26 September 1917, RG 24, vol. 1252, HG 593-1-82; PC 2850, 5 October 1917, RG 24, f. 1252, HG 593-1-82.
67 NAC, Mrs A.S. Seeley to Canadian Militia Department, 1 January 1916, RG 24, vol. 1234, HG 593-1-12.
68 'Hysteria' was one of the contemporary euphemisms for 'shell shock' or post-traumatic stress. See Desmond Morton, *When Your Number's Up: The Canadian Soldier in the First World War* (Toronto: Random House, 1993), 197–8.

69  NAC, PC 2615, 28 October 1916, RG 24, vol. 1252, HG 593-1-82, vol. 1.
70  NAC, RG 24, 'A protest from Miss Helen Reid and the Montreal Patriotic Fund.' When W.G. Ferguson of Toronto asked whether his 'unmarried wife' of four years, could have separation allowance, not even the fact that the woman's husband was German softened the heart of Militia Department officials. SA could not be granted: C.F. Winter memo to Ferguson to Kemp, 20 February 1917, RG 24, vol. 1252, HG 593-1-82.
71  NAC, Minutes to L.S. Fraser to Lt-Col. C.S. McInnis, 22 August 1916, RG 24, vol. 1235, HG 593-1-12.
72  NAC, Charles S. Green to Sir Robert Borden, 9 May 1917; and Walter I. Gow, Deputy Minister, Overseas Military Forces of Canada to Green, 17 May 1917, RG 24, vol. 1252, HG 593-1-82, vol. 2.
73  NAC, Carson to Hughes, 8 June 1916, RG 9 III ('Carson File'), vol. 178, 6-M-377.
74  NAC, Col. W.R. Ward to Director of Personal Services, 19 July 1917, and accompanying correspondence, and Perley to Kemp, 17 May 1917, RG 24, vol. 1252, HG 593-1-82.
75  NAC, PC 1872, 11 July 1917. See documents in RG 24, vol. 1252, HG 593-1-82.
76  NAC, J.W. Borden to Militia Council, 1 July 1917, and Philip Morris to Secretary, Militia Council, 20 June 1917, RG 24, vol. 1252, HG 593-1-82.
77  Morton, 'Entente Cordiale?' 234–9.
78  'There is reason to believe that the agitation against the voluntary method might be laid at the door of the foreigner, who naturally wished to escape as much of the burden of the war as possible, or of the socialistic official who regarded taxation as the best method of placing the burden upon the hated rich ... The generosity with which they had subscribed during previous years justifies the conclusion that their judgement rather than their loyalty was at fault and that they had yielded too easily to the misleading and perverted arguments of their leaders' (Morris, *Canadian Patriotic Fund*, on British Columbia, 89–106, especially 97).
79  NAC, Borden Papers, Memorandum No. 3 on the work of the Department of Militia and Defence, 56, OC 333, In testimony to the Special Committee on Returned Men in 1917, Major Ingalls claimed that his branch had held 148,049 SA accounts on 31 December 1916 and 170,000 on 30 April 1917. He estimated that half the soldiers had double SA and AP accounts and a third had a triple account (since they could divide their assigned pay). See 'Returned Men, 1917,' 1159.
80  NAC, Borden Papers, Memorandum on the Work of the Department of Militia and Defence, 57–8.

81 NAC, Borden Papers, Memorandum No. 4 respecting the work of the Department of Militia and Defence, 1 January 1917 to 31 December 1917, OC 333, 39157, 24–25; Special Committee on Returned Men, 1917, 1158.

82 'Returned Men, 1917,' 1161.

83 NAC, PC 2501, 13 September 1917. On background, see Margeson testimony, Canada, Parliament, *Proceedings of the Special Committee ... on the Pension Board, the Pension Regulations ... 20 May 1918* (Ottawa, 1918), (hereafter *Special Committee on Pensions*, 1918), 131.

84 'Returned Men, 1917,' 1169–70. See also J.W. Borden to Colonel Ward, 8 May 1917, RG 24, vol. 1252, HG 593-1-82. On 'lady district investigators,' see f. 4323 2D 34-1-133, 2 vols. On Diprose: W.S. Edwards, Assistant Deputy-Minister of Justice, to the Militia Council, 2 April 1918, RG 24, vol. 1234, HG 593-1-12.

85 NAC, May B. Morris to AAG, MD No. 2, 29 November 1918, RG 24, vol. 4286, 34-1-10, vol. 3., 'Investigation of Mrs. Smith.'

86 NAC, Borden Papers, T.S. Ewart to Borden, 19 December 1917, OC 323, 37158.

87 NAC, MacNeil & Beattie to Kemp, 10 March 1917 and Ingalls to A/APMG, 27 March 1917, RG 24, vol. 1235, HG 593-1-12.

88 NAC, PC 508, 24 February 1917, provided rules for payments to cease at death.

89 Ingalls testimony, 'Returned Men, 1917,' 1171.

90 Margeson testimony, *Special Committee on Pensions, 1918*, 180; PC 2375, 23 November 1917.

91 Linda Kealey, *Enlisting Women for the Cause: Women, Labour and the Left in Canada, 1890–1920* (Toronto: University of Toronto Press, 1998), 203.

92 'Returned Men, 1917,' 1158, 1162–3.

93 See *Labour Gazette*, December 1914–19, for estimates of weekly living costs for a family of five. See Kealey, *Enlisting Women*, 203–4.

94 See Nesbitt, *Special Committee on Pensions, 1918*, 131. The organ of the National Council of Women of Canada, chided women for complaining about the CPF effect on domestic labour. See *Women's Century* 4, 2 (1916); Calgary *Herald*, 15 November 1916, and reply, 22 November 1916.

95 See Hamilton Papers, Ernest Hamilton to Mrs Hamilton, n.d.

96 Soldiers' Wives Leagues and other associations for 'Next of Kin' are reported briefly in the yearbooks of the National Council of Women, 1914–15 to 1918–19. SWL branches are described as existing in Montreal, Ottawa, Kingston, Cobalt, Saint John, Saskatoon, and Prince Albert, among other places.

97 Morton, 'Entente Cordiale?' 228.

98 Alberta *Non-Partisan*, 15 March 1918, 6; 10 May 1918, 5.

99 Kealey, *Enlisting Women*, 205–6.

100 *Western Labour News*, 16 August 1918.

101 'Great War Next of Kin Associations,' *The Yearbooks of the National Council of Women of Canada*, 1918–19, 262; Vancouver *Daily World*, 22 March 1917, 8; ibid., 13 Sept. 1917, 14; ibid., 25 October 1917, 9.

102 Many Canadian wives joined husbands in Britain, and no separate count was kept of marriages of 'war brides' overseas. In 1917–18, 17,000 CEF dependants were persuaded to return to Canada, relieving pressure on Britain's food supply and on the eventual military repatriation. Including repatriation after 11 November, a total of 54,500 dependants is comparable to the 65,000 wives and children repatriated to Canada after the Second World War. See Albert Carman, *The Return of the Troops* (Ottawa: King's Printer, 1920), 331–3; Joyce Hibbert, *The War Brides* (Toronto: PMA Books, 1978) 156, Desmond Morton and Glenn Wright, *Winning the Second Battle: Canadian Veterans and the Return to Civilian Life, 1915–1930* (Toronto: University of Toronto Press, 1987), 110.

103 By 1925 there were 20,015 pensions for dependants, the maximum for the war. These included orphans and mothers as well as war widows and their children. See *Canada Year Book*, 1940, 1066.

104 On pensions, see Desmond Morton, 'Resisting the Pension Evil: Bureaucracy, Democracy and Canada's Board of Pension Commissioners, 1916–1933,' *Canadian Historical Review* 68, 2 (1987), 199–224; Morton and Wright, *Winning the Second Battle*, 44–61.

105 Morton and Wright, *Winning the Second Battle*, 112; Carman, *Return of the Troops*, table 1.

106 See C.P. Stacey, *Six Years of War: The Army in Canada, Britain and the Pacific* (Ottawa: Queen's Printer, 1955), 52; J.F. Londerville, *The Pay Services of the Canadian Army Overseas in the War of 1939–45* (Ottawa: Runge Press, 1950) 215–16; Serge Durflinger, 'Verdun during the Second World War,' PhD thesis, McGill University, 1996), 311 ff.; Barry Broadfoot, *Six Years of War: Memories of Canadians at Home and Abroad* (Toronto: Doubleday Canada, 1974), 21–9.

# 9 Ontario and the Great War

ADAM CRERAR

The traditional rendering of Ontario as a province unified by the Great War cannot be dismissed as a mere caricature. 'Rule Brittania' did indeed reverberate in the streets of Woodstock and Berlin in the hours after Britain's declaration of war against Germany. Crowds gathered around newspaper bulletin boards for the latest word from Europe. Male clerks, factory workers, miners, lumbermen, and university students lined up at recruiting offices in search of adventure, the opportunity to serve, and a little money in tight times. Veterans of the ill-fated expedition to relieve Gordon at Khartoum trained volunteers in Southampton's town hall, while in Toronto the cavalry drilled on the snow-dusted exhibition grounds, beneath the eerie scaffolding of idle roller coaster tracks. At railway stations couples embraced fiercely under the muted sounds of brass in the open air. From the pulpit clergymen exhorted men to enlist and comforted the bereaved with thoughts of Christian sacrifice and certain resurrection. Strange new words and the places they evoked – first Ypres, then Passchendaele, later Vimy – entered thoughts and conversations from Copper Cliff to Amherstburg. The newspapers that introduced these words recounted the triumph of individual valour and courage in the mud of France and Flanders as on the football fields of peacetime autumns. At one recruiting rally in Toronto in 1915, 100,000 participants sang 'Abide with Me,' their voices rising from the banks of the Don River in the August air.

At Queen's Park, Tory premier William Hearst and Liberal opposition leader Newton Rowell shelved partisanship on war issues and competed only in their respective pursuit of recruits and donations to war charities. The province sent relief to Belgium and food to the mother country, erected a military hospital in England, and contributed

Tents on the main campus of the University of Toronto (ca. 1914), with an aeroplane overhead; the plane is a Jenny JN4, built at Leaside (City of Toronto Archives, Fonds 1244, Item 752)

to a fund for the acquisition of machine guns. By 1917 only spending for education outstripped the annual provincial allocations for war-related initiatives, which ultimately totalled almost $10 million. But these expenditures were dwarfed by the $51.5 million donated by individual Ontarians, who together contributed about half of the amount raised for the Canadian Patriotic Fund for soldiers and their families and bought roughly half of the war bonds issued by the federal government in 1917 and 1918. Among many others, the Orangemen of North Huron, St Matthew's Anglican Church in Ottawa, and Mrs James Young of Galt each donated a machine gun to the troops. Women, excluded from military service because of prevailing conceptions of their essential weakness, spearheaded wartime benevolent activities and made clothes for those overseas; worry, fear, and frustrated ambition powered a murderous clicking of needles in halls and homes across the province.

At universities, scientists trained pilots, produced antitoxins, and counselled victims of shell shock. In the north, miners unearthed iron for shells, sulphur for explosives, zinc and copper for brass bullet casings, and nickel for steel alloys in shells and armour. Employees on the line at Ontario munitions factories ensured that by the third year of the war Canada was producing one-quarter to one-third of the ammunition and half of the shrapnel used by British forces overseas. The public spirit of wartime self-sacrifice and the desire to put barley and rye to good use led the province to introduce prohibition in 1916. Thereafter at the Gooderham distillery in Toronto workers produced acetone for cordite where once the whisky flowed.

As the war stretched into its second year and the reality of casualties and the emergence of well-paying industrial jobs to produce the goods of war made military service less attractive, recruiting leagues from across the province turned to employers, fraternal orders, athletic clubs, and churches for lists of eligible recruits among their employees and members. Women in Blyth and Seaforth issued white feathers of shame to unenlisted men while wearing badges that taunted recipients to 'Knit or Fight.' In Berlin, groups of twenty to thirty soldiers seized potential recruits and 'escorted' them to the city's recruiting office. Far from objecting to these coercive measures, municipal councils from Port Arthur to Parkhill, boards of trade in Ottawa and Chatham, and churches, women's organizations, fraternal societies, business and political clubs, and most of the province's major anglophone newspapers called for government-enforced enlistment months, or even years, before Prime Minister Borden's decision in the spring of 1917 to proceed with conscription.

Professionals and businessmen, aided by their allies in academe, the clergy, and the women's movement, spearheaded the recruiting and conscription campaigns, but the enthusiasm for the war effort was by no means an exclusively middle-class one. Almost four out of every ten Ontario men between the ages of eighteen and forty-five signed up for overseas service before the formal introduction of conscription in October 1917, and many more attempted to enlist only to be turned away for medical reasons. Possibly as many as two-thirds of Toronto men of military age volunteered for service; even if the press gang tactics of recruiters made some of these attempts less than truly voluntary, such a figure nevertheless indicates a remarkable degree of social mobilization for war in the city even prior to the introduction of state compulsion. Furthermore, the vast majority of soldiers were clerks and factory workers, most of whom judged that the Trades and Labour Congress was right in 1915 to characterize the war as 'the mighty endeavour to secure early and final victory for the cause of freedom and democracy' and to oppose, two years later, active resistance to conscription over the objections of more radical western delegates. In the federal election held in December 1917 to confirm Borden's new Union Government and its policy of conscription, Ontario voters handed the prime minister's candidates seventy-eight of the eighty-two seats at stake. By the time church bells, fire sirens, and factory whistles signalled news of the armistice in November 1918, Ontarians in uniform totalled approximately 240,000 men and women – almost 9 per cent of the population – and over 68,000 of them had been killed or wounded. Communities across the province raised civic memorials to remember the dead and monumental hospitals to care for the blasted minds and bodies of the living.[1]

In the great narratives of the Canadian experience on the home front during the Great War – of French-English battles over conscription, Maritime and western resentment at Ottawa's allocation of wartime resources, and conflicts between labour and capital – Ontario stands as the mainstay of a generally conservative anglophone patriotic fervour: the leading source of recruits, industrial hub of the country's war machine, fount of charity, champion of conscription, and heart of the Union Government and the English Canadian war effort. Ontarians' determination to wage a war over lands most of them had never previously imagined, let alone looked upon, is indeed both breathtaking and sobering. But the consensus in the province about the justness of the Allied cause can leave the false impression that Ontarians responded homogeneously to the war, marching in lockstep to the rhythm of a common patriotic tune. In fact, the intensity of people's support for the war, and even their reasons for offering it, varied considerably from group to group, with implications that were anything but predictable. In the heart of British Canada, in the country's most industrialized province, among the most interesting responses to the war emerged outside the parlours of the Imperial Order Daughters of the Empire (IODE) and beyond earshot of the cheering in public squares.

The western world's capacity in the Great War to apply technology and organize manpower to the single purpose of obliterating an enemy makes it easy to regard that conflict as an instance of industrialism gone mad. But wars also require food to thrive: without it hungry soldiers relinquish their weapons and famished civilians topple their governments. Since Britain was a net importer of food in peacetime and was isolated from traditional suppliers in central Europe in war, Canada's pork and wheat arguably contributed as much to the Allied war effort as its shells and bullets. One might not think of Ontario as having been capable of playing an important role in the wartime production of food, but in fact agriculture had remained central to the province's economy and society in the early twentieth century, even as it continued to industrialize and as a majority of its citizens came to live in towns and cities. More Ontarians worked around barns than in factories in 1914; Ontario's first war gift to Britain came not in the form of shells or guns – there were none yet to be given – but of 250,000 pounds of flour.[2]

Ontarians had always romanticized farming in their literature, religion, and politics, but food's strategic significance in war meant that agricultural labour became idealized as a duty akin to military service. 'The farmer at work in the field,' proclaimed Premier Hearst with typical agrarian hyperbole, 'is doing as much in this crisis as the man who goes to the front.' The province accordingly increased the number of agricultural advisers in its country districts, provided a thousand tractors for use at cost, and arranged for seed loans for cash-strapped farmers. Determined to make two blades of grass flourish where one had grown before, the provincial Department of Agriculture papered the Ontario countryside with 100,000 flyers and pamphlets in 1917 alone.[3]

Few Ontarians traded full-time jobs – even with promises of equal pay on the farm – for summers of trudging behind teams and mucking out barns. But for those with flexible summer schedules and the desire to make a little money while serving their country, the idea of farm work held considerable appeal. In 1918, 18,000 to 19,000 high school students – roughly 70 per cent of those enrolled province-wide – signed up as 'Soldiers of the Soil.' In the same year, about 2,400 female teachers and university students and married women, known as 'farmerettes,' picked fruit and vegetables on the Niagara Peninsula in place of Six Nations men drawn to higher-paying jobs in war industries. Their memoirs suggest that many of those involved in the farm work – bent double in berry fields with special badges sewn on sweat-soaked uniforms – found an opportunity for service and sacrifice otherwise denied to them on account of their sex.

Those unwilling to move to the country were encouraged by federal and provincial officials to plant gardens and even raise pigs in an effort to free up food for soldiers and civilians overseas. *Saturday Night* humorist Peter Donovan mocked the notion of urban pig-keeping – he conjured up fur-clad society women with pigs on leashes – but through their cultivation of vacant lots across the province, women's and businessmen's clubs and baseball and bowling teams raised millions of dollars of produce in 1917 and 1918. However, this wartime gardening frenzy indicated more than participants' patriotism; it also reflected town and city dwellers' desire to reduce food costs in a time of high inflation. Among the economizers were the future Group of Seven artists Arthur Lismer and J.E.H. MacDonald, who gardened coopera-tively on the latter's small property in Thornhill. This cultivation pro-vided a degree of household self-sufficiency and inspired one of MacDonald's most memorable paintings – *The Tangled Garden.*

That Ontarians responded so effectively to calls for agricultural mobilization suggests how close to its agrarian origins the province remained in the war years. After all, many town and city dwellers themselves had grown up on farms or were only a generation removed from farm families that remained on the land, so they possessed both the skills and the inclination to make this mobilization possible. Clergy-men and reporters embraced farming and gardening as prompts to family unity, fitness, and the levelling of class barriers; boys in reform schools who agreed to work on beet or flax farms were deemed to be 'cured' as a result of their time in the fields and discharged upon completion of their duties. So, far from seeing the war as promoting the triumph of industrialism, many Ontarians hoped that it would re-awaken urban citizens' appreciation of the value of farming and rural life.[4]

From the start, enthusiasm for the war effort was not as intense in the country as in the city. The *Hamilton Herald* complained as early as September 1914 that Ontario farmers were benefiting from high com-modity prices boosted by wartime conditions, but failing to meet tar-gets for Patriotic Fund contributions. In the years that followed, urban newspapers continued to flag farmers' apparent stinginess towards the war charities, the Victory Loan campaign, and the farmerettes. Farmers' enlistment lagged behind that of the general population as well, and some county councils refused to finance recruiting efforts as substan-tially as did their urban counterparts. When businessmen, professors, clergymen, and labour leaders founded the Central Ontario branch of the Speakers' Patriotic League in March 1915, they did so – according to one of the league's co-founders – because 'in many parts of the country districts they have not yet come to realize that we are at war.'[5]

Farmers' lack of engagement in campaigns to raise money for war charities can be explained in part by their economic circumstances. With their wealth tied up in land, buildings, and animals, most lacked the disposable income upon which the Patriotic Fund and Victory Loan campaigns relied. Furthermore, farming communities' charity came largely in the form of knitted goods and care packages frequently overlooked by the accountants of patriotism. By contrast, the generosity of urban dwellers was inflated by the large contributions of businesses that suffered no shortfall of income in the overheated wartime economy. Moreover, the Patriotic Fund's small allowances to soldiers' families compensated for an *urban* problem – the loss of income following husbands' and fathers' transition from regular employment to military service – and thus had less appeal to farm families, to whom enlistment meant the loss of a pair of male hands. Indeed, clerks and factory workers could leave their employment for military service on the understanding that their families would be supported, at least minimally, by the fund and that in peacetime they could return to their jobs, or ones like them, with few consequences for their future livelihoods. For the unemployed, the option of military pay followed by a return to work in better times was especially appealing. Farmers, on the other hand, wondered whether their properties – their businesses *and* their homes – could survive their absences.[6]

Age, the recording practices of military officials, and ethnicity each contributed to the discrepancy between urban and rural rates of enlistment in Ontario. Soldiers tended to be single and in their twenties, but since most Ontario farm owners inherited their properties and worked the land in families, the vast majority of the latter were married and at least in their thirties. Non-inheriting farm boys of military age who had established themselves in non-farm occupations likely remained connected to their home farms in one way or another, but they were not registered as farmers by recruiting officials. Finally, in a conflict about which British-born Canadians were the most enthusiastic on account of their strong identification with the mother country, rural Ontarians tended to be native born. In 1911 the British born represented one-quarter of the men living in cities and towns with populations of 7,000 or greater and fully 31 per cent of men living in Toronto but just one-tenth of those residing in rural southwestern Ontario.[7]

The separation of farming Ontarians from their urban counterparts was not merely a matter of demography. When E.C. Drury learned of the outbreak of war in the summer of 1914 on his farm north of Barrie, he discussed the news with his wife and then walked out into his fields to read the *Globe* to his hired men around the binder. No one cheered; no band kicked up dust on the local concession road or startled the livestock. Isolated from the parades, rallies, impressments, and general military presence that imbued public life in the streets of the province's towns and cities, farmers remained at a remove from the most frenzied expressions of martial fervour in Ontario and were able to retreat from it to the relative quiet of their farmsteads.[8]

Furthermore, the businessmen and professionals who led the recruiting societies mounted campaigns with a distinctly urban bias. To be sure, calls for young men to fight German barbarism in defence of British liberty and in response to Christian duty could appeal to farm boys and machinists alike. But much recruiting propaganda offered the trials and excitement of war as antidotes to the dangers and boredom of modern urban existence – substitution of athletic soldiering for scrawny clerkdom, the masculine rigours of military life for the pampering of urban middle-class domesticity. Such messages, perhaps popular among male audiences at football and hockey games, had a limited appeal to those in the countryside, who faced no shortage of fresh air, exercise, or proximity to patriarchy.[9]

The principal issue that set the country against the city in Ontario during the war was conscription. Most urban Ontarians, especially those in the middle class, saw the introduction of conscription in 1917 as a long-overdue measure that ensured that overseas troop strengths would be maintained while shirkers received their due at home. But behind the exuberant newspaper headlines and urban rallies in support of the measure there lay a large and inchoate agrarian population opposed to it. Farmers feared that conscription would exacerbate a farm labour shortage that had been building since 1914, owing to mass enlistment, the drying up of immigration, and the emergence of high-paying employment in war industries that drew prospective labourers away from the countryside to the towns and cities in which it was located. Indeed, the average annual cost in wages of a farmhand nearly doubled in the first three years of the war, from $323.00 to $610.00. The acuteness of these conditions in Ontario – in which there was both a concentration of war industry and a high rate of enlistment – accounts in part for why agrarian concerns about conscription were more intense in the province than in any other part of the country. Despite increased labour costs, Ontario farmers' concerns about conscription were not rooted in imminent impoverishment. Wartime demand for food precipitated high commodity prices that helped to offset, if not surpass, rising costs and left most farmers in the province better off in 1917 than at the beginning of the war. Ontario farmers' relative self-sufficiency in food and fuel helped to insulate them from the harshest effects of wartime inflation. Throughout the war farmers continued to drain their fields and settle mortgages, keep levels of acreage under crop and stockholding relatively stable, and run thriving agricultural clubs and Women's Institutes.[10]

But conscription threatened to interfere with the free functioning of the family farm economy by removing sons whose labour was essential to the wood-cutting and repairs, seeding and harvesting, and care for livestock that dominated men's work on the farm. This was true both for sons based permanently at home and for non-inheriting sons. The latter tended to leave their families in stages, departing the farm for schooling and employment but returning periodically to sustain the farm that helped to finance their non-farm ventures and to allow siblings their own opportunities to establish lives elsewhere. It was precisely this reciprocal emigration – which allowed farm families to reconcile the interests of both departing and remaining members – that conscription disrupted by proposing to remove sons from the equation. In the later war years dramatically escalated rhetoric appeared in the farm press about the effects of 'rural depopulation' on country districts, not so much because the rate of farm children's departures was escalating – it was not in any significant way – but because conscription limited farm families' capacity to negotiate those departures.[11]

Although most Ontario Liberal MPs initially voted for the Military Service Act in the early summer of 1917, their support for conscription and Borden's proposal to unite the Conservatives and Liberals in a national wartime government to implement the new policy wavered when they began to hear the reservations of their rural constituents. In the west, the Borden government's disenfranchising, through the Wartime Elections Act, of tens of thousands of immigrants from enemy countries who had been naturalized since 1902 affected people who for the most part had come to Canada when Laurier was prime minister and tended to vote for his party; without their names on the voters' lists, western Liberals flocked to the Union Government. In Ontario, however, those disenfranchised represented a much less significant portion of the electorate. Farmers' anti-conscription attitudes made Liberals' loyalty to their much-loved chief politically viable, a sentiment that scuttled the prospects for general political union among the federal parties in Canada's largest province.

Newton Rowell helped to salvage Borden's plans for Union Government by agreeing to make the jump to Ottawa to serve as the senior Liberal and Ontario minister in the new federal cabinet that was unveiled in October, but the Toronto lawyer's move failed to assuage the concerns of Ontario farmers. The federal election to confirm the new government, called for mid-December, quickly came to be seen as a referendum on conscription. 'Shall Canada continue to take her part in the war, and support the men she has sent to the front?' asked the Orillia *Packet*, in summing up the views of the government's urban middle-class supporters; 'or shall the Dominion quit, and shamefully abandon the brave men who have been battling for civilisation amid the mud and carnage in France and Flanders?' Anti-conscription rallies in rural Ontario in the first days of the campaign led Union Government strategists to fear that Ontario farmers were preparing to embrace the second of the *Packet's* options, so they appointed the great Liberal political organizer and bagman, Clifford Sifton, to spearhead the Ontario campaign. Installed in the less than pastoral setting of Toronto's King Edward Hotel, Sifton developed a two-pronged strategy to win over the support of the province's farmers.

First, Sifton persuaded Borden to announce that the local tribunals enforcing conscription would more adequately acknowledge farmers' need for labour. Then, in a speech to farmers in Dundas three weeks prior to the vote, the minister of militia and defence, General S.C. Mewburn, declared that farmers' sons would be completely exempt from the Military Service Act. Following further anti-conscription rallies by farmers suspecting an election ruse, the government issued on 3 December one order-in-council confirming Mewburn's announcement and a second requiring the appointment of agrarian representatives to tribunals to protect the nation's agricultural interests. A few days later the central appeal judge of the Military Service Act upheld the first of the agricultural exemptions.[12]

The Union Government's remarkable accommodation of farmers' demands was accompanied by vicious attempts to discredit Laurier and the opposition as a group of papist Germanophiles in league with Quebec nationalist and isolationist, Henri Bourassa. Rural Ontarians were primary targets of this propaganda: 'Slander!' asserted a fist-shaking son of the soil on one poster. 'That man is a slanderer who says that the farmers of Ontario will vote with Bourassa, pro-German[s], suppressors of free speech and slackers. Never! They will support Union government.' As events transpired, Union supporters proved to be no strangers to slander. As the Laurier Liberal candidate in Simcoe North, E.C. Drury found himself subjected to virulent attacks: his opponents called the abstaining and liberal-minded candidate a drunk and a member of the Ku Klux Klan and his Methodist wife a Catholic. In Toronto, members of the Great War Veterans' Association roughed up Laurier Liberals in the streets. With the exception of the Brockville *Recorder* and the *London Advertiser*, local dailies sided with the government and inundated readers with Union propaganda. A few days prior to the election, some local weeklies devoted almost a third of their pages to advertising for the Union government and its local candidates. In North Waterloo, the *News Record* and the *Telegraph* failed to publish or even report on any opposing campaign material in the last three and a half weeks of the election.[13]

Given the virulent rhetoric of the Union forces, their support by leading businessmen and professionals, their control of the press, and their one-sided electoral reforms – including the enfranchisement of female relatives of military personnel overseas and the above-mentioned disenfranchisement of 'enemy aliens' – it is hardly startling that the campaign culminated in a huge victory for the government in Ontario. Nor was German- and Franco-Ontarians' support for Laurier a surprise, given their treatment by the government's propaganda machine. What is most remarkable is the relative failure of the Union Government in rural southwestern Ontario, where it won just 50.7 per cent of the vote, compared with 62 per cent province wide.[14]

The meaning of this result is subtle. The government's problems in this region had little effect on the outcome of the election because its solid support among urban and military voters ensured victory in all but a few ridings. Furthermore, not all of those voters who chose non-government candidates were opposed to the war effort or even to the Military Service Act; although Laurier personally rejected conscription, he insisted only that his candidates agree to a referendum on the matter. Also, agrarian scepticism about the government did not extend to eastern Ontario: evidently the proximity of rural anglophone voters to expanding French-Canadian populations made the former more amenable to the anti-French Catholic rhetoric of the Union campaign.[15]

Nevertheless it is significant that despite their exemption of farmers' sons from conscription, shameless smear campaigns against their opponents, manipulation of the ballot, domination of the press, and at least theoretical claim to represent both Liberals and Conservatives, Union candidates captured only a bare majority of voters in the rural southwest. Distanced geographically and emotionally from the public atmosphere of war in the province's towns and cities, the primarily agrarian residents of the rural heartland of the province remained aloof from the promises and threats of the government. The results, incidentally, did not stem from a regional antipathy to the Tories or passion for Laurier. In the preceding federal election in 1911 Conservatives actually won a *greater* proportion of votes in the region than Union men did in 1917 – 51.5 per cent of the total – even though they ran on partisan lines and opposed reciprocal trade with the United States, a policy supported by most of the province's farm leaders.[16]

That urban workers generally did not share farmers' lack of enthusiasm for the war effort suggests that the urban-rural divide proved a more crucial determinant of attitudes to the war in Ontario than the gap between haves and have-nots. Despite grievances that surpassed those of farmers – such as the erosion of wages by wartime inflation, shop-floor speed-ups in the munitions and textile industries, government strike-breaking policies and initiatives against radicals, and the failure of the state to impose more than symbolic profits and income taxes – the Union Government captured the support of almost 60 per cent of urban civil voters in southern Ontario, and almost 70 per cent of those in the Toronto ridings. Independent labour candidates won roughly 2 per cent of the provincial vote and merely 8 per cent of the ballots in the ridings they contested. Moreover, although wartime business-labour conflict peaked in 1918, in that year there were about the same number of disputes as in 1913, which in the industrial south involved only 9,155 people. One might attribute these relatively low figures to government repression, but the federal government's ban on strikes was in place for only the last month of the war, and labour unrest in the workplace and at the ballot box would explode in 1919 despite the government's escalating repression of the labour movement in the months after the armistice. The complicated history of working-class patriotism in Ontario has yet to be fully explored, but it seems clear that most workers, immersed in the province's urban culture of war, chose to support the Union Government and stay on the job rather than derail a national enterprise in which they believed. That many profiteering employers failed to show comparable restraint only intensified the post-war reaction.[17]

Although the Union Government's exemption of farmers' sons from conscription did not win the avid support of Ontario farmers, it did bring a halt to their protests and allow them to begin making preparations for the coming agricultural season, a task in which they were encouraged by furious government rhetoric about the importance of increasing production. But while farmers repaired fences and obtained seed in the early spring of 1918, German forces bore down on Allied positions on the Western Front and made all the talk about food somewhat moot. On 19 April Borden announced that, in the light of the German offensive, the terrible casualties it wrought, and the resultant need to reinforce Canadian troops, the government was giving itself the power to cancel all exemptions, including the one for farmers' sons.[18]

Most farmers were stunned by the government's action. A wave of local and regional protest meetings designed to force a reconsideration of the policy culminated in a mass meeting in Ottawa in mid-May, but to no avail. Borden told the gathering of 5,000 farmers – 3,000 from Ontario and 2,000 from Quebec – that his most 'solemn covenant' was to Canadian men at the front, not to Canadian farmers, and that the very real possibility of defeat in France made it 'to say the least, problematical whether any of this production would be made of service to the Allied nations overseas or to [the] men who [were] holding that line.' In response, the pages of the agrarian press filled with cases of conscripts leaving widowed mothers, 'imbecile' fathers, and lone sisters or baby brothers to fend for themselves on otherwise empty farms. In some regions, potential conscripts moved away from highways and into neighbouring fields and woods, where they lived off the goodwill of the surrounding population.[19]

Prior to May 1918 urban dwellers' criticism of what many of them regarded as their rural counterparts' somewhat lackadaisical commitment to enlistment, war charities, and Victory Bonds had been muted, but with Ontario farmers' rejection of conscription in the Allies' darkest hour, the gloves were off. *Saturday Night's* H.F. Gadsby portrayed the Ottawa protestors as dirty, grass-eating hicks, who smelled of the barnyard and had about as much right to address Parliament as the animals they raised. A number of convictions of anti-conscription farmers accused of violating a federal order prohibiting the expression of anti-war opinions were upheld by the Ontario supreme court, even though the local magistrate in the case had said before the trial that 'a lot of farmers need[ed] to be jailed,' and that he was 'going to put the agitation of the farmers down.' Tory MPP J.A. Currie even mused publicly about his willingness to use machine guns on the protesting farmers. Queen's University political economist O.D. Skelton later remarked to farm leader and author W.C. Good that he was 'astounded by the violence of the anti-farmer sentiment among even educated city people.' As Skelton's comment implies, the sentiment that he describes was by no means universal – the *Toronto Star* even expressed some sympathy for farmers' labour problems – but it was sufficiently widespread to convince tens of thousands of Ontario farmers that the days of their political accommodation with urban Ontario were over.[20]

Most farmers were not pacifists: they genuinely believed in government efforts to increase food production in the interests of the war effort and felt that the conscription of their sons served only to undermine those endeavours. In their remonstrance to Parliament in May, the farmers in Ottawa acknowledged that they were appearing 'at [the] most critical moment of the deadly struggle for the preservation of the liberties of the world.' But how on earth, they asked, could the esteemed members of the Woodstock Bowling Club and the Arts and Letters Club of Toronto raise more food in their spare time than experienced farmers working full time? While the campaigns to provide urban farm labourers worked reasonably well in the limited and controlled work of berry-picking, they did not always provide farmers with labourers who had the expertise – or the stamina – to conduct even general farm work. W.C. Good, a man renowned for his tremendous capacity for hard work, had been 'driven almost to death' by fourteen-hour days in the absence of labour in the fall of 1916. One 'Soldier of the Soil' sent out to Good's Brantford-area farm went AWOL after a day and a half, owing to exhaustion. With farmers struggling to simply maintain levels of production, the Department of Agriculture's tips on increasing them felt impractical and patronizing. The government-supplied tractors remained expensive and insufficiently reliable to be good investments. A few farmers, like Good, even began questioning the benefits of the greater production campaign itself. Why grow more food if the resulting increase in supply only lowered commodity prices? One could work oneself into the ground and be no further ahead.[21]

For protesting Ontario farmers the government's cancellation of exemptions represented a political betrayal. 'Many farmers accept the principle of conscripting single men with a fairly good grace,' remarked one Burlington farmer just after the announcement of the change, ' – but most of them are indignant with the Govt for breaking faith with them after having promised them exemption.' In calling up farmers' sons the government broke a critical election promise within five months of its victory and undermined a production policy that had been encouraging farmers to pull out all the stops until just days before the announcement. In explaining their political impotence, many farmers pointed to the dominance of urban businessmen and professionals at Queen's Park and Parliament Hill and the absence of their own from the corridors of power. Although the pre-war census had declared the province half-rural and half-urban, farmers represented only 18 of 111 provincial MPPs and perhaps as few as 6 MPs from the province. 'Profiteering urban millionaires have been robbing the farmers of their sons, and robbing them of their representation in Parliament, and they will continue to do so,' concluded the agrarian *Weekly Sun*. 'Isn't it time farmers organized politically?'[22]

Those farmers who agreed with the *Sun* increasingly turned for institutional support to the United Farmers of Ontario (UFO), an agrarian organization founded in 1914 to pursue the social, political, and economic interests of the province's farmers. The UFO had the support of most existing farmers' clubs within a few years, but when it became associated with the anti-conscription movement, its membership took off, expanding from 200 clubs and 8,000 members in March 1917 to 615 clubs and 25,000 members by the end of the war. At a convention at Massey Hall in Toronto in early June, 3,000 farmers subscribed $15,000 to fund the creation of a farmers' paper to ensure non-partisan coverage of farm issues along the lines of the Winnipeg-based *Grain Growers' Guide*. By the following month, the Wiarton *Canadian Echo* was describing the North Bruce United Farmers as part of the 'rising of a total wave' of farmers that was creating a 'transition stage' in the province's politics.[23]

The war emergency and farmers' fundamental support for the war constrained agrarian political action for the duration – but not completely. When the Hearst Tories refused to nominate a farmer candidate for a provincial by-election scheduled for 24 October in the riding of Manitoulin and provincial Liberals failed to propose *any* candidate to honour a wartime political truce, the local United Farmers put forward their own man, a Mennonite farmer named Beniah Bowman. The Tories sent Premier Hearst and several heavyweight ministers to Manitoulin, attacked the UFO for causing what they regarded as an unnecessary election, and smeared Bowman as a 'Mennonite Menace' not worthy of 'those priceless privileges which are the heritage of the people of the Anglo-Saxon race'; these privileges were not enumerated, but presumably fair treatment was not among them. Bowman, who ran on a vague platform of 'equality for all,' won the election as the farmer candidate with 54 per cent of the vote, a victory that presaged further UFO successes in Ontario North and Huron North over the next few months.[24]

With the coming of peace, conscription itself ceased to be a central matter in provincial politics. Owing both to local conscription officials' willingness to repeatedly issue short-term agricultural leave to farmers' sons and to the happily abrupt end to the war, relatively few farmers were actually conscripted for overseas service. But the war cast a long shadow over Ontario politics in the year following the armistice. Premier Hearst saw his stature among his fellow Conservatives eroded by his wartime policies of prohibition and fiscal restraint on the publicly owned Hydro-Electric Power Commission, which respectively alienated the less temperate members of his party and his most popular minister, Hydro czar Adam Beck. Lacking the experienced Rowell and in any event badly split between pro- and anti-Union factions, the Liberals failed to offer a coherent alternative. Most important, the agrarian political mobilization for political representation that had been sparked by the conscription issue did not fade. The United Farmers movement doubled in size over the next year and precipitated a grassroots campaign that culminated in the stunning election of forty-five UFO MPPs in the provincial election of October 1919. With the support of eleven Labour MPPs, elected by urban voters similarly looking for a new political order commensurate with the country's wartime sacrifice, the United Farmers formed Canada's first third-party government. The war had been generally popular, yet within a year of the armistice those who had led the war effort in Ontario were in political exile, and the group at the greatest remove from the conflict now occupied Queen's Park. The new premier, so recently vilified as a racist and a drunk, was E.C. Drury.[25]

In 1914 Ontarians' identification with Britain and the empire was considerably less partial and ambivalent than their associations with urban life. Most were – and, more important, saw themselves as – British subjects. In Ottawa, British traditions and influences shaped both the procedures of government and the neo-Gothic architecture of the parliament buildings themselves. Prior to the war Ontario voters consistently rejected proposals for reciprocal trade with the United States out of respect for the imperial connection, and in their efforts to sort out how Canada could best play a role in the Empire, social reformers and intellectuals felled forests of newsprint. Men served in militia units steeped in British military culture and fought for the mother country in the Boer War; women, banned from the troop ships in that conflict, formed branches of the IODE to support the British cause from home.

Soldiers in the trenches, civilians watching, CNE camp, ca. 1914 (City of Toronto Archives, Fonds 1244, Item 966)

Across the province, students struggled to memorize important dates and passages from British history and literature, and from 1899 public school patriotism culminated in the speech-making and cadet parades of Empire Day, held on 23 May before the holiday celebration of Queen Victoria's birthday on the 24th. Postage stamps depicting a map of the world reminded correspondents that Canada's pink mass was part of the greatest empire that had ever been.[26]

Ontarians' fundamental support for the war effort and identification with British culture in the broadest sense can give a misleading impression of the province's cultural homogeneity in the early twentieth century. In fact, when Britain committed Canada to war in 1914, almost one-quarter of Ontarians were not, according to the census conducted in 1911, of Scottish, English, Irish, or Welsh descent. Prior to the conflict these Canadians had been regarded by the majority according to a hierarchy of supposedly racial characteristics that favoured peoples from northern and central Europe as fellow 'nordics'; cast southern and eastern Europeans as problematic citizens who could be assimilated into British-Canadian social and political norms only with considerable effort; and dismissed Blacks, Asians, and Aboriginal peoples as fundamentally incapable of adapting to these norms. Inspired by contemporary theories of nationalism that held racial purity and linguistic uniformity to be prerequisites of national strength, and concerned about the possible erosion of that uniformity by the wave of non-British immigration coming to Canada's shores in the Laurier years, the federal government increasingly limited the entry of visible minorities, and provincial governments – including that of Ontario – restricted the schooling rights of non-anglophones.[27]

The Great War's effects on these relationships were contradictory. On the one hand, the conflict threatened to further isolate minorities within a society whose identity seemed increasingly defined by a war-inspired British-Canadian nationalism. On the other hand, the war provided opportunities for groups previously alienated to demonstrate through their war service their claim to equal citizenship and a place in the main narrative of the Canadian experience. The case of ethnic minorities in the war in Ontario is particularly interesting because, in contrast to the West, where debates about pluralism centred on the assimilation of foreigners, minorities in this province were largely Canadian born. Aboriginal peoples had the greatest claim to original residency, of course, although French communities established on the Detroit River prior to the Conquest actually predated the settlement of the Six Nations on the Grand River following the American Revolution. German-speaking settlers came to Markham township and Waterloo county in the first years of Upper Canada's existence, and most African-Ontarians in 1914 were descended from men and women who had migrated to the province from the United States to escape slavery prior to emancipation in that country's Civil War.[28] Inasmuch as the war has been seen as a coming of age for Canadian nationalism, what did it mean for these Ontarians, whose attachments to their home communities were at least as strong and long-standing as those of their British-Canadian counterparts?

The pre-war understanding between France and Britain in the face of German expansionism in Europe saw no corresponding entente between French and English on the western side of the Atlantic. In Ontario, the Conservative J.W. Whitney government just prior to the war moved, through a policy known as Regulation 17, to limit French-language education in the public schools to the first two primary years, and to allow this limited instruction only in institutions where French was already being taught. As Patrice Dutil effectively illustrates in chapter 5, the effect of the war was to exacerbate this conflict over language in Ontario schools.

But even as the debate over Regulation 17 became a battleground of the war itself, as French Canadians marched in support of francophone education in the streets of Ottawa and provincial minister of education and Orangeman Howard Ferguson condemned the protests as a 'national outrage' that threatened to undermine the foundations of the dominion, there were yet demonstrations of moderation on both sides. Among them were the arguments made in 1917 by two prominent Toronto university professors, C.B. Sissons and George Wrong, for at least some tolerance of French education and the merits of bilingualism. For their part, Franco-Ontarian leaders began to acknowledge the legitimacy of the government's concern that in a primarily anglophone province all children should become fluent in English. Meanwhile, the actual experiences of francophone students varied widely from region to region: in the province's oldest French-Canadian communities, in Essex and Kent, French-language schooling was curtailed by order of the region's Irish Catholic bishop, Michael Fallon, while in northern Ontario French Canadians were so much a part of the region's social fabric and sufficiently removed from provincial opinion leaders in the south that Regulation 17 was ignored in practice. In the end, despite the tensions it exacerbated, the war did not displace long-standing local relationships between the two linguistic communities.[29]

Although Irish Catholics like Bishop Fallon shared with the Anglo-Protestant Orange Order a common desire to limit the influence of French Catholics in Ontario society, their feelings for Great Britain were anything but mutual. Most Irish Catholics resented Britain's colonial policy towards Ireland and might have been expected in 1914 to regard the Union Jack more as symbol of oppression than as an emblem around which to rally in war. Yet despite the British government's execution of Irish nationalists following the Easter uprising of 1916 and the Canadian government's virulent anti-Catholic rhetoric in the federal election of the following year, Irish Catholics shared with Protestants the conviction that the Allied war effort represented a crusade for Christianity and the liberty of Canada. Having reconciled Canadian patriotism with continuing opposition to British policies in their home country, Irish Catholics in Toronto enlisted in greater proportions than Protestants and played a leading role in the city's recruiting and charitable efforts, thus definitively demonstrating their love of country and claim to citizenship on equal terms with their fellow Canadians. The unprecedented support of the Young Men's Christian Association and the Salvation Army for a campaign in 1918 to provide overseas soldiers with Catholic facilities perhaps best indicates the acceptance of this claim by the Protestant majority. Although sectarian tensions would persist in Ontario for decades, especially in rural parts of the province, this final step in Irish Catholics' integration into the social fabric of Toronto – a city once known as the Belfast of North America – marked a step forward in the history of Canadian pluralism.[30]

Unlike Irish Catholics, Blacks in Ontario wholeheartedly embraced both the symbols of British patriotism and the British cause in the war itself. Hamilton newspaper editor George Morton tried to make Canada's minister of militia, Sam Hughes, comprehend the intensity of his people's desire to serve. It was rooted in their love for a country that had been 'their only asylum and place of refuge in the dark days of American slavery,' he contended, a place of 'consecrated soil, dedicated to equality, justice, and freedom ... under the all-embracing and protecting folds of the Union Jack.'[31] Morton's view was an idealized one – many escaped slaves had not, in fact, found equality and justice north of the border and had returned to the United States following the Civil War – but it affirmed his people's British citizenship in the face of those who questioned their humanity and was surely no more idealized than the myths of empire that led White Ontarians to Passchendaele and Amiens.

Despite the pleas of Morton and others, Ontario Blacks from large cities and small towns alike were turned away from recruiting stations by the units in which they aspired to serve. Most Whites, blinded by prejudice and the failure of their moral imaginations, supposed that Blacks lacked the requisite intelligence and character to be soldiers. Others thought that training non-Whites to kill Whites was ill advised, whatever the circumstances: it might start a trend. Most White soldiers could not imagine living with and serving alongside Black men. Even when the Toronto journalist J.R.B. Whitney raised forty men and promised 110 more for an all-Black unit, he was rebuffed by Hughes because no commander in Toronto's military district would take them, and Hughes refused to force integration. Only when the war dragged on and White enlistment began to dry up did the federal government in the late spring of 1916 authorize the formation of a construction battalion of Blacks based in Nova Scotia. Only about 350 Ontario men enlisted in the battalion, possibly in reaction to earlier rebuffs, but more likely because of the general decline in enlistment by this time in the war. Those who joined the battalion were paid the same as Whites conducting similar work and were given their freedom in France, unlike their counterparts in the U.S. army. But Canadian exceptionalism in race relations extended only so far: when a Black sergeant arrested a White enlisted man at a Canadian camp in England a couple of months after the armistice, White Canadian soldiers rioted in protest. Blacks' service did little to challenge local segregation, which persisted in some communities until the 1960s.[32]

While African Canadians' service was discouraged at the start of the war, Aboriginal enlistment was banned outright. The Canadian military justified its policy of racial purity in this instance by casting it as a protective measure: German soldiers would not adhere to the conventions of 'civilized' warfare when they encountered Aboriginals on the battlefield. In contrast to the case of Blacks, however, Canadian officials generally winked at this ban and then scrapped it altogether in December 1915, likely because of the well-known history of Natives acting as military allies of the Crown, which made Aboriginal service in the Canadian Expeditionary Force (CEF) seem feasible and appropriate. A century after the War of 1812, Native leaders recalled the political and economic advantages that had once accrued to their people in wartime alliances.[33]

Aboriginal peoples in Ontario embraced the war effort with great enthusiasm, but in ways that confound simple definitions of discrete 'Native' and 'White' experiences and interests. In the Brock Rangers' Benefit Society, the women of the Six Nations knitted socks as their White counterparts did in nearby Brantford – Canadian men of all backgrounds required dry feet in the trenches – but they also raised money through the sale of beadwork and other traditional crafts and embroidered a regimental flag that incorporated both British military and Iroquoian clan motifs. Some military leaders proposed that Aboriginals be placed into an all-Native battalion organized around Six Nations recruits, but the plan was dashed by opposition from commanders of other battalions around the province who objected to the proposed diversion of recruits from their own units – and, more important, from non-Six Nations Natives who refused to serve in a battalion dominated by Mohawks. These men enlisted in their local units, alongside their non-Aboriginal neighbours, in great numbers. Among the Nawash at Cape Croker, for example, *all* men of the age covered by the Military Service Act – twenty to thirty-four – volunteered.[34]

Aboriginal leaders understandably rejected the view, held by officials at the Department of Indian Affairs, that the exposure of Natives to non-Aboriginal Canadians on the front lines would promote the assimilation of native cultures to a superior Canadian norm, but they were otherwise divided on the implications of military service. The Grand Indian Council of Ontario, the central body of non-Six Nations chiefs in the province, hoped for advances for their people akin to those anticipated by African-Canadian leaders such as Morton and Whitney. 'We as Indians are at a crucial stage of our lives,' argued the council president, F.W. Jacobs, in 1917, 'whilst our young men are at the Front fighting the battles of our Noble King, and our Country, we cannot say that they are fighting for their liberty, freedom and other privileges dear to all nations, for we have none.' By encouraging enlistment and contributions to war charities and accepting the application of conscription to its peoples, the council strove to demonstrate that 'Indians, like all humanity are endowed with the same instincts [and the] same capabilities' as other Canadians. Jacobs enjoined the federal government to give Aboriginals the vote and abolish the treaty system in order to 'liberate' his people and allow them to 'become identified with the peoples of this country and become factors side by side with them in shaping [its] destinies.' As it happened, the council's own policies fell short of Jacobs's ringing appeal to a broader humanity; citing 'a natural dislike of association with negroes on the part of Indians,' it successfully lobbied for the transfer of five natives from a predominantly African-Canadian unit at Windsor in 1917.[35]

The Six Nations Council wanted nothing to do with the Grand Indian Council's rhetoric of liberal emancipation. Its members saw themselves as the spokesmen of a separate nation, and wanted to be called to war as such – as an ally of the British Crown. When the federal government refused to accommodate this request, the council objected to federal efforts to conscript band members and to hive off reserve lands for veterans' farm allotments. When the council raised $1,500.00 for 'patriotic purposes,' it sent the money directly overseas as a gift to the Crown rather than to the Canadian government or to one of the privately managed war charities. The council's attitude did not sit well with all on the reserve: some soldiers saw their military service for Canada as compatible with their aboriginal identities and petitioned the federal government to replace the traditional council with an elective one – to no avail. In fact, the council's position became the ideological rationale for an important post-war Aboriginal association, the Pan-Canadian League of Indians. The league's founder, Fred O. Loft, a Mohawk lieutenant in the CEF, argued that as a result of wartime service natives had 'the right to claim and demand more justice and fair play' – including greater control over band lands and funds *and* the franchise – though not at the expense of abandoning their heritage or their special status as Aboriginals.[36]

Although Loft's league failed to coalesce, it served as a model for future pan-Aboriginal associations. Furthermore the war did promote an unprecedented interaction among Natives from different parts of the province and the country, and wartime relations between Natives and Whites likely gave some among the former a sense of being treated as equals. When the people of Southampton erected a new town hall following the war and dedicated it to those who had served and died in the conflict, for example, they remembered and recognized veterans from the nearby Saugeen band. But such instances of interracial comradeship at personal and local levels proved fleeting, and for Aboriginal integrationists and separationists alike there would be little progress in the years ahead in Native-White relations and little sense of a positive legacy from the first war before the start of the second.[37]

For those non-British Canadians who did not have deep roots in the province, the cultural lenses through which they perceived the war were often calibrated to long-standing disputes and rivalries in their countries of origin. Most Jews in Ontario in 1914 had migrated from Europe since the turn of the century and had profound social, economic, and cultural associations with friends, family, and communities in the Old World. During the war, Canadian Jews' desire to promote the cause of their co-religionists overseas led them to initiate extensive fund-raising campaigns, often run by women, for European relief and for the promotion of Jewish settlements in Palestine. These efforts, which culminated in the founding of the Canadian Jewish Congress in March 1919, created a possible conflict with the majority culture: Canadian Jews had little sympathy for Britain's pogrom-fomenting ally in Russia, especially when Jews had generally thrived in the relatively liberal German and Austro-Hungarian empires. Even so, the Toronto Jewish Council of Women shared in the benevolent work of women across the province and became noted for their initiatives on behalf of the war effort. Furthermore, any potential source of conflict between British-Canadian and Jewish-Canadian agendas was dissipated by the

Balfour Declaration of 1917, which, by committing British support to the creation of a Jewish homeland in Palestine, married the cause of British imperialism in the region to the Zionist hope for a Jewish state. News of the British policy prompted huge rallies of Jews in the streets of Toronto and other Canadian cities and sparked interest among Jews in the CEF about serving in a 5,000–man strong all-Jewish legion under British command in Palestine. Unfortunately, the commonality of interest implied by the Balfour Declaration was not fully manifested in practice: four Toronto men in the group of 300 Canadian Jews who joined the new unit were court-martialled for protesting against the legion's anti-Semitic practices. Although the decisions were later reversed on appeal, they suggest the limited capacity of temporary circumstances, even those as dramatic as the ones emerging in wartime, to dislodge long-term prejudices.[38]

While Jews' aspirations were ultimately compatible with those of British Canadians in the war, the same was not the case for Finnish Canadians. Many Finns had been socialists in their home country and had found nothing in the rough conditions of Ontario's forests, mines, and factories to lead them to abandon their beliefs and vote for the Conservative party. Socialist community halls in places such as Toronto, Copper Cliff, and Port Arthur provided immigrants with social services and a sense of belonging that eased the adjustment to their new society. These beliefs and practices, regarded sceptically by the majority culture in peacetime, became doubly suspect during the war. First, many Ontario Finns opposed Britain's alliance with czarist Russia, the primary impediment to Finnish independence. Then, the successful Russian Revolution in 1917 and Red Finns' attempts to emulate it brought Ontario Finns' socialism into disrepute. When the federal government moved to shut down potentially revolutionary organizations in the last months of the war, the Finnish Socialist Organization of Canada was among them. Although socialist Finns were allowed to reconstitute themselves after the war, their movement had been significantly tainted by the brush of radicalism as a result of the ban, and many Finns thereafter eschewed radical politics in favour of more conservative institutions that sought to win the acceptance of the broader Canadian community.[39]

During the war itself, however, the people most at risk of harassment were of course those whose ethnicity seemed to associate them with the enemy. Germans, Austrians, and Turks might be loyal to king and country, some thought, but to which ones? The federal government quietly encouraged unnaturalized Canadians – those who had not yet become British subjects – from enemy nations to emigrate to the United States, at least for the duration of the war, and obliged those who remained to register with local officials, surrender their firearms, and make regular reports to authorities. Those who threatened the security of the country or lacked the resources to care for themselves were subject to internment.[40]

Prior to the war, few perceived that German Ontarians could be regarded as enemies of Canada. Most, after all, had been born in Ontario and had roots in the province extending back to a time when 'Germany' itself existed only in the feverish dreams of nationalist intellectuals. Furthermore, the pseudo-scientific gradations of the social Darwinists classified Germans as racial cousins of the British and thus worthy of the rights and responsibilities of citizenship in Canada. The fact that King George and Kaiser Wilhelm were, in fact, cousins and that the former was descended from the House of Hanover seemed rather apt.

Almost immediately, however, the circumstances of the war undermined German Canadians' relatively favourable status in Ontario. Accounts, true and false, of German war atrocities – of Germans killing nurses, crucifying soldiers, attacking hospitals, releasing poison gas, and murdering civilians by sinking the *Lusitania* – inflamed anti-German sentiment across the province, in part because many of the victims were Canadian. Wild reports of enemy action in Ontario itself further exacerbated these feelings. On one day the wary residents of New Liskeard spotted a German airship; on another, Parry Sounders caught wind of a German plot to bomb a Canadian Northern train; on a third, the vigilant citizens of Brockville alerted officials with news of planes winging their way from the U.S. border to Ottawa, having misidentified balloons released by Americans in celebration of 100 years of peace with their northern neighbours. Such rumours of improbable German actions were inflamed by the occasional discovery of an actual plot, as when in the summer of 1915 two German Americans were convicted in Detroit for scheming to destroy public buildings and factories across the river in Windsor and Walkerville.[41]

Despite the fact that there is no evidence of any German Canadian having been jailed for subversive activities anywhere in the province throughout the course of the war, it is clear that a growing antipathy towards all things German resulted in a dramatic reduction in the rights and freedoms of German Ontarians. Toronto's city council fired civil servants of German descent and closed the city's German-Canadian social clubs; its Board of Education purged its ranks of enemy alien teachers, forced others to resign who expressed unconventional views of the causes and course of the war, and even fired janitors and groundskeepers of questionable descent. While their Toronto counterparts were ensuring patriotic shrubbery, the Hamilton school board moved in 1915 to force teachers to reveal their citizenship and testify as to their views on the war.

German Ontarians soon found themselves in untenable positions. At the University of Toronto in September 1914 Professor Paul Wilhelm Mueller came under attack for coming to the defence of his sons, students at Harbord Collegiate, who had criticized their principal for making rabidly anti-German speeches at school assemblies. Mueller was hardly a threat to national security. Although, like many German Canadians, he was not officially naturalized, he was no longer a German citizen, was an alumnus of the University of Toronto, and had been resident in Canada for more than twenty years; his rabble-rousing sons were cadets at Harbord Collegiate. But local newspapers, led by the *World* and the *Telegram*, started a campaign to have Mueller and the two other German-born professors at the university dismissed, amid 'rumours' that the men were engaging in espionage. 'If we can't get university professors of British blood,' thundered Tory back-bencher Thomas Hook to the cheers of the North Toronto Conservative Club, 'then let us close the universities.' Well aware of the university's dependence on provincial grants, the board of governors asked the professors to take full paid leave to the end of June 1915; conscious of their precarious position, all three had moved on to other posts well before that date. When F.V. Riethdorf, a professor of German at Woodstock College, quit his post to offer his services to the Speakers' Patriotic League, his demonstration of loyalty was attacked as disingenuous. Claude Macdonell, the Tory MP for Toronto South, objected to someone who 'look[ed] like a German ... [and spoke] with a strong German accent playing such a role'; Riethdorf, he contended, should be seen not as a loyal British subject but as a turncoat whose disloyalty to 'his people' made him unfit to be a Canadian. Riethdorf left the league and joined the Canadian Medical Army Corps.[42]

The most profound wartime challenge to the status of German Canadians in Ontario took place in the city of Berlin and the surrounding region of North Waterloo, where three-quarters of the residents were of German ancestry, local anglophones had tolerated the teaching of German to most pupils in city schools, and the German names of pioneers marked the roads. Although German Berliners were enthusiastic about the war effort – they constituted about half of the soldiers of the local battalion, the 118th, and would consistently meet war bond and charity targets – they were on the defensive from the onset of the conflict. German disappeared from the city's streets and schools as anglophones objected to the public use of the enemy language and German Canadians sought to demonstrate their loyalty by suppressing overt demonstrations of their culture. As the war stretched on, and especially in the wake of the burning of the Parliament buildings in early 1916 – falsely assumed to be the work of German arsonists – questions began to be raised about the appropriateness of the name 'Berlin' for an ostensibly loyal Canadian city. 'The fact remains,' argued the chair of the North Waterloo recruiting committee, 'that Berlin was named after the capital of Prussia and is to-day the capital of the German Empire, whence have emanated the most diabolical crimes and atrocities that have marred the pages of history.' Proponents of a change also feared that patriotic Canadians would refuse to buy products made in Berlin. Opponents noted that the pages of history revealed that the city's name could not have honoured an Empire that, at its naming in 1833, had not existed, and that the booming war economy in the city was doing just fine.

Yet German Berliners found it difficult to come to the defence of their city's name. Few wanted either to convey an impression of disloyalty or to attract the attention of the soldiers of the 118th, some of whom had taken to assaulting those of German descent whose patriotism they questioned. In May 1916 soldiers stole a bust of Kaiser Wilhelm I from the German Concordia Club and later returned to sack the place, despite the fact that the club had contributed almost half of its members to the CEF and had closed its doors for the duration out of respect for the war effort. Authorities refused to press charges in the interests of 'racial harmony,' and in the wake of the incident the city council asked the province to authorize a name change.

The Hearst government was not particularly eager to accommodate a modification: it refused two requests from the Berlin council before passing a measure allowing any community to change its name following a majority vote in a referendum. In the bitter campaign that ensued, the 118th, free from worries about prosecution, kept potential opponents of the change away from the polls, and possibly hundreds of voters were disenfranchised on the grounds that they were not officially naturalized citizens, even though they had long voted in elections and in some cases had sent sons to Europe. In the end, corruption and intimidation tipped the scales in favour of the forces for change by a majority of 81 out of over 3,000 votes cast. A second referendum designed to elicit a new name drew so little enthusiasm that only one-third of the original electors bothered to vote. 'Kitchener,' added to the ballot at the last moment after the English field marshal of that name was lost in the North Sea just prior to the vote, edged out 'Brock,' the defender of Upper Canada in the War of 1812, by just eleven votes. Although over 2,000 petitioners – twice as many as those who *voted* in the second referendum – pleaded with the premier to consider their charges of electoral fraud in the first vote and to delay any change until after the war, Hearst let the decision stand.

Although the loss of the name of Berlin revealed the vulnerability of German Ontarians in wartime, those in North Waterloo remained in a better position than most of the province's other minorities. Once the 118th was shipped overseas, shortly after the second referendum, the German majority in the region began to reassert its traditional control over local politics. In the first municipal election after the referenda, in January 1917, the residents of Kitchener elected a full slate of anti-name-change candidates, though the new council declined to attempt to return to the original name in the interests of public order. In the federal election later in that year, voters repelled the Union Government's xenophobic campaign – even shouting Prime Minister Borden down at a rally – and supported an ex-mayor's candidacy under the banner of the Laurier Liberals by a two to one margin. In the short term, much bitterness followed this election; one veteran concluded that British Canadians should be cleared out of the riding and the remainder – presumably Germans and Liberal supporters – killed by firing squads or hand grenades. Resourceful Guelph city councillors offered their municipality as a refuge for Kitchener businesses seeking to depart their traitorous riding. But the businesses stayed; despite the loss of the name of its city, the German-Canadian community in the area was sufficiently large and well established, physically and culturally similar to the broader British-Canadian majority, and loyally supportive of the war effort to survive the indignities of the war and to rebuild.[43]

Ukrainian Canadians lacked German Ontarians' general prosperity and long-standing presence in the province and were thus more vulnerable to the effects of wartime prejudice. Most were single young men from the western Austro-Hungarian provinces of Galacia and Bukovyna who had come out to Canada at the end of the long pre-war years of prosperity to find their fortunes. A few Ukrainians initially favoured the Austrian cause against Russia in the war because like the Finns they feared a victorious Czar Nicholas II would crush their nationalist aspirations, but most supported Britain once it became involved in the conflict, and some even tried to pass *as* Russians in order to evade the ban on enemy alien enlistment and fight for their new country.

Just as the vagaries of imperialism transformed Ukrainians into 'Austrians,' those of the capitalist economy left many unemployed and destitute in the depression of 1912–13. Municipal councils, fearing social unrest and seeking to avoid heavy outlays for relief payments, called on military officials to use their authority to remove impoverished enemy aliens from their streets. Most of the 8,816 people detained in internment camps – about 6,000 of them were Ukrainian – were from the west, the central destination of such immigrants in better times. The largest single internment in Ontario occurred in the winter of 1914–15, when about 800 Ukrainians were taken from the streets of Fort William and Port Arthur, but dozens of enemy aliens, as they were called, were similarly removed from cities in the south as well. Most ended up in camps in northern Ontario, where they were safely removed from the country's major cities and forced to toil away in manual labour; the transportation of enemy aliens into the Ontario camps contributed to the doubling of the Ukrainian population in the province in the 1910s. At one of the biggest camps, in Kapuskasing, internees cleared land for an experimental farm; everywhere in the north they faced primitive conditions in a harsh climate that induced health problems ranging from frostbite to tuberculosis. Although only about 1.5 per cent of unnaturalized enemy aliens in the country were interned in this way, the very threat of internment – and the sense of rejection by Canadian society as a whole – was felt by all who were at risk.[44]

Through its internments, disenfranchising of enemy aliens naturalized since 1902 in the Wartime Elections Act, banning of foreign-language periodicals and radical organizations in the last weeks of the war, and tolerance of many private vigilante actions against minorities, the federal government did not live up to its early promise to treat enemy aliens with 'fairness and consideration.'[45] But then neither did the Canadian public. While most of the federal government's *active* repression of minorities was aimed at radicals and recent immigrants, the general British-Canadian public tended to be less discriminating.

One of the sorrier developments of the war was the extent to which British Canadians directed their prejudice in a general way against all immigrants. In Kingston, for example, the city's Dutch sanitary inspector, a Mr Timmerman, was harassed as an enemy alien by his fellow citizens; to the *Kingston Standard*'s evident amusement, Timmerman was 'kept busy denying he was a German.' In 1915 in Guelph, where the enemy alien population was just 1 per cent of the total, local officials registered about twenty-five Armenians as enemy aliens along with the local population of Turks, even though the Old World animosity between the groups was so great that it would result in the Turkish-led Armenian genocide of the next year. Amid news of the battle of Vimy Ridge in April 1917 about 500 veterans and soldiers marched up Yonge Street in Toronto and then broke up into groups of fifty to attack 'enemy' businesses and round up 'aliens.' The attacks hurt not only innocent Canadians of enemy descent, but also people originally from allied countries such as Russia, Italy, and Serbia, some neutral Swiss, and some Ukrainian veterans of the CEF who had passed as Russians in order to serve their new country.[46]

Those who harassed ethnic minorities in Ontario did so out of a combination of war-related animosity and fear of minorities as an economic threat. When most interned enemy aliens were released before the end of 1916, the rationale for the action was less the government's new-found appreciation of civil rights than its perception of the need for inexpensive labour in war industries. When interned Ukrainians were released from confinement to work at tanneries in Bracebridge, their new co-workers refused to work with them and burned their residence for fear of competition from cheaper labour. Ex-internees were given a similar welcome at the tannery in Acton.[47]

Given that veterans had faced death at the hands of foreigners overseas at the pay of $1.10 per day, unadjusted to inflation, it is hardly surprising that they were at the forefront of much anti-immigrant activity. What is more intriguing is the way in which their actions dislocated the traditional relationships between ethnicity and power in Ontario society. When veterans attacked the works of the Russell Motor Company in Toronto in April 1917 for employing about ninety former Kapuskasing labourers, the soldiers sent to the scene to restore order were initially sympathetic to the veterans. The state, however, sided with the enemy alien labourers and their employers: six veterans were eventually court-martialled for their roles in the attacks.[48]

On one August night in the last year of the war soldiers and civilians, ostensibly angry at low rates of enlistment of 'enemy aliens,' ransacked a total of fifteen minority-owned restaurants in Toronto, starting with the Greek-owned White City Cafe. On the following night, about 2,000 rioters refocused their wrath on the police, attacking officers and stations out of resentment at the police's attempts to protect the restaurants. Only the mayor's threat to read the Riot Act and the sending out of mounted police restored order. In the aftermath of the White City Cafe riots, protestors at public rallies, led by the Great War Veterans' Association, called for the government to conscript non-enemy aliens and single police officers, send enemy aliens to work farms, and plan after the war to revoke the business licences of aliens – naturalized, enemy, or otherwise – and deport them to their countries of origin. The federal government's banning of foreign-language periodicals and radical organizations at the end of the war was in part a response to these demands.[49] One can recognize that some of the government's motives for not proceeding further were related to its sympathy for the interests of employers seeking cheap labour – not the noblest of motivations, to be sure – and still be grateful that the complete platform of the veterans was not enacted.

Indeed, the association between power and prejudice that is suggested by an examination of the government's restrictive measures against enemy aliens was not so clearly manifested in the individual relations between members of the majority and minority groups. For example, although Professor Mueller was ultimately asked by the University of Toronto to leave his classes, his case was supported by the president of the university, Robert Falconer, by several prominent citizens, including Prime Minister Borden, and by the student newspaper the *Varsity*, which called for Mueller's critics to remember 'British fair play.' All objected to mainstream newspapers' vilification of Mueller and other law-abiding German Canadians. At Queen's, McMaster, Victoria, and Western universities professors of German descent continued to be employed without harassment because those institutions were less dependent on public finances than the provincial university, which relied on annual grants from the legislature, and thus they were less vulnerable to the attacks of the press and the vagaries of public opinion. The University of Toronto, city councils, and boards of education often were the sites of the most rabidly anti-German sentiment in Ontario, not because of the elites who ran them but because of their *greater* accountability to public fears and passions.[50]

By any measure – the purchase of war bonds, contributions to charities, rates of enlistment, electoral support for conscription – most Ontarians supported their country's engagement in the Great War and sought to see it through to victory. But this common cause did not produce shared purposes, and in the years from 1914 to 1918 patriotism in Ontario took many forms and was qualified to varying degrees. The nature of the war itself, of course, shaped Ontarians' responses to it: without conscription as a galvanizing issue, farmers would not have become a social and political movement capable of forming the provincial government; only the hostilities with Germany precipitated the nominal shift from Berlin to Kitchener. Yet one is struck, too, by the intractability of social relations in the face of wartime strains and upheavals. The farmers' revolt disrupted the political status quo in the province, but it was waged from a position of relative social and economic strength. By contrast, while some of the province's most disadvantaged citizens were among the war's strongest supporters – they had much to fight *for* if little to defend – their service failed to bring them the social inclusion to which many of them aspired. Patriotism boosted the fortunes of the Irish, but not those of Blacks and Aboriginals; Ukrainian Canadians likely rallied around the flag more enthusiastically than French Canadians, but of the two groups only the former were subject to internment; German Canadians in Waterloo County lost the name of their city but not, except briefly, their status in it.

The war has long been regarded as a catalyst in the expansion of the role of government in Canadian society, and indeed their commitment to the war effort led English Canadians generally, and Ontarians specifically, to support unprecedented state initiatives concerning taxation, the control of alcohol, and the mobilization of manpower. The story of the war in Ontario, however, is more than simply a narrative of state power and intervention. From the nativist campaigns of veterans to the varied responses of excluded minorities and farmers' grass-roots resistance to conscription, the province's citizens themselves frequently grasped the initiative of wartime response and acted apart from or at cross-purposes with their governments. The resulting impression of the province in these years is consequently less one of patriotic stasis than of a war experienced and imagined on many fronts.

NOTES

1 The preceding paragraphs are derived from the following sources. Barbara Wilson, *Ontario and the First World War, 1914–1918: A Collection of Documents* (Toronto: Champlain Society, 1977), xxi, xxiv–xxv, xvix, xxxix–xlv, xci, cvii, 3, 124, 160. Robert Rutherdale, 'Canada's August Festival: Communitas, Liminality, and Social Memory,' *Canadian Historical Review* (June 1996),

221–49. Mary Rubio and Elizabeth Waterston, eds, *The Selected Journals of Lucy Maud Montgomery*, vol. 2, *1910–1921* (Toronto: Oxford University Press, 1987), 91–2, 157. Desmond Morton, *When Your Number's Up: The Canadian Soldier in the First World War* (Toronto: Random House, 1993), 50–2. Morris Zaslow, *The Northward Expansion of Canada, 1914–1967* (Toronto: McClelland and Stewart, 1988), 3. Daphne Read, ed., *The Great War and Canadian Society: An Oral History* (Toronto: New Hogtown Press, 1978), 27. For pictures of the cavalry at the Canadian National Exhibition, and of soldiers leaving Toronto's Union Station, see photos 777J and 824–828E, respectively, in the William James Collection, City of Toronto Archives. Robert Allen Rutherdale, 'The Home Front: Consensus and Conflict in Lethbridge, Guelph, and Trois-Rivières during the Great War,' PhD thesis, York University, 1993, 48–9, 71–2. J.M. Bliss, 'The Methodist Church and World War I,' *Canadian Historical Review* (September 1968), 217–23. Michael Gauvreau, *The Evangelical Century: College and Creed in English Canada from the Great Revival to the Great Depression* (Montreal and Kingston: McGill-Queen's University Press, 1991), 262–4. Neil Semple, *The Lord's Dominion: The History of Canadian Methodism* (Montreal and Kingston: McGill-Queen's University Press, 1996), 395–402. Ian Hugh McLean Miller, *Our Glory and Our Grief: Torontonians and the Great War* (Toronto: University of Toronto Press, 2002), 15–18, 55–7, 60–2, 77–8, 89–91, 94–105, 107–20, 190–2. Jonathan F. Vance, *Death So Noble: Memory, Meaning, and the First World War* (Vancouver: UBC Press, 1997), 35–72, 90–102. Robert S. Prince, 'The Mythology of War: How the Canadian Daily Newspaper Depicted the Great War,' PhD thesis, University of Toronto, 1998, esp. 232–45. Jeffrey A. Keshen, *Propaganda and Censorship during Canada's Great War* (Edmonton: University of Alberta Press, 1996), 24–39, 124–5, 188–90. Peter Oliver, *Public and Private Persons: The Ontario Political Culture, 1914–1934* (Toronto: Clarke, Irwin: 1975), 18–27, 34, 42. Margaret Prang, *N.W. Rowell: Ontario Nationalist* (Toronto: University of Toronto Press, 1975), 158–227. J. Castell Hopkins, *The Province of Ontario in the War: A Record of Government and People* (Toronto: Warwick Bros and Rutter, 1919), 2–9, 15, 117. Ontario, *Public Accounts of the Province of Ontario*, 1914–15 (a16–19), 1915–16 (a16–19), 1916–17 (a12–15), and 1917–18 (a26–9). Christopher A. Sharpe, 'The Great War,' in Donald Kerr and Deryck W. Holdsworth, eds, *Historical Atlas of Canada*, vol. 3, *Addressing the Twentieth Century, 1891–1961* (Toronto: University of Toronto Press, 1990), Plate 26. J. Castell Hopkins, ed., *The Canadian Annual Review of Public Affairs, 1917* (Toronto: Annual Review Co. 1914–18), 301. Hopkins, *Canadian Annual Review ... 1915*, 210–12. N.E.S. Griffiths, *The Splendid Vision: Centennial History of the National Council of*

*Women, 1893–1993* (Ottawa: Carleton University Press, 1993), 125–30.
Alison Prentice et al., *Canadian Women: A History*, 2nd ed. (Toronto: Harcourt Brace 1996), 232–3. A.B. McKillop, *Matters of Mind: The University in Ontario, 1791–1951* (Toronto: University of Toronto Press, 1994), 265–70, 284. Ruby Heap, '"Salvaging War's Waste": The University of Toronto and the "Physical Reconstruction" of Disabled Soldiers During the First World War,' in Edgar-André Montigny and Lori Chambers, eds, *Ontario since Confederation: A Reader* (Toronto: University of Toronto Press, 2000), 214–34.
H.V. Nelles, *The Politics of Development: Forests, Mines, and Hydro-Electric Power in Ontario, 1849–1941* (Toronto: Macmillan, 1974), 349–61. Graham D. Taylor and Peter Baskerville, *A Concise History of Business in Canada* (Toronto: Oxford University Press 1994), 293. W. Robert Wightman and Nancy M. Wightman, *The Land Between: Northwestern Ontario Resource Development, 1800 to 1990s* (Toronto: University of Toronto Press, 1997), 190–1. Peter Oliver, *G. Howard Ferguson: Ontario Tory* (Toronto: University of Toronto Press, 1977), 83–4. Michael Bliss, *A Canadian Millionaire: The Life and Business Times of Sir Joseph Flavelle, Bart., 1858–1939* (Toronto: Macmillan, 1978), 308, 317. Robert Craig Brown and Ramsay Cook, *Canada, 1896–1921: A Nation Transformed* (Toronto: McClelland and Stewart, 1974), 299–302. Richard Allen, *The Social Passion: Religion and Social Reform in Canada, 1914–28* (Toronto: University of Toronto Press, 1990), 39. Robert Matthew Bray, 'The Canadian Patriotic Response to the Great War,' PhD thesis, York University, 1977, 154–6, 329–39, 346–54. Paul Maroney, '"The Great Adventure": The Context and Ideology of Recruiting in Ontario, 1914–1917,' *Canadian Historical Review* (March 1996), 62–79. Desmond Morton, *A Military History of Canada* (Edmonton: Hurtig, 1990), 136–7. J.L. Granatstein and J.M. Hitsman, *Broken Promises: A History of Conscription in Canada* (Toronto: Copp Clark Pitman, 1985), 39–40. Hopkins, *Canadian Annual Review ... 1915*, 331. Nikolas Gardner, 'The Great War and Waterloo County: The Travails of the 118th Overseas Battalion,' *Ontario History* (September 1997), 220–4. W.R. Chadwick, *The Battle for Berlin, Ontario: An Historical Drama* (Waterloo: Wilfrid Laurier University Press, 1992), 36, 46–7, 88. Vance, *Death So Noble*, 112–13. R. Matthew Bray, '"Fighting as an Ally": The English-Canadian Patriotic Response to the Great War,' *Canadian Historical Review* (June 1980), 151–68. John English, *The Decline of Politics: The Conservatives and the Party System* (Toronto: University of Toronto Press, 1977), 108–9. C.A. Sharpe, 'Enlistment in the Canadian Expeditionary Force, 1914–1918: A Regional Analysis,' *Journal of Canadian Studies* (Winter 1983–4), 16–22. Frederick H. Armstrong, *Toronto: The Place of Meeting* (Toronto: Windsor, 1983), 154–5. Randall White, *Ontario, 1610–*

*1985: A Political and Economic History* (Toronto: Dundurn Press, 1985), 210. For the views of the Trades and Labour Congress, see Martin Robin, 'Registration, Conscription, and Independent Labour Politics, 1916–1917,' *Canadian Historical Review* (June 1966), 102. Vance, *Death So Noble*, 12–34, 198–225. Desmond Morton and Glenn Wright, *Winning the Second Battle: Canadian Veterans and the Return to Civilian Life* (Toronto: University of Toronto Press, 1987), 130.

2 P.E. Dewey, *British Agriculture in the First World War* (London: Routledge, 1989), 4, 17, 31, 221. Avner Offer, *The First World War: An Agrarian Interpretation* (Oxford: Clarendon Press, 1989), 45–78, 366–70. Adam Crerar, 'Ties That Bind: Farming, Agrarian Ideals, and Life in Ontario,' PhD thesis, University of Toronto, 1999, 13–15. Prang, *N.W. Rowell*, 158.

3 For Hearst's views, see Hopkins, *Canadian Annual Review ... 1914*, 460–1. Crerar, 'Ties That Bind,' 242–52. Kerry Badgley, *Ringing in the Common Love of Good: The United Farmers of Ontario, 1914–1926* (Montreal and Kingston: McGill-Queen's University Press, 2000), 56–7, 146. Kerry Badgley, '"Co-operation Pays and Pays Well": Cooperatives and the State in Ontario, 1914 to 1930,' *Canadian Papers in Rural History* 10 (1996), 167. Margaret Evans and R.W. Irwin, 'Government Tractors in Ontario, 1917 and 1918,' *Ontario History* (June 1969), 99–109.

4 Crerar, 'Ties That Bind,' 130–1, 137–8, 253–77. Hopkins, *The Province of Ontario in the War*, 47.

5 Wilson, *Ontario and the First World War*, xx–xxi, xxix. For the Hamilton *Herald*, see Bray, 'Canadian Patriotic Response,' 49–50. Hopkins, *Canadian Annual Review ... 1915*, 321. Crerar, 'Ties That Bind,' 278–9. Bray, '"Fighting as an Ally,"' 147–8. George M. Wrong, 'The Bi-lingual Question,' in J.O. Miller, ed., *The New Era in Canada: Essays Dealing with the Upbuilding of the Canadian Commonwealth* (London: J.M. Dent & Sons, 1917), 244–5.

6 Hopkins, *Canadian Annual Review ... 1918*, 486–7, 510. Nancy Christie, *Engendering the State: Family, Work, and Welfare in Canada* (Toronto: University of Toronto Press, 2000), 47–89. Bray, 'Canadian Patriotic Response,' 49–50. Maroney, '"The Great Adventure,"' 67. Crerar, 'Ties That Bind,' 280.

7 Crerar, 'Ties That Bind,' 279–80. Morton, *When Your Number's Up*, 279.

8 E.C. Drury, *Farmer Premier: The Memoirs of E.C. Drury* (Toronto: McClelland and Stewart, 1966), 73. Robert Bothwell, Ian Drummond, and John English, *Canada, 1900–1945* (Toronto: University of Toronto Press, 1987), 128–9, 154–5. For local histories that suggest rural Ontario's isolation from most intense aspects of war atmosphere, see Elizabeth Bloomfield, *Waterloo Township through Two Centuries* (Waterloo: Waterloo Historical Society, 1995), 252, and Glenn J. Lockwood, *Montague: A Social History of an Irish*

*Township* (Kingston: Mastercraft, 1980), 469. In comparison, see Miller, *Our Glory and Our Grief*, for the intensity of war fervour in Toronto. See also Maroney, '"The Great Adventure,"' 77–9. Vance, *Death So Noble*, 112–13. Crerar, 'Ties That Bind,' 280.

9 Maroney, '"The Great Adventure,"' 79–96. Bruce Kidd, *The Struggle for Canadian Sport* (Toronto: University of Toronto Press, 1996), 37–41. Bray, 'Canadian Patriotic Response,' 118. Keshen, *Propaganda and Censorship*, 132.

10 Bray, 'Canadian Patriotic Response,' 365. English, *Decline of Politics*, 131. Granatstein and Hitsman, *Broken Promises*, 74–5. Robert Trowbridge, 'War Time Rural Discontent and the Rise of the United Farmers of Ontario, 1914–1919,' MA thesis, University of Waterloo, 1966, 71–2. W.R. Young, 'Conscription, Rural Depopulation, and the Farmers of Ontario,' *Canadian Historical Review* (September 1972), 299–300. Bothwell, Drummond, and English, *Canada, 1900–1945*, 173. Hopkins, *Canadian Annual Review ... 1918*, 497. Crerar, 'Ties That Bind,' 15–25.

11 That Ontario farming remained an essentially familial occupation is suggested by the 1911 census's recording of just one farm labourer for every four farm operators in the province; to each of the latter one could in most cases reasonably add the unpaid labour of wives and children. Crerar, 'Ties That Bind,' 26–39, 43–66. For public debate on rural depopulation in wartime, see Young, 'Conscription, Rural Depopulation,' 299–314. For an examination of the less detrimental effects of the war on the household economy of the urban working class, see Craig Heron, 'The High School and the Household Economy in Working-Class Hamilton, 1890–1940,' *Historical Studies in Education* (Fall 1995), 222, 231–3.

12 English, *Decline of Politics*, 131, 144–60, 163, 186, 191–2. Granatstein and Hitsman, *Broken Promises*, 73–5. Bray, 'Canadian Patriotic Response,' 456–64. Prang, *N.W. Rowell*, 191–210, 220–1. Robert Craig Brown, *Robert Laird Borden: A Biography*, 2 vols (Toronto: Macmillan, 1975, 1980), 2: 112, 120–1. J.M. Beck, *Pendulum of Power: Canada's Federal Elections* (Scarborough, Ont.: Prentice-Hall, 1968), 136. Badgley, *Ringing in the Common Love of Good*, 57–60. Trowbridge, 'War Time Rural Discontent,' 98–9. Hopkins, *Canadian Annual Review ... 1917*, 352. F.J.K. Griezic, '"Power to the People": The Beginning of Agrarian Revolt in Ontario: The Manitoulin By-Election, October 24, 1918,' *Ontario History* (March 1977), 36–7. Wilson, *Ontario and the First World War*, lvi–lvii. Quote from the *Packet* in Daniel T. Byers, 'The Conscription Election of 1917 and its Aftermath in Orillia, Ontario,' *Ontario History* (December 1991), 284.

13 Bray, 'Canadian Patriotic Response,' 491–6. For the fist-shaking pro-Union farmer poster, see Roger Hall and Gordon Dobbs, *Ontario: 200 Years in*

*Pictures* (Toronto: Dundurn, 1991), 177. Granatstein and Hitsman, *Broken Promises*, 76–8. Beck, *Pendulum of Power*, 143–6. Kathryn M. Bindon, *More Than Patriotism: Canada at War, 1914–1918* (Toronto: Personal Library/ Nelson, 1979), 149–53. E.C. Drury, *Farmer Premier*, 79. Miller, *Our Glory and Our Grief*, 152. Wiarton *Canadian Echo*, 12 December 1917. Adam Crerar, 'Filling the Dinner Horn of Peace: The North Bruce United Farmers and the Ontario General Election of 1919,' unpublished MA paper, University of Toronto, 1991, 13. W.H. Heick, '"If We Lose the War, Nothing Else Matters": The 1917 Federal Election in North Waterloo,' *Ontario History* (June 1980), 84–85.

14 English, *Decline of Politics*, 194–205. Beck, *Pendulum of Power*, 136–48. Brown, *Robert Laird Borden*, Vol. II, 123–5. Byers, 'Conscription Election of 1917,' 286–7. R. Haycock, 'The 1917 Federal Election in Victoria-Haliburton: A Case Study,' *Ontario History* (June 1975), 105–18. The 'rural' vote is calculated by adding up the results from township polls – in contrast to those located in hamlets, villages, towns, or cities. Not everyone who voted at a rural poll was a farmer, and some farmers living close to 'urban' polls likely voted there, but the calculation gives one a sense of regional inclinations. I've defined southwestern Ontario as the region lying south and west of and including Simcoe and Peel counties. Canada, Parliament, Sessional Papers (SP), 1920, vol. 4, no. 13, 1–132.

15 English, *Decline of Politics*, 134. Miller, '"Our Glory and Our Grief,"' 347–61. Granatstein and Hitsman, *Broken Promises*, 78–9. Hopkins, *Canadian Annual Review ... 1917*, 643.

16 Canada, SP, 1911–12, vol. 11, no. 18, 2–178.

17 For urban election return figures, see n.14, above. James Naylor, *The New Democracy: Challenging the Social Order in Industrial Ontario, 1914–1925* (Toronto: University of Toronto Press, 1991), esp. 255 for those involved in strikes and 39 for the strike ban in last month of the war. Gregory S. Kealey, 'State Repression of Labour and the Left in Canada, 1914–1920: The Impact of the First World War,' *Canadian Historical Review* (September 1992), 281–314. Hopkins, *Canadian Annual Review ... 1918*, 338–44, 494. Bryan D. Palmer, *Working-Class Experience: Rethinking the History of Canadian Labour, 1800–1991* (Toronto: McClelland and Stewart, 1992), 196–9. Desmond Morton, *Working People: An Illustrated History of the Canadian Labour Movement* (Toronto: Summerhill Press, 1990), 112–16. Myer Siemiatycki, 'Munitions and Labour Militancy: The 1916 Hamilton Machinists' Strike,' in David J. Bercuson, ed., *Canadian Labour History: Selected Readings* (Toronto: Copp Clark Pitman, 1987), 119–37. Craig Heron, 'The Crisis of the Craftsman: Hamilton's Metal Workers in the Early Twentieth

Century,' *Labour / Le Travail* (Autumn 1980), 30–40. Michael J. Piva, *The Condition of the Working-Class in Toronto, 1900–1921* (Ottawa: University of Ottawa Press, 1979), 46–7, 56, 162–4. Craig Heron and Myer Siemiatycki, 'The Great War, The State, and Working-Class Canada,' in Craig Heron, ed., *The Workers' Revolt in Canada, 1917–1925* (Toronto: University of Toronto Press, 1998), 11–42. James Naylor, 'Striking at the Ballot Box,' in Heron, ed., *Workers' Revolt in Canada*, 144–175. Craig Heron, *Working in Steel: The Early Years in Canada, 1883–1935* (Toronto: McClelland and Stewart, 1988), 114–21, 133–42. Bray, 'Canadian Patriotic Response,' 340–2, 359–61. Miller, *Our Glory and Our Grief*, 136–8, 174–7. Keshen, *Propaganda and Censorship*, 91–3.

18 Hopkins, *Province of Ontario in the War*, 20, 53–5. Crerar, 'Ties That Bind,' 283–4. Brown, *Robert Laird Borden*, Vol. II, 132–3. Young, 'Conscription, Rural Depopulation,' 307–8.

19 For Borden's covenant, see Hopkins, *Canadian Annual Review ... 1918*, 411–12. Trowbridge, 'War Time Rural Discontent,' 120–8. Read, *The Great War and Canadian Society*, 109–10.

20 Crerar, 'Ties That Bind,' 284–7. Young, 'Conscription, Rural Depopulation,' 307–13. For the anti-agrarian magistrate, see Griezic, '"Power to the People,"' 36–8. For Currie's views, see Badgley, *Ringing in the Common Love of Good*, 74. For Skelton's observations, see Brown and Cook, *Canada: 1896–1921*, 320. Jean Macleod, 'The United Farmer Movement in Ontario, 1914–1943,' MA thesis, Queen's University, 1958, 44. Trowbridge, 'War Time Rural Discontent,' 131–8.

21 For the farmers' remonstrance, see Trowbridge, 'War Time Rural Discontent,' 114, 130–8. For Good's struggles, see Crerar, 'Ties That Bind,' 223, 282–4. Young, 'Conscription, Rural Depopulation, 299–307. Griezic, '"Power to the People,"' 35. W.C. Good, *Production and Taxation in Canada: From the Farmers' Standpoint* (Toronto: J.M. Dent & Sons, 1919), 16–18.

22 For the Burlington farmer's indignation, see Charles M. Johnston, *E.C. Drury: Agrarian Idealist* (Toronto: University of Toronto Press, 1986), 51. Brian Tennyson, 'The Ontario General Election of 1919: The Beginnings of Agrarian Revolt,' *Journal of Canadian Studies* (February 1969), 27. For the views of the *Weekly Sun*, see Griezic, '"Power to the People,"' 40.

23 Tennyson, 'Ontario General Election of 1919,' 28–9. Badgley, *Ringing in the Common Love of Good*, 52–3. Trowbridge, 'War Time Rural Discontent,' 90–4. Wiarton *Canadian Echo*, 10 July 1918, cited in Crerar, 'Filling the Dinner Horn of Peace,' 16.

24 Griezic, '"Power to the People,"' 43–54.

25 Robert Craig Brown and Donald Loveridge, 'Unrequited Faith: Recruiting

the CEF, 1914–1918,' *Revue internationale d'histoire militaire* 54 (1982), 65–6, 79. Hopkins, *Canadian Annual Review … 1918*, 466. Peter Oliver, *Public and Private Persons: The Ontario Political Culture, 1914–1934* (Toronto: Clarke, Irwin, 1975), 18–42. Oliver, *G. Howard Ferguson*, 87. Tennyson, 'The Ontario General Election of 1919,' 30–5.

26  Robert M. Stamp, 'Empire Day in the Schools of Ontario: The Training of Young Imperialists,' *Journal of Canadian Studies* (August 1973), 32–41. See also Mark Moss, *Manliness and Militarism: Educating Young Boys in Ontario for War* (Toronto: Oxford University Press, 2001), 140–6.

27  Calculated from Canada, Census, 1911, vol. 2, table VII, 204–5. For the clearest contemporary discussion of racial hierarchies, see J.S. Woodsworth, *Strangers within our gates, or, Coming Canadians* (Toronto: F.C. Stephenson, 1909; reprint University of Toronto Press, 1972).

28  For brief accounts of the early histories of these groups, see Paul Robert Magocsi, *Encyclopedia of Canada's Peoples* (Toronto: University of Toronto Press, 1999).

29  Margaret Prang, 'Clerics, Politicians and the Bilingual Schools Issue in Ontario, 1910–1917,' *Canadian Historical Review* (December 1960), 281–307. Marilyn Barber, 'The Ontario Bilingual Schools Issue: Sources of Conflict,' *Canadian Historical Review* (September 1966), 227–48. Oliver, *G. Howard Ferguson*, 41–9, 72–8. Brown and Cook, *Canada: 1896–1921*, 262–4. C.B. Sissons, *Bi-lingual Schools in Canada* (Toronto: J.M. Dent & Sons, 1917), 209–15. George M. Wrong, 'The Bi-lingual Question,' 258–9. Oliver, *Public and Private Persons*, 97–100. Jack Cecillon, 'Turbulent Times in the Diocese of London: Bishop Fallon and the French-Language Controversy, 1910–1918,' *Ontario History* (December 1995), 369–95.

30  Mark G. McGowan, *The Waning of the Green: Catholics, the Irish, and Identity in Toronto, 1887–1922* (Toronto: University of Toronto Press, 1999), 250–84. Philip Currie, 'Reluctant Britons: The Toronto Irish, Home Rule, and the Great War,' *Ontario History* (Spring 1995), 65–76. Granatstein and Hitsman, *Broken Promises*, 76.

31  Wilson, *Ontario and the First World War*, 167–8.

32  James W. St G. Walker, 'Race and Recruitment in World War I: Enlistment of Visible Minorities in the Canadian Expeditionary Force,' *Canadian Historical Review* (March 1989), 1, 5–6, 9–12, 18, 21–6. Robin W. Winks, *The Blacks in Canada: A History* (New Haven, Conn.: Yale University Press, 1971), 314–19. Wilson, *Ontario and the First World War*, 166. Sarah-Jane (Saje) Mathieu, 'North of the Colour Line: Sleeping Car Porters and the Battle Against Jim Crow on Canadian Rails, 1880–1920,' *Labour / Le Travail* (Spring 2001), 9–41.

33 Peter Schmalz, *The Ojibwa of Southern Ontario* (Toronto: University of Toronto Press, 1991), 228. Walker, 'Race and Recruitment in World War I,' 3–9. Wilson, *Ontario and the First World War*, cx–cii.

34 Sally M. Weaver, 'The Iroquois: The Grand River Reserve in the Late Nineteenth and Early Twentieth Centuries, 1875–1945,' in Edward S. Rogers and Donald B. Smith, eds, *Aboriginal Ontario: Historical Perspectives on the First Nations* (Toronto: Dundurn, 1994), 246. Wilson, *Ontario and the First World War*, cx–cxiv, 171–4. Walker, 'Race and Recruitment in World War I,' 13. Schmalz, *Ojibwa of Southern Ontario*, 229–30. Edward S. Rogers, 'The Algonquian Farmers of Southern Ontario, 1830–1945,' in Rogers and Smith, *Aboriginal Ontario*, 153. Walker, 'Race and Recruitment in World War I,' 13.

35 As it happened, a federal order-in-council issued in mid-January 1918 declared Natives exempt from compulsory service, precisely on the grounds that those who were not full citizens (Aboriginals, conscientious objectors, enemy aliens, people of Japanese descent) should not have the responsibilities, as well as the privileges, of citizenship. This must have been a disappointment to the council, but other Natives felt that, since they weren't treated as full citizens, they should be exempt. Indeed, despite Jacobs's liberal rhetoric, the council did not advocate the complete abolition of Indian status. Schmalz, *Ojibwa of Southern Ontario*, 230–1. Vance, *Death So Noble*, 245–50. Wilson, *Ontario and the First World War*, cx–cxiv, especially 174–5 for Jacobs's views. For the council's efforts to transfer the aboriginal soldiers, see Walker, 'Race and Recruitment in World War I,' 14, 18–19.

36 Weaver, 'The Iroquois,' 245–7. Olive Dickason, *Canada's First Nations: A History of Founding Peoples from Earliest Times* (Toronto: Oxford University Press, 1997), 303–4. For Loft's words, see J.R. Miller, *Skyscrapers Hide the Heavens: A History of Indian-White Relations in Canada* (Toronto: University of Toronto Press, 2000), 319. Walker, 'Race and Recruitment in World War I,' 16.

37 Rogers, 'Algonquian Farmers of Southern Ontario,' 154–6. Schmalz, *Ojibwa of Southern Ontario*, 228. Dickason, *Canada's First Nations*, 301. Walker, 'Race and Recruitment in World War I,' 25–6. C.M. Johnson, *Brant County: A History, 1784–1945* (Toronto: Oxford University Press, 1967), 125.

38 Irving Abella, *A Coat of Many Colours: Two Centuries of Jewish Life in Canada* (Toronto: Lester and Orpen Dennys, 1990), 156–63. Gerald Tulchinsky, *Taking Root: The Origins of the Canadian Jewish Community* (Toronto: Lester, 1992), 193–200, 262. Hopkins, *Canadian Annual Review ... 1917*, 432.

39 Edward W. Laine, 'Finnish Canadian Radicalism and Canadian Politics:

The First Forty Years,' in Jorgen Dahlie and Tissa Fernando, *Ethnicity, Power and Politics in Canada* (Toronto: Methuen, 1981), 96–9. Keshen, *Propaganda and Censorship*, 89.

40 David Edward Smith, 'Emergency Government in Canada,' *Canadian Historical Review* (December 1969), 436–7. Brown and Cook, *Canada, 1896–1921*, 225. Wilson, *Ontario and the First World War*, lxx–lxxi. Kealey, 'State Repression of Labour and the Left,' 286.

41 Bliss, 'Methodist Church and World War I,' 215. Wilson, *Ontario and the First World War*, xxx–xxxi, lxx–lxxii. Bindon, *More Than Patriotism*, 46–8. Miller, *Our Glory and Our Grief*, 44–9. Keshen, *Propaganda and Censorship*, 7. Rutherdale, 'The Home Front,' 186–8, 194, 196.

42 Keshen, *Propaganda and Censorship*, 8. Larry Hannant, *The Infernal Machine: Investigating the Loyalty of Canada's Citizens* (Toronto: University of Toronto Press, 1995), 32. For Reithdorf, see Wilson, *Ontario and the First World War*, lxxi–lxxii. James G. Greenlee, *Sir Robert Falconer: A Biography* (Toronto: University of Toronto Press, 1988), 204–5. Rutherdale, 'The Home Front,' 206. For Hook, see Greenlee, *Sir Robert Falconer*, 201–13. McKillop, *Matters of Mind*, 258–62. Hopkins, *Canadian Annual Review ... 1914*, 266.

43 W.H. Heick, '"If We Lose the War, Nothing Else Matters,"' 68–86. Geoffrey Hayes, *Waterloo County: An Illustrated History* (Waterloo: Waterloo Historical Society, 1997), 115–21. Wilson, *Ontario and the First World War*, lxxvii–lxxxiv, 77–8, 81–9, especially 84–6 for the views of the chair of the North Waterloo recruiting committee. Chadwick, *Battle for Berlin, Ontario*, 17, 78–85, 122, 150–7. Hopkins, *Canadian Annual Review ... 1917*, 436.

44 Frances Swyripa and John Herd Thompson, eds, *Loyalties in Conflict: Ukrainians in Canada During the Great War* (Edmonton: Canadian Institute of Ukrainian Studies Press, 1983), vii. John Herd Thompson, 'The Enemy Alien and the Canadian General Election of 1917' in Swyripa and Thompson, eds., *Loyalties in Conflict*, 25, 40. Frances Swyripa, *Wedded to the Cause: Ukrainian-Canadian Women and Ethnic Identity, 1891–1991* (Toronto: University of Toronto Press, 1993), 8, 52. Andrij Mackuch, 'Ukrainian Canadians and the Wartime Economy,' in Swyripa and Thompson, *Loyalties in Conflict*, 70–1. Zaslow, *Northward Expansion of Canada*, 3. Orest T. Martynowich, *Ukrainians in Canada: The Formative Period, 1891–1924* (Edmonton: Canadian Institute of Ukrainian Studies Press, 1991), 309–28. Donald H. Avery, 'Ethnic and Class Tensions in Canada, 1918–1920: Anglo-Canadians and the Alien Worker,' in Swyripa and Thompson, eds., *Loyalties in Conflict*, 80. Keshen, *Propaganda and Censorship*, 10. For the numbers of internees, see Kealey, 'State Repression of Labour and the Left,' 293.

45  For the government's promise, see Brown and Cook, *Canada: 1896–1921*, 225. Kealey, 'State Repression of Labour and the Left,' 281–314.
46  For the harassment of Kingston's sanitary inspector, see Brian S. Osborne and Donald Swainson, *Kingston: Building on the Past* (Westport, Conn.: Butternut Press, 1988), 284. Rutherdale, 'The Home Front,' 196–7. Miller, *Our Glory and Our Grief*, 63–5. Martynowich, *Ukrainians in Canada*, 419–21.
47  Wilson, *Ontario and the First World War*, lxxiii.
48  Martynowich, *Ukrainians in Canada*, 421.
49  Miller, *Our Glory and Our Grief*, 178–82. Morton and Wright, *Winning the Second Battle*, 74, 82–3, 119–21. Keshen, *Propaganda and Censorship*, 330. Brown and Cook, *Canada: 1896–1921*, 226.
50  Greenlee, *Sir Robert Falconer*, 207–10, 220. McKillop, *Matters of Mind*, 262. Hopkins, *Canadian Annual Review ... 1914*, 266.

# 10 Ethnic and Class Relations in Western Canada during the First World War: A Case Study of European Immigrants and Anglo-Canadian Nativism

DONALD AVERY

## Introduction

The conventional wisdom holds that the years 1914–19 were a time of serious social and political disruption for Canada. But why was this the case? Was it because of the unique and devastating consequences of the Great War when Canada, a relatively small nation of 6 million people, suffered staggering battlefield losses on the Western Front? Or did the searing experience with total war only intensify already existing tensions and problems that divided Canadians on the basis of ethnicity, religion, class and region?[1]

In this chapter I attempt to address these questions in relation to one region – the Canadian west – and to focus on one social group: European immigrant workers whose status as 'foreigners,' or 'aliens' became more sharply defined within the context of total war. During the years 1914–19 individuals and groups were deemed loyal or disloyal, law-abiding or revolutionary, according to how their behaviour conformed to the values and norms of the middle-class Anglo-Canadian community. Being an enemy alien – from Germany, the Austro-Hungarian Empire, Bulgaria, or Turkey – was the most serious disability, at least until the latter stages of the war when fear of a 'Bolshevik' revolution in Canada gained momentum, particularly in those parts of western Canada where industrial conflict escalated.

The most spectacular confrontation occurred during the Winnipeg General Strike of May-June 1919, an event that polarized the city, the region, and the nation. In its desperate attempts to maintain social order the Union Government of Sir Robert Borden passed a series of draconian laws aimed at the radical alien. At the same time, members of the House of Commons seriously debated whether the country should continue to encourage European immigration, or whether the necessary numbers of industrial workers and agriculturalists could be secured from Great Britain and the United States. This cultural bias was reinforced by the growing popularity of eugenics arguments which stressed the supremacy of the Anglo-Saxon and Nordic 'races' – and the corresponding hereditary inferiority of eastern and southern Europeans. This debate paralleled developments in the United States, where Congress passed a series of quota laws, virtually excluding those immigrant groups deemed inferior on the basis of race and ethnicity.

What was most striking about the 1919 situation was the popularity immigration restriction enjoyed in the Canadian west, a rather surprising response given the region's pre-war dependence on foreign workers in both the agricultural and the industrial sectors of the economy. Many western spokesmen, however, regarded this exclusionist movement as a temporary phenomenon, directly related to wartime tensions. This viewpoint was aptly summarized in May 1919 by Thomas Crerar, a prominent prairie politician: 'A great majority of the people, as a result of the times we have lived through the last four years ... are not quite back to normal judgement.'[2]

## Social and Economic Background

Between 1896 and 1914 Canada in general and western Canada in particular experienced unprecedented economic growth: railway mileage doubled, mining production tripled, and wheat and lumber production increased tenfold. This economic expansion was accompanied by dramatic population growth; in the decade 1901–11 the nation's population increased by a remarkable 34 per cent. Much of this increase was due to immigration; in 1914 it was estimated that 3 million people had entered the country since 1896. Although a substantial number of these 'newcomers' settled on the land, the vast majority derived some portion of their annual income from the wage employment offered by the booming agricultural and industrial sectors of the western Canadian economy whose demand for labour, both skilled and unskilled, seemed insatiable.[3]

Led by the spokesmen for labour-intensive industries, including agriculture, public opinion in western Canada came to favour an immigration policy that went beyond the traditional open-door approach and encouraged the systematic recruitment abroad of men and women who could meet the challenge of a nation freshly embarked upon great enterprise. This opinion found expression in the immigration policies of successive dominion governments. Although the official pronouncements of the Immigration Branch in this period stressed that only farmers, farm labourers, and domestics would be recruited, exceptions were frequently made to accommodate the needs of businessmen in the expanding sectors of the economy of the three prairie provinces and British Columbia. That Canada's search for immigrant agriculturalists was largely in the hands of steamship agents in search of bonuses further altered official policy; many who entered the country as farmers and farm labourers quickly found their way into construction camps, mines, and factories.[4]

Faced with the demands of major projects, such as the building of two new transcontinental railways, Canada's 'captains of industry' required a workforce that was both inexpensive and at their beck and call.[5] To them the agricultural ideal which lay at the root of Canadian immigration policy increasingly appeared obsolete. Supply and demand should be the new governing principle of immigration policy. The best immigrants would be those willing to roam the country to take up whatever work was available – railroad construction in the Canadian Shield in the summer, harvesting in Saskatchewan in the fall, coal mining in Alberta in the winter, and lumbering in British Columbia in the spring.[6] This view ran against the deep-seated Canadian myth of the primacy of the land, but nevertheless it prevailed.[7] By 1914 it was obvious, even to immigration officials, that Canada had joined the United States as part of a transatlantic market.[8]

Statistics on the ethnic composition of this immigration and the regional concentrations of immigrants (settlers and resource workers) as well as their distribution within the occupational structure bring to the surface the contours of what could be called 'the specificity of the Canadian experience.' In 1891, at an early stage in Canada's industrialization, the foreign-born population accounted for 13.3 per cent of the total population, a figure that was roughly comparable to the ratio of immigrants in the United States. However, this foreign population came overwhelmingly (76 per cent) from British sources. By 1921 the percentage of foreign born had jumped to 22.2 per cent (which was about 7 per cent higher than that of the United States), while the foreign born other than British now accounted for 46 per cent of all the foreign-born population. After 1901 the spatial distribution of the foreign-born population was also modified as Ontario's share declined from 46.3 per cent to 32.8 per cent. In contrast, the surge of immigrants into western Canada greatly changed the demographic character of these four provinces. In 1901 it was home to 31.5 per cent of all foreign born in the country; by 1921 the figure had risen to 54 per cent![9]

Of the many immigration problems which faced the Laurier and Borden governments, none was more intractable and none politically more dangerous than that of the movement of Asians into British Columbia. Part of the problem, from Ottawa's perspective at least, was the concentration of the country's Asian population along the Pacific coast;[10] another was the fact that, as cheap expendable workers, they became a pawn in one of the rawest struggles between capital and labour in a region where the wishes of big business were rarely denied.[11] Yet by 1914 the large-scale entry of Chinese, Japanese, and Sikh immigrants for the most part had been curtailed because of the 1905 Chinese Immigration Act, which levied an exorbitant head tax of $500.00, and because of the regulations that were established after the 1907 Vancouver race riots.[12]

In many ways, the campaign for a 'White' British Columbia was similar to developments in the Pacific regions of the United States, where nativist organizations sought to exclude and marginalize Asian immigrants in their midst. Nor is this move surprising. Prior to the outbreak of war, Asian and White immigrants alike moved back and forth across the Canada–United States border in large numbers in search of work. There were also strong ties between labour unions and socialist organizations in the two countries, and radical organizations such as the Industrial Workers of the World (IWW) enjoyed considerable success in British Columbia and Alberta in a series of spectacular strikes in 1907 and 1912. As a result, American and Canadian security agencies were already sharing information about anarchist and socialist radicals even before the Great War.[13]

## The Coming of War

The economic status of immigrant workers on the eve of the First World War was not favourable. By 1912 the unsettled state of European affairs had helped to produce a prolonged economic slump in the transatlantic economy. This recession was particularly felt in western Canada, a region which was very dependent on foreign capital for its continued prosperity. By the summer of 1914 there was widespread unemployment in the area, the more so since over 400,000 immigrants had arrived in the previous year.[14] Before long many prairie and west coast communities were providing relief to unemployed workers.[15] But worse was to follow – especially for immigrants unlucky enough to have been born in those countries which took up arms against the British Empire.

The outbreak of war in August 1914 forced the dominion government into a unique situation; to implement a comprehensive set of guidelines for immigrants from hostile countries. Of the persons classified as enemy aliens there were 393,320 of German origin, 129,103 from the Austro-Hungarian Empire, 3,880 from the Turkish Empire, and several thousands from Bulgaria.[16] The dominion government's position was set forth in a series of acts and proclamations, the most important being the War Measures Act of August 1914, which specified that during a 'state of war, invasion, or insurrection ... the Governor in Council may do and authorize such acts ... orders and regulations, as he may ... deem necessary or advisable for the security, defence, order and welfare of Canada.' Specific reference was made to the following powers: censorship on all forms of communication and the arrest, detention and deportation of dangerous enemy aliens. Subsequent orders-in-council in October 1914 and September 1916 prohibited enemy aliens from possessing firearms and instituted a system of police and military registration. By end of the war over 80,000 enemy aliens had been registered, though only 8,579 of these were actually interned. This number included 2,009 Germans, 5,954 Austro-Hungarians, 205 Turks, 99 Bulgarians, and 312 classified as miscellaneous. These 8,579 prisoners of war were located in some twenty-four different camps, although most were placed in either Kapuskasing, Ontario, or Vernon, B.C.[17]

Although there were very few incidents of sabotage or espionage on the home front during the war, enemy aliens soon became the object of intense Anglo-Canadian hostility.[18] This was particularly true of those enemy aliens categorized as Austrians, since most of them were immigrants of military age who retained the status of reservists in their old homeland.[19] Throughout the fall of 1914 there were also alarming reports about what was afoot in the German-American communities of several American cities; one agent reported from Chicago that 'should the Germans achieve a single success I believe that we in Canada are in danger of a repetition of the invasion of 1866 on a larger scale.' What made the threat from the United States even more ominous was the steady flow of migrant labourers across a virtually unpatrolled border; many of those on the move were either enemy aliens or members of alleged pro-German groups such as Finns.[20]

The fear of a fifth column among unemployed and impoverished enemy alien workers was widespread.[21] Conversely, they gave strong support to the notion that enemy aliens who had jobs should be turned out of them: in 1915 there were many dismissals for 'patriotic' reasons. This policy was popular among both Anglo-Canadian workers and immigrants from countries such as Italy and Russia, now allied with the British Empire.[22] Some labour-intensive corporations, however, held a different point of view.[23] The Dominion Iron and Steel Company, for example, resisted the pressure to dismiss their enemy alien employees on the grounds that Nova Scotia workers 'would not undertake the rough, dirty jobs.'[24] It was only when the company obtained an understanding from the dominion Immigration Branch that it could import even more pliable workers from Newfoundland that it agreed to join temporarily in the patriotic crusade.[25] Elsewhere corporate resistance was even stronger. In June 1915 English-speaking and allied miners threatened strike action at Fernie, B.C., and Hillcrest, Alberta, unless all enemy alien miners were dismissed. The situation was particularly tense at Fernie, where the giant Crow's Nest Coal Company initially baulked at this demand. Eventually a compromise was achieved: all naturalized married enemy alien miners were retained; naturalized unmarried enemy aliens were promised work when it was available; the remainder of the enemy alien work force, some 300 in number, were temporarily interned. Within two months, however, all but the 'most dangerous' had been released by dominion authorities.[26]

This action indicated that, despite severe local and provincial pressure, the Borden government was not prepared to implement a mass internment policy. The enormous expense of operating the camps and an antipathy to adopting 'police state' tactics partly explain the dominion government's reluctance. There was also a suspicion in Ottawa that many municipalities wanted to take advantage of internment camps to get rid of their unemployed. Solicitor General Arthur Meighen articulated the view of the majority of the cabinet when he argued that instead of being interned, each unemployed alien should be granted forty acres of land which could be cultivated under government supervision; he concluded his case with the observation that 'these Austrians ... can live on very little.'[27] By the spring of 1916 even the British Columbia authorities had come around to this point of view. One provincial police report gave this account of how much things had quieted down: 'From a police point of view, there has been less trouble amongst them [aliens] since the beginning of the war than previously;

Internment Camp No. 2, Edgewood, British Columbia, ca. 1916 (National Archives of Canada, PA127065)

the fact that several of them were sent to internment camps at the beginning of the war seemed to have a good effect on the remainder. ... In my opinion, if there is ever any trouble over the employment of enemy aliens, it will be after the war is over and our people have returned.'[28]

Yet the changed attitude in British Columbia also reflected a dramatically altered labour market. As the war progressed, serious labour shortages developed in both the province and the country. In the summer of 1915 there was a demand for about 10,000 harvest labourers in the Prairie provinces. Many of those who came to do the harvesting were unemployed enemy alien workers from the slums of Vancouver and Winnipeg who had their transportation subsidized by the dominion and western provincial governments.[29] Government involvement in the recruitment of such workers was increased in 1916 when it became apparent that the supply of labour available on the Prairies would again be insufficient to meet the harvest demands. The dominion Immigration Branch now began placing advertisements in United States newspapers urging Americans to look northward for employment. Instructions were also issued to the agents of the branch that the money qualifications of the Immigration Act were to be relaxed. By the end of September 1916 over 5,000 harvesters had crossed the international border, attracted by generous wages ($3.50 a day) and cheap (1 cent per mile) rail fares from border points.[30]

Increasingly, the practice of securing industrial workers from the United States was also regarded as essential to the maintenance of the Canadian war economy. By an order-in-council of August 1916 the Alien Labour Act was temporarily shelved in order to facilitate the movement of industrial labour northward. Thousands of American residents were soon streaming into Canadian industrial communities,[31] but after the entry of the United States into the war in 1917 this source of labour supply was abruptly cut off. Of necessity the focus of Canadian recruitment efforts now shifted overseas, most notably towards East Asia and the West Indies. The most ambitious proposal called for the importation of thousands of Chinese labourers on a temporary basis. But this solution met with the same violent objections it had always encountered from organized labour and nativist opinion, and it was ultimately rejected by the dominion government.[32]

Since an overseas solution seemed impossible, the new labour situation put a premium on the surplus manpower available in the country. As a result, the alien worker, whether of enemy extraction or not, became a very desirable quantity indeed. The implementation of conscription in the summer of 1917 only aggravated an already difficult situation; by the end of the year it was estimated that the country faced a shortage of 100,000 workers. From the spring of 1917 on, foreign workers found themselves not only wanted by Canadian employers, but actually being drafted into the industrial labour force by the dominion government.[33] As of August 1916 all men and women over the age of sixteen were required to register with the Canadian Registration Board, and in April 1918 the so-called anti-loafing act provided that 'every male person residing in the Dominion of Canada should be regularly engaged in some useful occupation.'[34]

As early as 1916 the dominion government had adopted the practice of releasing non-dangerous interned prisoners of war (POWs) under contract to selected mining and railway companies both to minimize the costs of operating the camps, and to cope with labour shortages. Not surprisingly, this policy was welcomed by Canadian industrialists, since these enemy alien workers received only $1.10 a day and were not susceptible to trade union influence.[35] One of the mining companies most enthusiastic about securing large numbers of the POW workers was the Dominion Iron and Steel Corporation. In the fall of 1917 the president of the company, Mark Workman, suggested that his operation be allocated both interned and 'troublesome' aliens, since 'there is no better way of handling aliens than to keep them employed in productive labour.' In December 1917 Workman approached Borden, before the latter left for England, with the proposal that the POWs interned in Great Britain be transferred to the mines of Cape Breton Island. Unfortunately for the Dominion Steel Company, the scheme was rejected by British officials.[36]

The railway companies, particularly the Canadian Pacific, also received large numbers of POW workers. The reception of these workers harked back to some of the worst aspects of the immigrant navvy tradition of these companies. During 1916 and 1917 there was a series of complaints from POW workers, and on one occasion thirty-two Austrian workers went on strike in the North Bay district to protest dangerous working conditions and unsanitary living conditions. Neither the civil nor the military authorities gave any countenance to their complaints; the ultimate fate of these workers was to be sentenced to six months' imprisonment at the Burwash prison farm 'for breach of contract.'[37]

This coercion was symptomatic of a growing concern among both Anglo-Canadian businessmen and dominion security officials about alien labour radicalism. Not surprisingly, a 65 per cent increase in food prices between August 1914 and December 1917 created considerable industrial unrest, and the labour shortages which began developing in 1916 provided the trade unions with a superb opportunity to strike back. In 1917 there were a record number of strikes and more than 1 million man days were lost. Immigrant workers were caught up in the general labour unrest. In numerous industrial centres in northern Ontario and western Canada they demonstrated a capacity for effective collective action and a willingness to defy both the power of management and the state. The onset of the Russian Revolution in 1917 added to the tension in Canada by breathing new life into a number of ethnic socialist organizations.[38]

By the spring of 1918 the dominion government was under great pressure to place all foreign workers under supervision, and, if necessary, to make them 'work at the point of a bayonet.' The large-scale internment of radical aliens and the suppression of seditious foreign-language newspapers was also now widely advocated.[39] In June 1918 C.H. Cahan, a wealthy Montreal lawyer, was appointed to conduct a special investigation of alien radicalism. In the course of his inquiry Cahan solicited information from businessmen, 'respectable' labour leaders, police officials in both Canada and the United States, and various members of the anti-socialist immigrant community in Canada. The report which Cahan submitted to cabinet in September 1918 was the basis of a series of coercive measures: by two orders-in-council (PC 2381 and PC 2384) the foreign language press was suppressed and a number of socialist and anarchist organizations were outlawed. Penalties for possession of prohibited literature and continued membership in any of these outlawed organizations were extremely severe: fines of up to $5,000.00 or a maximum prison term of five years could be imposed.[40]

**The Red Scare**

The hatreds and fear stirred up by the First World War did not end with the Armistice of 1918; instead, social tension spread in ever-widening circles. Anglo-Canadians who had learned to despise the Germans and the Austro-Hungarians had little difficulty in transferring their aroused passions to the Bolsheviks. Though the guns were silent on the Western Front, Canadian troops were now being sent to Siberia 'to strangle the infant Bolshevism in its cradle.'[41] Within Canada, there was widespread agitation against potentially disloyal aliens and those involved in socialist organizations. An editorial in the Winnipeg *Telegram* summed up these sentiments: 'Let every hostile alien be deported from this country, the privileges of which ... he does not appreciate.'[42]

In the early months of 1919 the Borden government was deluged by a great wave of petitions demanding the mass deportation of enemy aliens. Enquiries were actually made by the dominion government concerning the possible implementation of a policy of mass expulsion. Surveys by the Department of Justice revealed that there were over 88,000 enemy aliens registered, 2,222 of whom were located in internment camps. There were also 63,784 Russian subjects in Canada, many of whom officials in Ottawa believed to be potentially hostile.[43] The policy of mass deportation was rejected, however, because of both its likely international repercussions and the demands it would make on the country's transportation facilities at a time when the troops were returning from Europe.[44]

The need to find jobs quickly for the returning soldiers also affected the situation of the foreign worker. Both politicians and businessmen faced a powerful argument in the claim that all enemy aliens should be turned out of their jobs to make way for Canada's 'heroes,' but their actions were also motivated by the fear that the veterans would be radicalized and lured into socialist organizations if their economic needs were not immediately satisfied. By February 1919 the British Columbia Employers' Association, the British Columbia Manufacturers' Association, and the British Columbia Loggers' Association all had announced that their memberships were prepared to offer employment to returned soldiers by dismissing alien enemies. This pattern was repeated in the mining region of northern Ontario, where in the early months of 1919 the International Nickel Company, for instance, dismissed 2,200 of their 3,200 employees, the vast majority of whom were foreigners.[45] Even the CPR joined the 'patriotic crusade' of dismissals. As Vice-President D.C. Coleman put it, 'The aliens who had been on the land when the war broke out and who went to work in the cities and towns, taking the jobs of the men who went to the front ... [should] go back to their old jobs on the land.'[46]

But not even the land of the 'men in sheepskin coats' was now safe for the immigrant worker; rumours were abroad that the dominion government intended to cancel large numbers of homestead patents, and assaults on aliens by returned soldiers were commonplace.[47] Even the usually passive *Canadian Ruthenian* denounced the harsh treatment which Ukrainians and other foreigners were receiving from the Anglo-Canadian community and the dominion government: 'The Ukrainians were invited to Canada and promised liberty, and a kind of paradise. Instead of the latter they found woods and rocks, which had to be cut down to make the land fit to work on. They were given farms far from the railroads, which they so much helped in building – but still they worked hard ... and came to love Canada. But ... liberty did not last long. First, they were called "Galicians" in mockery. Secondly, preachers were sent amongst them, as if they were savages, to preach Protestantism. And thirdly, they were deprived of the right to elect their representatives in Parliament. They are now uncertain about their future in Canada. Probably, their [property] so bitterly earned in the sweat of their brow will be confiscated.'[48] By the spring of 1919 the Borden government had received a number of petitions from ethnic organizations demanding either British justice or the right to leave Canada. The *Toronto Telegram* estimated that as many as 150,000 Europeans were preparing to leave the country. Some Anglo-Canadian observers warned, however, that mass emigration might relieve the employment problems of the moment, but in the long run it would leave 'a hopeless dearth of labour for certain kinds of work which Anglo-Saxons will not undertake.'[49]

Concern about the status of the alien worker led directly to the appointment by the dominion government of the Royal Commission on Industrial Relations on 4 April 1919. The members of the commission travelled from Sydney to Victoria and held hearings in some twenty-eight industrial centres. The testimony of industrialists who appeared before the commission reveals an ambivalent attitude towards the alien worker. Some industrialists argued that the alien was usually doing work 'that white men don't want,' and that it would 'be a shame to make the returned soldier work at that job.' But in those regions where there was high unemployment among returned soldiers and where alien workers had been organized by radical trade unions, management took a strikingly different view. William Henderson, a coal-mine operator at Drumheller, Alberta, informed the commission that the unstable industrial climate of that region could be reversed only by hiring more Anglo-Canadian workers, 'men that we could talk to ... men that would come in with us and co-operate with us.' Many mining representatives also indicated that their companies had released large numbers of aliens who had shown radical tendencies; there were numerous suggestions that these aliens should not only be removed from the mining districts, but actually be deported from Canada.[50]

In the spring of 1919 Winnipeg was a city of many solitudes. Within its boundaries, rich and poor, Anglo-Saxon and foreigner lived in isolation. The vast majority of the white-collar Anglo-Saxon population lived in the south and west of the city; the continental Europeans were hived in the north end. This ethno-class division was also reflected in the disparity between the distribution of social services and the incidence of disease. Infant mortality in the North End, for example, was usually twice the rate in the Anglo-Saxon South End. The disastrous influenza epidemic which struck the city during the winter of 1918–19 further demonstrated the high cost of being poor and foreign.[51]

During January and February 1919 there was a series of anti-alien incidents in the city. One of the worst occurred on 28 January, when a mob of returned soldiers attacked scores of foreigners and wrecked the German club, the offices of the Socialist Party of Canada and the business establishment of Sam Blumenberg, a prominent Jewish socialist.[52]

Reports of the event in the *Winnipeg Telegram* illustrate the attitude adopted by many Anglo-Canadian residents of the city towards the aliens. The *Telegram* made no apologies for the violence; instead, the newspaper contrasted the manly traits of the Anglo-Canadian veterans with the cowardly and furtive behaviour of the aliens: 'It was typical of all who were assaulted, that they hit out for home or the nearest hiding place after the battle.'[53] Clearly, many Anglo-Canadians in the city were prepared to accept mob justice. R.B. Russell reported that the rioting veterans had committed their worst excesses when 'smartly dressed officers ... [and] prominent members of the Board of Trade' had urged them on. Nor had the local police or military security officials made any attempt to protect the foreigners from the mob.[54]

At the provincial level, Premier Norris's response to the violence was not to punish the rioters, but to establish an Alien Investigation Board, which issued registration cards only to 'loyal' aliens. Without these cards foreign workers not only were denied employment, but were actually scheduled for deportation. Indeed, the local pressure for more extensive deportation of radical aliens increased during the spring of 1919, especially after D.A. Ross, the provincial member for Springfield, publicly charged that both Ukrainian socialists and religious national-ists were armed with 'machine guns, rifles and ammunition to start a revolution in May.' The stage was now set for the Red Scare of 1919.[55]

The Winnipeg General Strike of 15 May to 28 June 1919 brought the elements of class and ethnic conflict together in a massive confronta-tion. The growing hysteria in the city was accompanied by renewed alien propaganda, a close cooperation between security forces and the local political and economic elite, and finally, attempts to use the immi-gration machinery to deport not only alien agitators but also British-born radicals. The sequence of events associated with the Winnipeg Strike has been well documented: the breakdown of negotiations be-tween management and labour in the building and metal trades was followed by the decision of the Winnipeg Trades and Labour Council to call a general strike for 15 May. The response was dramatic: between 25,000 and 30,000 workers left their jobs. Overnight, the city was di-vided into two camps.[56]

On one side stood the Citizens' Committee of One Thousand, a group of Anglo-Canadian businessmen and professionals who viewed them-selves as the defenders of the Canadian way of life on the Prairies. Their purpose was clear: to crush the radical labour movement in Winnipeg. In their pursuit of this goal the Citizens' Committee engaged in a

Crowd gathered outside the Union Bank of Canada building on Main Street during the Winnipeg General Strike, Winnipeg, Manitoba, 21 June 1919 (National Archives of Canada, PA163001)

ferocious propaganda campaign against the opposing Central Strike Committee, both through its own newspaper, the *Citizen*, and through the enthusiastic support it received from the *Telegram* and the Manitoba *Free Press*. The committee's propaganda was aimed specifically at veterans, and the strike was portrayed as the work of enemy aliens and a few irresponsible Anglo-Saxon agitators.[57] John W. Dafoe, the influential editor of the *Free Press*, informed his readers that the five members of the Central Strike Committee – Russell, Ivens, Veitch, Robinson, and Winning – had been rejected by the intelligent and skilled Anglo-Saxon workers and had gained power only through 'the fanatical allegiance of the Germans, Austrians, Huns and Russians.' Dafoe advised that the best way of undermining the control which the 'Red Five' exercised over the Winnipeg labour movement was 'to clean the aliens out of this community and ship them back to their happy homes in Europe which vomited them forth a decade ago.'[58]

The Borden government was quick to comply. On 15 June the commissioner of the Royal North-West Mounted Police (RNWMP) indicated that one hundred aliens had been marked for deportation under the recently enacted section 41 of the Immigration Act, and that thirty-six were in Winnipeg. In the early hours of 17 June officers of the force descended on the residences of two Winnipeggers: six Anglo-Saxon labour leaders and four 'foreigners.' Ultimately, none of these men was summarily deported, as planned.[59] In the case of the Anglo-Saxon strike leaders an immediate protest was registered by numerous labour organizations across the country. Alarmed by this uproar, the Borden government announced that it did not intend to use section 41 against British-born agitators either in Winnipeg or in any other centre.[60]

The foreigners arrested were not so fortunate. The violent confrontation of 21 June between the strikers and the RNWMP, in which scores of workers were injured and two killed, encouraged the hard liners in the Borden government. On 1 July a series of raids was carried out across the country on the homes of known alien agitators and the offices of radical organizations. Many of those arrested were moved to the internment camp at Kapuskasing, Ontario and subsequently deported in secret.[61] In their attempts to deport the approximately 200 'anarchists and revolutionaries' rounded up in the summer raids of 1919 the Immigration Branch worked very closely with United States immigration authorities. This cooperation was indicative of a link which was being forged between Canadian and American security agencies; the formation of the Communist Labour Party of America and the Communist Party of America in the fall of 1919 further strengthened this connection.[62] The RNWMP and Military Intelligence also maintained close contact with the British Secret Service. Lists of undesirable immigrants and known communists were transmitted from London to Ottawa. Indeed, the Immigration Branch had now evolved from a recruitment agency to a security service.[63]

In time the repression of militant foreign workers took many different forms. In combating the woodworkers unions, the British Columbia Loggers' Association implemented an extensive blacklisting system, particularly after the December 1919 loggers' strike, calculated to purge all members of the IWW and One Big Union (OBU), as well as those 'known to have seditious, radical or disloyal leanings.'[64] In the Rocky Mountains coal-mining district the companies were also successful in withstanding a lengthy strike and purge of local radicals. In this effort both the international headquarters of the United Mine Workers of America (UMWA), now concerned over the number of wildcat strikes and the growing radicalism in District 18, and the dominion government provided assistance. This meant that all members associated with the OBU were rejected for employment, while the political records of the remainder of the mining population were thoroughly investigated. A considerable number of alien workers in this region were also placed in internment camps.[65] One of them, Timothy Koreichuk, a leading organizer for the Ukrainian Social Democrats in District 18, died while interned at Vernon, British Columbia. To the *Ukrainian Labor News* Koreichuk was a heroic victim of capitalist oppression: 'Sleep and dream martyr! Your fervour for the struggle which you have placed in the hearts of all Ukrainian workers will remain forever.'[66]

## Immigration 'Reform'

The events of 1918–19 produced a spirited national debate on whether Canada should continue to maintain an open-door immigration policy. Since many Anglo-Canadians equated Bolshevism with the recent immigration from eastern Europe, support grew for policies similar to the quota system under discussion in the United States.[67] The Winnipeg strike, the surplus of labour, and a short but sharp dip in the stock market sharply reduced the incentive for industrialists to lobby for the continued importation of alien workers. Even the Canadian Manufacturers' Association, a long-time advocate of the open-door immigration policy, sounded a cautious note: 'Canada should not encourage the immigration of those whose political and social beliefs unfit them for assimilation with Canadians. While a great country such as Canada possessing millions of vacant acres needs population, it is wiser to go slowly and secure the right sort of citizens.' Ethnic, cultural, and ideological acceptability had temporarily triumphed over economic considerations. Whether Canada was prepared to accept a slower rate of economic growth in order to ensure its survival as a predominantly Anglo-Canadian nation now became a matter of pressing importance.[68]

The wartime national security provisions were extended to the Immigration Act during its 1919 revisions. Of paramount importance was section 41, which stipulated that 'any person other than a Canadian citizen who advocates ... the overthrow by force ... of constituted authority' could be deported from the country.[69] This sweeping provision reinforced section 38 of the act, which gave the Governor General in council authority 'to prohibit or limit ... for a stated period or permanently the landing ... of immigrants belonging to any nationality or race deemed unsuitable.' By order-in-council PC 1203, Germans, Austrians, Hungarians, Bulgarians, and Turks were excluded because of their wartime association; PC 1204 barred Doukhobors, Mennonites, and Hutterites because of 'their peculiar customs, habits, modes of living and methods of holding property.'[70]

Among European immigrants themselves the enemy alien hysteria and the Red Scare produced great bitterness, and many considered returning home during the summer of 1919, since their future prospects in Canada looked anything but promising. Certainly, there seemed little reason to believe that they could ever become part of the mainstream of Canadian life. In these circumstances Ukrainian, Finnish, and Russian organizations offered an alternative to the 'Canadian Way of Life' – an alternative that found sustenance in the achievements of Soviet communism.[71] The distinctive outlook of Slavic and Finnish socialists in Canada was described as follows in a 1921 RCMP intelligence report: 'If in earlier years they came sick of Europe, ready to turn their back on their homelands, and full of admiration for the native Canadian and Canadian civilization, they have changed their point of view. The war and revolution have roused their intense interest in Central Europe. They belong almost wholly to the poorest element in the community, and it is highly exciting to them to see the class from which they come, composed in effect of their own relatives, seize control of all power and acquire all property.'[72] Such was the legacy of the year 1919 – the floodtide of radical labour politics in Canada.

## Conclusion

Why was there such strong anti-immigrant sentiment among western Canadians during the First World War? And why did the federal government find it necessary to launch so many repressive measures, particularly during the period 1917–19, against groups deemed 'un-Canadian?' In part, this nativist campaign can be regarded as an intensification of pre-war bias when negative stereotypes of central Europeans was widespread. In these years, even prominent social reformers such as Reverend Charles W. Gordon (Ralph Connor) and James S. Woodsworth tended to equate immigrant poverty with immorality and ethnic festivals with debauchery and violence.[73] RNWMP reports from western Canada also stressed the tendency of foreign workers to take the law into their own hands, the prevalence of knives and guns turning even minor disagreements into violent confrontations. The RNWMP also were distressed by their inability to apprehend labour agitators and 'criminals,' largely because ethnic communities often viewed the Law as 'the enemy.' This conspiracy of silence appeared particularly threatening in large ethnic 'ghettos' such as North End Winnipeg.

Yet another pre-war stereotype was the spectre of foreign agitators and demagogues who sought to disrupt and corrupt western Canadian society. Industrial unrest among immigrant workers, for instance, was usually blamed on anarchists, socialists, and syndicalists who, it was alleged, were able to mobilize the latent violence of the foreign worker. The possibility that the west would become 'balkanized' into a series of ethnic fiefdoms also preoccupied reformers prior to 1914  particularly in Manitoba, where the willingness of the Roblin government to exchange immigrant bloc votes for cultural concessions was vigorously denounced by prominent regional spokesmen such as John W. Dafoe, the influential editor of the Manitoba *Free Press*. These allegations about 'un-Canadian' activities gained even greater intensity during the 1917 wartime general election, when recent immigrants from Europe were disfranchised in the name of national security.[74]

Although the pre-war legacy is important, one should not underestimate the extent to which the war itself dramatically turned western Canadian public opinion against enemy aliens during the war years. As casualties mounted, propaganda about Germany and its allies became more and more vicious, and, according to one account, by 1917 'most Canadians ... believed that they were fighting a people that inoculated its captives with tuberculosis, decorated its dwellings with human skin, (and) crucified Canadian soldiers.' Not surprisingly, retaliation against the large and diversified German Canadian community was widespread, including internment, press censorship, confiscation of property, public ostracism, and mob violence. Throughout the war years punitive measures were also directed at Ukrainians and other former citizens of the Austro-Hungarian empire because of their dual loyalty, their predominantly working-class status, and their identification with Bolshevism, particularly during the 1919 Red Scare.

Yet it is instructive that the 1919 immigration restrictions were designed only as emergency measures. This was evident when the Union Government refused to impose a statutory prohibition against German immigration and instead relied upon more flexible orders-in-council. As a result, once the economy had recovered, Canada became an immigration nation once again, and between 1923 and 1930 over 400,000 Germans, Ukrainians, and other European immigrants entered the country, most of them gravitating towards the farms and resource industries of western Canada. In contrast, the numbers of overseas Chinese, Japanese, and East Indians allowed into the country were sharply reduced, while Asian Canadians living in British Columbia were still denied full civil rights.[75] As 'White' immigrants, central Europeans were immediately candidates for Canadianization, although language, culture, occupation, and place of residence clearly set them apart from Anglo-Canadian society. This social distance was lengthened by the suspicion and hostility many newcomers felt when they discovered that Canada regarded them as second-class citizens. The words of Sandor Hunyadi, the fictional character created by John Marlyn in his book *Under the Ribs of Death*, vividly describe what Anglo-Winnipeg looked like from the immigrant North End: "'The English," he whispered. "Pa, the only people who count are the English. Their fathers got all the best jobs. They're the only ones nobody ever calls foreigners. Nobody ever makes fun of their names or calls them 'bologny-eaters,' or laughs at the way they dress or talk. Nobody," he concluded bitterly, "cause when you're English it's the same as bein' Canadian.'"[76]

**Postscript**

Since the publication of *Dangerous Foreigners* in 1979, the scholarship dealing with ethnic and class conflict in western Canada during the First World War has greatly improved. In terms of scholarly debates, there are two subjects that have particular relevance for this chapter. The first was the specific wartime experience of the different European ethnic groups – notably those branded as enemy aliens. Not surprisingly, given their numbers and their strong sense of community, Ukrainian Canadians have been in the lead, demanding a redress of the wartime wrongs,[77] a campaign that has been greatly enhanced by a range of historical studies on this topic.[78] A second intriguing debate involves questions about the 'exceptional' radical character of the western Canadian labour movement, particularly during the period 1914–19.[79] Although the full scope of the controversy cannot be assessed here, these revisionist studies have provided valuable insights into the role immigrant workers assumed, both in western Canada and elsewhere.[80]

Yet despite this impressive scholarship, there are still important themes that remain unexplored. For example, there is a great need to reassess how Chinese and Japanese residents of British Columbia coped with wartime harassment, how the ideological and religious differences within various European ethnic groups were intensified by four years of conflict, and what role immigrant women assumed in the various labour confrontations of that period, including the Winnipeg General Strike.[81] These challenging subjects – and many others – await the attention of future historians of the Canadian west and the First World War.

NOTES

1 The author has written extensively on this subject. See Donald Avery, *'Dangerous Foreigners': European Immigrant Workers and Labour Radicalism in Canada, 1896–1932* (Toronto, 1979); *Reluctant Host: Canada's Response to Immigrant Workers, 1896–1994* (Toronto, 1995); 'The Radical Alien and the Winnipeg General Strike of 1919,' in C. Berger and R. Cook, eds, *The West and the Nation: Essays in Honour of W.L. Morton* (Toronto, 1976).

2 Queen's University Archives, Thomas Crerar Papers, Crerar to George Chipman, 15 April 1919.

3 O.J. Firestone, *Canada's Economic Development, 1867–1953* (London, 1958), 65.

4 *Fifth Census of Canada, 1911* (Ottawa, 1912), 2, 42–4; Robert England, *The Central European Immigrant in Canada* (Toronto, 1929); George Haythorne and Leonard Marsh, *Land and Labour: A Social Survey of Agriculture and the Farm Labour Market in Central Canada* (Toronto, 1941), 213–30.

5 For early studies of the experience of European immigrant workers in the Canadian frontier see James Fitzpatrick, *University in Overalls* (Toronto, 1920), and Edmund Bradwin, *The Bunkhouse Man* (Toronto, 1928).

6 Ukrainian Rural Settlements, *Report of the Bureau of Social Research* (Winnipeg, 25 January 1917); J.W. Dafoe, *Clifford Sifton in Relation to His Times* (Toronto, 1931), 318–19; Canada, *House of Commons Debates*, 1905, 7686; ibid., 1911, 1611. There are also extensive references to this trend in National Archives of Canada (NAC), Immigration Branch (IB) Records, ff. 29490 and 195281.

7 For the more traditional view of the primacy of agricultural immigrants see Norman Macdonald, *Canada, Immigration and Colonization, 1841–1903* (Toronto, 1968); Robert England, *The Colonization of Western Canada* (Toronto, 1936); and Harold Troper, *Only Farmers Need Apply* (Toronto, 1972).

8 American scholarship on the transatlantic movement of European immigrant workers is extensive. Two of the most useful studies are John Brodar, *The Transplanted: A History of Immigrants to Urban America* (Bloomington, Ind., 1987), and Gerald Rosenblum, *Immigrant Workers: Their Impact on American Labor Radicalism* (New York, 1973).

9 M.C. Urquart and K.A.H. Buckley, eds, *Historical Statistics of Canada* (Toronto, 1965), Series A, 133–42; Canada Manpower and Immigration, *Immigration and Population Statistics*, (Ottawa, 1974), 3: 7–15.

10 In 1891 approximately 98 per cent of the Chinese population was in British Columbia; although numbers declined somewhat during subsequent decades, 60 per cent of Canada's Chinese were still in the province in 1921. In contrast, over 90 per cent of the Japanese and East Indian population lived in British Columbia until the Second World War. Peter Li, *The Chinese in Canada* (Toronto, 1982), 51.

11 Peter Ward, *White Canada Forever: Popular attitudes and Public Policy towards Orientals in British Columbia (Montreal, 1978);* Edgar Wickberg, ed., *From China to Canada: A History of the Chinese Communities in Canada* (Toronto, 1982).

12 Patricia Roy, *A White's Man's Province: British Columbia's Politicians and Chinese and Japanese Immigrants, 1858–1914* (Vancouver, 1989); Hugh Johnston, *The Voyage of the Komagata Maru: The Sikh Challenge to Canada's Colour Bar* (Delhi, 1979).

13 Ross McCormack, *Reformers, Rebels and Revolutionaries: The Western Canadian Radical Movement, 1899–1919* (Toronto, 1978); Mark Leier, *Where the Fraser Flows: The Industrial Workers of the World in British Columbia* (Vancouver, 1990).

14 *Labour Gazette* (1914), 286–332, 820–1.

15 This report appeared in the Winnipeg-based Ukrainian newspaper *Robotchny Narod*, 14 March 1914. Other newspapers claimed that over 3,000 Bulgarian navvies had returned to Europe during the fall of that year.

16 *Fifth Census of Canada, 1911* (Ottawa, 1912), 2: 367; J.C. Hopkins, ed., *Canadian Annual Review of Public Affairs (CAR) 1915* (Toronto, 1914–18), 353.

17 Revised Statutes of Canada, 1927, chap. 206, vol. 4, 1–3; *Canadian Gazette,* 15 August 1914. NAC, Sir Robert Borden Papers (BP), 56666, C.H. Cahan to C.J. Doherty, 14 September 1918.

18 Canadian citizens of African-Canadian, Chinese, Japanese, East Indian, and Aboriginal backgrounds also encountered discrimination during the war years. One of the most blatant was the way volunteers from these groups were treated by the Canadian military establishment. Although about 5,000 Indians, 1,000 Blacks and several hundred Chinese and Japa-

nese enlisted in the Canadian forces, they were predominantly assigned to low-status jobs in the construction or forestry units overseas. See James Walker, 'Race and Recruitment in World War I: Enlistment of Visible Minorities in the Canadian Expeditionary Force,' *Canadian Historical Review* 70, 1 (March 1989), 26.

19 Major General W.D. Otter, *Internment Operations, 1914–20* (Ottawa, 30 September 1920), 2, 6, 12; *CAR*, 1916, 433.

20 *CAR, 1916*, 433; Joseph Boudreau, 'The Enemy Alien Problem in Canada, 1914–1921,' unpublished PhD thesis, University of California, 1964, 50–103.

21 *Canadian Ruthenian*, 1 August 1914.

22 NAC, Department of Militia and Defence Headquarters (DND), f. C-965 #2, Report, Agent J.D. Sisler, 9 August 1914. There were numerous other reports in this file.

23 Some of the strongest support for internment camps came from prominent citizens in heterogeneous communities. In Winnipeg, for example, J.A.M. Aikins, a prominent Conservative, warned that the city's enemy aliens might take advantage of the war 'for the destruction of property, public and private.' NAC, BP, 106322, Aikins to Borden, 12 November 1914.

24 *Canadian Mining Journal*, 15 August 1914.

25 NAC, IB, f. 775789, T.D. Willans, travelling immigration inspector to W.D. Scott, 9 June 1915; D.H. McDougall, general manager, Dominion Iron and Steel Corporation, 29 May 1915.

26 *Northern Miner* (Cobalt) 9 October 1915; *CAR, 1915*, 355; NAC, DND, file 965, No. 9, Major E.J. May to Colonel E.A. Cruickshank, district officer in command of military district #13, 28 June 1915.

27 Otter, *Internment Operations*, 6–12; NAC, Arthur Meighen Papers (MP), 106995, Meighen to Borden, 4 September 1914. The European dependants of these alien workers obviously had to live on even less, because after August 1914 it was unlawful to send remittances of money out of the country. NAC, Chief Press Censor Papers, vol. 196, Livesay to Chambers, 4 December 1915.

28 British Columbia Provincial Archives (BCPA), British Columbia Provincial Police (BCPP), file 1355–7, John Simpson to Chief Constable of Greenwood to Colin Campbell, supt of the BCPP, 26 January 1916.

29 NAC, IB, f. 29490, No. 4, W. Banford, Dominion immigration officer to W.D. Scott, 13 May 1915; BCPA, Sir Richard McBride Papers, McBride to Premier Sifton (Alta), 30 June 1915. About 20,000 Canadian troops had also been used in gathering the harvest during 1915.

30 NAC, IB, f. 29490, No. 6, W.D. Scott, 'Circular Letter to Canadian Immigration Agents in the United States,' 2 August 1916.

31  NAC, Sir Joseph Flavelle Papers, 74, Scott to Flavelle, director of imperial munitions, 11 August 1916; IB, f. 29490, No. 6, J. Frater Taylor, president of Algoma Steel to Flavelle, 17 August 1917. The number of American immigrants entering the country was 41,779 in 1916 and 65,739 in 1917.

32  China provided over 50,000 labourers to the Allied cause. They were transported from Vancouver to Halifax in 1917 for service in France. British Columbia *Federationist*, 18 January 1918; *Vancouver Sun*, 7 February 1918; Harry Con et al., *From China to Canada: A History of the Chinese Communities of Canada* (Toronto, 1982), 119.

33  NAC, IB, f. 75789, A. Macdonald, Employment Agent, Dominion Coal Company to Scott, 25 July 1916.

34  *CAR, 1918*, 330; ibid., 1916, 325–8; Statutes of Canada, 9–10 Geo. v, xciii. The reaction of the Trades and Labor Congress to the treatment of enemy alien workers varied. On one hand, they endorsed the 'patriotic' dismissals in 1915; by 1916, however, the congress executive was concerned that the dominion government intended to use large numbers of enemy aliens as cheap forced labour. *Proceedings of the Thirty-First Annual Session of the Trades and Labor Congress of Canada, 1915* (Ottawa, 1915), 16–17; ibid., *1916*, 43.

35  Otter, *Internment Operations*, 9–14; NAC, Secretary of State Papers, Internment Operation Section, file 5330, No. 7, Major Dales, Commandant Kapuskasing to Otter, 14 November 1918; Desmond Morton 'Sir William Otter and Internment Operations in Canada During the First World War,' *Canadian Historical Review* 55 (March 1974), 32–58.

36  NAC, BP, f. 43110, Mark Workman to Borden, 19 December 1918; ibid., 43097, Borden to A.E. Blount, 1 July 1918.

37  *CAR, 1915*, 354; Internment Operation Papers, Otter to F.L. Wanklyn, CPR, 12 June 1916.

38  McCormack, *Rebels, Reformers and Revolutionaries: The Western Canadian Radical Movement, 1899–1919* (Toronto, 1977), 143–216; Francis Swyripa and John Herd Thompson, eds, *Loyalties in Conflict: Ukrainians in Canada During the Great War* (Edmonton, 1983).

39  NAC, DND, C-2665, Major-General Ketchen, officer commanding Military District 10, to secretary of the Milita Council, 7 July 1917; Department of Justice Papers, 1919, file 2059, Registrar of Alien Enemies, Winnipeg, to Colonel Sherwood, Dominion Police, 17 August 1918; CPC, 144–A-2, Chambers to secretary of state, 20 September 1918.

40  NAC, BP, f. 56656, C.H. Cahan to Borden July 20, 1918; BP, f. 56668, Cahan to Borden, 14–20 September 1918, 45; BP, f. 56668, Cahan to Borden, 14 September 1918. The fourteen illegal organizations also included the

IWW, the Group of Social Democrats of Anarchists, the Chinese Nationalist League, and the Social Democratic Party; the latter organization was removed from the list in November 1918. NAC, BP, f. 56698, Cahan to Borden, 21 October 1918; Statutes of Canada, 1919, 9–10 Geo. v, lxxi–lxxiii.

41 James Eayrs, *In Defence of Canada: From the Great War to the Great Depression* (Toronto, 1967), 30.

42 *Winnipeg Telegram*, 28 January 1919.

43 NAC, Internment Operations, f. 6712, Major General Otter to acting minister of justice, 19 December 1918; Justice Records, 1919, vol. 227, Report, chief commissioner Dominion Police to director of public safety, 27 November 1918.

44 NAC, BP, f. 83163, Sir Thomas White to Borden, 31 February 1919. On 28 February 1919 the German government lodged an official complaint with British authorities over 'the reported plan of the Canadian government to deport all Germans from Canada.' IB, f. 912971, Swiss ambassador, London, England to Lord Curzon, 28 February 1919.

45 *Vancouver Sun*, 26 March 1919; Department of Labour Library, Mathers Royal Commission on Industrial Relations, 'Evidence,' Sudbury hearings, 27 May 1919, testimony of J.L. Fortin, 1923.

46 *Montreal Gazette*, 14 June 1919.

47 In April 1918 an amendment to the Dominion Land Act denied homestead patents to non-naturalized residents; the subsequent amendments to the Naturalization Act in June 1919 also made it extremely difficult for enemy aliens to become naturalized. NAC, Department of Justice Papers, 1919, f. 2266, Albert Dawdron, acting commissioner of the Dominion Police, to the minister of justice, 28 July 1919; Statutes of Canada, 1918, 9–10 Geo. v, c. 19, s. 7; *House of Commons Debates*, 1919, 4118–33.

48 NAC, Chief Press Censor, 196–1, E. Tarak to Chambers, 11 January 1918 (translation), 91; IB, f. 963419, W.D. Scott to James A. Calder, minister of immigration and colonization, 11 December 1919; *Toronto Telegram*, 1 April 1920; MP, f. 000256, J.A. Stevenson to Meighen, 24 February 1919; *Canadian Ruthenian*, 5 February 1919.

49 NAC, IB, f. 963419, W.D. Scott to James Calder, minister of Immigration and Colonization, 11 December 1919; *Toronto Telegram*, 1 April 1919; NAC, Meighen Papers, 0000256, J.A. Stevenson to Meighen 24 February 1919.

50 Department of Labour Library, Mathers Royal Commission, 'Evidence,' Victoria hearings, testimony of J.O. Cameron, president of the Victoria Board of Trade; ibid., Calgary hearings, testimony of W. Henderson; ibid., testimony of Mortimer Morrow, manager of Canmore Coal Mines.

51  Alan Artibise, *Winnipeg: A Social History of Urban Growth, 1874–1914* (Montreal, 1975), 223–45, Manitoba *Free Press*, 3 November 1918.

52  NAC, DND, C-2665, Secret Agent No. 47, Report (Wpg), to Supt Starnes, RNWMP, 24 March 1919.

53  *Winnipeg Telegram,* 29 January 1919.

54  Public Archives of Manitoba, OBU Collection, R.B. Russell to Victor Midgley, 29 January 1919.

55  Manitoba *Free Press*, 7 May 1919; *Western Labor News*, 4 April 1919. The Alien Investigation Board was legitimized by the passage of order-in-council PC 56 in January 1919, which transferred authority to investigate enemy aliens and to enforce PC 2381 and PC 2384 from the dominion Department of Justice to the provincial attorney general. Between February and May the board processed approximately 3,000 cases, of which 500 were denied certificates. RCMP Records, Comptroller to Commissioner Perry, 20 March 1919; Manitoba *Free Press*, 7 May 1919, 83. NAC, MP, 000279, D.A. Ross to Meighen, 9 April 1919.

56  D.C. Masters, *The Winnipeg General Strike* (Toronto, 1959), 40–50; David Bercuson, *Confrontation at Winnipeg* (Montreal 1974), 103–95.

57  Murray Donnelly, *Dafoe of the Free Press* (Toronto, 1968), 104; RCMP Records, 1919, vol. 1, Major-General Ketchen to secretary of the Militia Council, 21 May 1919; *Winnipeg Citizen*, 5–20 June 1919.

58  Manitoba *Free Press*, 22 May 1919.

59  NAC, BP, 61913, Robertson to Borden, 14 June 1919; BP, diary entries 13–17 June; RCMP Records, CIB, vol. 70, J.A. Calder, to Commissioner Perry, 16 June 1919; IB, f. 961162, Calder to Perry, 17 June 1919.

60  Tom Moore to E. Robinson, 24 June 1919 cited by Manitoba *Free Press*, 21 November 1919; NAC, BP, diary entry 20 June 1919; NAC, BP, f. 61936, Robertson to Acland, 14 June 1919; Manitoba *Free Press*, 18 June 1919.

61  *Ukrainian Labor News*, 16 July 1919; Norman Penner, ed., *Winnipeg: 1919: The Strikers' Own History of the Winnipeg General Strike* (Toronto, 1973), 175–81; NAC, IB, f. 912971, No. 3, T.J. Murray, Telegram to J.A. Calder, 30 October 1919; Department of Justice Records, 1919, file 1960, deputy minister of justice, to Murray and Noble, 5 November 1919.

62  In October 1918 the United States Congress had passed an amendment to the 'Act to Exclude and Expel from the United States Aliens Who Are Members of the Anarchist and Similar Classes'; Emma Goldman, Alexander Berkman and 247 other 'Reds' were deported to Russia under this measure in December 1919. John Higham, *Strangers in the Land* (New York 1966), 308–24; NAC, IB, f. 961162, No. 1, F.C. Blair, secretary of immigration and colonization, memorandum to J.A. Calder 24 November 1919;

ibid., John Clark, American Consul-General, Montreal, to F.C. Blair, 19 June 1920.

63  NAC, IB, f. 961162, assistant director RCMP (CIB division) to F.C. Blair 4 August 1920; William Rodney, *Soldiers of the International: A History of the Communist Party of Canada, 1919–1929* (Toronto, 1968), 7–21.

64  UBC Archives, British Columbia Loggers' Association Minute Book, 8 August, 12 December 1919.

65  Glenbow Institute (Calgary), Western Coal Operator Association Collection (WCOA). W.R. Wilson, president of the Crow's Nest Coal Company to W. McNeill, president of the WCOA 2 September 1919; ibid., Samuel Ballantyne, chairman of the UMWA International Commission to MacNeill 2 September 1919. See also Allen Seager, 'Class, Ethnicity and Politics in the Alberta Coalfields, 1905–1945,' in Dirk Hoerder, ed., *Struggle a Hard Battle: Essays on Working-Class Immigrants* (DeKalb, Ill., 1986).

66  *Ukrainian Labor News*, 29 October 1919.

67  In addition to the pressure to exclude enemy aliens and pacifists, there was considerable support for the suggestion that Canada should not accept immigrants from certain regions because of their alleged racial deficiencies. Hume Conyn, MP for London, Ontario, cited the writings of eugenist writer Madison Grant as justifying the exclusion of 'strange people who cannot be assimilated.' Higham, *Strangers in the Land*, 308–24; *House of Commons Debates*, 1919; 1916, 1969, 2280–90.

68  *Industrial Canada* (July 1919), 120–22. *Maclean's* (August 1919), 46–9. Wellington Bridgman's *Breaking Prairie Sod* (Toronto, 1920) is an extreme example of the western Canadian backlash towards European immigrants.

69  'An Act to amend an Act of the present session entitled An Act to amend The Immigration Act 1919,' Statutes of Canada, 1919, 9–10 Geo. V, ch. 26, s. 41.

70  PC 1203 and PC 1204 were enacted on 9 June 1919. Statutes of Canada, 1919, 9–10 Geo. v, vols 1–11, X; NAC, IB, f. 72552, no. 6, F.C. Blair, secretary, Department of Immigration and Colonization, to deputy minister, 11 August 1921.

71  NAC, DND, C-2817 Major General Gwatkin to S.D. Meuburn, minister of militia, 5 August 1919; IB, f. 563236, No 7, deputy attorney general of Ontario to F.C. Blair 6 November 1919; Ivan Avakumovic, *The Communist Party in Canada: A History* (Toronto, 1975), 1–53.

72  Surveillance of communist 'infiltrators continued throughout the 1920s. NAC, Department of Justice, 1926, file 293, C. Starnes to deputy minister of justice, 27 October 1926; Avakumovic, *Communist Party in Canada*, 1–53; Barbara Roberts, *Whence They Came: Deportation from Canada, 1900–1935* (Ottawa, 1988), 71–97, 125–58.

73  Ralph Connor, *The Foreigner* (Toronto, 1909); J.S. Woodsworth, *Strangers Within Our Gates* (Toronto, 1909).

74  John Herd Thompson, 'The Enemy Alien and the Canadian General Election of 1917,' in Swerpa and Thompson, *Loyalties in Conflict*, 25–47.

75  Li, *Chinese in Canada*, 50–65; Kay Anderson, *Vancouver's Chinatown: Racial Discourse in Canada, 1875–1980* (Montreal and Kingston, 1991), 49–160.

76  John Marlyn, *Under the Ribs of Death* (Toronto, 1957), 18.

77  L.Y. Luciuk, *A Time for Atonement: Canada's First Internment Operations and the Ukrainian Canadians, 1914–1920* (Kingston, 1988); L.Y. Luciuk and S. Hryniuk, eds, *Canada's Ukrainians: Negotiating an Identity* (Toronto, 1991); L.Y. Luciuk and R. Sydoruk, *In My Charge: The Canadian Internment Camp Photographs of Sergeant Willian Buck* (Kingston, 1997); L.Y. Luciuk, N. Yurieva, and R. Zakaluzny, eds, *Roll Call: Lest We Forget* (Kingston, 1999); Lubomyr Luciuk, *Searching for Place: Ukrainian Displaced Persons, Canada, and the Migration of Memory* (Toronto, 2000).

78  Other studies on the internment of Ukrainian Canadians include M. Lupul, ed., *A Heritage in Transition: Essays in the History of Ukrainians in Canada* (Toronto, 1982); O. Martynowych, *Ukrainians in Canada : The Formative Years* (Edmonton, 1991); F. Swyripa, *Ukrainian-Canadians: A Survey of Their Portrayal in English-Canadian Works* (Edmonton, 1978); P. Yuzyk, *The Ukrainians in Manitoba: A Social History* (Toronto, 1953).

79  The major advocates for western radical exceptionalism were Masters, *Winnipeg General Strike*, McCormack, *Reformers, Rebels, and Revolutionaries*, Martin Robin, *Company Province*, Vol. 1, *The Rush for Spoils* (Toronto, 1972), and Bercuson, *Confrontation at Winnipeg*, and *Fools and Wisemen: The Rise and Fall of the One Big Union*. This viewpoint has been challenged by a number of historians, notably Greg Kealey, '1919: The Canadian Labour Revolt,' *Labour / Le Travail* 13 (Spring 1984) 11–44; David Frank and Nolan Reilly, 'The Emergence of the Socialist Movement in the Maritimes, 1899–1916,' in R.J. Brym and R.J. Sacouman, eds, *Underdevelopment and Social Movements in Atlantic Canada* (Toronto, 1979); Suzanne Morton, 'Labourism and Economic Action: The Halifax Shipyards Strike of 1920,' *Labour / Le Travail* 22 (Fall 1988), 67–98; and James Naylor, *The New Democracy: Challenging the Social Order in Industrial Ontario, 1914–25* (Toronto, 1991).

80  Since the mid-1970s there have been a number of studies dealing with the convergence of ethnicity and class within the western Canadian labour movement. They include Stanley Scott, 'A Profusion of Issues: Immigrant Labour, the World War, and the Cominco Strike of 1917,' *Labour / Le Travail* 2 (Spring 1977), 54–78; Jim Tan, 'Chinese Labour and the Reconstituted Social Order in British Columbia,' *Canadian Ethnic Studies* 19, 3 (1987),

68–88; Gillian Creese, 'Organizing against Racism in the Workplace: Chinese Workers in Vancouver before the Second World War,' *Canadian Ethnic Studies* 19, 3 (1987), 35–46; Allen Seager, 'Socialist and Workers: The Western Canadian Coal Miners, 1900–21,' *Labour / Le Travail* 16 (Fall 1995); John Kolasky, *The Shattered Illusion: The History of Ukrainian Pro-Communist Organizations in Canada* (Toronto, 1979).
81 There are a number of important studies in which the pivotal role immigrant women assumed within the Canadian labour movement is analyzed. For three different perspectives see Ruth Frager, *Strife, Class, Ethnicity, and Gender in the Jewish Labour Movement of Toronto, 1900–1939* (Toronto, 1992); Varpu Lindstrom, *Defiant Sisters: A Social History of Finnish Immigrant Women in Canada* (Toronto, 1988); Frances Swyripa, *Wedded to the Cause: Ukrainian Women and Ethnic Identities, 1891–1991* (Toronto, 1993).

## 11 The Crusade for Science: Science and Technology on the Home Front, 1914–1918

ROD MILLARD

In his presidential address to the Royal Society of Canada on the eve of the millennium in 1899, T.C. Keefer, civil engineer and transportation philosopher, predicted that Canada would have a magnificent second industrial revolution based on abundant, cheap hydroelectricity.[1] Keefer did not live to see his electrical utopia.[2] He died in January 1915, about a year after Henry Ford improved mass production with the moving assembly line. Just as Ford had revolutionized production, science applied to modern warfare in the form of the machine gun, high explosives, and poison gas, showed, as Carroll Pursell notes, 'that death, too, could be mass-produced.'[3] A century of belief in the constructive power of science was shaken; a devastating critique would follow the war. Canadian scientists and engineers, however, did not lose their faith in science. No less horrified than other Canadians by the macabre spectacle of death and destruction on the Western Front, they knew they had an important role to play in winning the war, while still hoping some day to create the kind of world Keefer only dreamed of. The war gave them an unprecedented opportunity to promote science and, more important, to promote themselves.

From the outset of the war, serious scientific and technological problems were encountered.[4] In September 1914, for example, Canadian manufacturers could not produce a complete round of artillery ammunition because they lacked sophisticated machine tools and proper gauges. Also, while Canada produced concentrates of zinc and copper matte – metals essential for making the brass parts of shells – refining was done in the United States, not Canada. As a result, machinery, gauges, refined zinc and copper, including fabricated copper shell bands and, for a time, shell fuses, had to be purchased by Canadians directly from the United States.[5] Manufacturers also complained that they were unable to produce many articles essential to various trade processes because of German monopolies.[6] Scientists ruefully observed that for the past forty years, Germany had systematically established many state-supported, science-based industries – some once dominated by Britain – through the clever use of synthetics. With German efficiency and aggressive business tactics, these industries became monopolies, leaving Britain and its allies dependent on various German chemical, electrical, and glassware commodities. Distinguished British scientists credited German industrial success to the organization of its scientific resources, particularly the application of science to industry.[7] In Canada, Professor A.B. Macallum, a University of Toronto biochemist and eminent researcher, attributed the neglect of science to a long tradition of amateurism and laissez-faire individualism in science.[8] Had Britain developed its industries scientifically, he argued, Germany would not have become strong enough to wage war.[9]

In spite of Macallum's misgivings, some important scientific and technological developments took place in wartime Canada. Although Canadian troops were victims of the first gas attack at Ypres in 1915, no chemical warfare research was conducted in Canada until 1937.[10] Researchers focused instead on projects such as the production of acetone and helium, achieving some significant innovations at home and abroad.[11] In 1915 British authorities realized that their strategic supplies of acetone, a solvent used to make cordite, the standard British military propellant, were inadequate for an expanded war effort. Anxious to secure a reliable supply, and because Canada had the only carbide and acetylene plant in the British Empire, the Imperial Munitions Board (IMB), the British government's purchasing agent in Canada, asked Shawinigan Water and Power, Quebec, to manufacture acetone from acetylene, using German patents commercially unexploited before the war. Towards the end of 1915 a team of chemists – T.H. Matheson, H.S. Reid, A.F.G. Cadenhead, W.C. Harvey, and F.H. Andrews – began experiments at Shawinigan Falls. Solving many difficult chemical and mechanical problems, they synthesized acetone from acetylene in commercial quantities. By January 1917 the first shipment of acetone was sent to Britain. The whole process, from experiment to shipment, took just over a year.[12] The company also produced the first commercial quantities of metallic magnesium in North America, whereas Germany previously had been the world's sole supplier.[13] Earlier, in the spring of 1916 the IMB had set up its second national factory, British Acetones,

Toronto Ltd, to produce acetone from corn by a fermentation process at the Gooderham and Worts distillery in Toronto. This method was discovered by Chaim Weizmann during an experiment at the Royal Naval Cordite Factory in Poole, England. British Acetones developed the technology to bring Weizmann's discovery into commercial production. The Toronto plant became the largest supplier of acetone in the British Empire.[14]

Helium, like acetone, was scarce and expensive. Sir Richard Threlfall and Sir Ernest Rutherford suggested that helium could be substituted for hydrogen, then commonly used in balloons and dirigible airships, if an adequate supply could be secured. Unlike hydrogen, helium was less dangerous to use because it was non-flammable. In December 1915 the British asked J.C. (later Sir John) McLennan, head of physics, University of Toronto, to conduct a survey of the empire's helium resources. Following experiments in 1917 in Hamilton, McLennan and a team of Canadian scientists and engineers recovered large quantities of inexpensive helium from natural gas at a plant in Calgary. Although this supply of helium was developed too late for the war effort, the knowledge gained from its production enabled McLennan and his colleagues at the University of Toronto to conduct pioneering research in low temperatures after the war.[15]

Aircraft, like acetone and helium, were not produced in quantity in Canada until the war. While the technology used to build them was imported, significant innovation did take place in Canada. In June 1915, for example, Canada's first aircraft factory, Curtiss Aeroplanes and Motors Ltd of Canada, located in Toronto, began to produce the Curtiss Canada, or Model C. The original plan was to duplicate the American-designed America, a large twin-engine flying boat intended for transatlantic flight. Such profound changes occurred during production, however, that a new plane, different in design and appearance soon emerged – the Curtiss Canada. A similar, but less dramatic change happened with the JN4, a single-engine, two-seat biplane used for military flight training. Built by Canadian Aeroplanes Ltd, Toronto, an IMB factory that had absorbed much of the Curtiss plant, the JN4 was the first mass-produced aircraft in Canada. Some 2,918 were built during the war. Like the Curtiss Canada, the JN4 was modified during production and was known as the Canadian JN4; pilots and mechanics called it simply the 'Canuck.'[16]

The most extraordinary technical achievement in wartime Canada was the rebuilding of the Quebec Bridge in 1917. The first attempt to span the St Lawrence River near Quebec City ended tragically on 29 August 1907, when the bridge, nearing completion by the Phoenix Bridge Company of Phoenixville, Pennsylvania, collapsed, killing seventy-four men. It was one of the world's most spectacular engineering disasters. After a royal commission investigation blamed the disaster on faulty design and inadequate on-site engineering supervision, the St Lawrence Bridge Company, a Canadian business headed by Phelps Johnson was awarded the contract to rebuild the bridge. Using Johnson's new K-truss bracing system, the bridge was finished in 1917, but not without another accident, which resulted in the death of eleven men. Opened officially on 22 August 1919 by the Prince of Wales, the Quebec Bridge attracted worldwide attention as the world's longest cantilever bridge.[17]

Overseas, McLennan and other Canadians made important scientific contributions to the war effort. McLennan served as a scientific adviser to the Admiralty. He assembled a team of his former assistants and students (some drawn from active duty) to work on what McLennan believed was the most difficult problem assigned to scientists – the detection and destruction of enemy submarines.[18] A.S. Eve, a McGill physicist, served as scientific director at the Admiralty Experimental Station in Harwich, and his colleague, Louis V. King, also worked on anti-submarine devises, developing a continuous tuneable diaphragm for sending and receiving underwater sound.[19] In 1916 Robert W. Boyle, head of physics at the University of Alberta, was placed in charge of a group working on submarine detection by echo methods, which used high-frequency sound waves and was later known as ASDIC. Another Canadian, Reginald Fessenden, inventor of radio, while working in Boston developed the Fessenden Oscillator, an apparatus used for underwater telegraphy and echo sound ranging to determine the distance of submerged objects, such as icebergs, or submarines.[20] On the Western Front, another McGill physicist, J.A. Gray, was in charge of locating enemy artillery by sound-ranging. He developed the technique for making important corrections for wind velocity.[21]

Notwithstanding these achievements, Canadian scientists and engineers were painfully aware that relatively little scientific research was conducted in Canada. The Connaught Laboratories, established in 1917 in Toronto, produced vaccines and sera, but basic scientific medical research, concentrated mainly at the University of Toronto and McGill University, lacked facilities and funding. Little industrial research was conducted. Reporting on a survey of industrial research facilities in

May 1918, A.B. Macallum declared that provision for pure or applied scientific research in Canadian industry was 'utterly inadequate.'[22] Only thirty-seven industrial firms, with a total staff of 161, reported having research facilities; their total annual research expenditure was $135,000.[23] Macallum later estimated that the country had only fifty pure researchers.[24] Making matters worse, enlistments for military service had seriously depleted the scientific staff of government, industry, and university research establishments.[25] '[R]esearch in Canada,' economist Adam Shortt reported to Prime Minister Borden, 'has been largely suspended except in a few of the leading industrial establishments.'[26]

Most private organizations were not capable of conducting industrial research. The Royal Society of Canada, the country's premier scientific society, founded in 1882, was a learned society dedicated to literary and philosophical as well as scientific pursuits. In 1914 it did not possess a permanent headquarters in Ottawa, much less an industrial research laboratory or laboratories of any kind.[27] Although the Canadian Society of Civil Engineers, Canada's pre-eminent national professional engineering society, had conducted research on engineering standards and specifications,[28] the society was primarily a professional body organized officially to raise the standard of engineering practice by the exchange of professional knowledge. Other engineering societies, such as the Canadian Mining Institute, served professional and business interests.[29] An exception was the Royal Canadian Institute, Canada's oldest surviving scientific society founded in 1849.[30] In 1914 the institute organized the Bureau of Scientific and Industrial Research and School of Specific Industries, as a private research agency to apply science to industry by means of 'industrial fellowships' modelled after the highly successful system created by a University of Toronto graduate, Dr Robert Kennedy Duncan, at the University of Kansas and the Mellon Institute of Industrial Research.[31] Lacking its own laboratories, the bureau was designed to act as an intermediary between manufacturers needing research, and universities – specifically the University of Toronto – providing laboratories and researchers.[32] Unfortunately, the University of Toronto was not yet ready to engage in the pure research that would allow the bureau to function.

By 1914 the University of Toronto was attempting to meet the practical needs of a rapidly expanding industrial economy through scientific research. In 1897 it offered the research degree of Doctor of Philosophy and the degree of Master of Applied Science in 1913. The creation of the School of Engineering Research within the Faculty of Applied Science and Engineering in 1917 represented the university's main contribution to industrial research. In spite of these initiatives, the university was not fully committed to institutionalizing industrial research. The Faculty of Applied Science and Engineering still believed that education was its principal function. This view was shared by the larger university community. Although useful in promoting the university's science and graduate programs, industrial research would remain subordinate to its wider educational ideals.[33] Government offered no better prospects for research.

Before the war, no government agency was specifically mandated to coordinate and promote industrial research. The Geological Survey of Canada, founded in 1842, surveyed mineral, forest, and water resources before it was absorbed into other government departments by 1890. The Dominion Experimental Farms (1886) improved farming methods, while the Biological Board (1912), which eventually became the Fisheries Research Board, operated several marine biological stations.[34] The Commission of Conservation (1909) advised the government on the scientific management of the country's natural resources. It represented the first attempt to use science and technology to solve problems created by rapid industrialization and urbanization.[35] Commission head, Clifford Sifton, wanted to coordinate industrial research. By 1918, however, the tide of public opinion in Canada and elsewhere had turned against the conservation ethic to embrace notions of maximizing natural resource production through science for commercial ends. Sifton resigned in 1918, and the commission was abolished in May 1921.[36] What was needed was some new government body to coordinate industrial research. British and American wartime initiatives provided an example of the kind of state-supported research many Canadian scientists, engineers, and industrialists wanted to see in Canada.

On 5 July 1915, amid complaints in Britain that science was not being fully mobilized for war, the Admiralty set up the Board of Invention and Research, an independent body of eminent civilian scientists, to evaluate new inventions submitted to the government. On 25 July an order-in-council created the Advisory Council for Scientific and Industrial Research to promote the application of science to industry; in the following year it became the Department of Scientific and Industrial Research. In France, the Ministry of Inventions was formed in November 1915 to promote scientific research for the Ministry of War and of the Marine.[37] Before the United States entered the war, the National Advisory Committee for Aeronautics was organized in March 1915 to improve American aircraft. In the same year, a Naval Consulting Board, chaired by the sixty-nine-year-old Thomas Edison, was established to assess new technology, and in an attempt to centralize research in the United States, the National Research Council was founded in June 1916.[38]

In Canada during 1915 and 1916 prominent scientists, engineers, and industrialists urged the dominion government to appoint a commission on industrial research. Engineering and scientific societies offered their help;[39] prominent individuals, such as J.W. Flavelle, head of the IMB, strongly favoured the idea.[40] Correspondence and meetings with Sir George Foster, minister of trade and commerce, however, produced no results until 20 January 1916, when the British minister of munitions issued a circular letter, which included certain Canadian universities, asking for help with scientific military research.[41] Alarmed by the prospect of Canadian universities' acting independently of the government, on 23 May 1916 Foster submitted a report to the Privy Council recommending the appointment of a committee of council consisting of the ministers of trade and commerce, interior, mines, inland revenue, labour, and agriculture, together with a nine-member advisory committee representing scientific and industrial interests. Foster argued that there was an urgent need to mobilize and coordinate existing scientific and industrial resources to eliminate waste and to promote efficiency.

On 6 June an order-in-council created a cabinet subcommittee on scientific and industrial research, chaired by Foster, with a provision for an advisory council.[42] On 29 November 1916 another order-in-council appointed the members of the Honorary Advisory Council for Scientific and Industrial Research, or, the National Research Council (NRC), as it was named officially in 1925. The members included some of the most distinguished engineers, scientists, businessmen, and university administrators in Canada: J.C. McLennan; R.F. Ruttan, professor of chemistry, McGill; Frank Adams, dean of applied science, McGill; R.A. Ross, consulting engineer, Montreal; A.S. Mackenzie, president, Dalhousie University; W.C. Murray, president, University of Saskatchewan; T. Bienvenu, vice-president and general manager, La Banque Provinciale du Canada; and R. Hobson, president, Steel Company of Canada. Later, S.F. Kirkpatrick, professor of metallurgy, Queen's University, and Arthur Surveyer, consulting engineer, Montreal, joined the council. Bienvenu attended only one meeting; Hobson was too busy with wartime duties to attend. Civil engineer J.B. Challies, superintendent, Dominion Water Power Branch, Department of the Interior,

Ottawa, was made secretary; A.B. Macallum was appointed administrative chairman; he was the Advisory Council's only paid member. On 29 August 1917 Bill 83 established the Advisory Council by act of Parliament. Its creation represented the first attempt in Canada to organize scientific research on a national basis.

Few noticed the appointment of the Advisory Council. Foster confided to his diary that most members of cabinet were 'utterly indifferent or antagonistic';[43] Borden did not take note of it when he wrote his memoirs after the war. Given the times, this was not unexpected. In its third year, the war was not going well: casualties mounted, enlistments sagged, and a conscription crisis loomed. French and English Canadians quarrelled over the war and the treatment of French-speaking schoolchildren outside Quebec. While Foster's volunteer council of earnest professors may have lacked much public notice, they nevertheless were important because they were part of a larger trend in wartime Canada. By late 1916 the voluntary and private nature of Canada's war mobilization gave way, under the stress of war, to coercion and the intervention of the state in nearly every aspect of public and private life. Between 1916 and 1918 various government control agencies, appointed under the government's emergency powers, tended to centralize Canada's wartime economy. As in other countries, these activities helped to undermine laissez-faire attitudes and prepared the way for the greatly expanded role of government in economic and social life.[44] The Advisory Council was no exception. Its creation was not only a bureaucratic manifestation of a country with a conservative and statist political tradition, but also the inevitable outcome of wartime conditions.

Organized to study and coordinate industrial research, the Advisory Council had no clearly defined role and status, apart from advising a cabinet subcommittee. There was little significant military research to coordinate, and the council did not have laboratories to conduct industrial research. Conflict with other government departments and agencies was inevitable. Awarding student scholarships and research grants to professors helped to avoid friction; the studentships and fellowships were a simple, direct, and highly effective way the Advisory Council assisted universities to produce researchers while it supported individual research projects. Collective research was conducted by associate committees, three of which were permanent: chemistry, mining and metallurgy, and forestry.[45] In the summer of 1918, in spite of the relentless opposition of Queen's University, the Advisory Council decided to lobby for the building of a central research laboratory in Ottawa. The cabinet initially rejected the idea, but in April 1919 it appointed a Commons committee headed by Hume Cronyn to investigate the matter. A year later, when the committee recommended a central research laboratory, the House of Commons passed the necessary legislation, but the Senate returned the bill in 1921.[46] Not until 1932, in the depth of the Great Depression, were laboratories opened in Ottawa. The NRC then flourished during and after the Second World War.

The NRC's success, however, has created one of the central myths in the history of Canadian science and technology: there was no industrial research in Canada before the First World War, the war forced the government to establish the NRC in 1916, and the NRC then became the focus of industrial research. Writers, such as Mel Thistle and Wilfrid Eggleston, have perpetuated this myth. James Hull and Philip Enros, however, argue that the movement for industrial research in Canada dates from a meeting in Toronto in 1897 of the British Association for the Advancement of Science, and that the lobby for industrial research led by engineers, scientists, and businessmen was large and vigorous. The NRC myth, according to Hull and Enros, originated with the NRC's indictment of the poor state of industrial research in Canada, particularly its 1917 survey of the industrial research facilities, which, they argue, underestimated the country's research potential. As the principal promoter of industrial research, it was in the NRC's interest to project a gloomy picture of the state of industrial research in Canada.[47]

The war may not have been the great catalyst to industrial research, but scientific and engineering leaders were clear about one point: the war had demonstrated the importance of science to Canada and had given scientists greater recognition and self-confidence. 'One of the most remarkable and perhaps unexpected results of the great war,' Frank D. Adams noted in 1917, 'is that there has been in every country in the English-speaking world a sudden awakening to the importance of scientific research.'[48] In his presidential address to the Royal Society of Canada in 1920, R.F. Ruttan stated that the world was 'ringing with appreciation of what science had accomplished in the great struggle.'[49] Intimidated by German science before the war, Canadian scientists no longer felt inferior; victory had given them new confidence. Liberal scientific methods – cooperation coupled with freedom of effort and the power of initiative – not 'German drill-sergeant, dogmatic and cast iron methods,'[50] helped British scientists to match and surpass German achievements. In two years Britain had accomplished in every branch of science what Germany had taken forty years to attain. Scientists were not blind to the horror of modern warfare created by science. They considered the new weapons of war as necessary evils to defend the empire. They were more positive about the power of science to serve humanity: science had entered a new era. A.S. Mackenzie, president of Dalhousie University, declared: 'science has fallen upon the most momentous period of its history.'[51] The time was right to promote science and to take advantage of public support.

At the same time, however, scientists were concerned about whether Canada had the means to fulfil its scientific destiny. Mackenzie characterized Canadian research facilities as a 'disgrace,' adding that Canada was a 'parasite' on the research facilities of friends and neighbours.[52] Pure research had suffered during the war. Ruttan estimated that only two or three university laboratories and one or two government departments could conduct research.[53] Lack of research facilities was not only disgraceful, but a potential threat to Canada. There was a widely held belief among engineers and scientists that economic competition with Germany after the war would be fierce, or, as Macallum put it, 'merciless.'[54] Germany's defeat on the battlefield would not necessarily destroy its formidable science-based industries. Aided by government subsidies and cheap labour, Germany would aggressively apply science to industry to dominate once again whole industries and world markets. 'The present war,' the *Contract Record and Engineering Review* asserted, 'is a mighty effort by Germany to gain not only a military, but also a commercial supremacy ... Tomorrow the military struggle will end and then the real and permanent business of nations will begin – *industrial war*. No one doubts that our military enemies of today will be, in equal strength, our commercial enemies of tomorrow.'[55] If Canada hoped to pay off its enormous war debt and be competitive after the war, it should take advantage of Germany's wartime isolation, conserve its natural resources, and follow Germany's example of applying science to industry, rather than rely on tariff and patent laws. Science, business, and government had to cooperate to promote science and industrial research. Canada had no alternative.[56] Germany was not the only potential threat to Canada. Danger also loomed from the republic to the south. With its well-endowed private industrial research laboratories, the United States not only had established a Naval Consulting Board and its own National Research Council, but was acquiring commercially useful German technology by confiscating enemy patents and industrial assets in the United States.[57]

The key to national prosperity was research. This was the great lesson engineers and scientists had drawn from Germany and the war. German governments subsidized universities; science graduates applied science to industry to create wealth and power. Similarly, American universities, with their German-trained professors, provided American industry with scientific and technological 'know-how' through their science and engineering graduates. Macallum explained the relationship between education and industry: 'when the universities of a nation become permeated with the research spirit, as in Germany and the United States, its industries become endowed with it also ... If the British Empire is to organize its industries on the research basis, it must promote research first in its universities.'[58] Unfortunately, Canadian universities lagged far behind German and American universities. Macallum observed, for example, that the 'annual budget of the Massachusetts Institute of Technology exceeded the total of the annual expenditures of all the Faculties of Applied Science in Canada.'[59] Macallum was dismayed that no systematic attempt had been made to find and train Canadian researchers. There were not enough researchers in Canada before the war; more would be needed after. In the meantime, he hoped that the Advisory Council's studentships and fellowships would address the problem and even revolutionize the universities by helping them to become research institutions.[60] For J.C. Fields, funding universities was of national importance: 'How can we tolerate the thought that in Germany provision is made for training men in advanced research which is not made in Canada; that positions exist for men so trained which do not exist in Canada! What excuse can we Canadians offer in extenuation of the fact that the leading universities of the United States have left our universities far behind in the matter of research? If the people of Canada realized the significance of the modern scientific movement, they would see to it that the necessary funds were forthcoming, and they would surely insist, as a matter of national pride, on our universities taking their place alongside the foremost in the world.'[61] Given the poor state of Canadian graduate education, Fields's anger is understandable. Beginning in the late nineteenth century, graduate training emerged on a small-scale, haphazard basis and was confined mainly to the University of Toronto and McGill University. These institutions had few graduate students and awarded fewer advanced degrees. Between 1906 and 1913, for example, the number of students enrolled in PhD science disciplines at McGill ranged from seven to fifteen. From 1906 to 1912 only four science doctorates were awarded; six between 1913 and 1920. During a typical year at the

University of Toronto, 1910–11, only twenty-four PhD students were enrolled in science disciplines.[62] The Advisory Council claimed that less than a dozen PhD degrees in pure science had been awarded in Canada by 1918.[63]

Founded originally as denominational colleges to train clergy, most of the older Canadian universities did not recognize the need for advanced degrees. Few university posts were available to graduates in a young country emerging from its rural-agrarian roots. Universities were chronically underfunded and understaffed. They possessed scant library and laboratory facilities and awarded few graduate scholarships. Aspiring graduate students went to Britain and, especially, to the United States. Prestigious eastern American graduate schools, a mere two-day train ride from Toronto, attracted eager Canadian graduate students because of their prominent faculty members, generous scholarships, and the increasingly coveted PhD degree.[64] Although some Canadian professors helped their students to obtain American scholarships, others were concerned about the exodus of Canada's best students. Establishing a Canadian graduate program that offered the PhD, like Johns Hopkins in Baltimore, seemed to be an obvious solution. The leading advocate of this view was James Loudon, the University of Toronto's first Canadian-born president (1892–1906). During an acrimonious debate in the late nineteenth century over the place of science in the university, this ambitious and aggressive president championed the cause of German-style research at Toronto, but failed to have the PhD degree introduced in 1883. Macallum (who was graduated from Johns Hopkins in 1888 with a PhD) and other Toronto alumni returned to Canada from the United States with American degrees to fill appointments at Toronto. Together with their mentor, Loudon, they lobbied for the establishment of the PhD, and in 1897 the university senate approved the degree. Loudon attributed this achievement mainly to Macallum's efforts.[65] Macallum later supervised Toronto's first completed PhD thesis.[66]

A man with a vision and a mission, Macallum worked tirelessly to expand the PhD offerings at Toronto and to create a graduate school. In 1916 he declared that the University of Toronto was at a crossroads: it could remain a reputable provincial university, or it could become a national university recognized abroad for research. But unless Canadian universities offered facilities for graduate work, students would turn to the United States. It would be 'disastrous' for Canadian unity, Macallum warned, if younger Canadian universities, especially the

A.B. Macallum of the University of Toronto, n.d. (University of Toronto Archives, B1966-0005/003(01))

western universities, recruited their faculty members either in part or wholly from among American university graduates. It was the patriotic duty of the older universities, particularly the University of Toronto, to develop graduate courses. In a few years, Macallum predicted, Toronto would become a national university, 'organized to mould and unify the intellectual life of Canada.'[67] In the meantime, more scholarships and library facilities were needed.[68]

Apart from patriotic ideals, the research ethic, and the University of Toronto's destiny, Macallum and other scientists were troubled by more practical problems – the lack of status and jobs. Emerging from a highly pragmatic frontier society more concerned with subduing the wilderness than conducting laboratory experiments, science, especially pure science, had never been highly regarded other than for its immediate practical value, such as discovering mineral wealth. Scientists complained that science was badly taught in schools and looked down upon by universities. Oxford and Cambridge, not the German-style American universities, were represented as the highest university ideal.[69] McGill economics and political science professor Stephen Leacock satirized scientists and engineers in *Arcadian Adventures with the Idle Rich* (1914); Queen's English Professor James Cappon referred to his colleagues in the physics building as 'educated plumbers.'[70]

Scientists could live without respect, perhaps, but not without jobs. Before the war, few opportunities existed in Canadian universities for ambitious young scientists. Some found government work; more – especially chemists – obtained jobs in industry; most were forced to seek employment in the United States. In 1895, Loudon complained to George Ross, Ontario minister of education (1883–99), about the loss of forty Toronto graduates to posts in American colleges and universities. Three years later, he published a list of eighty graduates who had obtained American fellowships, scholarships, and teaching positions in American universities.[71] The most vocal critic of Toronto's 'brain drain' was J.C. McLennan, Macallum's former student who had been awarded the University of Toronto's first PhD degree in physics (1900). McLennan rarely missed an opportunity to scold Canadian businessmen for not recognizing how science could improve productivity. He warned that Canadian-trained scientists, forced to work in the United States, were, in effect, strengthening competitive foreign industries at Canada's expense. Complaining in 1916 that he had lost thirteen or fourteen of his ablest students to the United States, McLennan believed that Canada should conserve its scientific talent by creating attractive career opportunities at home.[72] Earlier, in 1914, the Royal Canadian Institute had attempted to do just that.

The loss of Canadian scientific talent to the United States aroused the institute's nationalist indignation. As the University of Toronto had earlier established the PhD degree to help to stem the flow of students to American graduate schools, the institute hoped that its Bureau of Scientific and Industrial Research would help to curb the loss of Canadian scientists to American research laboratories by creating career opportunities for young scientists and engineers. 'The Bureau,' declared the Institute's secretary-treasurer, F.M. Turner, an industrial chemist, in 1915, 'exists solely to try to get Canadian industrialists to avail themselves to a larger extent than they have in the past of the chemical and engineering talent we are developing in our universities.'[73] Although the Bureau conducted some minor research and disseminated useful technical information to various manufacturers, apart from an extraordinary offer from the Mellon Institute of Industrial Research to administer five of its industrial fellowships at the bureau it could not obtain financial support after the appointment of the Advisory Council.[74]

Engineers were faced with status and employment problems similar to those of scientists. As salaried employees of large public and private corporations, engineers could neither control their professional lives nor protect themselves from competition, as doctors and lawyers could do. To this extent, they found themselves in relatively the same economic predicament as most other industrial wage and salary earners. They felt unrecognized and unrewarded. The war, however, changed everything. Taking to heart David Lloyd George's 1915 remark that the war was a terrific contest between the engineers of the warring nations,[75] Canadian engineers took up arms with patriotic zeal and soon earned distinction in rank and decoration.[76] The war gave engineers an unprecedented opportunity to demonstrate their usefulness, not only at the Front, building fortifications and providing logistical support, but also at home, producing munitions and maintaining essential services. It brought engineers to public attention, and, for the first time in the history of the profession, they received the recognition they thought they deserved. By 1918, however, the prospect of peace threatened to deprive engineers of the source of their prominence. Overcrowding in the profession intensified competition for scarce jobs; wartime inflation threatened to undermine them financially. Various earlier initiatives, such as promoting industrial research, designed to enhance their prestige by identifying their expertise with the public interest, had failed to raise their status. Rejecting unionization for social and philosophical reasons, they campaigned instead for restrictive provincial licensing laws to obtain the same ends as unionization. Posing as enlightened professionals protecting the public interest, they received substantial monopoly powers through licensing to restrict competition, without resorting to any professionally undignified restrictive trade practices such as strikes.[77]

Scientists, by contrast, were not disposed to political action. Few in number, they were scattered throughout a handful of universities, government departments, and private industries. Highly individualistic, they possessed little group consciousness of themselves as a distinct occupation, much less as a profession. (There was, for example, no separate category for scientists in the 1911 and 1921 censuses.) Scientists tended to identify instead with their employers, as professors, civil servants, or company employees. Unlike engineers, they had no national organization to represent them. Nevertheless, by controlling university degrees and appointments, academic scientists had, in some respects, more control over their working lives than engineers. What scientists needed were more jobs and research facilities. Macallum and the Advisory Council provided both.

Macallum always insisted that industrial research could be furthered only by research in pure science at well-equipped graduate schools.[78] The training of researchers was a necessary precondition; the Advisory Council's studentships and fellowships provided the means. Promoting graduate teaching allowed Macallum and his colleagues to appeal to the university's traditional teaching role while advancing their own research agenda. Universities increasingly came to recognize the importance of research, and by the end of the war, they saw scientific research as a fundamental part of the university.[79]

For several decades, Macallum had mounted his own personal crusade for scientific research through the University of Toronto, the National Conference of Canadian Universities, the Royal Society of Canada, and, especially, the Advisory Council. A few days after his appointment to the Advisory Council, Macallum told the Empire Club in Toronto: 'We must develop and all of us must crusade for research. I have been crusading in this country; I have been crusading in the University, and now I am going out into the larger field to crusade ... I am going to be a sort of Peter the Hermit to get you all to join me in the crusade.'[80] By the onset of the Great War, Macallum had emerged as the principal propagandist and lobbyist for scientific research in Canada. Envisioning a terrible industrial war after the conflict, Macallum and other scientists and engineers effectively extended the war effort into peacetime to make industrial research a national priority. They were the essential workers in the struggle for national survival: only scientists and engineers could apply science to industry. The Advisory Council was the institutional expression of the wartime anxiety over industrial efficiency. Created to foster industrial research, it also served the interests of scientists by promoting scientific research in the universities.

The National Research Council, according to Frank Underhill, was one of the two most important things to emerge from the Great War. Although Canadian scientific and technological accomplishments were relatively modest, the first attempt to organize science on a national basis through the creation of the NRC was, in many respects, the most significant wartime scientific and technological achievement. Starved for resources in the 1930s, the NRC expanded dramatically during the Second World War[81] and emerged at the centre of Canadian science in the post-war era. No other organization had such influence on the development of Canadian science and technology.

The Great War changed Canadian attitudes towards science, as a force for both good and evil. It brought scientists and engineers to public attention and rewarded them with jobs, NRC grants, expanded research facilities, graduate schools, and, most important, prestige. At the end of the Great War, in an increasingly secularized world, scientists emerged as modern-day crusaders.

NOTES

1  T.C. Keefer, 'Presidential Address,' *Proceedings and Transactions of the Royal Society of Canada (PTRSC)*, 2nd ser., 5 (1899), 4–18.
2  See Nelles, Introduction, in H.V. Nelles, ed., *Philosophy of Railroads and Other Essays by T.C. Keefer* (Toronto: University of Toronto Press, 1972), ix–lxiii.
3  Carroll Pursell, *The Machine in America: A Social History of Technology* (Baltimore: Johns Hopkins University Press, 1995), 228.
4  Although in use before 1914, the term 'technology' did not gain much usage until the Great Depression. Karl Marx and Arnold Toynbee, for example, did not use the term. See Leo Marx, 'The Idea of Technology and Postmodern Pessimism,' in M.R. Smith and Leo Marx eds, *Does Technology Drive History?* (Cambridge, Mass.: MIT Press, 1994), 242–52. The term 'science' often referred to both science and technology.

5  David Carnegie, *The History of Munitions Supply in Canada, 1914–1918* (London: Longmans, Green, 1925), 29, 33, 59–60, 77, 80, 216; H.H. Vaughan, 'The Manufacture of Munitions in Canada,' *Transactions of the Engineering Institute of Canada* 33 (1919), 1–5.

6  See Editorial, 'Development of Industrial Research,' *Industrial Canada* 18 (May 1917), 54.

7  R.O. Wynne-Roberts, 'The War and its Relation to Engineering Work,' *Contract Record and Engineering Review* 29 (3 November 1915), 1127–8; Ian Varcoe, 'Scientists, Government and Organized Research in Great Britain, 1914–16: The Early History of the DSIR,' *Minerva* 8 (1970), 192–5; Michael Pattison, 'Scientists, Inventors and the Military in Britain, 1915–19: The Munitions Inventions Department,' *Social Studies of Science* 13 (November 1983), 527.

8  For an account of Macallum's career in physiology and biochemistry at the Faculty of Medicine, University of Toronto, see Sandra F. McRae, 'The "Scientific Spirit" in Medicine at the University of Toronto, 1880–1910,' unpublished PhD dissertation, University of Toronto 1987, 117–44.

9  A.B. Macallum, 'The Old Knowledge and the New,' *PTRSC*, ser. 111, 11 (1917) appendix A, 66.

10  John Bryden, *Deadly Allies: Canada's Secret Little War, 1937–1947* (Toronto: McClelland and Stewart, 1989), 13; Gradon Carter and Graham S. Pearson, 'North Atlantic Chemical and Biological Research Collaboration, 1916–1995,' *Journal of Strategic Studies* 19 (March 1996), 74.

11  For an interpretation of what constitutes 'Canadian' technology, see Bruce Sinclair, 'Canadian Technology: British Traditions and American Influences,' *Technology and Culture* 20 (January 1979), 108–23; on the importance of technology transfer and the distinction between invention and innovation in the Canadian context, see Christian de Bresson, 'Have Canadians Failed to Innovate? The Brown Thesis Revisited,' *HSTC Bulletin* 6 (January 1982), 10–23.

12  Carnegie, *History of Munitions Supply*, 154–5; G.J.J. Warrington and R.V.V. Nicholls, *A History of Chemistry in Canada* (Toronto: Sir Isaac Pitman and Sons, 1949), 172–3.

13  R.C. Fetherstonhaugh, *McGill University at War, 1914–1918, 1939–1945* (Montreal: Gazette Printing, 1947), 87.

14  Carnegie, *History of Munitions Supply*, 154–5; for a detailed account of British Acetones, Toronto, Ltd, from an engineering point of view, see especially J.H. Parkin, *Aeronautical Research in Canada, 1917–1957* (Ottawa: National Research Council of Canada, 1983), 1: 82–98.

15  Robert Craig Brown, 'Sir John Cunningham McLennan, PH.D., F.R.S.,

O.B.E., K.B.E., 1867–1935,' *Physics in Canada / La Physique au Canada* 56 (March/April 2000), 95; H.H. Langton, *Sir John Cunningham McLennan: A Memoir* (Toronto: University of Toronto Press, 1939), 46–7; Yves Gingras, *Physics and the Rise of Scientific Research in Canada*, trans. Peter Keating (Montreal and Kingston: McGill-Queen's University Press, 1991), 71–2.

16  Carnegie, *History of Munitions Supply*, chap. 21; K.M. Molson, 'Aircraft Manufacturing in Canada during the First Great War,' *Canadian Aeronautical Journal* 5 (1959), 47–52 and M.R. Riddell, 'The Development and Future of Aviation in Canada,' *Journal of the Engineering Institute of Canada* 2 (March 1919), 200, 202.

17  J. Rodney Millard, 'Phelps Johnson,' *Dictionary of Canadian Biography* (Toronto: University of Toronto Press), Vol. 15 (forthcoming).

18  Brown, 'Sir John Cunningham McLennan,' 95–6; Langton, *Sir John Cunningham McLennan*, 48–50.

19  J.S. Foster, 'Louis Vessot King,' *Biographical Memoirs of Fellows of the Royal Society* (London: Royal Society, 1957), 3: 104.

20  David A. Keys, 'Robert William Boyle, 1883–1955,' *PTRSC* 3rd ser., 49 (1955), 63–4. Gary L. Frost, 'Inventing Schemes and Strategies: The Making and Selling of the Fessenden Oscillator,' *Technology and Culture* 42 (2001), 462–88.

21  Louis V. King, 'The Development of Modern Acoustics,' *Transactions of the Royal Society of Canada*, 3rd ser. (1919), 5.

22  Canada, *Report of the Administrative Chairman of the Honorary Advisory Council for Scientific and Industrial Research of Canada*, Ottawa, 23 May 1918, 22.

23  Mel Thistle, *The Inner Ring: The Early History of the National Research Council of Canada* (Toronto: University of Toronto Press, 1966), 29.

24  Wilfrid Eggleston, *National Research in Canada: The NRC, 1916–1966* (Toronto: Clarke, Irwin, 1978), 7.

25  Canada, *Report of the Administrative Chairman*, 22.

26  Quoted in Eggleston, *National Research in Canada*, 7.

27  Carl Berger, *Honour and the Search for Influence: A History of the Royal Society of Canada* (Toronto: University of Toronto Press, 1996), 53.

28  'Report of the Annual Meeting,' *Transactions of the Canadian Society of Civil Engineers* 28 (1914), 14; 'Canadian Engineering Standards Committee,' ibid. (February 1920), 42.

29  See: J. Rodney Millard, *The Master Spirit of the Age: Canadian Engineers and the Politics of Professionalism, 1887–1922* (Toronto: University of Toronto Press, 1988), chap. 2.

30  The Geological Survey, founded in 1842, was a government advisory body,

not a learned society. For a historical profile of the Canadian Institute (as it was called until 1914), see W. Stewart Wallace, 'A Sketch of the History of the Royal Canadian Institute, 1849–1949,' in W. Stewart Wallace, ed., *The Royal Canadian Institute Centennial Volume* (Toronto: Royal Canadian Institute, 1949), 121-67.

31 See Philip C. Enros, 'The Bureau of Scientific and Industrial Research and School of Specific Industries: The Royal Canadian Institute's Attempt at Organizing Industrial Research in Toronto, 1914–1918,' *HSTC Bulletin* 7 (January 1983), 14–26.

32 Royal Canadian Institute, *Co-operation between Science and Industry in Canada: The Royal Canadian Institute as an Intermediary for its Promotion; Establishment of a Bureau of Scientific and Industrial Research* (Toronto 1914); *Bureau of Scientific and Industrial Research and School of Specific Industries of the Royal Canadian Institute* (Toronto, n.d.).

33 Philip C. Enros, 'The University of Toronto and Industrial Research in the Early Twentieth Century,' in R. Jarrell and A. Roos, eds, *Critical Issues in the History of Canadian Science, Technology and Medicine* (Thornhill, Ont.: HSTC Publications, 1983), 155–66.

34 G. Bruce Doern, *Science and Politics in Canada* (Montreal and Kingston: McGill-Queen's University Press, 1972), 2.

35 Ibid., 3; Bruce Sinclair, Norman R. Ball and James O. Petersen, *Let Us Be Honest and Modest: Technology and Society in Canadian History* (Toronto: Oxford University Press, 1974), 261.

36 Michel F. Girard, 'The Commission of Conservation as a Forerunner to the National Research Council, 1909–1921,' in Richard A. Jarrell and Yves Gingras, eds, *Building Canadian Science: The Role of the National Research Council* (Ottawa: Canadian Science and Technology Historical Association, 1992), 19–40.

37 Roy M. MacLeod and E. Ray Andrews, 'Scientific Advice in the War at Sea, 1915–1917: The Board of Invention and Research,' *Contemporary History* 6 (1971), 4–7; Pattison, 'Scientists, Inventors,' 527–51.

38 Daniel J. Kevles, *The Physicists: The History of a Scientific Community in Modern America* (New York: Alfred A. Knopf, 1978), 102–12.

39 National Archives of Canada (NAC), Foster Papers, MG 27 II D7, vol. 18, f. 1929, T.H. Wardleworth to Sir George Foster, 17 June 1915, 30 July 1915, 3 November 1916; A.T. Drummond to Foster 24 November 1915; H. Mortimer-Lamb to Foster, 6 March 1916. See also ibid., vol. 34, f. 74, schedule 'A,' 1–5; *Proceedings of the Royal Society of Canada*, Duncan C. Scott to Alfred Baker, 21 February 1916, XVI; 'National Industrial Preparedness Memorandum' printed in *Canadian Engineer*, 32 (8 February 1917), 127–9;

NAC, Engineering Institute of Canada Papers, MG 28 1-277, Annual Minutes, 20 March 1917, 26.

40 NAC, Foster Papers, J.W. Flavelle to Foster, 6 June 1917.

41 NAC, PC 1266, 6 June 1916.

42 'Report of the Privy Council,' 6 June 1916, printed in *Transactions of the Royal Canadian Institute*, 11 (1916), 178–9.

43 NAC, Foster Papers, Diaries, MG 27 II D7, vol. 1, 23 Nov. 1916.

44 See: J.A. Cory, 'The Growth of Government Activities in Canada, 1914 – 1921,' Canadian Historical Association, *Report of the Annual Meeting* (1940), 66–75. For a discussion of the impact of the government's emergency powers on the economy, see David Edward Smith, 'Emergency Government in Canada,' *Canadian Historical Review* 50 (December 1969), 432–5.

45 Jarrell and Gingras, 'Introduction,' *Building Canadian Science* 1, 4; Canada, *Report of the Administrative Chairman*, 8–10.

46 Philip C. Enros, '"The Ornery Council of Scientific and Industrial Pretence": Universities in the Early NRC's Plans for Industrial Research,' in Jarrell and Gingras, *Building Canadian Science* 45–50; Eggleston, *National Research in Canada*, 9–20.

47 James P. Hull and Philip C. Enros, 'Demythologizing Canadian Science and Technology: The History of Industrial R&D,' in Peter Karl Kresl, ed., *Topics on Canadian Business* (Montreal: Association for Canadian Studies, 1988), 1–21.

48 Frank D. Adams, 'The Work of the Advisory Council for Scientific and Industrial Research,' *Canadian Engineer* 3 (15 March 1917), 234.

49 R.F. Ruttan, 'International Co-operation in Science,' *PTRSC*, 3rd ser., 14 (1920), appendix A, 40.

50 A. Stanley Mackenzie, 'The War and Science,' *PTRSC*, 3rd ser., 12 (1918), 2.

51 Ibid., 1.

52 Ibid., 4–5.

53 R.F. Ruttan, 'A Plan for the Development of Industrial Research in Canada,' Canada, *Honorary Advisory Council for Scientific and Industrial Research*, Bulletin No. 10 (Ottawa, 1921), 1.

54 Macallum, 'Old Knowledge and the New,' 65.

55 Editorial, 'Industrial Research and its Relation to Commercial Supremacy,' *Contract Record and Engineering Review* 30 (22 November 1916), 1101; italics added.

56 Wynne-Roberts, 'The War and Its Relation to Engineering Work,' 1127–8; Editorial, 'The Need of Industrial Research,' *Contract Record and Engineering Review* 31 (20 June 1917), 531; Frank D. Adams, 'The Work of the

Advisory Council For Scientific and Industrial Research,' *Canadian Engineer* 32 (15 March 1917), 234–5.

57 Editorial, 'Competition after the War,' *Canadian Engineer* 34 (6 June 1918), 519.

58 Macallum, 'Old Knowledge and the New,' 69.

59 Canada, *Report of the Administrative Chairman*, 24.

60 A.B. Macallum, 'The New Organization for Industrial and Scientific Research,' *Empire Club of Canada Addresses Delivered to the Members during the Sessions of 1915–16, 1916–17* (Toronto, 1917), 323; Macallum, 'Research Council and its Work,' 265–6.

61 J.C. Fields, 'Science and Industry,' Canada, *The Honorary Advisory Council for Scientific and Industrial Research*, Bulletin No. 5 (Ottawa, 1918), 11.

62 See W.T. Thompson, *Graduate Education in the Sciences at Canadian Universities* (Toronto: University of Toronto Press, 1963), 4–6.

63 Thistle, *Inner Ring*, 29.

64 Thompson, *Graduate Education*, 5–7; Peter N. Ross, 'The Establishment of the Ph.D. at Toronto: A Case of American Influence,' *History of Education Quarterly* 12 (Fall 1972), 366–7.

65 Ross, 'Establishment of the Ph.D.,' 365–6, 370, 372–3.

66 J.M. Neclin, 'Archibald Byron Macallum, pioneer of biochemistry in Canada,' *Canadian Journal of Biochemistry and Cell Biology* 62 (June 1984), viii.

67 A.B. Macallum, 'The Foundation of the Board of Graduate Studies,' *University of Toronto Monthly* (February 1916), 223–4.

68 *The First, Second, Third and Fourth Conferences of the Canadian Universities* (Saskatoon, 1917), 23–4.

69 Mackenzie, 'War and Science,' 5–6.

70 Berger, *Honour and the Search for Influence*, 64.

71 Ross, 'Establishment of the Ph.D.,' 366.

72 J.C. McLennan, 'Industrial Research in Canada,' *Transactions of the Royal Canadian Institute* 11 (Toronto 1917–18), 154; McLennan, 'The Problem of Industrial Research in Canada,' *Industrial Canada* 17 (July 1916): 254–5; J.C. McLennan, 'Science and Industrial Research,' 284.

73 Ontario Archives, Royal Canadian Institute Papers, No. II, F.M. Turner to C.L. Burton, 23 August 1915.

74 J.C. Fields to editor, *Canadian Engineer* 40 (23 June 1921), 4.

75 Walter J. Francis, 'The Engineer and the War,' *Canadian Engineer* 30 (6 April 1916), 417.

76 On the engineers' war service see 'The Engineer in Peace and War – The

Increasing Value of Trained Men,' *Contract Record and Engineering Review* 30 (5 April 1916), 324–5; 'The Work of the Canadian Engineers in France,' *Contract Record and Engineering Review* 31 (21 March 1917), 261–2.

77  See Millard, *Master Spirit of the Age*, chaps 8 and 9.

78  Macallum, 'The New Organization for Industrial and Scientific Research,' 324.

79  Gingras, *Physics*, 57–8.

80  Macallum, 'The New Organization,' 324.

81  See, especially, Donald H. Avery, *The Science of War: Canadian Scientists and Allied Military Technology during the Second World War* (Toronto: University of Toronto Press, 1998).

# 12 Canada Invaded! The Great War, Mass Culture, and Canadian Cultural Nationalism

PAUL LITT

When he stepped to the podium to address the Canadian Club of Montreal in December 1913, B.K. Sandwell had a novel topic for his audience. They were used to hearing about pressing political issues – imperial unity, the tariff, labour unrest – not frivolities like the theatre. But the drama critic maintained that his beat was 'a realm in which a vast and ever-increasing number of Canadians acquire a large part of their ideas and opinions.' Unfortunately, the plays Canadians saw were selected by 'two groups of gentlemen from New York City' who had come to dominate the business over the previous ten or fifteen years. They saw the continent as an open field in which to reap profits from their investments and had consolidated the sector so efficiently that Canadian theatre companies were squeezed out. 'The situation is without a parallel in history,' Sandwell complained, 'You may look in vain in a country such as Poland, occupied and administered by an alien conqueror, for any such foreign domination of the Polish stage as exists in Canada, although Canada has not been even invaded for the last hundred years, to say nothing of being conquered. Such a situation could only have come about by a gradual process – have stolen upon us, as it were, unawares.'

However it came about, the situation was, to Sandwell's mind, unhealthy for a 'nation in the making.' American productions purveyed interests and values that were American, not Canadian (or British, which were equally acceptable). Representative of the base republican culture of their origin, this 'pabulum' featured 'grafting aldermen,' 'brutal detectives,' and 'odoriferous garbage collectors.' The only silver lining Sandwell could see was that Canadian audiences were, in his estimation, more scrupulous than their Yankee counterparts and therefore less likely to be influenced by such trash.[1]

Sandwell's complaint fit into a tradition of Canadian nationalist concern about the influence of American culture that stretches from before Confederation to the present day. What makes his concerns interesting for our present purposes is the historical moment at which they were expressed. Less than a year later, Canada would be swept up in the Great War, a cataclysm that would consume the country for half a decade, spurring Canadian nationalist sentiment to new heights and generating some of the most intense anti-Americanism in the country's history. In this context one might have expected to see Canadians take action on Sandwell's complaint. In fact, they proved relatively ineffectual in dealing with the issue. In this chapter I explore why this was so. I focus on the main channels through which culture flowed in wartime Canada, the cultural products that flowed along them, and the interests that controlled the channels – specifically the voluntary sector, the private sector, and government.[2] I argue that nationalist responses to continental mass culture were limited by the biases of leading cultural nationalists, by the economic interests of Canadian cultural industries, and by government reluctance to intervene in the marketplace. These factors determined how cultural nationalism would affect Canadian society both during and after the war.

## I

Three months after Sandwell's appearance, the Canadian Club of Montreal invited another representative of the arts to speak. This time the topic was literature; the speaker, popular historian and journalist Beckles Willson, fresh from a sojourn in England, where he had achieved a modest fame by publishing popular fiction and ingratiating himself into polite society. Willson's talk amplified many of Sandwell's themes, spelling out more explicitly the cultural critic's view of the role of culture in Canadian society. Material things were trivial, he contended, compared with 'the mind and intellectual tastes, tendencies and achievements' that confirmed Canadians' 'status as a civilized people.' Culture had work to do in improving Canadians and bolstering their country's international status. It also gave them 'heroism, love, suffering, romance,' essential ingredients of a collective identity. 'Romance adds to a country,' Willson explained, 'peoples it with good spirits, invests it with associations, endears it to those who dwell in it and call it home!'[3]

Humanism, a sense of social responsibility, and anglophilia characterized Canada's leading cultural nationalists. For them, culture was the arts and letters; its purpose was not merely to entertain, but to edify. Canada, they believed, should develop a refined cultural life that would improve the minds and hone the aesthetic sensibilities of its citizens and win it recognition among civilized nations. To do so it need only build upon the rich cultural tradition it had inherited from Britain and gradually wean itself from those crude pastimes of frontier days perpetuated so regrettably by its republican neighbour.

For all their firm ideas on matters cultural, neither Sandwell nor Willson offered much in the way of a practical program for promoting the type of superior Canadian culture they advocated. Both recognized that Canada's cultural predicament was the result of the oligarchical workings of free markets, but neither questioned the fundamentals of the economic system. Instead, they appealed to their audiences to exercise their buying power as consumers in support of Canadian products. They also felt that government should do something to foster Canadian culture. Their conception of what government *could* do, however, was extremely limited: it could give awards, perhaps, or subsidize artists – although neither Sandwell nor Willson seemed to hold out much hope that it ever would. Willson had an additional, somewhat specific proposal: the Canadian Clubs should sponsor a circulating library of Canadian literature in every town. When neither the workings of the market nor government intervention offered any hope, the only recourse lay in the voluntary sector.

The idea that a circulating library of instructive Canadiana could counter the effects of continental mass culture may seem quaint, but it reflected the culturati's equation of culture with the artistic and intellectual life of a community. No two communities were alike, of course; their character varied with their size, region, economy, ethno-cultural character, and other variables. But it is possible to identify some common features of community cultural activities in Edwardian Canada. Much of this type of cultural activity was amateur, participatory, and integrated with community traditions and institutions. Church choirs, for example, played a prominent role in the local music scene. They trained a roster of singers, who could be drawn upon for musical productions ranging from concerts of religious or classical pieces to Gilbert and Sullivan operettas. The local opera house, music hall, or theatre often hosted such productions, along with plays staged by amateur theatrical societies. The importance of performing arts in community life was demonstrated by the existence of these venues in centres small and large, the larger communities boasting purpose-built, stand-alone facilities, the smaller ones a multi-purpose hall, sometimes part of the town hall or a downtown commercial block, and frontier towns making do with whatever they could find. These spaces also served as meeting places for painting classes or arts and crafts clubs. In some towns they provided rehearsal space for the town band.

Local cultural activities often were run on a voluntary basis by middle-class community leaders such as the librarian, the church organist and choirmaster, the minister, or the schoolteacher. The presence of these religious and educational leaders in community activities associated with character formation was not surprising. For similar reasons, convention accorded women fuller participation in the arts than they enjoyed in other parts of public life. Such pursuits had social purposes congruent with the middle-class woman's role as guardian of family respectability and community moral standards. They articulated aesthetic distinctions that signalled social status and demarcated class. They also served the evangelical impulse to save the lower orders and wayward bourgeois by offering a salutary alternative to the pool hall, the tavern, or the cockfight.

The resolute high-mindedness of cultural leaders from the local to the national levels was a response to the dangers they perceived in contemporary culture. Indeed, their insistence on cultural propriety belied the temptations of pleasurable entertainment that were available everywhere in wartime Canada. 'Serious' theatre presented everything from stark tragedies to light-hearted comedies, while vaudeville offered a serial carnival of minstrel shows, song-and-dance men, patter comedians, balladeers, acrobats, jugglers, and animal acts. It was, as Robertson Davies later remarked, the light-entertainment equivalent of television today. Canadians took steamboat excursions, visited amusement parks, rocketed around roller rinks, danced to the latest song, or – prior to Prohibition – fraternized in the hotel bar. The world of print was equally diverse. There were magazines and newspapers for different ethnic groups, regions, religious denominations, trades, professions, classes, and industries. The public consumed vast amounts of sentimental and sensational pulp fiction, including romances, adventures, detective and crime stories, westerns, mysteries, even anthropomorphized animal stories. Those who wanted at least the appearance of being more cultured could acquire cheap reprints of literary classics with decorative matching covers that looked impressive on the bookshelf. Variety distinguished the music scene as well. Records offered performances by famous opera stars such as Caruso, Adelina Patti, or Francesco Tamagno, but consumers could also buy ragtime, jazz, folk, or comedy. Sheet music for popular hits was stored in the piano bench alongside classics by composers such as Mozart and Beethoven.

The rage for ragtime music during the war was an example of mass culture's capacity for absorbing new styles from subcultures for mainstream consumption. Ragtime took the 'ragged' beat of southern Black music and applied it to European song styles, creating a popular new musical style. It served as accompaniment for faster, more sinuous dances – similarly adapted from southern Black culture and popularized by minstrel shows, vaudeville, dance bands, and movies.[4] Music and dance went together, of course. Dance crazes such as the foxtrot, the crab-step, even the tango – once deemed the 'dance of the brothel' – swept North American cities. Bob Edwards, editor of the Calgary Eye Opener, was not amused: 'It is said that modern music is merely a reversion to the cave man's foot-stamping and tom-tom beating,' he commented. 'This is quite likely. Anyone who visits a cabaret may hear not only the tom-tom beating but the footstomping – yes, and see the cave man dragging the cave lady about the floor.'[5] But Edwards was behind the times; the growing acceptance by the middle class of dancing in commercial dance halls was a notable development of the war years. Times were changing.

The cornucopia of contemporary cultural offerings was consumed, of course, in different ratios and quantities by different individuals in different settings and circumstances. As a general rule the more urban and affluent were exposed to novelty earlier and more often than were their poorer or more rural compatriots. Journalist Bruce Hutchinson, who grew up 'poor but comfortable' in suburban Victoria, recalled that his family's one extravagance was serious theatre. His mother would scrimp to buy gallery tickets for the touring production at the local quality playhouse, the Royal Victoria. Hutchinson's cultural tastes might be labelled highbrow: he was a member of the debating team at his high school, acted in the dramatic society's productions, and read 'Scott, Dickens, Thackeray, Maupassant, and Conrad' (all purchased second hand or borrowed from the public library). But he also played lacrosse and hockey, and his family attended movies more often than the theatre because it cost them only 10¢ each to see the latest feature.[6]

The novelty, diversity, and affordability of cultural products was but one manifestation of the constant and accelerating change affecting all facets of Canadian society. Canadian cities, and then towns, were increasingly wired for electricity and telephone ('Oh! What a Difference since the Hydro Came' ran the title of a 1912 hit song by Claude Graves, a printer from London, Ontario). South of the border, Henry Ford compressed the time it took to build a Model T automobile from twelve hours and twenty-eight minutes in 1910 to one hour and thirty-three minutes in 1915. Prices plummeted, making tin Lizzies affordable for the average family. By war's end, 276,000 Canadians owned a car, four times as many than at the beginning of the conflict. Social mores were changing, as well. Moral arbiters such as the Methodist Church had proscriptions against the theatre, dancing, card playing, and drinking, but these injunctions weren't followed religiously by Methodists, let alone the public at large.[7] The flouting of traditional mores was symbolized by the New Woman, a media caricature of unconventional new female behaviour. The New Woman dared to bicycle, play tennis or golf. She dared to don a duster, goggles, and cap and go motoring. She dared to abandon stiff, layered dresses in favour of looser, lighter, more natural clothing. Out went the corset in favour of a new invention, the practical brassiere ('A very dainty piece of lingerie designed to impart beauty and grace,' according to one ad). On went rouge and lipstick. The New Woman did all of this, yet she still went to church. Perhaps she had more reason to go than ever before.

Arts organizations were themselves changing along with the changing times. New transportation and communication links were allowing them to network over larger territories. The voluntary sector took advantage of these developments to organize on a regional scale. Music festivals, for example, developed in various regions in the years before the war (the same type of growth was evident in contemporary sports leagues).[8] The next step up from regional networks was, of course, national organization. The various Christian churches – with their national executives, regional administrations, and chapters in almost every community – provided a model for organizing on a national scale that was emulated by voluntary organizations such as the Women's Institute, the Imperial Order Daughters of the Empire, and the Woman's Christian Temperance Union, all of which promoted variations of the churches' social agendas. The Canadian Club of Montreal, the organization that Sandwell and Willson addressed before the war, was part of a national voluntary organization founded twenty years earlier to foster national consciousness. These organizations had blazed a trail that voluntary arts organizations would follow.

In the war years, however, the organization of Canada's voluntary cultural sector paled in comparison with the continent-spanning achievements of the entertainment businesses. As Sandwell had noted in his indictment of theatre, cultural industries had been reconstituted on a continental scale through a process of technological innovation, capital investment, and rationalization that characterized the growth of big business in the late nineteenth and early twentieth centuries. Touring circuses, minstrel acts, Wild West shows, and vaudeville companies followed the rail lines from the United States into Canada, circulating from major cities out to regional centres. There were no Canadian equivalents operating nationally because it was impossible to compete with American productions financed and produced for a market ten times as large.

Examples of this economic logic at work were evident across the mass media and in all the cultural products they carried. Universal public schooling had boosted literacy rates to higher than 90 per cent of the population by the time the Great War began, creating in the process a mass market for print. Big city evening papers, such as the *Toronto Star* or Montreal's *La Presse*, had built up huge circulations by offering a product with broad appeal. They aimed low with sensationalistic and sentimental material; they simultaneously aimed wide with a variety of offerings to satisfy many different tastes.[9]

Newspapers were local insofar as each served a particular city and its hinterland, printed news about that area, and reflected its interests. Nevertheless, continental cultural economics shaped their product. 'Not only is the Canadian newspaper built on American lines,' complained one observer, 'it is crammed with American "boiler plate" of all kinds, American illustrations, American comic supplements.'[10] He could have added columns, features and sports news. The big dailies also carried international news gleaned from American news services, which, one contemporary feared, gave Canadians 'impressions which, day by day, trained their minds imperceptively but surely.'[11]

Nationalist expectations of the press concentrated on magazines; for unlike newspapers, they served a national market. Unfortunately, the magazine market was dominated by American product more directly than that of the newspaper. In the late nineteenth century, American entrepreneurs had responded to rising literacy rates with general-interest magazines that offered a varied menu of short stories, topical non-fiction, commentary, business reports, poetry and arts reviews, all packaged with illustrations, photographs, and advertising in a colourful, attractively designed format. Middlebrow mass-market magazines, such as *McCall's*, the *Saturday Evening Post*, and the *Ladies' Home Journal*, were read by tens of thousands of Canadians. English-Canadian entrepreneurs imitated them with publications such as *Maclean's*, *Saturday Night*, and *Canadian Magazine*, but they found themselves competing in a domestic market already saturated with American product and dominated by American distributors. The smaller French-Canadian market, protected by language, managed to sustain its own general-interest magazines, such as *Le Samedi* and *Revue populaire*.[12] But even these publications, like their English Canadian counterparts, were American in that they mimicked the American formula for mass market success, substituting Canadian for American content.

Advertising constituted a substantial portion of newspapers and magazines and underwrote most of their cost. Ephemeral publications were inexpensive to purchase because they made most of their money by delivering large audiences to advertisers. Some popular publications, such as the store catalogues, were wholly commercial in content. The field of advertising was evolving from a haphazard commercial practice into a profession with a repertoire of increasingly sophisticated psychological techniques. While each advertisement was intended only to sell a particular product, collectively they promoted consumerism and associated values such as materialism and self-indulgence.

The one form of print communication in which advertising was not intermingled with editorial content was the book.[13] The Canadian book market was inundated with products from both British and American publishers. North American rights usually went to American publishers. Canadian publishers, concentrated in Toronto, survived by publishing textbooks for Canadian schools, by acting as agents for British and American publishing houses, and by publishing Canadian editions of foreign books. Patriotic publishers put out Canadian works for a Canadian audience as well, but there were easier ways to make money.

Print was also the medium through which plays and music were transmitted. New songs, for instance, were distributed primarily as sheet music. Songwriters who could afford to lose their investments had local job printers reproduce sheet music of their compositions. Sometimes a local instrument manufacturer or music academy would sponsor the printing as a sideline to its business. Canada's music publishers did not have the marketing clout required to routinely generate hits. Only New York's Tin Pan Alley, the music production centre that had grown up around the Broadway musical theatre, wielded that kind of influence. It advertised in mass-market magazines and major newspapers and cross-promoted popular performers and songs. The result was that hit songs could become well known across North America, heard often enough to be known by heart even by people who could not read music. The mass-marketed ditty took on the character of a folk song as it became incorporated into the popular repertoire and was sung for private as well as public entertainment.[14]

During the war years Canadians became accustomed to a new cultural convenience: music on demand. The piano, long a middle-class symbol of taste and refinement, had been modified by inventors in the late nineteenth century to overcome the inconvenience of not knowing how to play it. The result was the player-piano, a high-tech marvel that brought the sounds of the finest pianists into the home and satisfied 'all that is fastidious and discriminating in taste,' in the words of a contemporary ad. Over half of all pianos sold during the war were players.[15] Enterprising telephone companies offered Sunday afternoon musical concerts over their networks, but this service did not catch on. More successful was the record player, which was replacing the gramophone. It was produced in polished wood cabinets that fit in with the finest parlour furniture. At first the 'Victrola' and its imitators were too expensive for any but the well-to-do, but over the war years mass production made them affordable for the middle class. ('He suggested furs,' confided a stylish young lady in one ad, 'and I suggested a phonograph.') In the process, a market for 78-rpm records developed, opening a new channel of mass communication. For those who did not have a player piano or record player, the nickleodeon offered a similar experience on a pay-per-listen basis. These commercial coin-operated music machines, located in various public venues such as restaurants, ice-cream parlours, drugstores, pool halls, and saloons, could simulate drums, tambourine, whistle, xylophone, and banjo as well as the piano.[16]

As diverting as it was, the new music was upstaged by the cultural phenomenon of the decade: the movie. Moving pictures had been around for twenty years, but it was during the war that the feature film was developed and gained acceptance as a mainstream popular entertainment. D.W. Griffith's *Birth of a Nation* (1915), often credited as the breakthrough production in the popularization process, was merely the first in a pack of increasingly sophisticated products. One of the big hits of the war years was *Tarzan of the Apes* (1918), promoted as 'The Amazing Narrative of a She-Ape that Nursed an Orphan English Child to Astounding Manhood.' Movie 'palaces,' designed to add class and glamour to the movie-going experience, already far outnumbered stage theatres. A star system developed, turning actors like Charlie Chaplin and Canada's Mary Pickford into household names across North America. Canadian newspapers carried celebrity gossip like the *Saint John Globe*'s 'News of the Stage and the Motion Picture World.' Although most of the movies Canadians saw were American, a large minority came from Britain and France, both of which had burgeoning film industries.

The continental structure of the cultural industries affected Canadian artists as much as consumers. Canadian writers might use Canadian settings, but they worked in internationally popular genres. It was possible to stay in Canada and make a living as a writer, but only if you were an extraordinarily popular author such as Lucy Maud Montgomery or Ralph Connor. Lesser lights moved closer to the big publishers in New York or London and wrote for magazines and newspapers as well as books, always targeting 'the great middle band in the spectrum of the reading public.'[17] The same pattern was true in other areas of cultural production. Canadian theatre troupes survived by serving smaller towns instead of going head to head with the big American shows. This was the approach taken by the Marks Brothers, one of the best-known Canadian touring theatre operations of the era, and by 'Doc' Kelley, whose medicine show peddled patent medicines through song and dance, comedy skits, and tricks (and who merits immortality as the originator of the 'pie-in-the-face' routine).[18] Both acts worked both sides of the border. Similarly, Canadians who wanted to become successful recording artists had to go to the United States to do so. Wartime hits written by Canadians, such as 'Keep Your Head Down, Fritzie Boy' and 'K-K-K-Katy,' were published in New York. The hit-making machinery behind the popular song was in the States. In all of these cases, it was a challenge to discern what was uniquely Canadian about a cultural product produced and consumed within the continental cultural context.

Clearly, the trends that had prompted Sandwell's pre-war complaint were not restricted to theatre alone, and they grew stronger across the different cultural sectors throughout the war years. Canadians were increasingly plugged in to broader communications networks carrying cultural products around the continent. Styles and slang from the stage and screen were soon seen and heard on the street. In the summer, Canadians played baseball as well as cricket and lacrosse. In the winter, the well-to-do vacationed at American resort hotels from Florida to California. Traditional elements in Canada's local, regional, and national cultures were not necessarily displaced, but they were increasingly juxtaposed with new influences that flowed faster and more profusely with each passing year. However traumatic the experience of being at war, most Canadians lived the experience from the other side of the Atlantic Ocean, immersed in a North American cultural context in which it was business as usual. Continental channels of distribution continued to feed them a steady diet of new cultural products, and they continued to consume them. There was a thickening layer of shared continental culture in the average Canadian's life.[19]

## II

When war broke out in 1914, many cultural enterprises in Canada either ceased or scaled back operations. Some artists stopped working, either because they were temporarily transfixed by events in Europe or because they felt that making art was self-indulgent when lives were on the line overseas and the future of civilization hung in the balance. In Halifax, the Canadian Bioscope Company dissolved and auctioned off its films as personnel dispersed to war service at home and abroad. Many voluntary organizations also diverted their energies from cultural activities to supporting the war effort. Music festivals in the west suspended operations for the duration of the war. Choirs and orchestras lost members. In Toronto, the symphony orchestra stumbled along, then finally disbanded in 1918.

The operations of the continental cultural industries in Canada were restricted in some ways by the outbreak of war. In the performing arts sector, there were fewer shows on tour, owing to wartime exigencies. American theatrical troupes had to contend with disrupted train schedules, unheated theatres, and special wartime taxes. In 1918 the federal government even closed theatres across the country for one day a week to save fuel. After conscription was instituted, it was not unknown for police to arrive at a theatre or dance hall, seal the exits, and march young men who lacked registration papers off to the enlistment office. A raid at the Gaiety Theatre in Toronto in 1918, for example, culled 150 of the 1,000 men in attendance. Such incidents were bad for business.

Nevertheless, the outbreak of war did not substantially alter the channels along which culture flowed or the nature of the cultural products that flowed along them. The continental cultural industries were not flexible enough to accommodate the special needs created by the belligerent status of a small fraction of their market. The themes of shows staged in Canadian theatres were indistinguishable from those put on in peacetime, offering little, other than escapism, to address the cultural needs of a nation engaged in total war.[20] Those American cultural products that did deal with the war treated it as a topic of great contemporary interest rather than an all-encompassing cataclysm. It was used as a backdrop to give standard genres added topicality and poignancy. Magazines published informative articles about various aspects of the war effort alongside sentimental short stories about Daddy going off to the front or young lovers torn apart by epic events beyond their control. Advertisers used the war in a similar fashion to sell their goods. 'In these troubled days,' read a Columbia record player ad, 'the comfort and solace that only good music can bring is more than ever needed.'

British cultural products offered a counterbalance. British plays with war-related themes were brought to Canada, including the London hit *Under Orders*, the spy drama *The White Feather*, and its sequel, *The Black Feather*. British film documentaries about the war, such as *Britain Prepared* (1915) and the *Battle of the Somme* (1916), played to packed houses across the country. The Canadian public's interest in the war made it possible for publishers to market otherwise obscure offerings such as *The Kaiser as I Know Him* by Arthur N. Davis, advertised as 'Vivid pen-pictures of the Great Enemy of Democracy in action, painted by a man who was for fifteen years the German Kaiser's personal dentist.'[21] Such imports were supplemented with a host of cheaper but no less significant items such as trinkets, postcards, Union Jacks, and portraits of the king and queen.

These products filled a void, but they could not directly address Canada's unique experience of the war. Ultimately, Canadians were thrown back on their own resources for information and commentary. The crowd gathered around the newspaper office for the latest reports from Europe became a common sight at critical junctures in the conflict. Canadian newsreel producers sprang up to feed the public appetite for knowledge about the Canadian war effort, providing footage of Canadian troops training and staged representations of what was happening at the front. Over time they added material on the British and other Allies' war efforts, providing a broad view of the war with a Canadian perspective and emphasis. Canadian magazines put the war on their covers and provided thorough coverage, leveraging the rare opportunity to provide a distinctive product valued by their national market.[22] Although many arts organizations abandoned their cultural activities at the outbreak of war, their expertise was subsequently recruited to serve the war effort. War causes were supported by patriotic pageants and concerts at which the audience was both entertained and motivated to give more – be it in money, work, or able-bodied sons.

The war gave such domestic productions a comparative advantage over American cultural products. When the war began, book publishers had scrambled to meet the demand for books that could help to explain it, and they reaped commercial rewards for bringing out Canadian works such as Billy Bishop's *Winged Warfare*, F.M. Bell's *First Canadians in France*, and Gilbert Parker's *The War in the Crucible*. A Canadian publisher estimated that over 1,000 different war-related titles were marketed in Canada during the war and that they sold, on average, about ten times as well as the average pre-war publication, some going into print runs of up to 40,000 copies.[23] Most fit the mould of Ralph Connor's *The Sky Pilot in No Man's Land*, later characterized as 'the epitome of a prevalent Anglo-Saxon Canadian view of the War – idealistic, Protestant, evangelical, and British tribal.'[24] A Canadian market for war songs temporarily made domestic music publishing a more viable economic proposition. Canadians penned hundreds of tunes about the war, some of them general morale-boosters ('What the Deuce Do We Care for Kaiser Bill'), others with specific aims such as boosting recruitment ('We'll Love You More When You Come Back Than When You Went Away'), and others encouraging efforts on the home front ('He's Doing His Bit – Are You?').[25]

The advertising industry was another significant domestic producer of war-related culture. The leading experts at commercial persuasion applied their talents to raising money for wartime charities such as the Belgian Relief Fund, the Canadian Patriotic Fund, the Salvation Army and the Canadian Red Cross. They also devised campaigns to promote recruiting, Victory Bonds, and thriftiness on the home front. Some copywriters went over the top to reach their objective:

> The invasion of Canada sounded like 'bosh' six months ago.
> Today, serious men no longer laugh.
> This time next year the Battle of Halifax, the Sack of St. John, the Massacre of Montreal, and the Siege of Toronto, may be writing their red histories on the breast of civilian Canada.

Certain commercial campaigns associated themselves with the cause by glamorizing military service while selling men's products such as razor blades or wristwatches. In newspapers, magazines, posters, and

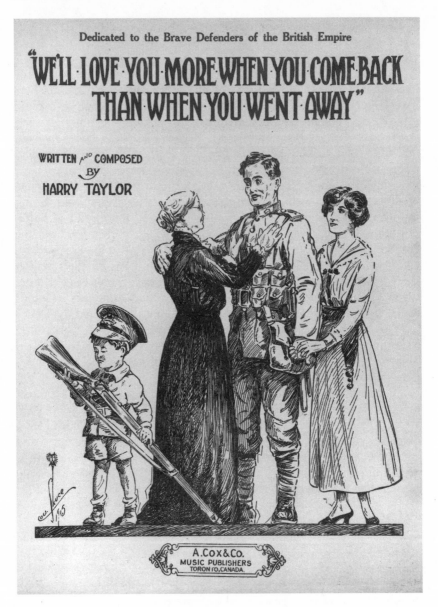

'We'll Love You More When You Come Back Than When You Went Away,' by Harry Taylor, © Public Domain (National Library of Canada, Music Collection, CSM 08071)

'Nursing Daddy's Men,' by Jean Munro Mulloy, © Public Domain (National Library of Canada, Music Collection, CSM05625)

billboards, advertising in the service of war cajoled, pulled at the heartstrings, and frightened readers. It sold the war to Canadians. Conversely, its usefulness in promoting the war effort helped to make advertising more socially and commercially acceptable.[26]

The federal government's primary concern in the cultural realm was to censor information that could be deemed useful to the enemy or could undermine the morale of Canadians.[27] When it came to using culture to encourage the war effort, it was less certain of its role. It had relied heavily on the press to help to mobilize the country for war in 1914 and sponsored advertising to mobilize human and financial resources. Max Aitken (later Lord Beaverbrook), a Canadian millionaire who had moved to London and ingratiated himself into circles of privilege and power, stepped into the breach, creating the Canadian War Records Office (CWRO), ostensibly to document Canada's war effort. Under Aitken's guidance – and with increasing government support – the CWRO also became a publicity office. It chronicled Canada's war exploits in books, photo-pictorials, paintings, and documentary film. Its publication *Canada in Khaki* exemplified how the contemporary formula for a successful mass-market magazine could be used to produce a popular, topical chronicle of Canada at war. It included sentimental poems about heroes and sacrifice, light-hearted cartoons, dramatic illustrations, and stories from the front such as 'Canada in Hunland,' 'The Knight Errant from Saskatchewan,' 'In Memoriam of A Good Fellow,' and 'Christmas Day on Vimy Ridge.' Prominent, too, were pitches for buying something special for soldiers overseas. 'Your boy at the front may not like to ask you for them,' ran one, 'but cigarettes are everything for him out there.' Profits from *Canada in Khaki* went to the Canadian War Memorials Fund. Its success was evidence of how government subsidy could produce a product that suited Canada's unique circumstances.

Canadians, then, were able to improvise their own cultural products to make up for their usual supplier's inability to meet their requirements. Had American mass culture been merely inadequate, perhaps such import substitutes would have seen Canadians happily through the war years. But in fact, American cultural products were not merely lacking – they were offensive. Canadians are known for their ability to consume American culture, but the heightened emotions of wartime and the differences in points of view of a belligerent Canada and a neutral United States fomented an unusual cultural indigestion. In movies, for example, U.S. directors had a habit of deploying shots of

American patriotic symbols to stir emotions. Audiences in Canada were stirred, but not in the way that was intended. In 1914 the British Columbia censor board banned fifty reels of American film for gratuitous display of the Stars and Stripes. Only seduction and infidelity were snipped more frequently that year.[28] In other cases it was U.S. boastfulness that was hard to stomach. A letter to the editor of the *Toronto Star* complained about 'moving picture shows that laud American characters and hold up to ridicule Englishmen and women ... Everything American is lauded to the skies, from President to the soldier. This is all right for the United States, but entirely out of place in Canada.'[29] Canadian theatre-goers were similarly appalled by American stage shows that derided the British Empire and mocked its war effort.

Canadians were ready to be offended by these productions because of their disappointment with the United States for staying on the sidelines during their desperate struggle to save civilization. Most knew little of how America's neutrality represented a balance between competing factions in its domestic politics. They interpreted Irish-American and German-American anti-British propaganda as indicative of American opinion in general. They gagged on smug pronouncements by American politicians that equated American neutrality with moral superiority, even as U.S. businesses prospered from war orders and the Allied powers grew increasingly indebted to New York bankers. The immense power of their neighbour, a seemingly natural ally, was denied to Canadians for reasons they could not comprehend. Small wonder the American flag was hissed at in Canadian theatres.[30]

The nature of the problem changed when the United States joined the war in April 1917, but not for the better. As U.S. cultural industries cranked up production of war-themed songs, magazine pieces, movies, and plays, American producers blithely exported domestic war propaganda with no adaptations to accommodate Canadian sensibilities. Canadians suddenly found themselves asked to believe that the United States was saving the world single-handedly. The *Passing Show of 1917* at the Gaiety Theatre in Toronto, for instance, featured the American patriotic number 'Goodbye Broadway, Hello France,' accompanied by a display of national flags in which the Union Jack was barely visible. Such presumption and insensitivity on the part of eleventh-hour adherents to the cause bred a deep resentment in Canada. Newspaper editors printed indignant editorials. Feelings ran so high that whole audiences walked out of productions. The result was an 'agitation,' as one observer put it, 'to control or modify the United States' flag-waving tendency.'[31] Sandwell's pre-war complaint about American plays was being rendered in starker tones across a broader cultural landscape. By heightening the contrast between the two countries' interests and values, the war emphasized the drawbacks of Canada's dependence on popular culture that largely emanated from outside its borders.

The problem was all the more evident because of Canadians' war-induced sense of accomplishment, identity, and independent destiny. When Canada turned fifty in 1917, the war was widely regarded as the maturing nation's rite of passage to full independence and status in international affairs. Canadians took pride in having fought hard for a righteous cause in Europe. Vindicated by victory, they revelled in a sense of accomplishment and maturity. The 'old bitch gone in the teeth,' Ezra Pound's famous characterization of the civilization capable of the carnage of the Great War, did not apply here. Canada was a frisky pup with a sharp bite.

The war and its aftermath also demonstrated the impracticality of pre-war schemes for imperial federation and nudged Canada towards greater constitutional autonomy. While still valuing their British cultural heritage, Anglo-Canadians gained a keener consciousness of the ways in which they were not British, and they would increasingly support autonomist foreign policies and imperial devolution. This trend only made Canada's dependence on continental mass culture all the more problematic. If Canada became less British, mass culture and the American values it bore would become relatively more influential, increasing the danger of what one contemporary called 'spiritual bondage,' a condition he defined as 'the subjection of the Canadian nation's mind and soul to the mind and soul of the United States.'[32]

## III

The offence given by American cultural products reinforced cultural nationalists' determination to foster a Canadian culture that would offset the influence of continental culture in the marketplace. The feasibility of this project varied widely from one cultural sector to the next. The cultural industries in Canada during the war years can be categorized roughly into two types. There were some that had Canadian producers serving their domestic market. In others, Canadian producers were scattered, small, and lacking in collective consciousness or power. Often the political clout in these sectors lay with distributors or retailers whose interest lay in a steady supply of American product.[33]

The significance of this distinction was evident in the publishing, the-atre, and movie industries, three high-profile cultural sectors targeted by nationalist initiatives in the wake of the war. In the first, nationalist and business interests combined with some success, while in the latter two they did not.

It was no coincidence that Canadian producers were entrenched most firmly in the older print media. Newspapers were a special case in which a local product would exist under most circumstances. The maga-zine and book publishing industries in Canada, for their part, pre-dated the rise of big business on a continental scale in the late nineteenth century. Despite the dominance of external producers, there were Cana-dian producers serving a Canadian market in this sector. Moreover, literature, the high culture in this medium, was considered a funda-mental aid to nationalism because it both proved the existence of and disseminated national identity. Thus, there was a shared interest be-tween nationalists and Canadian cultural industries in reserving some space in the domestic market for Canadian publishers.

In the past these factors had occasionally moved the government to set aside its laissez-faire principles and intervene in the marketplace. During the 1870s and 1880s the federal government had done its best to avoid enforcing international copyright conventions, thereby subsidiz-ing the Canadian publishing industry by allowing it to profit from publishing cheap editions of foreign works.[34] After it was forced to toe the line in the 1890s, the government toyed with protectionist measures on the rationale that Canadian publishers were frequently frozen out of their own market by the British and American practice of granting North American rights to American publishers.[35] It also subsidized Canadian newspapers and magazines with low second-class mail rates, a policy designed, as Sir Wilfrid Laurier put it, 'to foster a national consciousness.'[36] In 1917 the federal government played a role in break-ing Canadian newspapers' dependence on American news services, providing a $50,000 annual subsidy to support Canadian Press.[37] The magazine industry would campaign successfully in the post-war pe-riod for a protective tariff, demonstrating once again the sector's ability to move the government to defend its interests.

In cultural sectors where there was no established Canadian produc-tion industry, fostering Canadian content was much more of a chal-lenge. Nevertheless, efforts were made. In 1919 Canadian investors launched the Trans-Canada Theatre Society to secure 'complete control of a professional theatre route entirely in Canada.' Their business plan was to buy up theatres to create a chain across the country that would show touring versions of British plays (which presumably would offset the influence of U.S. plays, creating a balanced 'Canadian' theatre scene). Things did not work out as planned. Trans-Canada faced competition not only from American stage productions, but also from movies, which grew tremendously in popularity in these years. It went bankrupt in 1924.[38]

Nationalist impulses in the movie business followed a somewhat different path to the same dead end. A number of film producers were inspired by the post-war climate of cultural nationalism – and the possibilities it created for raising funds – to make movies in Canada on subjects both Canadian and non-Canadian. The most successful was Ernest Shipman, a Canadian with Hollywood experience who produced a clutch of films over half a decade following the war. Shipman's modus operandi was to raise money in the city closest to the locale in which he was filming. 'A New Industry in Canada,' proclaimed his Calgary newspaper ad in March 1919. He offered locals a piece of the action for *Back to God's Country*, with the assurance that his wife, Nell, 'the greatest outdoor girl on the screen today,' would be the star.[39]

The movie business was still in a state of flux, and it was possible for independent producers like Shipman to find distribution in North America and return profits to investors. But in the early 1920s Hollywood studios began buying up film distributors and theatres in order to guarantee a market for their products. Vertical integration shut Canadian productions out of domestic and international markets, blocking the development of a Canadian feature film industry before it got properly started.[40] Other western nations responded to the flood of cheap and attractive film imports from Hollywood in the post-war period with protectionist policies aimed at reserving a slice of their own markets for domestically produced films. In Canada's case, however, there was no established domestic production industry for the government to protect. Exhibitors were the dominant economic interest in the sector, and they wanted a steady supply of cheap and popular American product. The general public may have been interested in seeing Canadian movies, but there was no economic 'interest' backing a Canadian movie production industry.

The cultural nationalist impulse produced more tangible results in the voluntary sector. The organizational impulse evident in the sector in the pre-war years was just as strong in the post-war period and, energized by war-induced nationalism, spurred the development of a nation-wide web of cultural nationalist groups in the 1920s. There were new and revived professional associations in the arts, music festivals, academic organizations, and service clubs, all bound together with newsletters, journals, conferences, and national executives.[41] 'The war itself had broken down the barriers of mountain, lake and sea,' Brooke Claxton would recall in his memoir. 'Right across Canada were associations and individuals concerned about the same kind of things and working to the same goals.'[42]

This expanding network extended beyond voluntary organizations in the arts and letters to universities, cultural institutions, and the few cultural industries where Canada had domestic producers. Its activities in the post-war period reflected its power base. The painters of the Group of Seven, Canadian nationalism's poster boys of the post-war era, were nurtured by the Canadian advertising graphics industry, then promoted by the National Gallery and the Canadian press. *Maclean's* magazine pledged to print only Canadian non-fiction and a minimal amount of non-Canadian fiction. The *Canadian Magazine* went farther, promising 100 per cent Canadian content. A new firm in Ottawa, Graphic Press, dedicated itself to only Canadian works – an ideal it pursued for the better part of a decade before collapsing into bankruptcy. Other Canadian publishers devoted themselves to fostering a native literature in addition to publishing the foreign trade books and textbooks that still brought in most of their money. A flurry of anthologies, literary histories, and other published proof of national identity followed.

## IV

While such projects gave cultural nationalists a sense of accomplishment, they did little to offset the influence of continental mass culture. Despite American wartime provocations, Canadians had negligible success challenging continental mass culture on its own turf in the immediate post-war period. One is tempted to conclude that if nothing happened under these circumstances, nothing ever would happen. More to the point is to ask why this dog didn't bark – or, to put it more accurately, why it merely whimpered.

One possible explanation is that Canadian-American cultural relations simply returned to the status quo ante bellum: once the war ended, the gap between American and Canadian sensibilities closed, and the problem faded into a distant memory. But this was not, in fact, the case. In the 1920s America kept churning out 'how we won the war' productions, and Canadians continued to find them offensive. Sensitivities were still raw enough that Canadian advertising executives advised U.S. companies to carefully review their advertisements to ensure that they did not provoke Canadian customers. Late in the decade, an ambitious Canadian film production, *Carry On Sergeant*, was produced in large part as a Canadian rejoinder to American war movies.

A more significant factor was Canada's tendency to think of itself as British – if no longer as a British colony, at least as a British North American nation. This perception fostered the practice of depending on British books, music, theatre, and film to offset American products instead of producing Canadian equivalents. Canadians maintained an unwarranted faith in the mother country's continuing economic power and international influence, and they assumed that British cultural products would win in the marketplace, owing to their inherent superiority. Continued reliance on British culture as an antidote to American influence obscured the need for made-in-Canada solutions to Canada's unique cultural predicament.

This anglophilic reflex was reinforced by the tendency of the upper classes to associate British culture with high culture and American culture with low culture. Their model for a national culture was British culture or, at least, what they thought of as British culture: the canon of literature, fine art, serious theatre, and classical music. It was a model moulded to offset their negative impressions of mass culture. The class dimensions of this concept, high versus low, were conflated with nationalism, creating a parallel dichotomy of Canadian versus American. This bias was accommodated by the fact that the locus of Canadian cultural nationalism lay in the voluntary sector. Even if leading cultural nationalists had been interested in competing with American cultural producers in the marketplace of mass culture, they lacked the ability to do so. They were not business people with market knowledge, economic power, and political influence. The technologies that facilitated media transmission of culture were foreign to them. Indeed, as we have seen, the print media were the only Canadian cultural producers that had the economic significance and political clout – with the support of nationalists – to move the government to act against American cultural imports.

The Canadian cultural nationalism forged by the wartime experience would be influential in Canadian cultural policy for the next half century. A generation of cultural nationalists for whom the war was a formative experience would launch the Radio League, create the Canadian Broadcasting Corporation, support the National Film Board, champion the Massey Commission, and breathe life into the Canada Council.[43] All of these key components of the Canadian cultural establishment would be shaped by the voluntary sector's brand of cultural nationalism. Not until the 1960s would a new generation rethink its predecessor's assumptions and try again to Canadianize the more popular forms of culture purveyed in the continental cultural marketplace. By that time continental mass culture had had another half-century to entrench itself in the northern half of North America. As Canadian compromises go, this wasn't such a bad deal. Canadians enjoyed unfettered access to the mass culture that defined them as North Americans while developing parallel means of distinguishing themselves as above all that. Cultural nationalism flowed along the paths of least resistance, complementing rather than confronting continental mass culture.

NOTES

1 Bernard K. Sandwell, 'Our Adjunct Theatre,' *Addresses Delivered before the Canadian Club of Montreal, 1913–1914* (Montreal, 1914), 97. Sandwell noted that theatre, once suspect as a lowbrow, immoral diversion, was on its way upmarket and was increasingly being accepted in proper society. His assertion about Canada's not having been invaded, of course, excluded the War of 1812, various rebel incursions, and the Fenians. For an earlier, more wide-ranging analysis of the various ways in which American influences were affecting Canada, see Samuel E. Moffatt, *The Americanization of Canada* (Toronto: University of Toronto Press, 1972 [1906]).

2 The main exception was, of course, francophone Quebec, where anglophobia prevailed over anglophilia, and a relatively compact population with a distinctive culture and language created a viable regional market for locally produced cultural goods and impeded American cultural imports. Some of what follows applies to Quebec, but the province was, as always, a special case.

3 Beckles Willson, 'Canada's Undeveloped Literary Resources,' *Addresses Delivered before the Canadian Club of Montreal, 1913–1914*, 192.

4 Elaine Keillor, *Vignettes on Music in Canada* (Ottawa: Canadian Musical Heritage Society, 2002), 217.

5 Calgary *Eye Opener*, 2 December, 1916.

6 Bruce Hutchinson, *The Far Side of the Street* (Toronto: Macmillan, 1976), 41–2, 46–7. See Daphne Read, ed., *The Great War and Canadian Society: An Oral History* (Toronto: New Hogtown Press, 1978), for a variety of

individuals' memories of the war, some of which deal with cultural activities.

7 The Methodists' rules were relaxed somewhat by doctrinal reforms in 1914. See Ann Saddlemyer and Richard Plant, eds, *Early Stages: Theatre in Ontario, 1800–1914* (Toronto: University of Toronto Press, 1990), 48, 346. For a discussion of the degree to which the church effectively exercised moral leadership in small town Ontario of the late nineteenth century, see Lynne Marks, *Revivals and Roller Rinks: Religion, Leisure, and Identity in Small-Town Ontario* (Toronto: University of Toronto Press, 1996), 210.

8 Maria Tippett, *Making Culture: English-Canadian Institutions and the Arts Before the Massey Commission* (Toronto: University of Toronto Press, 1990), 55–6. Organizational networks had been built up in previous decades through postal and telegraph communication and rail transportation. During the war, two new technologies, the telephone and the automobile, accelerated this trend. Both were overcoming range limitations in these years. Transcontinental long-distance telephone service had just become available but was not yet routine, while the road system required to make the car a viable alternative for long-distance travel would come in the years following the war.

9 Paul Rutherford, *The Making of the Canadian Media* (Toronto: McGraw-Hill Ryerson, 1978), 49.

10 Archibald McMechan, 'Canada as a Vassal State,' *Canadian Historical Review* 1, 4 (December 1920), 349.

11 J. Castell Hopkins, ed., *Canadian Annual Review of Public Affairs, 1918* (Toronto: Annual Review. Co., 1914–18), 123.

12 Rutherford, *Making of the Canadian Media*, 46, 49.

13 It should be noted, however, that some books had ads, particularly for other books, inside their covers.

14 Keillor, *Vignettes*, 161.

15 So popular was the player piano that some Canadians could not leave home without it. During the war years, Robert J. Flaherty, the Arctic explorer and filmmaker who made the famed documentary, *Nanook of the North*, took his player piano with him on one of his expeditions. On departing the Belcher Islands, Flaherty gave his 'singing box,' as the Inuit called it, to a Native friend who subsequently suffered a common piano-owner's dilemma when he found it would not fit into his igloo. Enterprising in his returns policy, he transported it over 280 miles south to Fort George to give it back to its original owner. Wayne Kelly, *Downright Upright: A History of the Canadian Piano Industry* (Toronto: Natural Heritage / Natural History Inc., 1991), 38.

16 Keillor, *Vignettes*, 142–5.

17  Gordon Roper, Rupert Schieder, and S. Ross Beharriell, 'The Kinds of
     Fiction, 1880–1920,' in Carl Klinck, ed., *The Literary History of Canada*
     (Toronto: University of Toronto Press, 1965), 312.
18  Ann Saddlemyer and Richard Plant, eds, *Later Stages: Essays in Ontario
     Theatre from the First World War to the 1970s* (Toronto: University of Toronto
     Press, 1997), 128.
19  How were Canadian interests served by this situation? The answers vary
     by cultural sector and according to whether the interest in question was
     that of the consumer, producer, distributor, or cultural nationalist. The
     mass cultural milieu exposed Canadian consumers to a broader world. It
     was possible to appreciate Latin dance or southern Black music without
     ever leaving the country, even if one was fuzzy on their provenance.
     Canadians might end up with a watered-down or caricatured version of
     these styles, but they were exposed to something different from what they
     were likely to experience within their local cultural milieu.
        There was also a place for Canadian identity in international mass
     culture. Enough was published on the various regions of Canada to give
     Canadians and foreigners a sense of the diversity of their country and the
     character of its various parts. However, most people entertained vague
     impressions rather than a detailed knowledge based on extensive reading.
     The stereotype of a timeless, picturesque, pre-modern Quebec, for ex-
     ample, prevailed despite the growth of cities and industry in the province.
     Gilbert Parker's romance *The Money Maker* (1915), set in a fictitious Quebec
     parish, took this approach because that was its author's understanding
     of this part of his native country. 'I think the French Canadian one of the
     most individual, original, and distinctive beings in the modern world,'
     wrote Parker. 'He has kept his place, with his own customs, his own Gallic
     views of life, and his religious habits, with an assiduity and firmness';
     Roper, Schieder, and Beharriell, 'The Kinds of Fiction, 1880–1920,' 290.
     The other dominant image of Canada was the great northwest, otherwise
     known as 'God's Country,' a snowbound realm on the margin of civiliza-
     tion peopled by noble savages, mad trappers, gold-crazed prospectors,
     strapping lumberjacks, and dauntless Mounties. Caricatures like these
     projected an image of Canada to foreign lands that was as skewed and
     partial as those Canadians had from their imported impressions of other
     parts of the world.
        Allan Smith has written extensively on the North American dimension
     of Canadian identity in the late nineteenth and early twentieth centuries.
     See Smith, *Canada – An American Nation?* (Montreal and Kingston: McGill-
     Queen's University Press, 1994), particularly the essays 'The Continental
     Dimension in the Evolution of the English-Canadian Mind' (originally

published in the *International Journal* 31, 3 [1976], 442–69), and 'Samuel Moffatt and the Americanization of Canada' (first published as the Introduction to a reissue of Moffat, *Americanization of Canada*, vii–xxxi.

20  The *Toronto Evening Telegram* of Saturday 9 December, 1916, for instance, listed *H.M.S. Pinafore*, *The Merry Wives of Windsor*, *Charley's Aunt*, Irving Berlin's comedy *Watch Your Step*, and a 'thrilling story,' *Yellow Pawn*, at a variety of theatres – the Royal Alexandra, the Grand Opera House, Shea's, Loew's Yonge Street, and the Regent.

21  *Canada in Khaki. A tribute to the officers and men now serving in the overseas military forces of Canada* (Toronto: published for the Canadian War Records Office by Musson, n.d.), 2: 189. Davis's book was published in the United States and Britain by Harper & Brothers, a firm with offices in New York and London, but in an arrangement typical of the publishing industry in the English-language world, it was offered in Canada by the Musson Book Company of Toronto.

22  In the process, they tended to vacillate between courageous optimism and bleak despair, if only to exploit all available modes of sensationalism. *Maclean's*, for example, ran a cover illustration of a Canadian soldier strangling a German in November 1918, with the caption, 'Buy Victory Bonds and Strengthen His Grip.' Just a few months earlier it had featured an article entitled 'Why We Are Losing the War.'

23  Hugh Eayrs, president of Macmillan, in *Canadian Bookman*, 1919, as quoted in George L. Parker, 'A History of a Canadian Publishing House: A Study of the Relation between Publishing and the Profession of Writing, 1890–1940,' PhD thesis, University of Toronto, 1969, 59.

24  Roper, Schieder, and Beharriell, 'The Kinds of Fiction, 1880–1920,' 311.

25  See 'Canadian Sheet Music of the First World War,' *Music on the Home Front: Sheet Music from Canada's Past*, on the Web site of the National Library of Canada: http://www. nlc-bnc.ca/sheetmusic/m5-170-e.html.

26  H.E. Stephenson and C. McNaught, *The Story of Advertising in Canada* (Toronto: Ryerson Press, 1940), 171, 185.

27  Jeffrey Keshen, *Propaganda and Censorship during Canada's Great War* (Edmonton: University of Alberta Press, 1996), 107.

28  Peter Morris, *Embattled Shadows: A History of Canadian Cinema, 1895–1939* (Montreal and Kingston: McGill-Queen's University Press, 1978), 55.

29  *Toronto Daily Star*, 25 November 1916, as cited in Saddlemyer and Plant, *Later Stages*, 105n20.

30  Hugh L. Keenleyside, *Canada and the United States* (New York: Knopf, 1929), 365–8.

31  Hopkins, *Canadian Annual Review, 1918*, 123.

32 McMechan, *Canada as a Vassal State*, 347.
33 Ted Magder explains the lack of a feature film production industry in post-war Canada in these terms, and same explanation seems to apply to other cultural sectors with the same industry structure. See Magder, *Canada's Hollywood: The Canadian State and Feature Films* (Toronto: University of Toronto Press, 1993), 25. This categorization is somewhat speculative and may require revision once more research on these cultural sectors during this period becomes available. Moreover, it is a generalization that has to be qualified with regard to Canadian publishers, because they could (and did) easily lapse into the role of mere 'distributors' for British or American books. Many, however, entertained greater ambitions, using profits from publishing foreign works to invest in Canadian works.
34 George L. Parker, *The Beginnings of the Book Trade in Canada* (Toronto: University of Toronto Press, 1985), 167–93.
35 Parker, 'History of a Canadian Publishing House,' 25.
36 Fraser Sutherland, *The Monthly Epic: A History of Canadian Magazines, 1789–1989* (Toronto: Fitzhenry & Whiteside, 1989), 27.
37 Rutherford, *Making of the Canadian Media*, 55.
38 John Herd Thompson with Allan Seager, *Canada: 1922–1939: Decades of Discord* (Toronto: McClelland and Stewart, 1985), 171. Just prior to the war, the British Canadian Theatrical Organization Society had been formed to bring in English touring companies to counteract U.S. influence. See Patrick B. O'Neill, 'The British Canadian Theatrical Organization Society and The Trans-Canada Theatre Society,' *Journal of Canadian Studies* 15, 1 (Spring 1980).
39 Calgary *Eye Opener*, 15 March 1919.
40 The federal and some provincial governments established film bureaus to produce documentaries, but the feature film business remained an American free-market monopoly.
41 Mary Vipond, 'The Nationalist Network: English Canada's Intellectuals and Artists in the 1920s,' *Canadian Review of Studies in Nationalism* 7, 1 (1980), 32–52.
42 Claxton as quoted in Sandra Gwyn, *Tapestry of War: A Private View of Canadians in the Great War* (Toronto: HarperCollins, 1992), 488.
43 In the case of radio, the government was spurred to action, despite the existence of a Canadian distribution industry plugged into American supply lines. However, in this case the nationalist cause enjoyed the support of Canadian print industries that feared competition from broadcasting.

# 13 Eastern Approaches: Maritime Canada and Newfoundland

DAVID MACKENZIE

The people of Newfoundland and the Maritimes responded to the outbreak of the Great War in a fashion similar to Canadians elsewhere. Talk of war arose unexpectedly in late July 1914, and in the newspapers stories on the deteriorating European situation swept aside local politics, imperial affairs, and the 'Irish problem.' Even the rioting and violence that erupted during the street railwaymen's strike in Saint John, New Brunswick, faded from public attention as 'headlines concerning Sarajevo, the Kaiser, the British fleet, and Belgium drove Saint John's labour troubles out of everyone's mind.'[1] The outbreak of war sparked an outburst of patriotism that spanned the divisions in Maritime society based on language, religion, class, gender, race and between rural and urban society. As one Maritime historian has written, 'apart from a few eccentrics, almost everybody – workers, employers, Acadians, Blacks, Catholics, Protestants, Liberals, Conservatives, men and women – supported the Empire in its struggle against the Germans. Certainly, in August 1914 there were no important dissenters. Most Maritimers were intensely loyal to a Britain they identified with Christianity, civilization, and progress; for them, loyalty to King and Empire overshadowed loyalty to Canada or to region.'[2] Before it was over the Atlantic region would contribute to the military over 72,000 enlisted men and women.[3]

Governments responded immediately to the declaration of war with pledges of support for Britain and the war effort. In New Brunswick, Acting Premier George Clarke announced that his province would 'give whatever aid is deemed best for the empire to the utmost extent of the province's ability in the present crisis,'[4] and his government donated 100,000 bushels of potatoes for war relief. In Charlottetown, the

Conservative government offered 100,000 bushels of oats to Britain and cut short the celebrations marking the fiftieth anniversary of the 1864 Charlottetown Conference. In Nova Scotia, Liberal Premier George Murray pledged 100,000 tons of coal on behalf of his province, but ended up giving $100,000 in its place. The Newfoundland government immediately pledged its support to Great Britain and within days, amid the public rallies and outbursts of patriotic enthusiasm, helped to create the Newfoundland Patriotic Association, an independent and non-partisan organization charged with the raising, equipping, and shipping of troops for the war effort. The first contingent of approximately 500 Newfoundland volunteers sailed for Britain on 4 October 1914.[5]

At the start of the war there were just under 1 million Maritimers, and they were a diverse group of people – English and French, Protestant and Catholic, White and Black, Aboriginal and non-Aboriginal, men and women, farmers, fishers, workers, managers, and many more. For most, allegiance went to province over region, empire over nation. This was also the era of progressive reform in North America, and, as Maritime historians have been quick to point out, it was no different in the Maritimes. The old notion of Maritime conservatism has been put to rest and the pressing issues of the day – women's suffrage, prohibition, urban and social reform, labour regulation – were debated across Atlantic Canada in legislatures, church groups, universities, community centres, and at home.[6]

The Maritime economy continued to rely on the traditional primary products of the farm, forests, and ocean, but the real story of the new century was the growth in coal production and the rise of an iron and steel industry centred in Cape Breton Island and Pictou County, Nova Scotia. Thanks to railway construction and the protection of high tariffs on iron and steel imports, by the outbreak of the war the Maritimes were producing close to half the primary iron and steel in Canada. This industrial expansion was accompanied by the growth of a significant manufacturing sector in Nova Scotia and New Brunswick. By 1915 Nova Scotia manufacturing produced over $70 million worth of material and employed almost 34,000 people.[7] But there also were reasons for concern about the future. The out-migration of Maritimers was already a significant issue and, when combined with the population and economic growth of the west and central Canada, was gradually eroding the relative influence of the region in Confederation, leading to repeated government efforts to maintain Maritime representation in

Ottawa.[8] As news of the outbreak of the Great War spread across the region, however, the people of the Maritime provinces were generally optimistic about their future.

Newfoundlanders also had reason for optimism in 1914. It was not unusual for the pre-war governments of Newfoundland, a self-governing colony of 240,000 in 1911, to run a surplus. The long-standing problem of the French Shore (dating from the 1713 Treaty of Utrecht, which gave landing rights on parts of Newfoundland's coast to French fishers), was finally settled in Newfoundland's favour in 1904. In addition, the completion of the island-wide Newfoundland Railway and the 1905 establishment of the Anglo-Newfoundland Development Corporation and subsequent construction of a pulp and paper mill at Grand Falls led to some resource development and economic expansion and to even greater dreams of future growth and prosperity.

Nevertheless, there were great religious and class cleavages running through Newfoundland society. Most Newfoundlanders traced their ancestors to Ireland and the west of England, and the population mix of Catholic and Protestant was reflected in the denominational school system and in the fabric of Newfoundland society. Moreover, there were sharp class divisions in the fishing industry between the small, powerful merchant elite centred in St John's and the great mass of fishers, who scratched out a living year after year, disorganized, exploited, and usually heavily in debt.

The outbreak of war was welcomed in the Maritimes and Newfoundland with an outpouring of support for Great Britain and the empire, and although this original commitment was sustained through the war, the original enthusiasm began to evaporate as it dragged on. In both countries the war unleashed internal tensions and divisions that were exacerbated by a conscription crisis and ultimately led to the formation of national coalition governments. Newfoundlanders, like their Canadian cousins, made enormous sacrifices for the war effort and emerged in 1918 with a stronger sense of national identity. For Maritimers the experience was a little less certain. While the war was only one crucial moment in a long period of social change, the patriotic response to the war hastened the integration of the Maritimes into the larger Canadian economy and likely made Maritimers more 'Canadian.' At the same time, it accelerated the process that would lead to the creation of a strong regional identity and the explosion of Maritime discontent in the 1920s.

Atlantic Canada was the part of the country closest to the war in Europe and the one part directly touched by enemy activity. The fledgling

Royal Canadian Navy (RCN), small, neglected, and overshadowed by the much larger Canadian Expeditionary Force (CEF), pursued its wartime duties on the east coast with energy and determination. At the start of the war the RCN's Atlantic fleet comprised one ship – the HMCS *Niobe* (manned by Canadians, Newfoundlanders, and a majority of British sailors) – and at first the lack of coastal defence was not a serious problem. Nevertheless, throughout the war coastal artillery were maintained at Halifax, Sydney, and Saint John, while the protection of Canada's coastal waters was left to Great Britain and the Royal Navy.[9]

Fear of enemy activity off the Atlantic coast ran high for most of the war, and these fears were heightened by the success of German U-boats, which seemed able to roam across the Atlantic at will and with deadly success. In the early years the U-boat threat was a potential one only, but this was sufficient to raise concerns, and the RCN responded with coastal patrols all along the Atlantic coast and up the St Lawrence River. A direct enemy attack was unlikely, and coastal patrols ensured that no U-boat made use of any natural harbour. But the arrival of German U-boats off the coast of North America by the end of 1916, followed by Germany's adoption of unrestricted submarine warfare in 1917, brought the war to the shores of Atlantic Canada and Newfoundland. U-boats began to appear in Canadian waters and the RCN lacked the ability to stop them. RCN coastal patrols were stepped up, but even more important, a system of convoy escorts, based at Halifax and Sydney, was introduced. Later, in June 1918, the Canadian government established two air stations in Nova Scotia; a seaplane base at Halifax, which became operational in August, and one at North Sydney, operational in September 1918.[10] There were some questions over command on the east coast, but the impact of the convoys on the Maritimes was clear. A convoy system needed administrative support and people, and large port facilities were constructed at Sydney and Halifax, the latter becoming the administrative centre for the east coast.[11]

The war was perhaps more obvious in Halifax than anywhere else in the Maritimes. Halifax residents (numbering 46,619 in 1911 and some 7,000 more in Dartmouth) saw their city and port turned upside down with military construction and as a centre for convoy assembly, coastal patrols, and, by 1918, aerial activity. The port facilities were expanded and shipping activity was greatly increased: tonnage handled in the harbour jumped from $2 million in 1913 to over $17 million in 1917, and the value of exports passing through the harbour soared from less than $20 million in 1915 to over $140 million in 1917. The defence of Halifax became the responsibility of the army, and a garrison of troops was stationed there for the duration of the war. More important for the city, by 1915 Halifax became the main embarkation point for the Canadian forces heading overseas, and the influx of thousands of soldiers in transit put enormous strains on the city's resources. All these men needed hospitals and recreational facilities, as well as food and shelter, and their arrival sparked a construction boom. In addition, workers from across the province and country migrated to the city for the new jobs that appeared, increasing the population and introducing greater ethnic diversity. Halifax experienced its share of housing shortages and inflation, putting a great stress on a municipal government that was forced to deal with problems never before experienced.[12]

Despite the war off the Atlantic coast and the actions of the RCN, Maritimers, like most Canadians, looked to the army, not the navy, to conduct the war effort. Recruitment campaigns sprang up in the great wave of excitement, and thousands of young Maritime men responded to the call of empire. In each of the provinces Belgian Relief Committees and other charitable organizations were established to collect food and clothes for overseas relief, and public pressure was put on all eligible men to enlist. The divisions between politics, the press, church, and school blurred as politicians, preachers, university administrators, editors, and others used their influence and positions to encourage the youth of Atlantic Canada to heed the call. At first little pressure was needed. At Acadia University, for example, faculty resigned to take on war work and students enlisted in great numbers, so much so that financial problems resulted for the university. Of the class of 1918, twenty-seven of twenty-nine males who had enrolled in 1914 enlisted. Similar drops in student enrolment occurred at other universities. At Dalhousie, in 1914–15, one-third of registered male students joined up.[13] Coal miners and other workers also enlisted by the thousands, and if the number of strikes is any indication, working-class support for the war effort was evident. In both 1912 and 1913 there were thirty-two strikes in the Maritimes; that number dropped to seven in 1914 (before the outbreak of the war), and in 1916 there were only three.[14] In 1914 the Nova Scotia Provincial Workmen's Association issued a resolution approving 'the action taken by our Government and their determination to place all the resources of the country, our blood and our treasure, at the disposal of our Empire in order that this war may be prosecuted until the German Empire shall retain a place in history only.'[15]

Nova Scotia led the Maritime provinces in recruitment, contributing some 30,500 men. The battalions of the Nova Scotia Brigade were a source of great pride and were useful tools in recruitment drives, and any efforts to break up the Nova Scotians for reinforcements elsewhere were met with fierce opposition.[16] At Aldershot camp near Kentville, Nova Scotia, a crowd of 5,000 watched 'with thrilled hearts, and faces alight with pride, the Nova Scotia Highland Brigade swing past them in military manoeuvres.' For this author the moral value and purifying nature of the war was clear: 'a great miracle has been worked in Nova Scotia; the fisherman, the lumberman, the farmer, the clerk, the student of a year ago, was moving along that parade ground a part of a great human machine vibrant with determination surging with the manly blood of wholesome, keen eye, clear cut, clean limbed, sunburned manhood of the bluenose stock.'[17]

New Brunswick and Prince Edward Island lagged behind Nova Scotia in recruitment, and, indeed, Maritimers generally enlisted at a lower rate than English-speaking Canadians in Ontario and the western provinces. Whereas westerners and Ontarians enlisted at a rate of 15.52 per cent and 14.42 per cent, respectively, for the eligible age group, the rate of enlistment in the Maritimes was significantly lower at 9.96 per cent.[18] One explanation for the lower enlistment rate in the Maritimes was the presence of the large Acadian population, whose support for the war mirrored that of other francophone communities in the country. The Acadian press supported the war effort, and the creation of 165th Acadian Battalion in 1915 helped to raise support, but there were troubles in finding sufficient Acadian recruits to fill the ranks. Even more important were the migration of many service-age men to other parts of Canada and the United States combined with the lack of a large British-born population in the Maritimes; for it was the latter group that swelled the ranks in central and western Canada.[19]

One group of Maritimers who were not welcome, despite their willingness to serve, were Blacks. Maritime recruiters were no different from those across the country, in that visible minorities were discouraged from enlisting in the CEF. Although there were no specific regulations preventing minorities from enlisting, local commanders and recruiters ensured that this was to be a 'white man's war.' A handful of Nova Scotian Blacks served in the 106th Battalion, Nova Scotia Rifles, and several others saw action in France, but those who managed to get past the recruiters faced open and hostile racism from their officers, White soldiers, and in the local communities. Private Percy J. Richards from Saint John later recalled his experience: 'We would go to the recruiting centre in Sussex ... The recruitment officer, who was of German descent, told us that it was not a Black man's war. He questioned why we wanted to join the Army.'[20] This situation was unacceptable for the large Black communities in Nova Scotia and New Brunswick and led to protests against the blatant racism and discrimination. Finally, in the summer of 1916 Ottawa agreed to establish the No. 2 Construction Battalion, CEF, a Black labour battalion headquartered first at Pictou before moving to Truro, Nova Scotia. The great majority of recruits for the No. 2 Construction Battalion came from Nova Scotia and to a lesser degree from New Brunswick, but it was open to all African-Canadians and also included some recruits from the United States. On 28 March 1917 the battalion left Halifax for Britain with nineteen officers and 605 men. Because of its numbers the battalion was reduced to a company and attached to the Canadian Forestry Corps, CEF and served in France until the end of the war.[21] The Great War may have been about many things for Canadians, but racial equality was not one of them.

Across the Cabot Strait, a total of 11,988 Newfoundlanders volunteered for service in the war. Approximately 8,700 enlisted in Newfoundland and of this number 6,241 served in the Newfoundland Regiment (accorded the title 'Royal' Newfoundland Regiment in 1917 in response to its achievements and great sacrifices), 1,966 in the Royal Naval Reserve, and 494 in the Newfoundland Forestry Corps. The sailors in the Naval Reserve were dispersed into the Royal Navy, while the Forestry Corps was raised at the request of the British government to help to overcome the shortage of timber for ship-building in Britain. The Forestry Corps consisted of many recruits who were ineligible for other services as well as hundreds of experienced lumberjacks. At the same time, 3,296 Newfoundlanders enlisted in the CEF, meaning that well over 25 per cent of Newfoundlanders who enlisted chose the Canadian Army.[22] In addition, more than forty female nurses served overseas in hospitals in Great Britain and France.[23]

The focus of the Newfoundland war effort was the Royal Newfoundland Regiment (RNR). Enlistment in the RNR was at a rate no higher than that in the CEF, but if you subtract from the Canadian rate those who were born in the British Isles, it becomes clear that native-born Newfoundlanders volunteered at a rate higher than did native-born Canadians. Equally, the fatality rate in the Newfoundland overseas contingent was significantly higher than that experienced by the Canadians. Of the 5,046 Newfoundlanders sent overseas in the RNR, there were 3,565 casualties, including 1,281 fatalities. A front-line Newfound-

Royal Newfoundland Regiment just prior to sailing for Gallipoli; Aldershot, England, August 1915 (National Archives of Canada, PA127034)

land soldier had a 70 per cent chance of being killed or wounded during the war.[24] Given that the greatest source of recruits for the RNR came from the St John's area, the impact of this extraordinary casualty rate was felt the greatest there. This impact was felt not only through the suffering and despair of the families of the deceased, but also in the post-war era if only because of the absence of so many potential leaders of Newfoundland society.

Several companies served in the disastrous Gallipoli campaign, where disease was as much a foe as enemy fire, but it is the battle near Beaumont Hamel in northern France that lives on in the memory of most Newfoundlanders: on 1 July 1916 – the first day of the Battle of the Somme – close to 1,000 members of the RNR were met by German forces in what can only be called a massacre. In their effort to capture the German lines, the Newfoundlanders suffered 720 casualties, and about one quarter of the regiment was killed. Other battles followed, recording similar carnage: in October 1916 at Gueudecourt the RNR suffered 239 casualties; in the Battle of Arras on 17 April 1917 another 460 casualties; and at Cambrai in December 1917 more than 300.[25]

All these dead and wounded had names and families, and the rising number of casualties brought the war home to Newfoundland. Home defence, which had been largely ignored before the war, now became a matter of much concern if not a cause for much action. Fear and rumours of possible German submarine activity off the Newfoundland coast added to the tension at home and partly explains why the Newfoundland government arrested and/or deported some sixty enemy aliens and others deemed suspicious or untrustworthy.[26]

At home the war seeped into the fabric of Maritime society. Politically, it was an era of stable government, and despite the heated debates and rhetoric of election campaigns, from a distance it is the similarities rather than the differences that stand out. At the start of the war there were two Conservative and one Liberal governments. All were fundamentally conservative in nature while offering a mild degree of progressive reform. They dealt with fiscal issues, public works, workmen's compensation and employer's liability, temperance, women's suffrage, and, of course, the war effort.[27]

In Nova Scotia the Liberals, under the leadership of George Murray, were in office continuously from 1896–1923 and survived a wartime election in 1916. Likewise, in Prince Edward Island the Conservatives remained in office throughout the war and won a wartime election in 1915. The most significant change occurred in 1917, when Aubin-Edmond Arsenault was appointed premier, becoming the first Acadian premier in Island history. Only in New Brunswick did political power change hands, in an election that reflected the growing tensions within Maritime society. In 1912 the Conservatives under James Flemming won forty-six of forty-eight seats. Flemming resigned after being implicated in a scandal; his replacement, G.J. Clarke, died in 1917 and was replaced by James Murray, who called an election for February 1917. In that election the southern counties voted Conservative, but the Acadian counties voted strongly Liberal and helped to ensure a Liberal victory. Anglo outrage was expressed in the Fredericton *Daily Gleaner*: 'if the English-speaking electorate submit quietly to the humiliation, the Acadians and their church will soon be in absolute control of the government and the affairs of the province.'[28] The new Liberal government of W.E. Forster hardly threatened to transform New Brunswick society, but these divisions unleashed during the provincial campaign were repeated on the federal level later in that same year.

At the top of the political agendas of all three provinces was the issue of prohibition. The movement against alcohol prospered in the Maritimes as it did in parts of the rest of the country because it was embraced as part of the wide middle-class movement of progressive social reform before the war and after 1914 was linked to the war effort and patriotism. Church groups, women's groups, and national and local temperance organizations all clamoured for prohibition, using the war and the need for conservation as a justification. The Woman's Christian Temperance Union (WCTU) demanded tougher temperance laws; others called for plebiscites on the issue. The wartime debate varied from province to province, but in all provinces there was a constant battle over the introduction and amendment of temperance legislation. Prince Edward Island introduced prohibition in 1901 and toughened its law in 1918; New Brunswick introduced a prohibition law in 1917. In Nova Scotia a temperance bill that excluded Halifax was passed first in 1910, and, with the increase of support during the war, temperance legislation covered most of the province by 1916, but Halifax was always a hard sell on this issue. Moreover, all the provinces came under the federal law when it was passed in 1918. Nevertheless, while the war can be credited with introducting prohibition on the national level, it was not the whole story with respect to the Maritimes. There was strong public support for prohibition and provincial legislation was in place – especially in Prince Edward Island and Nova Scotia – before the war began, and the support lasted long after the war was over.[29]

In the vanguard of the prohibition movement were Maritime women, and it is no surprise that the prohibition movement was interconnected with the struggle for female suffrage. Before the war, Maritime women – like most Canadian women – found that their role was defined by society as being in the home, and when women worked, they earned less than men and maintained an inferior legal status. Most Maritime women, especially English-speaking middle-class women, were enthusiastic supporters of the war effort, and they threw themselves into war work and recruitment activities, including the Red Cross and hospital work, fund-raising, and food and clothes drives. In New Brunswick, for example, the provincial Red Cross, led by Lady Tilley, collected money and thousands of socks, shirts, handkerchiefs, and bandages for overseas, while the Girls' Home Efficiency Clubs collected 50,000 quarts of food in 1918 alone.[30]

The movement of women into the workplace and the monumental war work undertaken by women in organizations like the WCTU, the

Red Cross, the Imperial Order Daughters of the Empire (IODE), and the Victorian Order of Nurses did a lot to overcome the strong anti-suffrage and anti-feminist attitudes in the three Maritime provinces. It also gave a boost to the women's movements in the Maritimes, which at times in the past had been disorganized and in some cases almost non-existent. For some, the war played a key role in the granting of the franchise to women. One feminist journalist later wrote about her experiences in Nova Scotia, noting that 'at the end (the vote) came without struggle in recognition of women's services during the war. Things often work out that way I find.'[31]

Certainly in the political arena the contribution of women to the war effort was a constant factor in the suffrage debates, giving the male politicians a sound reason – and justification – for giving women the vote. But the extent of wartime influence must be assessed with some caution. In 1917 the Nova Scotia Local Council of Women supported a franchise bill, arguing that Nova Scotia should follow the lead of the western provinces that had given the vote to women, and Premier Murray himself announced that the vote for women was inevitable. Nevertheless, the bill was defeated. Similarly, in New Brunswick suffrage bills were defeated in 1917 and withdrawn in 1918, despite the great support from the WCTU and other women's organizations. Only the women of Nova Scotia had the provincial vote by the end of the war (1918); it became law in New Brunswick in 1919 and in Prince Edward Island only in 1922. There is little evidence to suggest that the war had any significant impact on attitudes about the place of women in Maritime society.[32]

Much the same could be said about Newfoundland, where the progressive movements of women's suffrage and temperance became the focus of considerable debate during the war. The temperance movement was influenced by developments in Canada and elsewhere, but wartime patriotism was likely the greatest impetus for success. In 1915 a national plebiscite went in favour of prohibition, and on 1 January 1917 the Newfoundland government outlawed the sale and use of alcohol.[33] Similarly, the women's movement, which had emerged from church basements and the WCTU into middle-class Newfoundland society, found fertile ground in wartime service. The outbreak of war was followed shortly by the creation of the Women's Patriotic Association (WPA), and by the end of the war it had formed over 200 branches across the island and had some 15,000 members. The WPA raised money, organized sales and bazaars, sponsored concerts and dinners, ran a club for returning soldiers, encouraged recruitment, and conducted special charity events to raise money for various causes. Even more important, the WPA undertook an island-wide knitting campaign for the war effort and in so doing immortalized the Newfoundland grey military sock.[34] The war experience may have also indirectly helped the suffrage cause, although the vote did not come until 1925.[35]

Both women and men benefited from the new jobs that opened up in war-related industries, and the war clearly helped to eliminate unemployment in the region, but gauging the impact of the war on the economy of Atlantic Canada as a whole is more difficult. On the surface the war probably helped the economy: Halifax and Saint John boomed with activity and construction; in 1917 the combined value of exports and imports through the port of Saint John was $206,087,220, up from approximately $30 million in 1912. In that same year, Halifax handled 1.7 million tons of freight and steel ship-building in Nova Scotia increased rapidly as well. Moreover, the value of manufacturing in Halifax alone topped $22 million. Munitions production went up, as did the prices for some of the products produced by Maritime industry; unemployment disappeared, and in some areas labour became scarce. 'Wartime prosperity extended beyond manufacturing,' McKay writes, 'the fisheries were more active than they had been for years; farmers throve on a higher demand for their products and higher prices; lumbermen exploited new market possibilities, such as supplying British collieries with the pit props they could no longer obtain in Europe. There even seemed to be new hope for wooden shipbuilding.'[36]

In other areas the economic benefits were less clear. The war had no significant impact on export patterns for the lumber industry, although it did produce higher prices and led to increased lumbering activity. Egg production increased, but not greatly; butter production rose and cheese production fell. The production of pig iron in Nova Scotia fluctuated, while exports of Nova Scotian apples rose dramatically, but this growth was part of a process of steady increase from the 1880s to the 1930s. Gypsum production in both Nova Scotia and New Brunswick slumped during the war, but revived and expanded in the 1920s. Pulpwood production in Nova Scotia and New Brunswick doubled between 1913 and 1920, but it doubled again in 1920s. In the important coal industry, output in Nova Scotia rose steadily up to 1915, then dropped over the next decade, only to revive in the late 1920s (output in New Brunswick, although on a much smaller scale, rose during the war). The sale of Maritime coal to the central-Canadian market, however, dropped significantly during the war, but even here the market revived after the war. More generally, the Maritimes fell further behind central Canada in manufacturing and industrial expansion, but this process had begun before the war and continued long after it was over.[37]

There is little question that the war was followed by severe economic problems in the Maritimes, but how the Great War fits into the equation is less clear. In chapter 6 Doug McCalla examines the economic impact of the war on the whole country, and it is clear that, like the rest of Canada, the Maritimes faced a period of economic readjustment after the war in trying to re-establish markets – in fish exports for the Caribbean, timber markets in Britain, coal for central Canada. But in most areas the economic problems following the war were caused by larger problems than those unleashed by the war. Railway construction in Canada had peaked before the war and was already in decline. With that decline came a drop in demand for steel rails produced in Nova Scotia and, consequently, a drop in demand for Nova Scotian coal. The out-migration of Maritimers to the west and elsewhere was a serious concern, and the rate of population growth in the Maritimes had already slowed down before the war. Likewise, manufacturing and banking were moving west, and central Canadian branch plants were moving in. The relative position of the Maritimes in Confederation was declining, and the region was increasingly becoming integrated into the larger Canadian economy.[38]

Nowhere was this process more apparent than in the amalgamation of the Intercolonial Railway into the Canadian National Railway, a process that lasted from 1917 to 1923. The Intercolonial – created as part of the Confederation agreement in 1867 – had long been an important factor in the Maritime economy. Low freight rates made it easier for Maritime business to compete with that of central Canada, but these same rates, combined with high costs and deficits made the Intercolonial an easy target for attack from central and western Canada. Maritime representation in the federal cabinet was weak and was unable to halt the merger that included the shifting of the Intercolonial head office from Moncton to Toronto. The impact of the demise of the Intercolonial on the Maritimes has been hotly debated, but the loss of control and the subsequent huge rise in freight rates undoubtedly contributed to the post-war sense of regional grievance in the region.[39] The loss of the Intercolonial and other factors contributed to the economic eclipse of the Maritime provinces, but they also pre-dated the outbreak of the war. The Great War did little more than interrupt a process of economic decline that was already underway. It did little to reverse these trends and, indeed, in some ways – such as the push for railway amalgamation – probably accelerated them.

The railway question was not a factor in Newfoundland, but the war had an equally mixed impact on the Newfoundland economy. On the surface it was an era of great prosperity, but the era was brief and ended with the war in 1918. Exports jumped in value from $13.136 million in 1914–15 to almost $37 million in 1918–19, and imports rose just as quickly. Government revenue and spending rose sharply as well.[40] In the fishery, foreign competition declined because of the war and the international price for fish rose along with demand. Fishers and merchants tried to benefit as much as possible from the advantageous wartime conditions, but in an odd way they became victims of this brief prosperity. As historian James Hiller writes, 'at the end of the war the fishing industry was over-extended and vulnerable. Fishermen and merchants alike had borrowed in order to expand operations and profit from the boom, and a number of the newer firms were undercapitalized. Fish prices began to drop, yet the price of imports remained high. Market conditions became difficult as competitors' fish began to arrive once again.'[41] In other ways Newfoundland's economy emerged relatively unchanged. There was fairly little industrial development, and, as a result, there was less of the influx of women and men into war production that was experienced in Canada, the United States and Great Britain.[42] For most women the focus of war work remained the Women's Patriotic Association, while for many other Newfoundlanders there were well-paying jobs to be had in Canada and the United States.

Financing the war was equally problematic. The main source of revenue for the government of Newfoundland was the tariff, and there were few direct taxes to speak of, although an income tax was introduced late in the war. The government borrowed heavily to finance its war effort, while expenses on public works rose considerably, and at the end of the war Newfoundland's public debt had risen to $43 million. This debt continued to rise after the war as fish prices fell and economic conditions worsened, and these circumstances set the stage for the eventual catastrophic financial problems of the 1930s. The war should not be blamed for the collapse of responsible government fifteen years later, however, since there were problems in the fishing industry and in an over-extended and expensive railway that pre-dated the war. At the same time, successive governments made little headway in dealing with these intractable problems either during the war or in the early post-war years.[43]

For Newfoundlanders and Maritimers things began to go sour in 1917. Casualty figures mounted and war weariness set in, anti-enemy feelings escalated into xenophobia at home, and old divisions in Maritime society that had been patched over by wartime patriotism and a sense of self-sacrifice reappeared. The rising cost of living began to eat away at the gains made by labour, and the calls to God and country lost their appeal the longer the war lasted and with each new revelation of wartime profiteering and corruption. Unions that had thrown themselves behind the war effort in 1914 began to reassert traditional demands for wages and working conditions. Others, like the steelworkers, went through a process of unionization during the war, buoyed by the confidence that wartime prosperity had produced. The number of strikes began to rise, leading to an explosion of union militancy once the war was over.[44]

Other tensions appeared, especially over conscription. Recruitment began falling. In September 1916, for example, a two-week, province-wide campaign was launched in New Brunswick with more than two dozen meetings (which included the carrying of a burning cross of St Andrew across the province on horseback, foot, and by auto), but it was largely unsuccessful. The meeting in Saint John produced only four recruits. As in other parts of the country, criticism appeared against the 'slackers' and, especially, those who spoke French.[45]

The debate over conscription unfolded along predictable lines, but Maritimers voted in their own way in the conscription federal election of December 1917. Some newspapers lined up solidly behind conscription and Borden's attempts to form the Union Government. The Saint John *Globe* said it was necessary to win the war, and that 'a further trial of voluntary enlistment means a further drain of the young manhood of Anglo-Saxon Canada, but no further assistance from Quebec. Is that more in the national interest than an act which fairly distributes the burden of service, and makes all who are sharers in the privileges and benefits of Canadian life contribute to its maintenance?'[46] Others were not so sure. The Acadians – who had never opposed the war – were generally opposed to conscription, even though some of their politicians and leaders were divided on the issue. The opposition may have been less vocal and the reaction to conscription less vociferous than in

Quebec, but that was likely because of the status of Acadians as a minority in each of the Maritime provinces.[47]

In the election campaign, however, support for conscription and the Union government was lower in the Maritimes than in the rest of English-speaking Canada. None of the three Atlantic premiers actively campaigned for the Union Government; Murray of Nova Scotia was offered a position in the new government but declined. On election day, New Brunswick divided along linguistic lines. The Liberals won the four ridings with large Acadian populations: Restigouche-Madawaska, Gloucester, Kent, and Westmorland; the rest of the province voted Union. Twelve of sixteen seats in Nova Scotia went to Borden, but only 48 per cent of the popular vote, compared with 45 per cent for the Liberals. Prince Edward Island returned two members for each party and split the popular vote. Even these numbers are a little deceiving. Political scientist J.M. Beck suggests that several of the ridings – two in Prince Edward Island and five in Nova Scotia – were won only with the questionable use of the military vote under the Military Voters Act.[48] The support for the Union Government and conscription was hardly overwhelming in Atlantic Canada.

The election campaign was punctuated on 6 December by the greatest domestic disaster of the war – the Halifax explosion. The French steamship *Mont Blanc* and the Belgian Relief steamer *Imo* collided in Halifax harbour soon after 8:00 a.m. The collision sparked a fire on board the *Mont Blanc*, which ignited the munitions cargo in its hold. The blast completely demolished the *Mont Blanc*; only one bent cannon was later found on the Dartmouth side of the Narrows, while parts of the anchor landed more than two miles away. The explosion and following tidal wave killed almost 2,000 and thousands more were injured, especially from the flying glass. It flattened the Richmond district, about one square mile, smashed windows and doors across town, and shook windows up to sixty miles away. To make matters worse for the approximately 10,000 homeless, a terrible early winter storm hit that night, leaving many to huddle in the shells of their wrecked homes.

The search for survivors and the clean-up began immediately, first by the local population, but as news spread, help began to pour in from across the province, the country, and internationally. Towns and cities across the region donated food and clothes, doctors and nurses made their way to Halifax to help the wounded, a ship with supplies came from Massachusetts, and money was raised from public and private sources across North America and Great Britain. The task of reconstruc-

View of Halifax after the explosion, looking south, Halifax, N.S., 6 December 1917 (W.G. MacLaughlan, National Archives of Canada, C19953)

tion and rehabilitation was given to the newly created Halifax Relief Commission, but it was difficult at first even to get glass for windows and lumber for walls. It took months to rebuild the city, and for many Haligonians the rest of the war was spent in temporary shelters. Many others were left with only the 'ugly blue scars' of their untreated wounds.[49]

1917 was equally dramatic in Newfoundland. Despite the heroic recruiting efforts of the various private organizations, maintaining the Newfoundland Regiment in the field proved to be a difficult task. By late 1916, thanks to the heavy casualty rates and dropping enlistments, a manpower shortage appeared. National pride was on the line, and, as in Canada, the call for conscription was heard, although not with the same enthusiasm across the country. The Newfoundland Patriotic Association ran its recruitment campaign from St John's and had had only limited success in the few recruitment drives it launched outside the city. This problem reflected one of the divisions in Newfoundland society: most of the enlistments came from the St John's area, while the fishers in the outport communities, who might more keenly suffer the loss of labour of a son or father who went off to war, were less enthusiastic about enlisting. It was in these outport communities that opposition to conscription was the greatest.

The divisions within the country were reflected in the House of Assembly and among those who would decide the conscription issue. The prime minister, Sir Edward Morris, had led his People's Party to victory in the election of 1913 by winning most of the seats in the Catholic parts of Newfoundland and in a few Protestant districts. The opposition consisted of a loose alliance of the old Liberal Party and the new Fishermen's Protective Union (FPU) led by the dynamic William Coaker. The FPU – part union, part cooperative movement, and part political party – appeared on the scene in 1908 and within a few years had expanded into a vigorous and progressive movement fighting for the rights of fishers and other workers in Newfoundland and Labrador. In 1914 the FPU was definitely on the rise, but when the war broke out, it was largely confined to the Protestant north and had already attracted the hostility of the Catholic Church and the business class centred in St John's.

This political alignment put Morris in a difficult position, and the introduction of conscription as a partisan issue threatened to divide the country. The unfolding of events mirrored developments in Canada. Morris represented Newfoundland at the Imperial War Conference in London in the early spring of 1917, and, like Borden, he turned to the idea of creating a national government of all parties as a way to avoid a messy wartime election. For Borden the key was Laurier; for Morris it was Coaker and the FPU, and Coaker was more open to the terms offered by Morris (which included the latter's eventual resignation) than Laurier was to those of Borden. Coaker accepted the invitation and the National Government was announced in July 1917.[50] At the end of that year Morris resigned as prime minister to become a British lord and was replaced by Liberal leader William Lloyd.

One of the first acts of the National Government in August 1917 was to take over responsibility for the Newfoundland Patriotic Association and to establish a Department of Militia to oversee recruitment in Newfoundland. The new department was equally unsuccessful in keeping up reinforcements by the volunteer method, and calls for conscription were heard once more, this time more strongly. Again, Coaker was the key. He realized that a great many of his supporters opposed conscription, but his ties to the empire, support for the war effort, and desire to prevent divisive outbursts – even violence – led him to accept conscription.[51] In May 1918 the Military Service Act was passed, calling up single men aged between nineteen and thirty-nine. By the end of the war some 3,629 men were called up; 1,573 were found fit for service and were sent to Britain in August 1918. They were still in training at the time of the Armistice. None saw combat or became casualties.[52] As in Canada, conscription had a greater political and social impact than a military one.

The biggest political loser in these developments was William Coaker. Prime Minister Lloyd represented Newfoundland at the Paris Peace Conference in 1919, but his National Government was already falling apart. Brought together by the exigencies of war, the initial cohesion evaporated quickly and old political divisions re-emerged. Coaker's leadership had been damaged by his support for conscription, and the growth of the FPU was stunted by its inability to attract support in the Catholic areas of Newfoundland. When the war ended, the National Government disintegrated, and Coaker found himself moving into an alliance with the revived Liberal Party (called the Liberal Reform Party) and its new ambitious leader, Richard Squires. Coaker was an influential minister in Squires's government, which came into office following the 1919 election, but he (and his party) never regained the stature or potential of the pre-war years.[53] In this respect the war had not been a moment of great change for Newfoundland politically; when it was over, the old denominational, class, and geographic divisions returned.

If anything, the war had stifled the great promise of change presented by Coaker and the Fishermen's Protective Union.

The war ended almost as unexpectedly as it had begun, and the people of Atlantic Canada and Newfoundland were hardly prepared for the peace, even though they had been longing for it for years. At first there were the usual celebrations, 'Bedlam let loose' in Digby, for example. 'The fire whistle first, then locomotive and boat whistles, bells, auto horns, guns, tin horns, fire-crackers and every conceivable noise-generator was put into operation with the throttle wide open. Digby never heard such a racket and never will again.'[54] Once the celebrations were over, however, people were left with the new realities of post-war life. Stories about the war and the peace settlement gradually faded from newspapers and were replaced by new concerns over labour unrest and the spreading influenza epidemic.

In some ways it was business as usual and a return to 'normalcy.' Soldiers returned to their homes to resume their lives, businesses reconverted to civilian production. Wartime production ended, war work ceased, jobs disappeared. For many women this meant a return to their pre-war lives, and in the post-war era women worked as domestic servants, teachers, and in factories, and they still earned less than men. But Canadian women now had the vote (and would have it provincially in all the Maritime provinces in a few years), and this change should not be underestimated.[55]

Halifax and Saint John saw their roles as embarkation ports reversed with the arrival home of thousands of soldiers. The pace of repatriation was hindered by the lack of available transport, and the trip home was never quick enough for the soldiers. There was some rioting by returning soldiers in Halifax in both 1918 and 1919. The cause of the rioting was usually a relatively insignificant incident that sparked anger and then spilled over into violence, but the turmoil itself was a reflection of the unrest and sense of dislocation that came with the ending of the war. As McKay nicely puts it: 'Everything seemed to be falling apart. The sky, once alight with patriotic fireworks as Maritimers headed for Europe, glowed with the light from incendiary fires set by rioting soldiers and civilians at the end of a war that had changed the world of 1914 beyond recognition.'[56]

For many workers it appeared that while they had made enormous sacrifices for the war effort, others had profited. Labour action, already on the rise in 1917, surged after the armistice; workers became more radicalized and new labour parties were organized. The number of strikes rose as workers resumed old struggles and fought to preserve the gains they had made during the war. In Halifax, for example, where labour tensions were already high, some 2,000 men in the building trades went on strike in May 1919. There was even less time for celebrations in the coal and steel industries. In 1919–20 the two steel companies were integrated into the British Empire Steel Corporation, and the following years were filled with cutbacks, lay-offs, and labour unrest. For some workers the war had been a period of union strength, but it did not last long.[57]

The war experience probably heightened the sense of Canadian nationalism in the Maritimes for both those who served overseas and those who stayed at home. For example, George Nowlan, who would later serve as minister of national revenue in the Diefenbaker government, was one veteran whose overseas experience increased his 'identification with a larger Canadian context.'[58] At home, Maritimers experienced the same problems engendered by the war – the dislocation, shortages, and tragedies – as other Canadians; they responded to the same calls for sacrifice, thrift, and volunteerism; and they were drawn into the national debates over conscription and Union government. The war also intensified the movement towards good citizenship as a goal of the public education system, transforming 'moral instruction from the promotion of fixed standards of individual morality to the fostering of a public morality.' Significantly, accompanying this transformation was a shift of emphasis from imperial to Canadian citizenship.[59]

At the same time, the war hastened the economic integration of the Maritimes into the Canadian economy, with the demise of the Intercolonial Railway serving as a symbol of the growing centralization of Canadian economic and political power. Even in areas of growth like manufacturing the Maritimes could not match the pace of industrialization in central Canada. This relative decline only sharpened the problems of the 1920s, which did so much to foster Maritime regionalism. In the process, what went missing was that air of progressive, open-minded optimism, reflected in the significant social movements of the day, that flowed through the Maritimes from the late nineteenth century. In its place, the post-war years offered depression, disillusionment, and sharper regional divisions.

The war did little to enhance the relationship between Canada and Newfoundland. On one level the links between them were growing stronger with each passing decade. Trade with Canada now almost equalled that with the United Kingdom, and Canada was an increasingly popular destination for Newfoundland emigrants, students, and seasonal workers. In addition, Canadian business and entrepreneurs were moving to and investing in Newfoundland, Canadian currency was legal tender, and Canadian banks monopolized Newfoundland's banking system.[60] Yet the prospects for the union of the two countries were slim. In 1912 Ottawa sent A.E. Kemp, minister without portfolio, to investigate, and he reported that there was 'no agitation going on in respect to this question, and that, so far as public opinion is concerned, the people may be said to be indifferent.'[61] The war did little to change this attitude. It had created a common cause and led to collaboration between the two nations, and clearly the war had accelerated the process of Americanization in Newfoundland,[62] but in no way could this process be interpreted as a step towards Confederation. Indeed, the opposite is probably closer to the truth. Before the war was over, government leaders began referring to Newfoundland as a 'dominion' like Canada, and Newfoundlanders emerged from the war with a stronger sense of their independence and heritage than had been the case in 1914.[63] The Great War heightened nationalism in both Maritime Canada and Newfoundland, but it was nationalism experienced and articulated for two very different countries.

Maritime Canadians and Newfoundlanders, despite their ethnic, linguistic, geographic, and economic diversity, responded to the war as others did across Canada and passed through waves of enthusiasm, patriotism, moral regeneration, and progressivism, to uncertainty, questioning, and, in some cases, anger punctuated by outbursts of hatred and violence. In both Newfoundland and the Maritime provinces the impact of these experiences would be felt for many years to come. In this way, the Great War was an experience that Newfoundlanders and Maritimers shared with all the people of Canada.

NOTES

1 Robert H. Babcock, 'The Saint John Street Railwaymen's Strike and Riot, 1914,' *Acadiensis* 11, 2 (Spring 1982), 27.
2 Ian McKay, 'The 1910s: The Stillborn Triumph of Progressive Reform,' in E.R. Forbes and D.A. Muise, eds, *The Atlantic Provinces in Confederation* (Toronto: University of Toronto Press, 1993), 203.

3 Margaret Conrad and James Hiller, *Atlantic Canada: A Region in the Making* (Toronto: Oxford University Press, 2001), 162.

4 *Saint John Globe*, 7 August 1914; see also *St John's Daily News*, 11 August 1914.

5 Frederick W. Rowe, *A History of Newfoundland and Labrador* (Toronto: McGraw-Hill Ryerson, 1980), 370–1.

6 See Ernest Forbes, *Maritime Rights: The Maritime Rights Movement, 1919–1927: A Study in Canadian Regionalism* (Montreal and Kingston: McGill-Queen's University Press, 1979), ix; McKay, 'The 1910s,' 193–5.

7 J. Castell Hopkins, ed., *The Canadian Annual Review of Public Affairs, 1916* (Toronto, Annual Review Co., 1914–18), 616. See also S.A. Saunders, *The Economic History of the Maritime Provinces*, ed. T.W. Acheson (Fredericton: Acadiensis Press, 1984), 30–1; Forbes, *Maritime Rights*, 4; McKay, 'The 1910s,' 194–5; Craig Heron, 'The Great War and Nova Scotia Steelworkers,' *Acadiensis* 16, 2 (Spring 1987), 4.

8 See Hopkins, *Canadian Annual Review, 1914*, 570; Patricia A. Thornton, 'The Problem of Out-Migration from Atlantic Canada, 1871–1921,' *Acadiensis* 15, 1 (Autumn 1985), 3–34; Forbes, *Maritime Rights*, 14–16.

9 Marc Milner, *Canada's Navy: The First Century* (Toronto: University of Toronto Press, 1999), 44–5. For a comprehensive look at Sydney during the war, see Brian Tennyson and Roger Sarty, *Guardian of the Gulf: Sydney, Cape Breton, and the Atlantic Wars* (Toronto: University of Toronto Press, 2000), 113–88.

10 S.F. Wise, *Canadian Airmen and the First World War: The Official History of the Royal Canadian Air Force*, Vol. I (Toronto: University of Toronto Press, 1980), 603–6.

11 Milner, *Canada's Navy*, 47–53.

12 Thomas H. Raddall, *Halifax: Warden of the North* (New York: Doubleday, 1965), 248–50, Milner, *Canada's Navy*, 45; see also Henry Roper, 'The Halifax Board of Control: The Failure of Municipal reform, 1906–1919,' *Acadiensis* 14, 2 (Spring 1985), 46–65.

13 Barry Moody, 'Acadia and the Great War,' in Paul Axelrod and John Reid, eds, *Youth, University and Canadian Society: Essays in the Social History of Higher Education* (Montreal: McGill-Queen's University Press, 1989), 149; Judith Fingard, Janet Guilford, and David Sutherland, *Halifax: the First 250 Years* (Halifax: Formac, 1999), 130; Hopkins, *Canadian Annual Review, 1916*, 607; see also Margaret Conrad, *George Nowlan: Maritime Conservative in National Politics* (Toronto: University of Toronto Press, 1986), 18–19.

14 Ian McKay, 'Strikes in the Maritimes, 1901–1914,' *Acadiensis* 13, 1 (Autumn 1983), 16; McKay, 'The 1910s,' 205–10.

15  Hopkins, *Canadian Annual Review, 1914*, 545–6; see also 544–5, 567, 570, 571.
16  For example, see National Archives of Canada (NAC), Robert Borden Papers, MG 26 H, I (a), vol. 45, 20219, S. Robertson to Borden, 3 September 1914.
17  *Digby Weekly Courier*, 8 September 1916; Moody, 'Acadia and the Great War,' 146.
18  Enlistment statistics taken from Robert Bothwell, Ian Drummond, and John English, *Canada, 1900–1945* (Toronto: University of Toronto Press, 1987), 14.
19  Phillippe Doucet, 'Politics and the Acadians,' in Jean Daigle, ed., *The Acadians of the Maritimes: Thematic Studies* (Moncton: Centre d'études Acadiennes, 1982), 245; Hopkins, *Canadian Annual Review, 1915*, 604; McKay, 'The 1910s,' 208.
20  Calvin W. Ruck, *The Black Battalion, 1916–1920: Canada's Best Kept Military Secret* (Halifax: Nimbus, 1987), 45; see also 22–6; James W. St G. Walker, 'Race and Recruitment in World War I: Enlistment of Visible Minorities in the Canadian Expeditionary Force,' *Canadian Historical Review* 70, 1 (March 1989), esp. 5.
21  Ruck, *Black Battalion*, 9–20; see also appendix A.
22  Christopher A. Sharpe, 'The "Race of Honour": An Analysis of Enlistments and Casualties in the Armed Forces of Newfoundland, 1914–1918,' *Newfoundland Studies* 4, 1 (Spring 1988), 28.
23  Margot Iris Duley, '"The Radius of Her Influence for Good": The Rise and Triumph of the Women's Suffrage Movement in Newfoundland, 1909–1925,' in Linda Kealey, ed., *Pursuing Equality: Historical Perspectives on Women in Newfoundland and Labrador* (St John's: Institute of Social and Economic Research, 1993), 27.
24  Sharpe, '"Race of Honour,"' 33–5.
25  Rowe, *History of Newfoundland and Labrador*, 373–4; see also Captain Leo Murphy, 'Newfoundland's Part in the Great War,' in J.R. Smallwood, ed., *The Book of Newfoundland*, Vol. I (St John's: Newfoundland Book Publishers, 1937), 351–451; P. Whitney Lackenbauer, 'War, Memory, and the Newfoundland Regiment at Gallipoli,' *Newfoundland Studies* 15, 2 (1999), 176–214; G.W.L. Nicholson, *The Fighting Newfoundlander: A History of the Royal Newfoundland Regiment* (London: Government of Newfoundland, 1965). See also Arlene King, 'Beaumont Hamel: Our Place in the Somme,' *Newfoundland Quarterly* 96, 2 (Summer 2003), 9–15.
26  See Gerhard P. Bassler, 'The Enemy Alien Experience in Newfoundland, 1914–1918,' *Canadian Ethnic Studies* 20, 3 (1988), 42–62. See also David Macfarlane, *The Danger Tree: Memory, War, and the Search for a Family's Past*

(Toronto: Macfarlane Walter & Ross, 1991); David Facey-Crowther, 'Home Is Where the Heart Is: The Correspondence of Newfoundland Soldiers in the Great War,' *Newfoundland Quarterly* 96, 2 (Summer 2003), 32–9.

27  See, for example, Hopkins, *Canadian Annual Review*, 1916, 602; *Canadian Annual Review, 1917*, 631.

28  Quoted in Doucet, 'Politics and the Acadians,' 255.

29  Hopkins, *Canadian Annual Review*, 1915, 596; *Canadian Annual Review*, 1916, 608; E.R. Forbes, 'Prohibition and the Social Gospel,' in Forbes, *Challenging the Regional Stereotype: Essays on the 20th Century Maritimes* (Fredericton: Acadiensis Press, 1989), 13, 29; McKay, 'The 1910s,' 210–11.

30  Hopkins, *Canadian Annual Review, 1915*, 605; *Canadian Annual Review, 1918*, 666; see also McKay, 'The 1910s,' 200–2.

31  E.M. Murray, quoted in Catherine Cleverdon, *The Women Suffrage Movement in Canada*, 2nd ed. (Toronto: University of Toronto Press, 1974), 176; see also 195–6, 202; Alison Prentice et al., *Canadian Women: A History* (Toronto: Harcourt Brace Jovanovich, 1988), 201–2.

32  See E.R. Forbes, 'Battles in Another War: Edith Archibald and the Halifax Feminist Movement,' in Forbes, *Challenging the Regional Stereotype*, 88–9.

33  Rowe, *History of Newfoundland and Labrador*, 367.

34  Duley, 'Radius of Her Influence,' 28–32; Gale Denise Warren, 'The Patriotic Association of the Women of Newfoundland: 1914–18,' *Newfoundland Quarterly* 92, 1 (1998), 23–32.

35  Duley, 'Radius of Her Influence,' 32–3.

36  McKay, 'The 1910s,' 205; statistics taken from Hopkins, *Canadian Annual Review, 1917*, 713; *Canadian Annual Review, 1918*, 648–9, 655.

37  Saunders, *Economic History*, 34, 77, 80–5, 106–7, 120–8.

38  John G. Reid, *Six Crucial Decades: Times of Change in the History of the Maritimes* (Halifax: Nimbus, 1987), 162–3; Saunders, *Economic History*, 26, 33, 38. See also T.W. Acheson, 'The Maritimes and "Empire Canada,"' in David Jay Bercuson, ed., *Canada and the Burden of Unity* (Toronto: Macmillan, 1977), 87–114; Gregory P. Marchildon, *Profits and Politics: Beaverbrook and the Gilded Age of Canadian Finance* (Toronto: University of Toronto Press, 1996).

39  See E.R. Forbes, 'The Intercolonial Railway and the Decline of the Maritime Provinces Revisited,' and Ken Cruikshank, 'With Apologies to James: A Response to E.R. Forbes,' *Acadiensis* 24, 1 (Autumn 1994), 3–34; Reid, *Six Crucial Decades*, 164.

40  S.J.R. Noel, *Politics in Newfoundland* (Toronto: University of Toronto Press, 1971), 130.

41  James Hiller, 'Newfoundland Confronts Canada, 1867–1949,' in Forbes and Muise, eds, *Atlantic Provinces in Confederation*, 365.

42  Duley, 'Radius of Her Influence,' 28. See also David Alexander, 'Newfoundland's Traditional Economy and Development to 1934,' in James Hiller and Peter Neary, eds, *Newfoundland in the Nineteenth and Twentieth Centuries: Essays in Interpretation* (Toronto: University of Toronto Press, 1980), 30.

43  Hiller, 'Newfoundland Confronts Canada,' 365–9; St John Chadwick, *Newfoundland: Island into Province* (Cambridge: Cambridge University Press, 1967), 126.

44  See Heron, 'Great War and Nova Scotia Steelworkers,' 21–2.

45  See for example, *Digby Weekly Courier*, 12 March 1915; Hopkins, *Canadian Annual Review, 1916*, 639.

46  *Saint John Globe*, 22 November 1917; see also 7 December 1917.

47  Quoted in Doucet, 'Politics and the Acadians,' 255; see also 253–4.

48  J.M. Beck, *Pendulum of Power: Canada's Federal Elections* (Toronto: Prentice-Hall, 1968), 141–5; Doucet, 'Politics and the Acadians,' 255.

49  Raddall, *Halifax*, 253; Suzanne Morton, 'The Halifax Relief Commission and Labour Relations during the Reconstruction of Halifax, 1917–1919,' *Acadiensis* 18, 2 (Spring 1989), 73–93; see Hopkins, *Canadian Annual Review, 1918*, 650–54; Janet Kitz, *Shattered City: The Halifax Explosion and the Road to Recovery* (Halifax: Nimbus, 1989); Joseph Scanlon, 'Myths of Male and Military Superiority: Fictional Accounts of the 1917 Halifax Explosion,' *English Studies in Canada* 24, 4 (December 1998), 387–411; *Digby Weekly Courier*, 14 December 1917; Saint John *Globe*, 7 December 1917.

50  Ian D.H. McDonald, *'To Each His Own': William Coaker and the Fishermen's Protective Union in Newfoundland, 1908–1925*, ed. J.K. Hiller (St John's: Institute of Social and Economic Research, 1987), 62.

51  Noel, *Politics in Newfoundland*, 124–7.

52  Sharpe, 'Race of Honour,' 41.

53  Noel, *Politics in Newfoundland*, 134–48.

54  *Digby Weekly Courier*, 15 November 1918.

55  McKay, 'The 1910s,' 224; D.A. Muise, 'The Industrial Context of Inequality: Female Participation in Nova Scotia's Paid Labour Force, 1871–1921,' *Acadiensis* 20, 2 (Spring 1991), 3–31.

56  McKay, 'The 1910s,' 222; see also Hopkins, *Canadian Annual Review, 1918*, 656.

57  Heron, 'Great War and Nova Scotia Steelworkers,' 33–4; Morton, 'Halifax Relief Commission,' 91; McKay, 'The 1910s,' 219–24. See also Ian McKay and Suzanne Morton, 'The Maritimes: Expanding the Circle of Resistance,' in Craig Heron, ed., *The Workers' Revolt in Canada, 1917–1925* (Toronto, University of Toronto Press, 1998), 43–86.

58  Conrad, *George Nowlan*, 24. For other examples of 'broadening horizons' and 'patriotic Canadians' from the Maritimes, see Susan Mann, ed., *The War Diary of Clare Gass, 1915–1918* (Montreal and Kingston: McGill-Queen's University Press, 2000), xiii, xxxiv; John Hawkins, *The Life and Times of Angus L.* (Windsor, N.S.: Lancelot Press, 1969), 42–53.

59  Robert Nicholas Berard, 'Moral Education in Nova Scotia, 1880–1920,' *Acadiensis* 14, 1 (Autumn 1984), 61–2.

60  See Malcolm MacLeod, *Kindred Countries: Canada and Newfoundland before Confederation*, Historical Booklet No. 52 (Ottawa: Canadian Historical Association, 1994).

61  NAC, A.E. Kemp Papers, MG 27 II D9, vol. 192, file: Borden, R.L., Correspondence, 1912–1914, Kemp to Borden, 10 October 1912. For wartime efforts to achieve Confederation, see McDonald, 'To Each His Own', chap. 4.

62  Noel, *Politics in Newfoundland*, 131.

63  Not everyone was impressed; the *St John's Daily News* editorialized on 5 December 1918: 'The Term ... is altogether too high falutin for a little country with a population of less than quarter of a million. Let's forget it, and go back to the good old title Ye Ancient Colony. It both looks and sounds better.'

# Part IV
# The Aftermath

# 14 Canada and the Peace Settlements

MARGARET MACMILLAN

In February 1919, when the great peace conference in Paris had been in session for almost a month, Sir Robert Borden, prime minister and leader of the Canadian delegation, had a rare interview with David Lloyd George, the British prime minister. An aide, probably Loring Christie from External Affairs, prepared an *aide mémoire*. It listed twelve subjects, some, such as Canada's representation on the allied food board or the date of Borden's departure for Canada, relatively small matters. Number six, however, dealt with a matter Borden had complained about frequently: 'Proceedings of Conference. Arrangement of work. Delay.' Canada cared deeply about a lasting peace settlement after the worst war the modern world had known, a war in which Canadians had fought and died. Borden, like many of the statesmen in Paris, also saw dangers in delaying the peace settlements. The other subjects for discussion included the demobilization of the Canadian army corps, important to both Canadian public opinion and the restless Canadian troops themselves; British slowness in reopening trade, something that was hurting Canada as a nation with a large war debt and much to sell; and the withdrawal of Canadian troops from Russia. Two pieces of territory were listed: the Alaska panhandle, whose award to the United States in 1903 still rankled with Canadians, and the British West Indies, where there had been some discussion of Canada and the islands forming at the very least an economic union. Finally, there were the subjects that from Borden's and Christie's perspectives were the most important of all: the appointment of governors general, Canada's representation on the council of the League of Nations, and its signature on the peace treaties and other international agreements.[1]

General Sir Arthur Currie, General Loomis, and officers in Grand Place, Mons, taking the salute of the march past, 11 November 1918 (National Archives of Canada, PA3524)

Canada's delegation to the peace conference was relatively small, about fifteen delegates and experts (Serbia, by contrast, sent over 100), but it was the most the country could spare. In addition to Borden himself, Canada sent three cabinet ministers: C.J. Doherty, the minister of justice; Sir George Foster, from trade and commerce; Arthur Sifton of Customs and Inland Revenue; and Oliver Biggar, the judge advocate general. Sir Arthur Currie, already in Europe as commander of the Canadian army corps, handled military questions, and John Dafoe, editor of the *Winnipeg Free Press*, managed press relations. Although the Paris peace conference marked the eruption of the academic expert into international relations, George Wrong offered his services to Borden in vain.[2]

The Canadian delegates had a relatively free hand in Paris, but they kept a wary eye on public opinion at home. Sir Thomas White, the acting prime minister, regularly cabled Borden with his concerns over the economic and political situation in Canada (and with requests that Borden hasten back to deal with it). 'Since women took such an enormous part in the war in every respect,' the Women's Party wrote to Borden from Toronto, 'they feel that in making peace and all that this infers [sic] in reconstruction, in which they will take their part, that they should have a voice through which to express their views.' Saskatchewan Ukrainians petitioned for Canadian support for Ukraine's independence, and in Paris Canadian Ukrainians called on Borden to ask for recognition by the powers, a request he duly passed on to Lloyd George. Send our husbands home, Canadian women wrote to Borden, or, at the very least, free them from the clutches of French women.[3]

Borden dominated his delegation. Lord Milner, British colonial secretary, wrote to the Duke of Devonshire, governor general of Canada, 'He is the only one of the Dominion P.M's, who, without ceasing to be a good Canadian, is capable of taking the wider view and whose judgement and influence are really useful on Imperial and International questions. He is not a showy man, but he is a man of weight. Not a provincial, as most of the Dominion Ministers still, almost inevitably are. And he is perfectly straight. Foster is very good too, but he belongs to an older school, and has not the same breadth of outlook.'[4] Borden, who had a well-developed sense of his own importance, would have agreed. When the new Royal Institute of International Affairs in London brought out a multi-volume history of the peace conference in the early 1920s, Borden was furious to discover that his name did not appear in the index, even though those of other dominion statesmen did. He demanded that Christie complain: 'I think I may safely claim that no Prime Minister of any British Dominion took more conspicuous or important a part in the work of the Peace Conference than I did.'[5]

Borden usually represented Canada in the meetings of the British Empire delegation and dealt with the leaders of the other delegations. Although the Canadian delegation met frequently, he did not always bother to brief it. 'Another of his inexplicable methods,' Foster complained.[6] Although Borden nominated Foster for committees, including the Supreme Economic Council, he had never taken his views seriously.[7] Sifton he found rather excitable.[8] Doherty, 'good-looking, but with an expression of limited intelligence,' in the view of Georges Clemenceau, the French prime minister, was in poor health and tended to fall asleep at meetings. He was generally regarded as a lightweight.[9]

As a number of participants noted later, the peace conference was good training for international affairs.[10] Paris, after all, was for the first six months of 1919 the world's centre of power, gathering together presidents, prime ministers, foreign secretaries, and generals from over thirty countries. The Canadians found themselves taking on new responsibilities. When neither Lloyd George nor Balfour turned up to a meeting of the British Empire delegation, which the British customarily chaired, Borden was asked to fill in, the first time a dominion premier had done so. He took the chair at the next eight meetings. Borden also chaired the commission determining Greece's borders, and Sifton was vice-chair of the one attempting to set up an international regime for ports, waterways, and railways. Biggar worked as one of the team under Maurice Hankey, the formidably efficient British secretary to the cabinet and the peace conference. As noted in the official history of the British Empire delegation, 'in all their functioning, the Canadian representatives were practically indistinguishable from the other national representatives present.'[11]

While the Canadians established some contacts with the French, their most lasting connections were with other English speakers. In the Hotel Majestic, where they were housed with the rest of the British Empire delegates, they sat at meals with their South African, Australian, New Zealand, Indian, and British colleagues. Biggar and Christie chatted about the German peace or the dangers of Bolshevism with Hankey, Philip Kerr, Lloyd George's personal assistant, and Lord Robert Cecil, a leading British expert on the League.[12] Borden played bridge regularly with the South African prime minister, Louis Botha, 'a fine noble sincere figure.'[13] Although several of the Canadians had mixed feelings about the Americans – Biggar complained to his wife about their 'pigheaded obstinacy and intellectual conceit' and ' their stupidity and a refusal to admit any view but their own'[14] – they usually got on well with individuals. 'We had a delightful time,' said Colonel Edward House, Woodrow Wilson's trusted adviser, after an hour with Borden, 'discussing governmental matters and the future of the Dominions.'[15] The Canadians often shared the Americans' impatience with Europe. In the future, Christie told one of the Americans at a particularly tense moment of the peace conference, 'America will let Europe stew in its own juice.'[16] The chief impression that he brought back from Paris, Dafoe told an audience in Canada, was that he was glad he was separated from Europe by the Atlantic Ocean.[17]

Most of the Canadians took the almost obligatory trip to the battlefields. 'Trop triste,' said Foster.[18] They bought souvenirs and the latest fashions for their wives. Biggar and Borden worked on their French with Mademoiselle Fifi Perret. (Borden switched to French in his diary and ventured a speech; according to Foster, 'There was about the space of one minute between the words and altogether it was a pretty crude attempt.'[19]) They went to restaurants and theatres and complained of the prices in the former and the scandalous nature of the latter. He and Christie saw one piece at the opera, so Biggar told his wife, which concluded with a young man embracing a married woman near a bedroom. 'Charming ideas the French have, have they not?' Better not mention it to Mrs Christie, he added, in case Christie had not owned up.[20] Borden and Dafoe took the normally sedate Foster out on the town with the Duchess of Sutherland for what Borden said was 'one of the friskiest evenings of Foster's life.'[21] They started with snails at a well-known restaurant ('I ate one plate full,' said Dafoe, 'so as not to be a quitter'[22]), attended a performance of Cyrano de Bergerac, and ended with a midnight dinner at the house of the leading actress. 'I can assure you that nothing outré or unusual took place,' wrote Foster to his wife.[23]

Although they chafed at the slow pace of the peace deliberations and worried about what was happening in Canada, the Canadians were aware that they were taking part in an epoch-making event. The peace conference was dealing with the mess left by the collapse of four empires; it was coping with new nations, such as Yugoslavia and Czechoslovakia, and re-emerging ones, like Poland. It was trying to adjudicate competing claims for territory and stop a score of small wars. Above all, it was trying to make a lasting peace. 'So here I am in the midst of things,' wrote Foster on 19 January, the day after the peace conference officially opened, 'representing Canada which takes a place on perfect equality of expression and direction with all the other nations.'[24]

The Canadian role in the peace settlements, for all Foster's enthusiasm, was modest. Canada supported the League of Nations, seen by many on both sides of the Atlantic, as the keystone of the peace settlements, but no Canadian delegates took part in the drafting of the League Covenant. When Borden mildly reproved Lloyd George for allowing four other small nations to sit on the League Commission and suggested that Doherty, who had devoted 'much study' to the issues be added, Lloyd George declined to act, using the excuse that the commission's work was too far along.[25] Doherty, like other dominion statesmen, resented his relative insignificance in Paris. As Biggar noted, 'They have been important people. Here they comparatively speaking do not matter in the slightest.'[26] Borden himself largely ignored Doherty's lengthy memorandum on the Covenant, turning instead to Biggar and

Christie, whose advice he valued, for the final draft of the Canadian position.[27]

Canada had little hope of making its voice heard partly because the great powers – Britain, France, Italy, the United States – were not prepared to share their authority with the two dozen smaller nations that were represented in Paris. 'We have had dead, we have wounded in millions,' said Clemenceau, when Canada, among others, complained. 'I make no mystery of it – there is a Conference of the Great Powers going on in the next room.'[28] While the formal structure of the peace conference had plenary sessions with votes, the real work was done by the Big Four, meeting with Japan as the Supreme Council. After the middle of March, Lloyd George, Clemenceau, Vittorio Orlando of Italy, and Wilson met as the Council of Four. The sheer volume of work and the range of crises before them, from the German peace terms to the fighting in the centre of Europe, added to their reluctance to complicate matters by consulting the lesser powers.

In any case, many of the issues did not affect Canada. 'With the defeat of Germany,' Milner wrote to Devonshire, 'Canada's interest in the European scene is visibly and rapidly wearing out.'[29] Canada's main concerns in Paris, Christie told Newton Rowell, acting secretary of state for External Affairs, were the League, disarmament, economic proposals, and reparations from the enemy.[30] Like the British, the Canadians wanted to punish Germany, but they also came to fear that too severe a punishment would drive the Germans to despair, even to Bolshevism, and, equally important, would damage British trade. The French, they agreed, were grasping and short-sighted in their insistence that Germany must pay up.[31] There was a danger, too, that the French would scoop the lion's share of reparations. 'Fear quite impracticable,' Borden cabled to White, when the latter pressed for including the Halifax explosion in a claim for Canadian war damages. 'If we put forward Halifax claims as suggested it would strengthen French demand that their extraordinary reparation claims shall have complete precedence.'[32] For the rest – the new borders in Europe and the Middle East, for example – the Canadian delegates were prepared to go along with the British.

Like most other people, the Canadians worried about the future. 'The world has drifted so far from its old anchorage,' Borden confided to his diary the day the German armistice was signed, 'and no man can with certainty prophesy what the outcome will be. I have said that another such war would destroy our civilization.'[33] Bolshevism was going to take Poland next, then Germany, and probably France and Britain as well, Biggar told his anxious wife.[34] The delay in getting peace settlements, Borden wrote to Lloyd George was 'fraught with the possibility of evil and even of disaster'[35] On the other hand, the Canadians were lukewarm about the allied intervention against the Bolsheviks and more than lukewarm about using Canadian troops. By the time the peace conference opened, Borden, with White's encouragement from Ottawa, had come to the conclusion that the Canadian contingents already in Siberia should be withdrawn.[36]

As far as the League of Nations was concerned, the Canadian delegation took a cautiously optimistic approach, but like many of their fellows in the British Empire delegation, they wondered whether such an organization would work. They pointed out that its success would depend on strong public support.[37] Borden warned House against putting too much detail in the covenant, because it would give the French and Billy Hughes of Australia, a leading critic, room to attack.[38] Borden and Doherty, informed by their legal training, easily picked holes in the draft Covenant and the Canadian delegation put a huge amount of effort into its memorandum on the League Covenant. Canada strongly opposed Article X, which obliged all League members to protect each other's territory and independence against outside aggression. The Canadians argued that this obligation would affect the future ability of members to determine their own foreign policy and, more specifically, their entry into a war (an issue that had particular resonance, since Canada had for some time been disputing the assumption that Canada inevitably was at war when Britain was).[39] The Article makes, said Doherty quoting the *Times*, 'a mutual guarantee society of unlimited Liability,' and he demanded that the offending article be taken out altogether.[40] Although one of the leading American experts on the League found the Canadian attack 'the most forcible argument against Article 10,' the Canadian criticisms had little impact.[41] Cecil, the British expert, said politely that the Canadian contribution was 'useful.'[42]

Canada's voice was also muted because it was not yet clear about what it was or what it wanted as an international player. Canada's move to independence was slow and tentative.[43] Unlike the United States, it had not had a defining act of rebellion to launch it onto the world stage as a fully independent force. Unlike Poland, it had not fought for generations against oppressors. In their first fifty years as a federation, Canadians had remained uncertain as to what they wanted. Was Canada to remain part of the British Empire, although with greater control over its own internal policies? Was the British Empire itself to become a tighter union, perhaps even with its own imperial parliament, bureaucracy, and cabinet? Among the Canadian delegates, opinions ranged from those of Foster, who took enormous pride in being part of the British Empire, to those of Dafoe, who looked forward to the eventual breakup of that empire and a fully independent Canada.[44] The majority had not yet made up their minds. Borden, who could write in his memoirs that he had 'a profound belief in the integrity of the Empire, in its future destiny, and in its influence for good,' could also say in his diary, after a dispute with the British, 'In the end and perhaps sooner rather than later, Canada must assume full sovereignty. She can give better service to G.B. & U.S. & to the world in that way.'[45]

Full independence was not something to be undertaken lightly. Membership in the British Empire was a useful counterbalance to the United States, and ambiguity had certain advantages. When there was some discussion about inserting provisions on freer trade in the German treaty (the idea was subsequently dropped), the Canadians hastily checked to make sure that they would still be entitled to imperial preference.[46] 'The position was difficult and in some respects delicate,' according to Borden. 'On the one hand we wished to be regarded as a unit for particular purposes, such as Imperial preference, and on the other hand we wanted to secure for the Dominions the right of separate representation in the Council and Assembly of the League. There was some danger of arousing the sensibilities of other nations.'[47]

Membership in the British Empire also gave Canada a status it would not otherwise have had. Ever since 1917, when Lloyd George had established the Imperial War Cabinet, the Canadian government, like those of its sister dominions and India, had been briefed fully on the conduct of the war and proposals for the peace. During the peace conference the Canadians had full access to the papers provided by the British foreign office and by Lloyd George's secretariat. In the words of Lloyd George himself, 'the Dominions were at the heart of the machine and would count.'[48] 'The world was pretty well gone over,' Christie told Wrong, in the meetings of the British Empire delegation, thirty-five in all between January and June 1919. 'All this experience certainly accounts in large measure for the prominent part taken by the Dominions at Paris. No small Power was in their class.'[49]

Nevertheless, even before the Great War, Canadians had realized that Canada's interests did not always coincide neatly with those of the empire or those of the mother country. In the Alaska panhandle dispute, for example, Britain had abandoned Canada's claims for the sake of better relations with the Americans. The Canadian government increasingly looked out for its own interests when it came to dealings with the United States. In the Great War, Canadians' awareness of their contribution as well as their disillusionment with the ability of the British to run a war properly altered permanently the relationship with Britain. As Borden told Lloyd George in 1917, 'The Dominions have fought in this war upon the principle of equal nationhood. It would be desirable to say that this principle has been consecrated by their effort and sacrifice and that it must be maintained.'[50] With Borden as mover, the Imperial Conference of that year called for a special meeting after the war to readjust the constitutional relations of the empire, 'based upon a full recognition of the Dominions as autonomous nations of an Imperial Commonwealth.'[51]

Borden sailed for Europe shortly after the armistice, determined that what had been achieved for Canada must not be lost in peacetime. He was taken aback (as was the irascible Hughes of Australia) to discover that the British government had already decided to accept Wilson's Fourteen Points as a basis for the negotiations.[52] He was more than taken aback when he realized that the British simply assumed that they would represent their dominions.[53] 'I had not come,' he told Hankey, 'to take part in light comedy.'[54] He threatened 'to pack his trunks, return to Canada, summon Parliament, and put the whole thing before them.'[55] The British suggested that Borden become one of their five plenipotentiaries, who, as the prime minister of the senior dominion, would represent the others. This offer in turn annoyed Hughes, who started to talk of separate representation for Australia. General Jan Smuts, foreign minister of South Africa, suggested that the dominions take turns as one of the British plenipotentiaries. Borden, who was under pressure from his own government, started to echo Hughes.[56] 'It would be regarded as intolerable in Canada,' he told the Imperial War Cabinet, 'that Portugal should have a representation in the Peace Conference which was denied to that Dominion.'[57] The Canadian press was full of references to the sacrifices Canada had made in the war and the recognition that it was owed.[58] 'Council today further considered Canadian representation at Peace Conference,' White cabled from Ottawa, 'and is even more strongly of opinion than when you left that Canada should be represented.'[59]

The final compromise, which Lloyd George worked out with the other great powers at the end of December 1918, was that the British

Empire delegation (the name was a victory in itself for the dominions) should have five plenipotentiaries, one of whom would be chosen from a panel of dominion representatives, and that, in addition, Canada, Australia, South Africa, and India would have two plenipotentiaries and New Zealand one at the peace conference. Although Britain's allies objected that this plan simply would give the British extra votes, others took the longer view. The French colonial ministry noted that the dominions had changed, 'de nations protégées à celui de nations participantes.' Britain was being forced out of its pre-war isolationism: if it wanted to protect its empire, it would have to do deals with its allies.[60] House hoped that, by granting a separate role to the dominions, the British Empire had moved closer to disintegration.[61]

When Serbia and Belgium were allowed extra representatives in January on the basis of their contribution to the war, the Canadian response was swift.[62] It was 'most unfortunate' Borden wrote to Lloyd George, that there had been no consultation with the dominions. 'It is hardly to be anticipated that Canadians will consider that their country is suitably recognized by being placed on an equality with Siam and Hedjaz.'[63] He permitted himself a joke with Botha: Canada must hold its own at least with Patagonia. Since the plenary sessions rarely held a serious vote, the dominions' struggle has sometimes been seen as a waste of time, but in international relations symbolism also plays a part. As Borden recorded in his diary, 'It was largely a question of sentiment. Canada got nothing out of War except recognition.'[64]

Borden remained alert for any suggestion that Canada (or he himself) was being slighted. He refused to go to the opening plenary session on 18 January 1919 because Lloyd George chose the prime minister of Newfoundland to represent the British Empire.[65] Canadian relief organizations, he grumbled, were not getting proper credit, because their donations were simply being lumped together with those of the British. Later that spring he wrote in dignified reproof to Cecil to complain that a morning newspaper had failed to list Foster as a Canadian representative on the Supreme Economic Council. 'I hope that something may be done to prevent such mischances in the future, as I am sure you will realise the unfortunate effects that might follow.'[66]

The Canadians did not test the limits as much as some of their dominion counterparts did. Hughes, for example, said openly in the Supreme Council (the remark was later edited out of the minutes) that Australia would make its own choice the next time Britain went to war. Botha echoed these sentiments in a private letter to Lloyd George of 15 May 1919, in which he said that the dominions had no obligation to add their names to the Anglo-American guarantee of protection to France against future attacks.[67] Borden contented himself with warning Lloyd George that the guarantee might be difficult for Canadians to support.[68]

When it came to the work of the peace conference, Borden and his fellow delegates accepted that when the Canadians sat on its committees and commissions, they did so as representatives of the British Empire, even sometimes of Britain alone. When it came to the composition of the Supreme Economic Council, set up in February 1919 to coordinate allied operations in areas such as shipping and finance, however, Borden and Foster agreed that there should be five representatives from the British Empire (with one from the dominions and India) and that they should be advised by a committee incorporating British and empire experts rather than two separate bodies as originally proposed.[69] Borden, for all his concerns about the spread of Bolshevism, accepted with alacrity Lloyd George's invitation to represent Britain at the proposed meeting with the Bolsheviks at Prinkipo – 'a great honour to Canada.' Appointed as vice-chair to the committee dealing with Greece's boundaries, Borden took his lead from British officials.[70] 'He is easy and intelligent,' Harold Nicolson wrote in his diary after his first meeting with Borden, 'and will make a good representative.'[71] In the committee meetings, which he occasionally chaired, Borden's interventions were generally limited to points of order and requests for information. When he did express an opinion, for example, on the desirability of Greece's receiving part of Asia Minor, he reflected the British viewpoint.[72]

When new international organizations were discussed, however, the Canadians remembered that they were a separate nation. Recognition of Canada's changed status came up again when the composition of the League of Nations and the International Labor Organization (ILO) were discussed. The Americans and the French at first assumed that the self-governing parts of the British Empire, which were not yet fully-fledged states, according to international practice, would not be members. They were soon disabused of this assumption by both the dominions themselves and the British speaking on their behalf. Cecil, who was lukewarm on the issue, told David Hunter Miller, his American counterpart, that Great Britain was obliged to ask for separate membership. Hughes, Smuts, and Borden all made it clear that their countries expected to belong to both the League and the ILO in their own right.[73] In response to American objections that the dominions would simply vote as the

British told them, Sifton, in an analogy which might have been better chosen, said that the United States was scarcely in a position to talk: 'There were many small States such as Cuba, Hayti, Liberia and Nicaragua and Panama, who were practically in the pocket of the United States, and would be dominated by Americans; so that the effect of the present proposal would simply be to redress the balance in some measure.'[74] The Americans chose not to make an issue of the matter. (House, who along with Wilson represented the United States on the League commission, again looked forward to the undermining of the British Empire.)[75]

The Canadians were also concerned about eligibility for membership on the executive councils of the League and the ILO. Under pressure from the smaller powers, the great powers reluctantly added four members to the League council to be chosen by vote of the League assembly.[76] Unfortunately, from the dominions' point of view, the wording again referred to 'states.' In the case of the ILO's council, the relevant clause lumped in colonies and self-governing dominions with the mother country and gave the latter the right to only one nominee. On 21 April, when Cecil presented the draft League covenant to the British Empire delegation, Sifton, Borden, and Hughes all complained. There would be 'unfortunate effects' back home, warned Sifton, when it was realized that Canada was not eligible for election to the League council. Cecil somewhat disingenuously replied that there had never been any intention of excluding the dominions and agreed to ask that the words 'member of the League' should replace 'state' throughout the document. A week later, Borden and Sifton raised similar concerns about the ILO. The provision, said Borden, would 'drive Canadian labour into the arms of the United States for the purpose of securing representation of the Governing Body.'[77] (In a memorandum to Borden, Sifton had described the reaction of Canadian workers: 'I rather anticipate that disregarding some views of theology they will say in their somewhat frank manner that they will see the Japanese and Italian delegates and their respective governments individually and collectively sizzling in the lowest depths of Hell before they will agree to accept a standing inferior to the negroes of Liberia.')[78] The British again were obliged to pursue the matter with the Americans and the French, both reluctant to start altering documents whose wording had given so much trouble.[79] As they were increasingly doing, the Canadians also lobbied on their own behalf.[80]

Borden returned to the attack on 5 May. Canada would reject the ILO convention in the plenary session that had been called to consider the Germany treaty, which included the League and the ILO, and although it would sign the treaty, it would immediately give notice of withdrawal from both bodies. 'Canada had led the democracies of the Western Hemisphere in the war and yet, in respect of this Labour Convention which, in view of her industrial importance, was of great concern to her, it was proposed to place her on a lower level than countries such as Liberia, Siam, Nicaragua, Panama, &c.'[81] A public disagreement at this stage was the last thing either the British or the other powers wanted. The plenary session took place on the following day, and the terms were to go to the Germans on the next. The Italians had only just arrived back in Paris after a very public walkout over their territorial claims, and the Belgians and the Japanese were threatening to leave.

Lloyd George promptly promised Borden that he would take up his concerns with the Council of Four. Borden sent him a reminder on the morning of 6 May. Clemenceau and Wilson reluctantly agreed to change the wording to make it clear that dominions such as Canada were eligible for the council of the ILO. When Borden learned that they had not also changed the wording on the League, he drafted a memorandum which was signed by Lloyd George, Wilson, and Clemenceau, in which they expressed their 'entire concurrence' with his view that the self-governing dominions were eligible to be named to the League council.[82]

Borden, who had been receiving increasingly panicky demands from White for his return, left Paris a few days later. 'It is most important' he told Foster and Doherty, who were to remain, 'that the status which has been secured for Canada at the present Conference should be maintained and that any proposal whether made through design, inattention or misconception, which might detract therefrom should be resisted and rejected.' The future should be plainer sailing, but 'it is necessary to bear in mind an inevitable tendency on the part of officials, and sometimes of Ministers, to forget that the United Kingdom is not the only nation in the British Empire.' Canadian proposals on the empire's adherence to the treaty, he added, had been accepted in 'most respects.'[83] Borden had been concerned about this issue for some time. The old practice, whereby the British representatives signed on behalf of the empire, no longer seemed congruent with Canada's status. In February 1919 he consulted his dominion colleagues and Lloyd George and got a general agreement that the treaties should be signed under the general

Allies around the conference table, Treaty of Versailles, Paris, France, 1919
(R. Simmons, National Archives of Canada, C242)

heading of British Empire delegation by the plenipotentiaries from the
dominions and India as well as by Britain, the former being identified
by their nations.[84] On 12 March Borden circulated a memorandum with
his view of the constitutional situation. The dominions should be parties and signatories to all treaties and conventions of the peace conference in recognition of the part they had played and also to record 'the
status attained.' Such a move, so Borden argued, was not a break with
the existing constitution of the empire: 'the Crown is the supreme
executive in the United Kingdom and in all the Dominions, but it acts
on the advice of different Ministries within different constitutional
units.' The lengthy Canadian memorandum on the League of Nations,
sent the following day, underlined this point: 'It is also assumed that the
Dominions of the British Empire are entitled to become Signatories of
the Covenant.'[85] The dominions were, in fact, moving on to new territory; their delegates were no longer signing merely as members of the

British Empire but on behalf of their respective nations. It was a technicality but, as officials in London realized, a highly significant one that granted the dominions greater autonomy in international affairs than they had hitherto possessed. Once conceded, it was difficult, if not impossible, to take back.[86]

The Canadians, who seem to have cared more about the issue than those from the other dominions, continued to press, requesting, for example, when the king, as was required, issued full powers to their plenipotentiaries, that he do so on the basis of a formal request from the Canadian government.[87] Sifton sent Dafoe a copy of his papers: 'the first tangible evidence of a recognition of the rights of Canadians to be alive. Of course the British Government and particularly the permanent service thereof, do not for a moment think it means anything more than a little flattery but possibly having once issued them, the habit may grow.'[88] On 28 June 1919 the dominion and Indian representatives – in the case of Canada, Doherty and Sifton – signed the Treaty of Versailles with Germany. The meaning of those signatures, however, remained as ambiguous as the status they were supposed to reflect. The five British plenipotentiaries signed first, on behalf of the United Kingdom *and* the British dominions and India. The remaining British empire signatures were underneath and indented, which suggests that they were subordinate to those of the United Kingdom.[89]

Ratification of the treaties induced a last flurry of activity. The question was simple but important: did the British Parliament and king ratify on behalf of the whole empire, or must each dominion Parliament meet and pass a separate ratification? Borden sent a testy cable to Sifton, now Canada's high commissioner in London: 'I am under pledge to submit the Treaty to Parliament before ratification on behalf of Canada.' Was Britain intending to ratify for the empire? 'If so our attendance at Paris and our signature to the Treaty was an utterly idle formality.'[90] The British took the opposing point of view, partly because they wanted to put the treaty with Germany into effect as soon as possible. Ratification by three of the big five powers was necessary, and although the French and the Japanese were prepared to move ahead quickly, the Italians were in the midst of a political crisis and the Americans were engaged in a bitter partisan debate. If each dominion Parliament had to be called – a procedure that would inevitably take time – the treaty would remain in limbo. 'It would be disastrous,' Balfour wrote to Milner, 'if whole of Peace of the world were to be hung up for months because Canadian Parliament had adjourned, and in order to give time for treaty to reach Australia and be discussed and approved by Australian Parliament.' He offered an elegant but ineffectual solution: the king could ratify on behalf of all the dominions, with the proviso that his doing so would not preclude his depositing further ratifications on behalf of each dominion as soon as their parliaments approved. Milner, whose own view was that ratification by Britain did indeed bind the empire, thought that this would only lead to more hurt feelings in the dominions. 'I can hardly suppose that it would be any particular satisfaction to them to go through what in that case would be a meaningless formality.' It was better, he thought, to encourage the dominions either to give Britain the authority to go ahead on behalf of the whole empire or to get their parliaments together as quickly as possible.[91] When the British tried to pressure the dominions by saying that the French, in particular, were demanding immediate ratification, Borden answered at once: 'I cannot emphasize too strongly the unfortunate results which would certainly ensue from ratification before Canadian Parliament has had an opportunity of considering Treaty.'[92] The British backed off, and the Canadian Parliament, along with the legislatures of its sister dominions, duly passed resolutions ratifying the treaty. A similar procedure was followed with the treaties signed subsequently with the other enemy nations.

The Canadians spent considerable time and effort in Paris on Canada's status. Borden and his advisers, such as Christie and Biggar, felt that their greatest achievement had been to get recognition, as Christie stated in a long paper he wrote in the summer of 1919, of Canada as an international person.[93] Christie felt that the empire, or as he preferred to call it, the British Commonwealth, was strengthened, although he had his moments of doubt. As he wrote to Wrong, 'It depends I suppose on whether the different parts of the Empire really make up their minds that they will play together, that they have in fact some important common objects, that there is actual business that they can transact better together than apart, or whether we, for example, are to be drugged by the unlovely miasma from the south and become "100% Canadian and the rest of the world be damned."'[94]

The peace conference was useful in another, less dramatic way, in that it obliged Canada to define its interests as an international player. Borden protested vigorously, for example, when the Canadians got wind of a proposal to restore a German submarine telegraph cable that had run via the Azores to New York. This line would divert traffic from a new link through Halifax and, even worse, hand it over to the Americans. Canada had suffered enough at the hands of American (and British) 'monopolists.' Canada wanted the cable left where it was and a share in its administration; Canada must also be represented at any future international telegraph congresses. Lloyd George raised the issue with Wilson, who was quick to reassure him that the United States had no intention of depriving Canada of its cable link.[95]

Canada recognized that it had considerable economic interests in Europe at the end of the war. A new trade mission in London under Lloyd Harris worked with the British to market Canadian products and to make sure that Canada received a share in European reconstruction. Canadian businessmen complained that the British were selfishly keeping their shipping to themselves.[96] Borden went directly to Balfour when he learned that only British and American firms were being asked to supply iron and steel to France: 'Canada has been fighting for nearly four years on French soil, with untold sacrifice in a war which concerned her, materially, as little as any country in the world. Under the circumstances, it seems incomprehensible that the French Government should utterly ignore Canada's capacity for supplying iron and steel.'[97] In February 1919 Borden and Harris saw Lloyd George to ask for an end to the wartime embargo on food shipments to neutrals and enemies: 'there would be deep dissatisfaction with Great Britain, both in the United States and Canada, if she persists in a policy which is considered to show disregard of her undertaking to accept food supplies which she called upon Canada and the United States to furnish.' Adequate food supplies, they added, would undercut the appeal of Bolshevism.[98]

During the peace conference, Foster made it his particular business to arrange credits with the French, Belgian, Greek, and Rumanian governments, so that they could buy Canadian products. 'There will be millions more to be fed and clothed to fend off widespread starvation,' he wrote enthusiastically in his diary. 'The call will still be on America to feed and supply.' He made sure that Canada was at the Lyons trade fair. The Australians, he noted with satisfaction, 'were hopelessly outclassed in exhibits and refused to attend our banquet.' (There was also a certain amount of rivalry between the two self-governing dominions.) He then brought the exhibits to Paris to reach the new nations such as Czechoslovakia.[99]

On international commercial aviation, then in its infancy, the Canadians argued that the special conditions in North America meant that Canada and the United States should be treated differently from European powers. Although there was no need for this issue to be settled by the peace conference, the powers took advantage of the presence of so many nations in Paris to set up a commission to work out an international convention. Canada was not directly represented, but Sifton sat on the British Empire's committee, where, he proudly told a Canadian friend, he made a nuisance of himself. He objected strongly to having merely British Empire representation on the proposed international board and threatened that Canada would not take part.[100] Indeed, he attacked the very idea of international regulation, arguing that conditions in North America were so special – the 4,000-mile undefended border with the United States; the prairies, where airplanes could land easily on either side of that border – that it would be absurd that a body largely staffed by Europeans would deal with them. 'The whole subject,' he wrote to Borden on 29 April, 'is so utterly unknown, that for anyone to sit down and attempt without consultation to include a country like Canada, where if commercial air traffic is a success it will be of vastly more importance than it is likely to be in any of the countries who are assuming to settle the matter, is a blunder that would generally be called a crime.' It would make much more sense for Canada and the United States to work out their own regulations. When one of the leading British experts was badly shaken in an air crash a few weeks later, he found it a clear demonstration that there was no point in trying to set up international standards.[101] Borden took Sifton's concerns, although in politer form, to the British Empire delegation.[102]

When the British showed few signs of budging, Sifton proposed on 6 May that Canada sign the convention with a reservation exempting air traffic between Canada and the United States from its provisions. The British reluctantly agreed to take the matter up with the aeronautical commission. As they had done on other issues, the Canadians also spoke directly to the Americans, whom they found sympathetic. In the summer of 1919 the American State Department contacted the Canadian government, via the British embassy in Washington, to ascertain Canadian views. 'They would not like to do anything,' the embassy reported, 'out of harmony with Canada's attitude.' Christie dealt directly with the Americans, and the Canadian government postponed signing the convention, with a view to working out a special arrangement with the United States.[103]

Although the Canadians insisted that, like the Americans, they were a disinterested party in Paris, they were also briefly tempted by the possibility of acquiring territory . Perhaps Canada should take over the little French islands of St Pierre and Miquelon? Possibly Newfoundland as well? Or the British West Indies? Management by the rich, energetic northern brother could only benefit the locals, Harry J. Crowe, a Toronto entrepreneur, assured Borden, and Canada's climate would deter Black immigration. As 'a striking and suitable commemoration of Canada's entry into World politics,' F. Perry of the Imperial Munitions Board wrote to Borden, Canada also should take over British Honduras and British Guinea. The subject had been discussed 'in a general way,' Borden replied, and he believed that Lloyd George might look on it favourably.[104] In his memoirs, Lloyd George claimed the problem was with the Canadians, who shrank from sharing in the responsibilities of the empire. 'I found Sir Robert Borden was deeply imbued with the American prejudice against the government of extraneous possessions and peoples which did not form an integral part of their own Union.'[105] There were, in fact, serious reservations on the British side, notably on the part of Milner, the colonial secretary. 'If the relations between Canada & Great Britain,' he wrote in the margins of a letter from Borden, 'are to remain those of intimate & indissoluble union – as partner nations in a Super-State – then I think Canada sh'd take over the West Indies. She will certainly develop them better than we can. But as long as these relations remain indefinite & even doubtful, I am unwilling to part – even to Canada – with any territory wh. is to-day indisputably British.'[106]

Borden chose not to push the matter, perhaps because the Canadians had another, more important, goal in sight: swapping British Honduras for the Alaska panhandle. The Americans and the British, who saw it as a way of removing a source of irritation between the United States and the British Empire, were sympathetic.[107] Borden talked to both Lloyd George and Milner as well as a 'very prominent' member of the American delegation towards the end of April 1919 and received some encouragement.[108] The matter went no further, partly because Lloyd George and Wilson were preoccupied with the German treaty and other crises and perhaps because Borden himself was already turning his attention back to Canada.

Canada's key relations at Paris were, as they had been even before the war, with Britain and the United States. The Canadians were determined that the two great powers in their world should get on. As Borden told the Imperial War Cabinet in 1917, the United States and the British Empire together 'could do more than anything else to maintain the peace of the world.'[109] If the League of Nations did not work out, he told Lloyd George just after the war ended, there might be a smaller one between 'the two great English speaking commonwealths who share common ancestry, language and literature, who are inspired by like democratic ideals, who enjoy similar political institutions and whose united force is sufficient to ensure the peace of the world.'[110] Throughout the peace conference, the Canadians took it upon themselves to explain the United States to other nations, especially to Britain.[111] As Borden told Lloyd George, 'Conditions in the United States and the policy of the United States Government from time to time are naturally of great moment to Canada by reason of the immediate proximity of the two countries and the constantly increasing commercial, industrial and social intercourse between them.'[112]

The United States, for its part, regarded Canada as a useful ally in its quest for a new diplomacy. House was 'very anxious,' he told the British representative Sir William Wiseman, as the peace conference was about to open, that 'BORDEN and SMUTS should "play in" with the President's policy.' Wilson had reservations about Borden – 'He is not a man who responds quickly, or with whom conversation is easy'[113] – but invited him to a meeting a few days later where the two men discussed the League of Nations and the disposition of the German colonies. Wilson, so Borden told his diary, 'agreed with me that good relations between B.E. and U.S. best asset either c'd have.'[114]

Borden took upon himself the role of conciliator when the United States and Britain differed. When the Americans, led by Samuel Gompers, head of the American Federation of Labor, wanted to include a labour charter in the preamble to the ILO and the British objected, it was Borden who worked out the final compromise.[115] When the British and American experts disagreed on Greece's borders with Albania, Borden tried to get a compromise.[116] In the British Empire delegation, he argued strongly against high reparations from Germany because they ran counter to Wilson's Fourteen Points, which they all had accepted. They must not, Borden warned, alienate the Americans. 'Otherwise the United States might unite with France to squeeze us out.'[117]

Canada and the United States briefly found themselves on opposite sides when it came to the eighth clause in the ILO charter, which provided that all foreign workmen lawfully in any country should receive the same treatment under labour legislation and social insurance as nationals. Borden, mindful of the prejudice at home against Asian labour, warned of 'great disorder, possibly rebellion on the Pacific Coast of the United States and of Canada.' Although the Americans shared his concern, Wilson, who himself may have drafted the clause, felt it necessary to get the charter accepted by the European countries, many of whose nationals worked in North America.[118] On 8 April Borden and the other dominion prime ministers thought they had prevailed upon the British to reconsider, but two days later they discovered the clause, still in the draft German treaty. In Borden's words, they took 'a very firm stand.'[119] At Lloyd George's request, Borden saw both Clemenceau and Wilson. The day before the plenary that was to approve the treaty, Borden held a meeting in his hotel room with, among others, George Barnes, the British minister of labour; Emile Vandervelde, the Belgian minister of justice and leader of the Socialist party; and Henry Robinson, a California banker representing the United States. It was agreed that on the following day he would move an amendment to the report of the labour commission. The offending clause was safely watered down to read: 'The standard set by law in each country with respect to the conditions of labour should have due regard to the equitable economic treatment of all workers lawfully resident therein.'[120]

Early in the peace conference, the Canadians acted as an intermediary between their fellow dominions, notably Australia, and the United States over the disposition of Germany's colonies. Wilson, who opposed territorial annexations, insisted that in the case of peoples not yet ready for self-government, the League of Nations should take on a mandated responsibility. Several of the British dominions, however, were determined to hang on to their wartime conquests. South Africa demanded German Southwest Africa (today's Namibia); Australia a number of islands south of the equator, including the northern part of New Guinea; and New Zealand German Samoa. The British, who did not object to mandates and, more important, had no wish to confront the Americans on this issue, found themselves obliged yet again to fight their dominions' battles.[121] At the Supreme Council on 24 January Lloyd George argued, rather half-heartedly, for annexation. Borden attempted to forestall the expected clash by arguing that the relations among the components of the British Empire were actually like those proposed for the League of Nations. Before the peace conference opened, Borden had warned the Imperial War Cabinet against quarrelling with the United States over the colonies. Like the rest of the Canadian delegation, he was rubbed the wrong way by Hughes. (There may also have been a certain amount of sibling rivalry. After all, Canada, as the oldest dominion, expected to take the lead, a prerogative Hughes tended to ignore.) Borden bristled at Hughes's attacks on Wilson and his League of Nations and was quietly pleased when Lloyd George consulted him on how to keep Hughes under control.[122]

Wilson said nothing in the Supreme Council.[123] To his intimates, however, he said he would not stand for 'dividing the swag.'[124] Intense discussions behind the scenes followed. Borden did not play a significant part, but he watched with disapproval as Hughes spurned the attempts by Smuts and House to come up with a compromise. After what Borden described in his diary as a 'pretty warm scene' at a meeting of the British Empire delegation, Hughes gave way and agreed to accept the territories he wanted as mandates, but he did so with ill grace (and an inflammatory newspaper interview), which infuriated Wilson.[125] Borden made a point of apologizing to the Americans and explaining that the British Empire delegation found Hughes equally troublesome.[126]

Borden took a much more active part in brokering a compromise on an another contentious issue between the British Empire and the United States a few months later. It arose when Japan tried to insert a clause on racial equality into the League's covenant. Although Britain had no objections to what was a rather anodyne clause, it found itself in an awkward position. On the one hand, it was allied to Japan, which expected support. On the other, its own dominions, notably Australia, New Zealand, and, to a lesser extent, South Africa and Canada, were panicky about what they saw, incorrectly, as a threat to their own limits on Asian immigration. The United States was also torn between seeing the justice of the Japanese demand as well as wanting to keep on friendly terms with Japan, and fearing its own domestic opinion, especially that on the west coast. A number of people, including House, Cecil, Smuts, and Borden, tried to come up with a formula that would appease both the Japanese, understandably sensitive about seeing their nationals treated as inferiors, and the hardliners, Hughes prominent among them. On 25 March the British Empire delegation met at Borden's apartment. Borden suggested new wording for the controversial clause, but Hughes rejected it. The Japanese delegates then joined the meeting, but the group was unable to reach a conclusion.[127] On 31 March Borden, who had discussed the matter with Smuts, carried new proposals to Hughes.[128]

When Smuts left on a mission to Hungary at the start of April, he and Cecil asked Borden to carry on for the British. Hughes, Cecil told Borden bluntly, was impossible. The Japanese were threatening to make a public protest. Indeed, there was a danger that they might refuse to sign the German treaty at all. 'It is possible,' Cecil added, 'that they may refuse to join the League of Nations.'[129] Borden took his responsibilities seriously, travelling back and forth between Cecil, the recalcitrant Hughes, and the Japanese delegates.[130] In the end, his efforts and those of everyone else came to nothing. The Japanese, to everyone's relief, decided not to press the issue. For all his distaste for Hughes and his methods, Borden recognized that Canada and Australia had a common interest in preserving the new status the dominions had won for themselves. The two men continued to meet until Borden sailed for Canada in May, leaving Doherty and Foster, himself about to leave, in charge.[131]

With the signing of the German treaty at Versailles on 28 June the main work of the conference ended. Christie believed that Canada had gained valuable experience. Before 1919, he argued, Canada's international relations were almost entirely economic in nature; the Paris gathering was the first occasion 'on which Canada became conscious that she was directly and vitally concerned in a world political conference.'[132] As Sifton saw it, 'We always took the position that while we were willing and anxious to help as far as possible in making it a good Treaty, we had no wish to raise questions that would cause trouble and only desired that in so far as our people were concerned and in regard to matters which especially interested them, we should have fair and equal treatment.'[133] Did that amount to full nationhood for Canada? Christie did not go quite so far. Canada had a 'new status'; it had been a member of the peace conference and signed the treaty with Germany, and it was now a member of the League of Nations and the ILO. 'The Dominions,' he concluded, 'have asserted a sovereign status of some sort and have for some purposes entered the Family of Nations.'[134]

Participation in the peace settlements was something of a false dawn for the dominions. They had made an exceptional effort, but none, not even Canada, had the diplomatic resources to sustain a role in international affairs. In addition, in the early 1920s Canada, like the others, was preoccupied with domestic affairs. Borden's successors showed little enthusiasm for the promised conference on imperial constitutional arrangements. In the end, it never took place. Nor did Canada show much interest in the round of conferences and meetings that followed Paris. It sent only a token delegation to the important Genoa economic conference in 1922 and was not represented at all at the Lausanne conference of 1923 that finally made peace between the Allies and the new Turkey. Canadian foreign policy was largely symbolic, in the words of Robert Bothwell, 'a policy that was genuinely unimportant to the majority of politicians in Ottawa, and one that could find no issue on which it could mobilize any interest, much less sentiment, in Canada.'[135]

On the other hand, Canada continued to manage its relations with the United States. By 1919, as the American legal expert Hunter-Miller rightly said, 'the practical situation was slipping away from the legal status.' Although matters affecting Canada were still technically dealt with by London and Washington, 'we knew, and London knew that we knew, and so on with all the possible permutations of this progression, that the matter could not be settled except in accordance with the wishes of the Ottawa government.'[136] Borden and his immediate successor, Arthur Meighen, pressed for Canadian representation in Washington. In 1920 Canada reached an agreement with a more or less willing Britain that a Canadian minister plenipotentiary, second in rank to the ambassador, should become part of the British embassy in the American capital. What the assignment meant in terms of authority was not spelled out. The Canadian view, which the British did not challenge, was that their minister would be responsible to and take instructions from the Canadian government. In the end, the new government of Mackenzie King chose not to make an appointment until 1927.[137]

Although imperial unity was maintained, the fault lines had become apparent in Paris. Dominions had gained the right to accept or withhold their assent to international agreements. Leaders such as Botha and Hughes had raised the question of whether London could commit the self-governing dominions to war. The answer was to come in 1922 during the Chanak crisis, when Lloyd George tried, unsuccessfully, to involve the dominions in its struggle with Turkey. Mackenzie King, now prime minister, firmly, if deviously, refused to commit Canadian forces. Canada's international status remained as unclear as ever. It was fortunate, perhaps, that the nation now had a prime minister who throve on ambiguity.

NOTES

1 National Archives of Canada (NAC), Borden Papers, vol. 157, Memorandum for Interview with Mr Lloyd George, 4.2.19.
2 Ibid., vol. 94, Wrong to Borden, 13.11.18; NAC, Christie Papers, vol. 4, Christie to Rowell, 1.1.19
3 NAC, Borden Papers, vol. 93, White to Borden, 11.4.19, 23.4.19, 26.4.19; vol. 157, letter of 16.12.18; vol. 94, petition forwarded by Arthur Meighen, 15.1.19; House of Lords Record Office (HLRO), Lloyd George Papers, F5/3/24, Borden to Lloyd George, 27.3.19; NAC, Borden Papers, vol. 157.

4  Bodleian Library (BL), Oxford, MS Milner, Deposit 383/1, Milner to Devonshire 25.3.19.
5  NAC, Christie Papers, vol. 3, file 6/6, Borden to Christie, n.d.
6  NAC, Foster Papers, vol. 8 (diary extracts), 11.1.19.
7  Robert Craig Brown, *Robert Laird Borden: A Biography*, Vol. 2, *1914–1937* (Toronto, 1980), 20, 208.
8  NAC, Borden Papers, C1864, diary entry 6.5.19.
9  Clemenceau, *Grandeur and Misery of Victory* (Toronto, 1930), 141; NAC, Oliver Mowat Biggar Papers, vol. 2, letter of 1.2.19; Foster Papers, vol. 106, letters to Mrs Foster, 21.12. 18, 1.1.19, 9.6.19; James Shotwell, *At the Paris Peace Conference* (New York, 1937), 165.
10  Clifford Lovin, *A School for Diplomats: The Paris Peace Conference of 1919* (Lanham, Md., 1997), 3 and passim.
11  NAC, Clement Jones, 'The Dominions and the Peace Conference. A New Page in Constitutional History,' copy in Christie Papers, vol. 7, f. 21, 30, 211.
12  See NAC, Biggar Papers, 12.3.19, 23.3.19, 28.3.19, 4.4.19.
13  NAC, Borden Papers, Borden diary entries 28.12.18, 16.1.19, 4.2.19.
14  NAC, Biggar Papers, 4.4.19.
15  Yale University Library (YUL), Edward M. House Diary, entry 1.2.19.
16  Library of Congress, George Louis Beer Collection, 13.5.19.
17  Murray Donnelly, *Dafoe of the Free Press* (Toronto, 1968), 99.
18  W. Stewart Wallace, ed., *The Memoirs of the Rt. Hon. Sir George Foster* (Toronto, 1933), 199.
19  NAC, Foster Papers, vol. 106, Foster to his wife, 3.2.19.
20  NAC, Biggar Papers, vol. 2, letter of 1.2.19.
21  Robert Laird Borden, *Robert Laird Borden: His Memoirs*, Vol. 2, *1916–1920* (Toronto and Montreal, 1969), 186.
22  Donnelly, *Dafoe of the Free Press*, 93.
23  NAC, Foster Papers, vol. 106, Foster to his wife, 5.2.19.
24  Ibid., vol. 8, entry for 19.1.19.
25  Canada, Department of External Affairs, *Documents on Canadian External Relations* (DCER), Vol. 2, *The Paris Peace Conference of 1919*, 53–4.
26  NAC, Biggar Papers, vol. 2, letter to Mrs Biggar, 1.2.19.
27  Robert Bothwell, *Loring Christie: The Failure of Bureaucratic Imperialism* (New York, and London 1988), 77, 173, 193; Brown, *Robert Laird Borden*, 155–6.
28  United States, Department of State, *Papers Relating to the Foreign Relations of the United States 1919: The Paris Peace Conference* (FRUS), 13 vols (Washington, D.C., 1942–7), 3, 188–93, 196–7.

29  BL, Milner MS. Deposit, 383/1, Milner to Devonshire, 25.3.19.
30  NAC, Christie Papers, vol. 4, Christie to Rowell, 1.1.19.
31  NAC, Foster Papers, vol. 2, diary entries 31.10.18, 2.12.18; vol. 8, diary entry 22.1.19; Borden Papers, diary entries 2.12.18. Biggar Papers, vol. 2, letter to Mrs Biggar of 23.3.19.
32  Canada, *DCER*, vol. 2, 88, Borden to White, 14.3.19.
33  NAC, Borden Papers, diary entry 11.11.19.
34  NAC, Biggar Papers, vol. 2, letter to Mrs Biggar of 16.2.19.
35  HLRO, Lloyd George papers, F5/3/21, Borden to LLG, 20.3.19.
36  See C.P. Stacey, *Canada and the Age of Conflict*, Vol. 1, *1867–1921* (Toronto, 1984), 276–82, for a discussion of Canadian intervention in Russia.
37  David Lloyd George, *War Memoirs* (London, 1933–8), 4: 1,754; Canada, *DCER*, 2: 63.
38  YUL, House Diary, entry 5.2.19.
39  See Brown, *Robert Laird Borden*, 2: 155–6.
40  Canada, *DCER*, 2: 58, 58–63 passim, 73–87.
41  David Hunter Miller, 'The Making of the League,' in Edward Mandell House and Charles Seymour, eds, *What Really Happened at Paris* (New York, 1921), 411.
42  NAC, Christie Papers, vol. 3, file 6/7, Christie to Clement Jones, 16.9.20; see also Bothwell, *Loring Christie*, 181–99.
43  See Gérard Bouchard, *Genèse des nations et cultures du Nouveau Monde* (Montreal, 2000), passim and  24–5, 230–7, 314–20.
44  NAC, Foster Papers, vol. 2, 24.12.18; Dafoe Papers, Letters 1919, Dafoe to Sifton, 26.8.19.
45  Borden, *Memoirs*, 2: 166; NAC, Borden Papers diary entry  1.1.2.18.
46  Public Record Office (PRO), London, Cabinet Minutes 28/29, British Empire Delegation (BED), 11 (1.3.19); NAC, Borden Papers, vol. 431, Borden memorandum to British Empire delegation, 1.4.19.
47  PRO, BED, 26 (21.4.19).
48  Ibid., 3 (23.1.19).
49  NAC, Christie Papers, vol. 3, 6/7, Christie to George Wrong, 30.12.19.
50  HLRO, Lloyd George Papers, F/5/2/4, memorandum of 26.4.17.
51  Lloyd George, *War Memoirs*, 4: 1,764–5; Borden, *Memoirs*, 2: 668.
52  Stephen Roskill, *Hankey: Man of Secrets*, Vol. 2, *1919–1931* (London, 1972), 29.
53  Borden, *Memoirs*, 2: 158; United States, *FRUS*, 1: 347–8.
54  NAC, Borden Papers, diary entry. 4.12.18.
55  Roskill, *Hankey*, 29–30.
56  L.F. Fitzhardinge, 'Hughes, Borden, and Dominion Representation at the Paris Peace Conference,' *Canadian Historical Review* 49, 2 (June 1968), 163–5.

57  David Lloyd George, *The Truth about the Peace Treaties*, 2 vols (London, 1938), 1: 206–7.
58  NAC, Borden Papers, vol. 115, White to Borden, 7.12.18; summary of press opinion, 9.11.18.
59  Canada, *DCER*, 2: 7, White to Borden, 4.12.18.
60  BL, MS Milner. Deposit, 388, Report No.12 from French Ministry of Colonies, 29.5.18.
61  YUL, House Diary, entries 28. 10.18; 6.2.19.
62  United States, *FRUS*, 3: 567–8; Lloyd George, *Truth about the Peace Treaties*, 1: 215.
63  Canada, *DCER*, 2: 30–1.
64  NAC, Borden Papers, diary entries 18.1.19, 13.1.19.
65  Roskill, *Hankey*, 49.
66  NAC, Borden Papers, vol. 94, Borden to White 7.3.19; vol. 433/62, Borden to Cecil 18.4.19.
67  David Hunter Miller, *The Drafting of the Covenant*, 2 vols (New York, 1928), 1: 490; HLRO, Lloyd George Papers, F/5/5.
68  Canada, *DCER*, 2: 148–9.
69  PRO, BED, 10 (27.2.10); BED, 13 (13.3.19); see also Borden's memorandum of 12.5.19 in ibid., 156.
70  NAC, Borden Papers, diary entry, 23.1.19; vol. 166, Borden to Eyre Crowe, 14.2.19, 20.3.19.
71  Harold Nicolson, *Peacemaking 1919* (London, 1964), 259.
72  NAC, Foster Papers, vol. 58, Minutes of the Greek Commission.
73  See Hunter Miller, *Drafting*, 1: 53–4, 57, 478–81; W.J. Hudson, *Billy Hughes in Paris* (West Melbourne, Australia, 1978), 51–2; Borden, *Memoirs*, 2: 179–80; Canada, *DCER*, 2: 35, 42–3, 70.
74  PRO, BED, 29 (28.4.19).
75  Edward Mandell House, *The Intimate Papers of Colonel House Arranged as a Narrative by Charles Seymour*, 4 vols (Boston and New York, 1926–8), 4: 311.
76  Hunter Miller, *Drafting*, 1: 53–5, 57–8; 2: 255–60; G.P. deT. Glazebrook, *Canada at the Paris Peace Conference* (London, Toronto, New York, 1942), 63–7.
77  PRO, BED, 26 (21.4.19); 29 (28.4.19).
78  NAC, Sifton Papers, vol. 7, folder on Labour Legislation, memorandum of 29.4.19.
79  Hunter Miller, *Drafting*, 1: 478–81, 487–8.
80  See, for example, Borden, *Memoirs*, 2: 205–6; Canada, *DCER*, 2: 228.
81  PRO, BED, 30 (5.5.19).
82  Canada, *DCER*, 2: 149–50; United States, *FRUS*, 5: 477–8, 478, 489–90; Canada, *DCER*, 2: 231.

83 Canada, 'Memorandum with respect to further work of Peace Conference,' *DCER*, 2: 155–6.

84 Borden, *Memoirs*, 2: 187, 193; Glazebrook, *Canada at the Conference*, 108–9; see also Philip G. Wigley, *Canada and the transition to Commonwealth: British-Canadian Relations, 1917–1926* (Cambridge, 1977), 84–9.

85 Canada, *DCER* 2: 72–3, 87.

86 Wigley, *Canada and the Transition*, 88–9.

87 Canada, *DCER*, 2: 118.

88 NAC, Sifton Papers, vol. 1, Sifton to Dafoe, 11.4.19.

89 See the note in United States, *FRUS*, 13: 62.

90 Canada, *DCER*, 2: 165.

91 BL, Milner MS, Deposit 390. Balfour to Milner 23.7.19; Milner to Balfour 26.7.19.

92 Canada, *DCER*, 2: 168–72.

93 Copy in NAC, Borden Papers, vol. 115.

94 NAC, Christie Papers. vol. 3, Christie to Wrong, 30.12.19.

95 Canada, *DCER* 2: 228–9; NAC, Borden Papers. vol 94, Borden to Lloyd George, 5.5.19; Paul Mantoux, *The Deliberations of the Council of Four*, 2 vols, trans and ed. Arthur S. Link (Princeton, N.J., 1992), 1: 462–5.

96 Canada, *DCER* 2, 5; NAC, Borden Papers, vol. 93; Christie Papers, vol. 4/ file 13; Foster Papers, vol. 2, entries 14.11.18, 25.11.18.

97 NAC, Borden Papers, vol. 93, Borden to Balfour, 28.11.18.

98 Canada, *DCER*, 2: 200–1.

99 See, for example, NAC, Foster Papers, vol. 8, entries 29.1.19, 30.1.19, 6.2.19, 7.2.19, 11.2.19, 4.3.19, 18.3.19; vol. 7. entry 5.11.18; vol. 8, entry 20.3.19.

100 NAC, Sifton papers, vol. 2, Sifton to Senator G.D. Robertson, 4. 6.19; vol. 1, memorandum of 14.4.19.

101 Canada, *DCER*, 2: 137–8, 143–4; NAC, Sifton Papers, vol. 7, folder Labour Legislation, Sifton to Borden, 5.5.19.

102 PRO, BED, 20 (13.4.19), 21 (14.4.19).

103 Canada, *DCER*, 2: 152–3, 232, 170–1 and fn 1, 185.

104 NAC, Borden Papers, vol. 444, Privy Council memorandum of 18.2.18; vol. 116. Crowe to Borden, 7.3.19, 1.4.19; vol. 159, Crowe to Borden, 23.5.18; vol. 116, Perry to Borden, 13.11.18; Borden to Perry 4.12.18.

105 Lloyd George, *Truth about the Peace Treaties*, 1: 554.

106 BL, additional Milner Papers. holograph note on Borden to Milner 16.5.19.

107 See, for example, Beer, entries 15.1.19 and 7.4.19; NAC, Christie Papers, vol. 7, file 20, memorandum of 15.1.19; Milner to Borden, 7.5.19.

108 BL, additional Milner Papers Borden to Milner 29.4.19; NAC, Borden Papers, diary entry 6.2.19.

109 Lloyd George, *War Memoirs*, 4: 1754.

110 HLRO, Lloyd George Papers, F/5/2/28, Borden to Lloyd George, 23.11.18.

111 See, for example, Borden's explanation of the Monroe Doctrine in PRO, BED, 27 (21.4.19).

112 NAC, Borden Papers, vol. 94, Borden to Lloyd George, 27.3.19.

113 YUL, Sir William Wiseman Papers, Series I, Box 7, Peace Conference Diary, 17.1.19, 21.1.19.

114 NAC, Borden Papers, diary entry 22.1.19.

115 Canada, *DCER*, 2: 130–1; Seth P. Tillman, *Anglo-American Relations at the Paris Peace Conference of 1919* (Princeton, N.J., 1961), 308–9.

116 YUL, House Diary entry 4.3.19.

117 PRO, BED, 19A (11.4.19, 9 a.m.).

118 Borden, *Memoirs*, 2: 197–8; PRO, BED 29 (28.4.19).

119 PRO, BED, 18 (8.4.19); Borden, *Memoirs*, 2: 197.

120 Borden, *Memoirs*, 2: 202; Shotwell, *Paris Peace Conference*, 295.

121 William Roger Louis, *Great Britain and Germany's Lost Colonies, 1914–1919* (Oxford, 1967), 7– 9.

122 Lloyd George, *Truth about the Peace Treaties*, 1: 116–17, 201; NAC, Foster Papers, vol. 7, 15.6.18, 11.7.18; Biggar Papers, vol. 2, 1.2.19; Borden Papers, diary entries 30.12.18, 11.1.19, 1.2.19; YUL, House Diary, entry 1.2.19.

123 United States, *FRUS*, 3: 718–28.

124 Woodrow Wilson, *The Papers of Woodrow Wilson*, 69 vols, ed. Arthur S. Link (Princeton, N.J., 1966–), 54, 308.

125 Borden, *Memoirs*, Vol. 2, 908; Robert Garran, *Prosper the Commonwealth* (Sydney, Australia, 1958), 265.

126 YUL, House Diary, entry 1.2.19; NAC, Borden Papers, diary entry 1.2.19.

127 Borden, *Memoirs*, 2: 195.

128 NAC, Borden Papers, diary entry 31.3.19.

129 Canada, *DCER*, 2: 104–5.

130 NAC, Borden Papers, diary entry 9.4.19, 10.4.19; Borden, *Memoirs*, 2: 195–6; Canada, *DCER*, 2: 216.

131 NAC, Borden Papers, diary entry 13.5.19.

132 NAC, 'Notes on the Development at the Paris Peace Conference of the Status of Canada as an International Person,' Borden Papers, vol. 115/6; Clement Jones, 'The Dominions and the Peace Conference. A New Page in Constitutional History,' 211, copy in Christie Papers. vol. 7, file 21.

133 NAC, Sifton papers, vol. 2, Sifton to Senator G.D. Robertson, 4. 6.19.

134 NAC, 'Notes on the Development at the Paris Peace Conference of the Status of Canada as an International Person,' Borden papers, vol. 115/6.
135 Bothwell, *Loring Christie*, 295.
136 Hunter-Miller, *Drafting*, 1: 489.
137 Stacey, *Canada and the Age of Conflict*, 311–17.

# 15 Remembering Armageddon

JONATHAN F. VANCE

It was 2 June 1919. The armistice had been concluded barely six months earlier; the peace treaty to end the Great War had not yet been signed. But on that sunny summer day, the people of Binscarth, Manitoba, came together to honour the eighteen men and one woman from the area who had given their lives in the war. They had chosen that day because on the first weekend in June 1916 the village had lost five of its young men, all killed in the bitter fighting around Sanctuary Wood. Three years later, they congregated before their memorial, a soldier standing at attention, carved from white Italian marble and placed on a plinth of red granite. It had cost $1,625.00 to erect, all of it raised through local subscription. The plot of land and the spruce trees that adorned it had been donated by townspeople; the metal ornamental fence was also a donation, crafted by a local veteran and blacksmith. The memorial was truly a community effort, motivated by the sorrow of a village.

Four years later, in August 1923, the citizens of Elmira, Ontario, gathered for a similar ceremony. The occasion this time was the Old Boys' and Girls' Reunion, held to celebrate the incorporation of the town and to mark the ninth anniversary of the beginning of the war. Linking the two events, and forming the centrepiece of the weekend's activities, was the unveiling of the war memorial erected by the citizens of Elmira and Woolwich Township. The Union Jack fluttered down to reveal another white marble soldier, virtually identical to the one in Binscarth. Below it were the names of fifteen local men who had given their lives in the Great War.

On a cool Sunday afternoon in September 1927 the ceremony was re-enacted at Arcola, near the Moose Mountains in southeastern

Saskatchewan. Some 1,500 people, better than twice the town's population, clustered around a small patch of grass off the main street; to one
side, aligned in neat ranks, stood nearly sixty local veterans. With the
Estevan Brass Band providing musical accompaniment, the province's
lieutenant-governor, Henry W. Newlands, drew the flag to reveal the
same white marble statue of a soldier standing at attention. Beneath the
figure, a plaque listed the names of twenty-three local men (including
two pairs of brothers) who had died during the war. Newlands
complimented the townspeople for keeping alive the memory of these
'dead war heroes with such a splendid monument' and then invited the
mayor, W.F. Youngblud, to accept the memorial on behalf of the citizens
of Arcola.[1]

Three towns, three virtually identical memorials – a citizen of Elmira
would not have felt out of place at Arcola's unveiling, while a farmer
from Binscarth might have experienced a welcome sense of familiarity
before Elmira's monument. Had these people travelled farther afield,
they would have recognized their own memorials in dozens of towns
across the country – Dorchester, New Brunswick; Huntingdon, Quebec;
Burks Falls, Ontario; Gladstone, Manitoba; Lunenberg, Nova Scotia, to
name but a few – and might have been comforted by a feeling of
community with other Canadians. For the standard monument served
a dual purpose. On the one hand, a mass-marketed marble soldier
could express local distinctiveness and individuality; the placement of
the monument in the town, the names on its pedestal, the inscription
selected all identified it as belonging uniquely to one community. But at
the same time, as Daniel Sherman tells us, the choice of a standard
figure allowed people to situate 'a sense of loss they shared with the
whole nation in the particular context of their own community.'[2] The
soldier could represent any of the local boys listed on the plinth (or
even, in Binscarth's case, Nursing Sister Margaret Lowe), but his uniform identified him as a member of Canada's national army, and his
similarity to other memorials across the country affirmed that the town
shared at least one common experience with a larger collectivity: death
in war.

This sense of personal grief was the most significant common de-
nominator linking the war memorials at Binscarth, Elmira, and Arcola.
Indeed, that single experience, the death of a loved one, came to under-
pin Canada's memory of the war, giving it a very specific character.
Certainly the memory reflected a desire to understand the war on a
rational level, to come to terms with its impact on Canada's economy,

politics, society, and culture. But perhaps more important, the memory sought to convey meaning on a less rational level; in short, it endeavoured to provide consolation. Never before had so many Canadians died violently in such a short period of time; never before had so many families shared the tragedy of losing two, three, four, or more relatives in quick succession. Death and mourning cast a darker shadow over post-1914 Canada than it had at any other time. What could assuage the grief? For many Canadians, the answer was expressed in the nation's collective memory of the war. They believed passionately that the fallen had died to save Christianity and western civilization from another dark age, and that the men and women who answered the country's call were ennobled by the experience. At the same time, the nation itself was raised to a higher level of existence because of its sacrifice in Flanders. Whether these assumptions would stand up in the cold light of critical enquiry was irrelevant. For that generation, at that time, the belief that their loss had meaning and purpose enabled them to cope with grief.

Because the human toll of the First World War, 60,000 dead and 140,000 wounded, was so catastrophic, it is easy to forget that Canadian society was not unfamiliar with the phenomenon of sudden, mass death before 1914.[3] Despite Victorian notions of progress and the overweening optimism of the Edwardian era, life in the early twentieth century remained nasty, brutish, and short for parts of the population. Little thought was given to safety in the workplace, and Canada's factories took a steady toll of lives. Vessels frequently disappeared off Canada's coasts, each taking with it a few men at a time. Even more dangerous were the nation's mines, which were hit by a series of disasters in the decades before the First World War. In 1891 a coal dust explosion ripped through a mine in Springhill, Nova Scotia, killing 125 men. It is not insignificant that the miners' memorial in Springhill stands near the memorial to the dead of the First World War; Springhill, like many other Canadian communities, clearly had far too much experience mourning the sudden death of young men before 1914.

Just as tragic were the disasters that killed less selectively. Man-made disasters, such as the streetcar accident in Victoria that left fifty-five people dead in 1896 or the 1910 train derailment in Sudbury that claimed forty-three lives, along with natural disasters, such as the July 1911 fire that killed seventy-three people in Porcupine, Ontario, or the June 1912 tornado that took forty-one lives in Regina, ensured that mass death was never very far from the minds of Canadians. The fact was deeply impressed on Haligonians in April 1912, when their city became a de facto morgue for the victims of the *Titanic's* sinking. Just months before the beginning of the war came an even bigger tragedy, at least as far as Canadians were concerned: the sinking of the *Empress of Ireland* in the Gulf of St Lawrence, with a toll of 1,012 lives.

Disease, too, remained a potent killer. The generation whose sons and daughters went to war in 1914 had seen cities ravaged by epidemic diseases, like the 1885 Montreal smallpox epidemic that killed as many as 5,800 people. Even into the twentieth century, the burgeoning urban centres were plagued by such intractable social problems that the threats to life were actually increasing for certain parts of the population. Between 1900 and 1914, for example, the mortality rate in urban Ontario climbed steadily.[4] But the available statistics are far from conclusive; short-term spikes in the death rate must be balanced against a long-term decline. Furthermore, one should not read too much into such statistics: as George Emery has shown, they are subject to a degree of social construction.[5] David Cannadine has suggested that those whose children came of age during the First World War were the first generation who could reasonably expect their children to outlive them. To have this comforting certitude wrenched away from them during the Great War was therefore a more profound shock than it might otherwise have been.[6] Historians of revolutions tell us that social upheavals are most likely to occur when a population's rising expectations are not met. Cannadine persuasively implies that the same notion can be fruitfully applied to the First World War: the impact of children's deaths on parents was especially profound because it was precisely the opposite of what they had come to expect.

By the same token, the natural or man-made disasters of the pre-war era had a limited impact on the public consciousness because they were infrequent and tended to be localized. The destruction of the town of Frank, Alberta, by a rockslide in 1903 certainly moved Canadians deeply, but their sympathy was detached because for most the experience was so far removed from their own. Death in the First World War was of a very different order. On any given day, dozens and perhaps hundreds of households might receive the fateful telegram that bore the news dreaded by all. The war was no respecter of class, or region, or religion, and the constancy of death may well have imparted an odd sort of unity to Canadian society as so many people tried to come to terms with the same experience. David Cannadine has argued that post-war society became a 'cult of the dead'; at the very least, we must admit that the losses of 1914–18 constituted a profound psychic shock, and made mourning an almost universal condition.

In conceptualizing the nature of that mourning, it is essential to understand its context. Two approaches have dominated the historiography: one looks back at the First World War from the modern age, seeing in it the roots of modernist idioms, cultural forms, and modes of expression; the other looks forward to the war from the Victorian age, emphasizing the persistence of nineteenth-century traditions, values, and sensibilities. This debate has produced an immense literature that has most recently leaned towards situating the war at the end of the age that preceded it rather than at the beginning of the age that followed it.

Certainly with respect to the nature of death and mourning, it is more helpful to place the Great War within the context of Victorian attitudes. David Marshall has shown that perceptions of death underwent a fundamental transformation in Canada through the nineteenth century. In the first half of the 1800s death was something to be feared and loathed; clerics preached a message of divine judgment and eternal damnation and urged the unrepentant to mend their ways before death overtook them. As the decades passed, however, this message began to change, as clerics realized that it offered little comfort to grieving relatives. In its stead, an avowedly consolatory image of death emerged. Death became a beautiful event, a passage from a life of strife to one of peace, happiness, and tranquility. It was not an end but a beginning, a new departure that should be welcomed by the moribund and celebrated by the survivors. As Marshall argues persuasively, the public demanded consolation, and this new vision of death provided it.[7]

Faced with loss on an unprecedented scale during the First World War, Canadians embraced this consolatory image of death. To use Marshall's phrase, they continued to draw the sting from death by affirming that their loved ones had died for a reason. The scale, hideousness, and apparent pointlessness of death in the Great War might seem to militate against such a response, but for many Canadians, the circumstances of the war in fact offered considerable scope for consolation. Victorians had coped with grief by believing that the dead had gone to a better place; the bereaved of 1914–18 could comfort themselves in the belief that their loved ones had died to defend western civilization and Christianity and to found a new nation from the ashes of war.

When news of the Armistice reached Canada on 11 November 1918, the first impulse of many Canadians was to celebrate. For almost four years, they had lived in the pressure-cooker of war. The stakes had been enormous: right must triumph, or the world would be plunged into another dark age of German *Kultur* and *Schrecklichkeit* (frightfulness), when Christianity, freedom, and justice would be banished from the earth. Also, there had often been cause for pessimism. Some people may have harboured secret doubts over the winter of 1917–18, when the triumph of the Allied armies seemed far from assured; others may have experienced a crisis of faith in March 1918, when Offensive Michael brought the German armies closer to victory than they had been at any time since 1914. The Armistice, however, restored that faith. Canadians could now see the defeat of the Central Powers as an affirmation. God *had* fought on the Allied side to preserve Christianity and western civilization from oblivion; the victorious conclusion of the war was proof. So, after the street parties, bonfires, and parades were over, Canadians heeded their second impulse and expressed their gratitude. Amateur poets across the country earnestly took up their pens to give thanks to God for the nation's deliverance. It seemed only fitting to offer up prayers on that momentous occasion; for, as Montreal poet C.L. de Roode proclaimed in his Armistice Day poem, 'Cette victoire, c'est la victoire de Dieu!'[8] The poet and tireless self-promoter Wilson MacDonald concurred, reminding readers of the proper course of action once the merry-making had subsided: 'Let us pour out our thanks in praise to Him / Who gave the peace we know.'[9] Many Canadians took MacDonald's advice to heart and congregated in chapel, church, or cathedral to join together in prayer, at least in those cities where the raging influenza epidemic had not brought a ban on public gatherings. For Canadians who were prevented from worshipping together, newspapers obligingly printed the texts of sermons from clergymen across the country. One way or another, people found a way to express their gratitude for the divine assistance that had brought the victory in a just war.

Validated in battle and sanctified by the church services of November 1918, this interpretation could now form the foundation of Canada's collective memory of the war. Despite any post-war concerns about petty national or political motivations behind the war, it affirmed that the very survival of western civilization had been at stake. L.M. Montgomery's characterization of the war as a 'death-grapple between freedom and tyranny, between modern and medieval ideals ... between the principles of democracy and militarism'[10] lost none of its resonance in the post-war years; it remained the norm to interpret the war as a

Warriors' Day Parade, 1920, CNE. Each day at the CNE was designated for special activities, and after the First World War, the first day was declared Warriors' Day. (City of Toronto Archives, Fonds 1244, Item 727)

struggle to save Europe from another dark age. Tales of German atrocities retained their appeal in post-war Canada (Claudius Courneloup, a veteran of the 22nd Battalion, was not alone in continuing to insist that he had joined up 'pour la sainte défense des veuves, des opprimes et des orphelins'[11]), and continued to be held up as justification for the nation's involvement. All of the values that Allied propaganda had emphasized during the war remained sacrosanct in Canada's collective memory afterwards – freedom, liberty, justice, democracy, truth, humanity. They could be found on war memorials, in school textbooks, in vaudeville songs, in poems and novels, and even in advertising, offering constant correctives to the few voices that deigned to suggest that the war had been fought for narrow political or economic motives.

Nevertheless, in 1926 Sir Arthur Currie, the former commander of the Canadian Corps, began to wonder if the 'just war' thesis was becoming stale. In his capacity as adviser to the Canadian Battlefield Memorials Commission, he vetted the inscriptions that would appear on Canada's official memorials in France and Belgium and expressed concern that they might record that the war had been fought, not 'for civilization' (which carried with it connotations of a noble and timeless struggle), but for 'the Allied cause' (which suggested short-term and perhaps tawdry political objectives). 'Is it possible,' he enquired of Colonel H.C. Osborne, the secretary-general of the Canadian agency of the Imperial War Graves Commission, 'that the presence of Miss Agnes Macphail at Ottawa makes you wish to eliminate from your monument any reference to fighting, or would such a reference be held to be at variance with the sentiments of Locarno?' Osborne's reply was mollifying: 'The idea that the Delilah of the House of Commons is cutting all our locks and taking the fight out of us is fine. However, it isn't true.'[12] What he might have said was that, in the collective memory of the war, Currie's concern was largely irrelevant; most Canadians would have accepted 'civilization' as a synonym for 'the Allied cause.'

The other synonym for 'the Allied cause' was, of course, 'right,' and this notion elevated the war above secular concerns such as democracy and freedom and into the spiritual realm. Not only did the collective memory interpret the war as a 'death-grapple' between civilization and barbarism; it was also another episode in the eternal struggle between right and wrong. 'Braves fils canadiens de Gaule et d'Albion,' wrote Quebec poet Alonzo Cinq-Mars. 'Vous aviez accepté la noble mission / De défendre le Droit contre la Barbarie.'[13] With similar rhetoric, the Brantford *Expositor* used the unveiling of the city's war memorial to remind its readers that 'the men of the Empire enrolled under the glorious banner of "God and My Right," for the most righteous crusade in the history of mankind.'[14]

Perhaps the clearest expression of this interpretation of the war is the prevalence of the St George and the dragon motif in Canada's collective memory.[15] Popular during the war with British and German propagandists alike, this centuries-old icon became a sort of visual shorthand for the meaning of the struggle: in spite of the modern weaponry and mass tactics, the Great War was like a medieval morality tale in which the good and virtuous knight triumphed over the forces of darkness, simply because his cause was just. The St George and the dragon motif was particularly suitable for use in war memorials, which sought to convey the strongest possible message with the simplest symbolism. For example, Percy Nobbs used it as the centrepiece of a memorial window to twenty-three members of the Delta Upsilon fraternity in Montreal who died during the war, and the figure of St George also graces the war memorial window in St Thomas's Church in Toronto. In the Peace

Tower in Ottawa, he can be seen in the central window of the memorial chamber as well as on the 1915 title page of the Book of Remembrance. In each case, the motif's impact lies in the fact that its meaning would have been so widely understood.

Given that the Allies represented the forces of good, it was axiomatic that Canada's soldiers were fighting with divine sanction and even with divine assistance. This notion is explicit in many Canadian war memorials, like the one in Quyon, Quebec, which declares that 'God gave the victory.' According to the *Ontario Reformer*, because of its tripartite construction the Whitby monument was 'in keeping with the great Three in One by whose aid we have been able to overcome these trials.'[16] The memorial inscription in Douglas, Manitoba, went a step further, placing God alongside Canadian infantrymen at the front:

They died unnoticed in the muddy trench,
Nay! God was with them, and they did not blench,
Filled them with holy fires that naught could quench
And when he saw their work on earth was done
    He gently called to them
    My sons, my sons.

On a slightly different level is the continuing resonance in post-war Canada of battlefield tales of visions or apparitions. Typically, they were based on purportedly eyewitness accounts by soldiers who had seen visions, most frequently of Jesus Christ (sometimes referred to as the White Comrade), angels, St George, or an army of medieval archers, which had comforted them and motivated them to fight on when their spirits were waning. In 'The White Comrade,' Katherine Hale tells of a glowing figure who visits desperately wounded soldiers on the battle-field as their spirits are ebbing. Any suggestion that the tale was fanciful was, in her view, absurd: 'You know the angels that appeared at Mons! / Many have seen bright angels in the field.'[17] Francis Cecil Whitehouse's poem 'The Archers of Mons' finds British soldiers in a desperate posi-tion, about to be overrun by German hordes; they are in danger of losing not only the battle, but their faith: '"There is no God!" they cry, and bite their lips, / "There is, indeed, no God!"' Suddenly, an army of ghostly bowmen appears in front of them, giving them the heart and strength to fight on: 'a Heavenly Guard, / Or old Crusaders sent once more to Earth / For His good purposes! / *They* – were the Will of God!'[18] For Whitehouse, whether or not this incident actually occurred was probably irrelevant. It was simply a literary device to verify what many Canadians knew to be true: that divine intervention had enabled Allied soldiers to triumph because their cause was just.

Many Canadians went a step further, however, by averring that, because Allied soldiers fought in defence of all that was good and right, they shared in a community of sacrifice with Jesus Christ. In this discourse, the comparison between the fallen soldier and Christ was made so direct and explicit that the distinction between the two became blurred. Canada's fallen soldiers were not simply labourers, clerks, and farmers who had died in battle; according to ex-soldier A.E. Johnson, they were 'joint heirs with Christ because they bled to save / His loved ones.'[19] When Ottawa journalist Grattan O'Leary observed in 1931 that Canada's soldiers had died 'for a free earth and as a ransom for mankind,' he placed their sacrifice on a par with 'One who gave His life as a ransom for many.' It was precisely the same metaphor that Mackenzie King had used eight years earlier, when he drew a parallel between the losses of the Great War and 'the tragedy of 1900 years ago, when the best life which the world has ever known was sacrificed.'[20] Writers and speakers extended the metaphor by comparing individual soldiers to Christ as a rhetorical technique to demonstrate their sterling qualities. McGill University professor John Macnaughton characterized as a kind of Christ Guy Drummond, the son of a wealthy and influential Montreal couple who was killed in action at the Second Battle of Ypres. Barry Dunbar, the protagonist of Ralph Connor's *Sky Pilot in No Man's Land*, saw the doomed and selfless Corporal Thom as 'just a common man, but uncommonly like God.'[21] In dedicating the memorial to George Baker, Canada's only member of Parliament to be killed in action, Mackenzie King asked listeners to ponder 'the God-like greatness of the human spirit' that found expression in Baker's life and death.[22] No matter how it was used, the message was the same: the Great War had brought forth a new generation of saviours.

Here, the collective memory of the war implicitly accepted the transformative power of war. Not all Canadians of the Edwardian era had the potential to reveal 'God-like greatness.' It took the test of battle to sort out the wheat from the chaff, to determine who was wanting in character and who would join, as King put it, 'that great company of the defenders of the right, the great Christian warriors of history.'[23] It went without saying that the fallen had passed the test; merely by dying they had proved their mettle and elevated themselves to saviour status. But survivors, too, could share in the curative power of war. They would never attain the stature of the dead, but they could demonstrate a magnitude of spirit that would forever set them apart. Furthermore, past conduct was not necessarily an indication of true character, and the memory of the war was careful to stress that saviours were found in the most unlikely places. 'There is many a man who came over in the first place a tough nut,' Lieutenant Colonel D.H.C. Mason told the Canadian Club of Toronto, 'who kicked around the world and fought his own way, who has learned that there is something bigger than that to fight for.'[24] Clarence Basil Lumsden, a Military Medal winner of the 25th Battalion, described one of those tough nuts in a short story entitled 'Two Men.' One was a pious, dutiful fellow who utterly failed the test of battle. The other was a hell-raiser who drank and swore too much; in the heat of battle, he redeemed his past ills and covered himself with glory by rescuing a wounded comrade.[25]

For such men, the war was a refining fire that 'revealed the pure gold' of Canadians,[26] and indeed this became the most popular metaphor to describe the experience of battle. Soldiers, 'like crude ore, went through the fire, and came out pure metal,' observed one memorial booklet; all that remained were the finest qualities.[27] The theme was implicit in the memorial cross in Mahone Bay, Nova Scotia. The dedication program echoed the press account of the Nova Scotia Highland brigade by informing spectators that the rough-hewn base recalled the province's rough and hardy sons, while the polished stone of remembrance suggested how 'the infallible human spirit was fashioned into heroism amid the fires of war.'[28]

Of course, war could work the same transformation on the nation that it worked on its citizens; the nation, too, could emerge from the crucible of war in finer form, in a process that was cast in the language of Christian salvation. In the imagery of a 1919 Victory Loan brochure, the war had been Canada's agony of the cross; emerging in November 1918, the nation had reached the resurrection morning. 'My Canada,' wrote the poet A.M. Stephen, was 'formed from the chastening soil of fire and tears / On Europe's battle mounds, of iron and flame.'[29] As Stephen's lines suggest, place came to have immense significance in this discourse, and the names with which Canadians had become so familiar during the war came to be endowed with immense symbolic importance afterwards. Valcartier, where the First Contingent had assembled before sailing for Europe, was transformed into 'the cradle of our national life.' Vimy Ridge was referred to as the nation's Golgotha, because it was the site of the 'sacrificial death' of so many of Canada's young men. Flanders, proclaimed John Macnaughton, was 'at once a Bethlehem and a Calvary,' because it was the site of Canada's martyrdom and its birth. Ypres became 'that place where Canada's soul, newfound, was born again.'[30] The transformation of these geographic locations into sites redolent with spiritual and moral significance was representative of Canada's entire collective memory of the war. All of the negative connotations of these places – the muddle of Valcartier, the hell of Ypres, the sucking mud of Flanders – could be effaced in favour of a positive, uplifting interpretation. The specifics of what had actually occurred during the Great War became less important than the symbolic meaning with which the conflict was endowed.

On one level, this entire process might suggest the invisible hand of elite manipulation in Canada's war memory. It might be argued that defending western civilization and Christianity was nothing more than defending the status quo, while the ideology of war as a transformative force, on either the individual or the national level, was a thinly veiled attempt to convince people to subordinate their own interests to those of the social and political elites. The fact that the entire memory played on emotion rather than rationality might make it seem even more sinister. But ironically, this is the very reason why it is so profoundly unsatisfying to see the collective memory simply as a product of elite manipulation. It assumes that the just war thesis, the defence of Christianity, or the creation of a new nation were ends in themselves. On the contrary, in the minds of Canadians who created and nourished the collective memory of the war, they were only means to a very different end: consolation, the same goal that had underpinned the response to death since the mid-Victorian era. Grief, not western civilization, Christianity, or the new nation, was the foundation of Canada's memory of the war.

The centrality of grief and consolation is clear in what were perhaps the most visible manifestations of the war memory in the interwar years: the proliferation of war memorials and the observance of Armistice (later Remembrance) Day. It is tempting to see these demonstrations as political, and there is no question that they were deeply contested: local elites squared off against each other over the design and location of war memorials; arts organizations attempted to exert centralized control over commemoration; lobby groups battled over the most fitting way to mark the annual observance of the war's end; and pacifist organizations derided both war memorials and Armistice Day as dangerous manifestations of militarism. But underlying these disputes was mutual agreement on their significance; regardless of how much bickering went on over commemorative practices, both sides of the debate accepted without question that such practices were central to the emotional response to the war. To borrow a phrase from American historian James Mayo, commemoration might be seen as a political landscape, but it was first and foremost a landscape of consolation.[31]

Canadians were no strangers to war memorials, and monuments from earlier conflicts dotted the country. The War of 1812 was commemorated most famously by the Brock Monument, which towered some 180 feet over Queenston Heights in the Niagara Peninsula. Less well known is the column erected in Allan's Corners, Quebec, where Lieutenant Colonel Charles de Salaberry and a small force of regular soldiers, militiamen, and Abenaki warriors routed an American invasion force at the Battle of Châteauguay in 1813. The old St Paul's Cemetery in Halifax was graced by Canada's finest memorial to the Crimean War, a massive stone arch erected in 1860 in memory of two local boys who died while in British service; parks in various other Canadian cities were adorned with cannons captured from Russian artillery units in the Crimea. The battles for New France, the rebellions of 1837–8, the Fenian Raids, and the rebellions of 1870 and 1885 each yielded a handful of memorials, but it was the South African War of 1899–1902 that produced the most concentrated burst of memorialization the country had yet seen. In a little over a decade, a rush of patriotic fervour and gratitude produced a wide variety of monuments across the country, from the splendid mounted horseman in Calgary to a more modest tribute to local soldier Corporal W.A. Knisley erected by the townspeople of Cayuga, Ontario.[32] Indeed, Knisley's memorial bears more than a passing mention; for it marked a shift in memorialization away from great captains. Knisley's only claim to fame was dying in the service of his country, but in the years following the First World War, that sacrifice would be what counted.

Taken together, these conflicts produced only a few dozen memorials, and it was evident very early in the Great War that commemoration would soon be taken to a whole new level. In 1915 A.Y. Jackson gloomily mused that before too many years had passed monuments to the war would 'disfigure every town and village in the country.'[33] Later writers have been equally dismissive of efforts at memorialization. James Stevens Curl had high praise for some of the Great War memorials, but lamented that the typical post-1945 monument would 'cause even the strongest to quail at the triviality of its mediocre language ...

Unveiling of the war memorial at Harbord Collegiate, Toronto, ca. 1920 (City of Toronto Archives, Fonds 1244, Item 978)

The terrors of death are made more terrible by the insults of present-day designs for funerary memorials.'[34] However, to judge memorials on aesthetic grounds was mistaken. Certainly every community wanted a memorial that was attractive, but aesthetic considerations were important only up to a point. What mattered for most communities was that the memorial spoke to the grieving heart, not to the discerning eye.

In this regard, it is important to understand the role of the memorial in the mourning process. Because of the nature and scale of the war, most Canadian families had no grave they could conveniently grieve at and so were denied access to an important source of consolation.[35] The Imperial War Graves Commission, established in 1917 to administer the burial of the British Empire's 1 million dead, steadfastly refused to allow the repatriation of bodies. Canadians who died in England while on active service could be brought home for burial (in the end, only about 5 per cent of the nation's war dead were buried in Canada); all others had to remain in IWGC-maintained cemeteries near the old battlefields. By the early 1920s most of the cemeteries were open to visitors, but cheap excursions organized by British and French tour companies were of little help to Canadians who had neither the time nor the money to undertake a costly and protracted transatlantic voyage. There were organized pilgrimages, and low-income Canadians could apply for subsidies to join the 1936 pilgrimage for the unveiling of the Vimy Memorial, but Canada had no program comparable to an American plan, which provided one free trip for a family to visit the grave of a relative in Europe.[36] For most Canadians the journey to a loved one's grave was simply not possible. Furthermore, since thousands of Canadian soldiers were listed as missing in action with no known burial place, many Canadians had no grave to mourn at.

For countless Canadians, the local war memorial came to fill that void; it provided a site for mourning to people who had no other site. The word cenotaph, after all, is derived from the Greek words meaning empty tomb, and many memorials, such as those in Bolton, Ontario, and Fredericton, New Brunswick, used a tomb shape to underline the meaning. Furthermore, much of the discussion surrounding the process of memorialization took as its starting point the notion that the community was erecting, not a piece of art to which aesthetic principles applied, but a substitute grave. For this reason, memorial committees often took great pains to solicit the opinions of grieving family members and to accord the greatest weight to their opinions. The memorial committee in Rimouski, Quebec, proclaimed proudly that the families of local soldiers had been well represented in their deliberations. In Kitchener, Ontario, a group of soldiers' mothers strongly opposed plans to erect a memorial carillon, insisting that bells did not constitute a fitting memorial. Despite some grumbling that they should not rule the process, the mothers prevailed and the carillon idea was dropped. When Winnipeg's committee rejected a memorial design submitted by Elizabeth Wyn Wood, the committee chair, R.D. Waugh, rationalized the decision on similar grounds, observing that the design 'did not convey to the relatives of our boys and girls who made the supreme sacrifice, that indescribable feeling of grief, pride and gratitude which only those who have suffered can understand ... [it] made no appeal whatever to the bereaved relatives, and therefore, was a complete failure as a suitable memorial.'[37]

A suitable memorial, in Waugh's view, was one that spoke directly to grieving family members, who would use the monument as the substitute for a grave they might never see. For this reason, many communities decided that their memorials should be dedicated, not to all who had served, but only to those who had died. In Guysborough, Nova Scotia, for example, the public notice announcing a fund-raising campaign stated that only the names of the dead would be inscribed on the monument; local veterans had to make do with being listed on a roll in the court house.[38] Even the most inclusive memorials established a hierarchy; pride of place went to the names of the fallen, with the names of returned soldiers being squeezed in on the sides or rear of the plinth.

Nowhere were these matters more hotly debated than in Toronto. As it was originally erected, the cenotaph paid tribute to all who had served, whether or not they had made the supreme sacrifice, but in 1925 the city's Board of Control circulated an enquiry to local veterans' organizations to determine if the inscription should be changed, to refer only to those who had died. Veterans' organizations, local militia units, and women's groups expressed wholehearted support for the proposed change, and in November 1925 the city council decided to alter the inscription.[39] The decision, however, did not go unchallenged. *Saturday Night* noted that 'the prevailing sentiment among objectors to the inscription ... seems to be that only those who fell in battle deserve commemoration and that they were necessarily more brave and self-sacrificing than those who survived.' This was nonsense, declared the editor, for every day a veteran died from wounds or illness sustained during service. 'Do they merit no memorial?' he queried. 'To think so is to yield to that false sentimentality which makes a fetish of death.'[40] Despite such objections, the fetish of death won out. Toronto's cenotaph is still inscribed 'To Our Glorious Dead.'

The same consideration was also behind the decision, taken by most smaller Canadian communities, that the memorial must list the names of the fallen. Obviously, this practice served a variety of purposes. The listing of names was a means to ensure the preservation of the memory of the fallen; if they were recorded in stone, they could not be forgotten. It would also bear witness to a community's contribution; the number of names on a memorial was a quick and easy way to determine if that town had acquitted itself well in the nation's time of need. But on another level, the names were essential because the memorial was to serve as a substitute grave; they allowed grieving relatives to make the direct link between the monument and the fallen who meant so much to them.

This conclusion is strengthened by the rituals connected with memorials, which mimicked those commonly associated with burial sites. It was customary to assert that memorials sat on hallowed or consecrated ground, adjectives that were typically applied to cemeteries. A speaker at the unveiling of the memorial in Yarmouth, Nova Scotia, for example, referred to it as a shrine. Relatives of the fallen were also accorded special privileges in unveiling ceremonies, just like the next of kin at a graveside service. They frequently occupied the best seating areas, and in many cases a relative was invited to perform the official unveiling. Usually, the local committee chose a mother, or occasionally a sister – fathers were only rarely called upon to perform unveilings.

Finally, it was not unusual to see memorials bedecked with floral tributes, often wreaths or flower arrangements of the same sort that would be left on a grave. Indeed, many communities observed Decoration Day, an American occasion dating from the U.S. Civil War, which involved the ritual placing of flowers on the graves of local heroes. In the early 1920s Decoration Day (observed on the Victoria Day weekend) was a significant event in the calendar of many communities, and large and impressive ceremonies were held in cities such as Montreal and Vancouver, usually organized by the Last Post Fund, the Great War Veterans Association, and the Imperial Order Daughters of the Empire (IODE).[41] A number of community groups and municipal organizations even suggested that the federal government institutionalize the ritual by formally proclaiming Decoration Day a statutory holiday.[42] This action was never taken, so Decoration Day remained the preserve of local groups like the James Baby Chapter of the IODE, which took it upon itself to decorate the graves of local heroes around Windsor, Ontario.[43] Perhaps ironically, the practice was also adopted by anti-war organizations. In Toronto in 1930, while thousands of people paid tribute to the fallen at the cenotaph, a small group of pacifists laid flowers on the graves of nurses, firefighters, policemen, and other 'heroes of peace.'[44]

However, it was on Armistice Day, much more than Decoration Day, when the local cenotaph was most important; if the local war memorial was a grave, then Armistice Day was a funeral. Just as most Canadians were prevented from seeking consolation at a grave, the vast majority of them had been denied the healing that went with a funeral; Armistice Day was a stand-in, allowing them to act one out every year. It was a time when Canadians from across the country would stop their daily labours, come together, and pause in common remembrance of the fallen.

Indeed, all of the rituals performed on 11 November suggest that it was conceived of as a substitute funeral. The hymns and scripture readings, typically used in service after service across the country, emphasized that lives were not lost in vain. Hymns like 'O Valiant Hearts' and 'O God Our Help in Ages Past' and readings such as Psalm 46 ('God is our refuge and strength') and 2 Timothy 2:3 ('Thou therefore endure hardness, as a good soldier of Jesus Christ') provided justification for death in war either by reflecting on historical antecedents or by placing it in the context of the eternal struggle between good and evil. Either way, the message was that death, however tragic, had meaning and purpose. The sermons and addresses, too, were frequently indistinguishable from eulogies, in that they attempted to cast death in the most favourable light, as Victorian clergymen had learned to do. The growing popularity at Canadian Armistice Day services of Laurence Binyon's 'For the Fallen' ('At the going down of the sun and in the morning / We will remember them'), itself strongly influenced by the tradition of English consolatory verse, also reflects the perception of Armistice Day as a kind of funeral.[45]

Virtually every other aspect of the typical Armistice Day service can be seen in the same light. The moment of silence, the centrepiece of the ceremony, was intended to replicate the ritual performed at soldiers' funerals at the front. The relatives of the fallen again enjoyed pride of place, just as they would at a funeral. The poppy quickly became a fixture in early November, as a replacement for the black armband that traditionally had been a part of funereal garb. As Marie Sylvia wrote, the poppy became a tangible promise that the memory of the dead would not be allowed to fade: 'Honneur! Honneur à toi, sang des heros vainqueurs! / Ton souvenir sacré restera dans nos coeurs!'[46] There were also floral tributes, a funerary ritual that allowed members of the community, whether or not they had personally experienced loss, to take an active role in the ceremonies. Indeed, this practice was jealously guarded: the Rev. F.C. Ward-Whate of Toronto reacted angrily to a British government suggestion that no wreaths be laid at war memorials: 'We can't forget and we won't forget,' he promised, making the implicit assumption that a floral tribute was a kind of mnemonic device. All of these rituals suggest that, through the interwar era, 11 November evolved into Canada's national funeral. 'This is the day of the Dead,' wrote an amateur poet from Vancouver on Armistice Day 1929. 'This is a day of mourning.'[47]

It is no wonder, then, that many people felt the name change from Armistice Day to Remembrance Day, which came into effect in 1931, was entirely fitting. As Sir Arthur Currie remarked in a speech in Toronto's

Massey Hall, Armistice Day referred to a specific point in history, 'the closing incident of the war.' Remembrance Day, on the other hand, was more general and called on people to honour a memory of the lives that were sacrificed.[48] In short, Armistice Day suggested a historical anniversary; Remembrance Day suggested a communal funeral.

Of course, it is possible to find politics at work on Armistice Day in the valuation of the sacrifice to the nation and the entrenchment of Christian values. There was also some criticism of the day for fostering an unhealthy and dangerous militarism. Still, even the sharpest critics of Armistice Day realized that they had to tread carefully. The ceremony, after all, offered a way to make 'public and corporate those unassuageable feelings of grief and sorrow which otherwise must remain forever private and individual.'[49] It was an integral part of the healing process, and few critics wanted to pick away at old scars. Just as it is considered unseemly to speak ill of the dead at a funeral, it was not proper to speak ill of the dead on 11 November.

So, when representatives of the Working Class Ex-Service Men's League appeared at the Toronto cenotaph in 1933 to lay a wreath that read 'In Memory of Those Who Died in Vain,' they were clearly offering a critique of the war, but they were also admitting the sanctity of the fallen.[50] Laura Goodman Salverson, whose two novels on the Great War encompassed both a traditional and a modernist interpretation, argued in a 1937 Remembrance Day article that peace and democracy made an 'honourable face to put upon a selfish wilfully engaged war of economic conquest,' but she, too, was careful to point out that her critique implied no disrespect to the dead. 'That they died under false colours,' she added, 'does not make their sacrifice less great. It merely multiplies our obligations.'[51]

Salverson and the Toronto workers, though they may not have realized it at the time, in fact shared significant common ground with the most vocal proponents of Canada's collective memory of the war. Both discourses were underpinned by a recognition of deep and profound grief. Regardless of whether the fallen had died in a righteous cause or had been sent to pointless deaths by stupid politicians and avaricious financiers, the real tragedy of the war was that so many young men and women had died. Grief became the *sine qua non* of post-war Canada, whether or not one agreed with the dominant memory; it could be used to justify either a restatement of the myth or a critique of it. In each case, the dead underpinned both the positive, traditional memory of war and the negative, modernist memory.

The centrality of grief and the need for consolation explain why Canada's memory of the war is punctuated by observations that seem, at first glance, to be strangely contradictory. For example, in 1934 official historian Colonel A.F. Duguid, in an assessment of Canada's war film *Lest We Forget*, averred that the film 'portrays the stark reality of war, its futility and its terrors, so that this method of settling disputes between nations may be dreaded and avoided,' but he took pains to stress that such frankness did not dim the glory of the fallen. On the contrary, the film paid them tribute with its 'scenes of self-sacrifice and heroism, of devoted service and of patriotic effort ... of self-forgetfulness and of loyalty.'[52] The London *Free Press*, for its part, also applauded the film for conveying the 'feeling that war is a sickening, stupid and silly affair ... [of] death and the destruction of everything that is beautiful,' but it, too, reminded readers that *Lest We Forget* also praised the fallen for their 'heroism and self-sacrifice, endurance, cheerfulness in suffering.'[53]

By the same token, Sir Arthur Currie often insisted that he never saw any glamour or glory on the battlefield: 'war is simply the curse of butchery, and men who have gone through it, who have seen war stripped of all its trappings, are the last men that will want to see another war.'[54] In 1924, at the dedication of War Memorial Hall at the Ontario Agricultural College in Guelph, Currie returned to the theme: 'There is no glory in it [war], as we understand it, in its methods or its results. The roll of the drum or the waving of the tattered flag no longer stirs the heart, as a perfect means of solving difficulties.' But this reality in no way compromised, he went on, 'the glory of sacrifice for the ideals involved.'[55] The following year, former divisional commander Sir Archibald Macdonnell spoke in similar terms at the unveiling of the war memorial in Saint John, New Brunswick: 'Modern warfare has lost that glamour which in centuries past stirred the imagination of people. When whole nations are aligned on the battle fields in a long mass of muddy burrows, war becomes horribly monotonous, yet officers and privates face the same dangers and they share the same fate. This memorial is not only the artistic expression of the gratitude of the people of this city to those whom they dearly loved, it is also a pious memento to all those young Canadians who, during four years of cruel agony, so prized liberty that, to save their country, no sacrifice was for them too great.'[56] The speeches are cut from the same cloth. They begin with a rejection of traditional assumptions regarding war, in terms that might almost be called modernist. Yet they end with an affirmation of the value of the conflict and a restatement of the notions that the traditional view had stressed: the glory of sacrifice for an ideal and a seemly piety towards the fallen who had died for liberty and their country. All the code words are there. Despite the muddy burrows, the monotony, and the cruel agony, war brought out the finest qualities of humanity.

It was not only old soldiers who were comfortable with this balancing act. When the *Globe* reviewed the exhibition of works of art from the Canadian War Memorials Fund, it praised the collection for hammering home the fact that 'war, in itself, is futile, horrible, sordid and evil' while at the same time proving that it was marked by 'individual heroism, devotion, sacrifice and nobility.'[57] The *Regina Daily Star*, in considering the first volume of Duguid's official history, admitted that the war was 'a series of mishaps, misconceptions, misunderstandings, misinformation,' but insisted that it had been 'redeemed in its most sordid stages by the gallantry, the almost superhuman courage of those pawns in the game, the common soldiery.'[58] It would be possible to cite countless other examples of the same mental process at work: an admission of the horrors of war accompanied by an insistence that they were not borne without nobility or purpose. What appears to be a paradox is, in fact, an entirely understandable human response to an unparalleled tragedy. There may have been disagreement about the meaning of the war, but there can have been no disagreement that the real tragedy was the loss of 60,000 Canadian lives. Providing consolation for that loss, rather than rational explanation for the war as a whole, was the goal of the nation's memory of the war.

In 1933 Sir Andrew Macphail was invited to give a Remembrance Day address to the Westmount Women's Club in Montreal. The venerable doctor from Orwell, Prince Edward Island, by then something of a grand old man of Canadian letters, had already made significant contributions to Canada's memory of the Great War. He had edited the bestselling collection of John McCrae's poetry in 1918 and in 1925 published a history of the Canadian Army Medical Corps that created a minor storm in political and military circles. Macphail was never one to shy away from controversy, but when asked to speak on the occasion of Canada's national funeral, he usually declaimed on the value of the sacrifice or the soldiers' joyful recollections of their service. On this occasion, however, Macphail injected a discordant note to remind his listeners that the fact of personal loss underpinned 11 November and

Canada's entire memory of the Great War. 'Are you women who are mothers of twelve-year-old boys,' he wondered, 'quite sure that you will not be called upon six years hence to face the problem that faced the mothers of 1914?'[59] Macphail died in 1938 and so did not live to see how eerily prophetic his comment was. Exactly as he predicted, Canadians in 1939 would be forced to embark on a quest for consolation for the second time in a generation.

NOTES

The author would like to extend thanks to the Social Sciences and Humanities Research Council and the Canada Research Chairs program for financial assistance, which made this research possible, and to Janet Maybury, Joel Porter, and Gordon Vance for their research assistance.

1 *Regina Leader*, 26 September 1927, 2.
2 Daniel J. Sherman, 'Art, Commerce, and the Production of Memory in France after World War I,' in John R. Gillis, ed., *Commemorations: The Politics of National Identity* (Princeton, N.J.: Princeton University Press, 1994).
3 I am grateful to Suzanne Morton for her thoughts on these matters.
4 Rosemary R. Gagan, 'Mortality Patterns and Public Health in Hamilton, Canada, 1900–14,' in *Urban History Review* 17, 3 (February 1989), 161–75; N.E. McKinnon, 'Mortality Reductions in Ontario, 1900–1942,' in *Canadian Journal of Public Health* 36, 7 (July 1936), 285–98.
5 George Emery, *Facts of Life: The Social Construction of Vital Statistics, Ontario, 1869–1952* (Montreal and Kingston: McGill-Queen's University Press, 1993).
6 David Cannadine, 'War and Death, Grief and Mourning in Modern Britain,' in Joachim Whaley, ed., *Mirrors of Mortality: Studies in the Social History of Death* (London: Europa, 1981), 217.
7 David Marshall, '"Death Abolished": Changing Attitudes to Death and the Afterlife in Nineteenth-Century Canadian Protestantism,' in Norman Knowles, ed., *Age of Transition: Readings in Canadian Social History, 1800–1900* (Toronto: Harcourt Brace, 1998), 370–87.
8 C.L. de Roode, 'La Victoire,' in *Victoire!* (Montreal: A.P. Pigeon, 1919), 3–4.
9 Wilson MacDonald, 'Peace,' in *Song of the Prairie Land and Other Poems* (Toronto: McClelland and Stewart, 1918), 142–4.
10 Letter of 12 January 1916, quoted in Owen Dudley Edwards and Jennifer

H. Litster, 'The End of Canadian Innocence: L.M. Montgomery and the First World War,' in Irene Gammel and Elizabeth Epperley, ed., *L.M. Montgomery and Canadian Culture* (Toronto: University of Toronto Press, 1999), 32.

11 C. Courneloup, *L'Epopée du Vingt-Deuxième* (Montreal: La Presse, 1919), 16.

12 National Archives of Canada (NAC), Arthur Currie Papers, vol. 12, f. 37, Currie to Osborne, 4 January 1926; reply, 11 January 1926.

13 Alonzo Cinq-Mars, 'Ypres,' in *De L'Aube au Midi* (Quebec: Édition de la Tour de Pierre, 1924), 6–7.

14 *Brantford Expositor*, 20 May 1933, 21.

15 See Alan R. Young, '"We Throw the Torch": Canadian Memorials of the Great War and the Mythology of Heroic Sacrifice,' *Journal of Canadian Studies* 24, 4 (Winter 1989–90), 5–28.

16 *Ontario Reformer*, 5 June 1924, quoted in Robert Shipley, *To Mark Our Place: A History of Canadian War Memorials* (Toronto: NC Press, 1987), 143.

17 Katherine Hale, *The White Comrade and Other Poems* (Toronto: McClelland, Goodchild and Stewart, 1916), 15.

18 Francis Cecil Whitehouse, 'The Archers of Mons,' in *The Coquihalla Wreck and Other Poems* (Toronto: Ryerson Press, 1932), 6–7.

19 A.E. Johnson, 'With a Vagabond around Vimy,' *Maclean's*, 1 April 1924, 16–17.

20 Hamilton Public Library, Clippings file, f. Armistice Day, speech over CNR broadcasting chain, 8 November 1931; *House of Commons Debates*, 9 February 1923, 181.

21 Quoted in E.B. Osborn, *The New Elizabethans: A First Selection of the Lives of Young Men Who Have Fallen in the Great War* (London: John Lane, 1919), 281; Ralph Connor, *The Sky Pilot in No Man's Land* (New York: George H. Doran, 1919), 257.

22 NAC, W.L.M. King Papers, series J5, vol. 21, f. 8, reel C-2792, speech dated 29 February 1924, 11574.

23 Ibid.

24 Canadian Club of Toronto, *Addresses Delivered before the Canadian Club of Toronto, 1918–19* (Toronto: Warwick and Rutter, 1919), 311.

25 Clarence Basil Lumsden, 'Two Men,' in *Acadia Athaneum* 45, 5 (May 1919), 216–19.

26 NAC, J.L. Ralston Papers, vol. 165, f. 1, address at Pictou war memorial, 11 July 1935.

27 UBC Special Collections, *A Short History of Captured Guns: The Great European War, 1914–1918* (Vancouver: n.p., n.d. [1934?]), finis.

28 Quoted in Shipley, *To Mark Our Place*, 134.

29 *The Victory Loan 1919*, brochure (Ottawa, 1919), 28; A.M. Stephen, 'Canada,' in *Canadian Bookman* 7, 3 (March 1925), 44.

30 Canon F.G. Scott, 'The Significance of Vimy,' in Empire Club of Canada, *The Empire Club of Canada Speeches, 1936–1937* (Toronto: Empire Club, 1937), 57; quoted in Osborn, *New Elizabethans*, 281; Major A. Graham, quoted in Manitoba *Free Press*, 21 April 1919, 8.

31 James M. Mayo, *War Memorials as Political Landscape: The American Experience and Beyond* (New York: Praeger, 1988).

32 Lieutenant W.H. Nelles is also mentioned, but it is clear that Knisley is foremost in the town's mind.

33 Quoted in Maria Tippett, *Art at the Service of War: Canada, Art and the Great War* (Toronto: University of Toronto Press, 1984), 76.

34 James Stevens Curl, *A Celebration of Death: An Introduction to Some of the Buildings, Monuments and Settings of Funerary Architecture in the Western European Tradition* (London: Constable, 1980), 337.

35 Pat Jalland, 'Victorian Death and its Decline, 1850–1918,' in Peter C. Jupp and Clare Gittings, eds, *Death in England: An Illustrated History* (Manchester: Manchester University Press, 1999), 247.

36 NAC, R.B. Bennett Papers, reel M-1463, f. W-15, vol. 2, Bennett to John R. MacNicol, MP, 2 February 1934.

37 Quoted in James H. Gray, *The Roar of the Twenties* (Toronto: Macmillan, 1975), 262.

38 Public Archives of Nova Scotia, Horatio Crowell Papers, MG23 vol. 27, f. 10, 'Soldier's Record Sheet, Soldiers' Memorial, Municipality of Guysborough, with notice of Soldiers' Memorial,' undated.

39 City of Toronto Archives, Board of Control minutes, 28 October 1925; City Council minutes, 2 and 3 November 1925.

40 *Saturday Night*, 14 November 1925, 1.

41 Serge M. Durflinger, *Lest We Forget: A History of the Last Post Fund, 1909–1999* (Montreal: LPF, 2000), 69–70; *Montreal Gazette*, 24 May 1924, 6.

42 NAC, Bennett Papers, reel M-1463, f. W-127 'Decoration Day,' letters from City of Stratford, Ontario Municipal Association, Premier of Saskatchewan, City of Kitchener, various dates [1930].

43 Windsor Municipal Archives, Hon. James Baby Chapter, IODE Papers, MS7 f. 14, Windsor GWVA to Baby Chapter, 25 April 1924.

44 *Globe*, 11 November 1930, 14; Thomas Socknat, *Witness against War: Pacifism in Canada, 1900–1945* (Toronto: University of Toronto Press, 1987), 127.

45 John H. Johnston, *English Poetry of the First World War: A Study in the Evolution of Lyric and Narrative Form* (Princeton, N.J.: Princeton University Press, 1964), 107.

46  Marie Sylvia, 'La fleur des soldats morts,' in *Vers le Beau* (Ottawa: private, 1924), 104–5.
47  S.C. Cain, 'Two in One,' *Vancouver Sun*, 9 November 1929, 9.
48  NAC, Canadian Legion Papers, MG28 I298, vol. 7, f. 8, Massey Hall, 13 November 1931, quoted in circular no. 31-2-57, 19 November 1931.
49  Cannadine, 'War and Death, Grief and Mourning,' 222, 227.
50  NAC, Brooke Claxton Papers, MG32 B5, vol. 1, f. 'Armistice Ceremony 1933,' article from *Atlantic Sun*, 16 November 1933.
51  Laura Goodman Salverson, 'Remembrance Day,' in *Canadian Association of Railwaymen Journal*, 3, 11 (November 1937), 242.
52  NAC, A.F. Duguid Papers, MG30 E133 ser. II, vol. 7, f. 22, memo from Duguid, 12 December 1934.
53  NAC, Department of National Defence (DND) Records, vol. 1746, f. DHS-5-5A, article from *London Free Press*, 4 April 1935.
54  Arthur Currie, 'The Last Hundred Days of the War,' in Empire Club of Canada, *Addresses Delivered to the Members during the Year 1919* (Toronto: Warwick Brothers & Rutter, 1920), 305.
55  *OAC Review*, 36, 11 (July 1924), 340.
56  NAC, Archibald Macdonnell Papers, MG30 E20, vol. 1, address of 10 June 1925.
57  NAC, A.E. Kemp Papers, MG27 IID9, vol. 1, f. C-7, pt 1, article from Toronto *Globe*, 30 October 1926.
58  NAC, DND Records, vol. 1506, f. HQ 683-1-30-18, article from *Regina Daily Star*, 28 June 1938.
59  NAC, Sir Andrew Macphail Papers, MG30 D150, vol. 6, f. 2, address to Westmount Women's Club, 10 November 1933.

# Contributors

**Donald Avery** is emeritus professor of history at the University of Western Ontario and the author of *'Dangerous Foreigners': European Immigrant Workers and Labour Radicalism in Canada, 1896–1932*, *The Science of War: Canadian Scientists and Allied Military Technology during the Second World War*, and *Reluctant Host: Canada's Response to Immigrant Workers, 1896–1994*.

**Ramsay Cook** is general editor of the *Dictionary of Canadian Biography*, the author of many books, including *The Regenerators: Social Criticism in Late Victorian English Canada*, and co-author, with Robert Craig Brown, of *Canada 1896–1921: A Nation Transformed*.

**Terry Copp** is professor of history at Wilfrid Laurier University. His publications include *The Anatomy of Poverty: The Condition of the Working Class in Montreal, 1897–1929* and *Fields of Fire: The Canadians in Normandy*.

**Adam Crerar** teaches at Wilfrid Laurier University. He recently completed his doctoral dissertation on the relationship between rural and urban Ontario, 1890–1930.

**Patrice A. Dutil** is director of research at the Institute of Public Administration of Canada. He is the author of *Devil's Advocate: Godfroy Langlois and Liberal Progressivism in Laurier's Quebec* and the founder of the *Literary Review of Canada*.

**John English** teaches at the University of Waterloo and is the author of many books on Canadian history, including *The Decline of Politics: The*

*Conservatives and the Party System, 1901–1920, Borden: His Life and World,* and a two-volume biography of Lester Pearson.

**J.L. Granatstein** writes on Canadian national history, most recently on the military. He taught at York University and was director and CEO of the Canadian War Museum.

**Paul Litt** teaches Canadian history and Canadian Studies at Carleton University. He has published on the Massey Commission, historic sites, and heritage issues in Ontario.

**David MacKenzie** teaches at Ryerson University and is the author of *Inside the Atlantic Triangle: Canada and the Entrance of Newfoundland into Confederation, 1939–1949, Canada and International Civil Aviation, 1932–1948,* and *Arthur Irwin: A Biography.*

**Margaret MacMillan** is the provost of Trinity College and professor of history at the University of Toronto. Editor of the *International Journal* from 1995 to 2003, she is also the author and editor of many books, including *Women of the Raj* and *Paris 1919: Six Months That Changed the World.*

**Douglas McCalla** has been Canada Research Chair in Rural History at the University of Guelph since 2002. He formerly taught at Trent University.

**Rod Millard** teaches Canadian history and the social history of technology in the Department of History at the University of Western Ontario. He is the author of *The Master Spirit of the Age: Canadian Engineers and the Politics of Professionalism.*

**Desmond Morton** is Hiram Mills Professor of History at McGill University. He is also professor emeritus at the University of Toronto, where he taught military, political, and industrial relations history for twenty-five years with his friend and colleague Craig Brown.

**Joan Sangster** is a professor of history and director of the Frost Centre for Canadian Studies and Native Studies at Trent University. She is the author of many books and articles, including *Earning Respect: The Lives* *of Working Women in Small-Town Ontario* and *Girl Trouble: Female Delinquency in English Canada.*

**Jonathan F. Vance** holds the Canada Research Chair in Conflict and Culture in the Department of History at the University of Western Ontario. His publications include *Death So Noble: Memory, Meaning, and the First World War* and *High Flight: Aviation and the Canadian Imagination.*

# Index